Waves of Change

Waves of Change

managing global trends in the financial services industry

Patrick Callioni

GLOBAL
professional
publishing

Global Professional Publishing
Random Acres
Slip Mill Lane
Hawkhurst
Cranbrook
Kent TN18 5AD
Email: publishing@gppbooks.com

ISBN 978-1-906403-38-6

Printed by Integrated Book Technology

Contents

Preface

I am writing this book during the Great Recession, as the head of the International Monetary Fund (IMF), Dominique Strauss-Kahn, has labeled the global economic crisis that has followed on from the US subprime crisis of 2007. While I will deal with current events insofar as I need to, this book is about the future, your future, my future, our children's future. I am not offering you the equivalent of a crystal ball or a horoscope. This is more like a long-range weather forecast, generally accurate in describing trends, but necessarily imprecise about some of the details. Long-range forecasting is an art, not a science, and those who practice it know that there are bound to be a few mistakes made and a few surprises lurking in the background. There, you have been warned. Use the material in this book with caution, but use it nonetheless, because my forecasting record, honed by a few decades of experience, is not bad. I expect that the broad trends I describe in the pages that follow are more likely than not to be accurate–and useful. In these difficult times, to be fore-warned is indeed to be fore-armed.

> *I think that we can now say that we've entered a Great Recession. This recession may last a long time unless the policies we're expecting are put in place, in which case 2010 can be a year of return to growth.* — Dominique Strauss-Kahn

To get us in the right mood, to curb my tendency towards the sin of hubris a little, allow me to share with you a quote from a report published in the March-April issue (2008) of *The Futurist*, a report prepared by the World Future Society, of Bethesda, Maryland, United States of America (USA).[1] This is what the Society said, "The economy of the developed world is on a path to grow for at least the next five years. Any interruptions will be relatively shortlived."

Viewing events from the perspective of early 2009, which is when I am writing these words, this forecast has turned out to be less than accurate, unless Dominique

1 *"Trends Shaping Tomorrow's World, Forecasts and Implications for Business, Government, and Consumers (Part One)", pages 35-52.*

Strauss-Kahn and countless other expert commentators turn out to be spectacularly pessimistic in their assessment of the economic crisis in which we are now immersed. I am not highlighting this particular prediction to embarrass the authors of the report, which, as we will see later, contains useful and reliable predictions about other matters. Rather, I am keen to show how dangerous it is to make forecasts about the future of the global economy, however sound the research and analysis underpinning those forecasts might be. Nevertheless, this is what I am doing in this book, comforted by the fact that in April 2008 I was finishing a book, eventually published in October 2008, which presented a somewhat different picture of the global economy from that entertained by the World Future Society.[2]

In that book I argued, among other things, that the subprime crisis in the USA, in tandem with the regulatory approach taken in the USA and given the size and importance of the US economy in the global financial system, presented an imminent and significant threat to the global economy. It is with little pleasure that I can say now that my diagnosis and prognosis were correct. I was also correct in forecasting that the economy of my home country, Australia, would be less affected by any global crisis, at least in part because of its approach to the regulation of the domestic financial services sector. We will return to this point later, in chapter 6.

They say that money makes the world go around and we all know that it is the financial services industry that makes money go around, ever faster, it seems. Recent events have also reminded us that a stable financial sector is fundamental to the well being of the economy and of society, especially in the developed world, where wealth is increasingly created in services industries, of which the financial sector is a large component. Any significant uncertainty in the world of finance is amplified hugely into economic disruption and social instability. Demagogues and populist politicians thrive in such circumstances and middle of the road, sensible politics tend to be pushed aside, often replaced by extremist left or right solutions. My fear in these times of turmoil is that government may want to remedy a flaw in regulatory frameworks by over-regulating.

Indeed, as I write this the British Government has effectively nationalized major banks and there are calls in the United States to nationalize the Bank of America and Citi, while the French Government argues for a global super-regulator and the Chinese want the US dollar replaced by special drawing rights as the de facto global currency.[3] If we follow any of these suggestions, we could trigger damaging events of equal import and gravity as did the failure of the authorities in the United States of America (USA) to

2 *Compliance and Regulation in the International Financial Services Industry*, Global Professional Publishing, Random Acres (UK) 2008.

3 See http://www.abc.net.au/news/stories/2009/01/19/2468680.htm and h ttp://curiouscapitalist.blogs.time.com/2009/01/15/the-case-for-nationalizing-citigroup-and-bank-of-america-and-getting-robert-reich-a-fact-checker/, where the case for nationalization is made, at least for Bank of America, and http://finance.yahoo.com/tech-ticker/article/yftt_157347/Stop-the-Charade,-Nationalize-Citi?tickers=C,AIG,BAC,JPM,XLF,^DJI,^GSPC, where a similar case is put for Citigroup.

manage risks in the financial markets during the last decade or so. On the positive side, I note that US Treasury Secretary Timothy Geithner is proposing to reform US regulatory structures to manage systemic risk.

What Geithner is proposing resembles the ideas for reform I put forward in 2008, in *Compliance and Regulation of the International Financial Services Industry*, to which I add in this book lessons I have learnt from the past few months. The gist of what I have to say is simply put: dying from a runaway investment fever or from sclerosis of the economic arteries has the same effect and we do not want either of the unpleasantly terminal outcomes that result from these conditions. What we need is regulation that is fit for purpose, balancing competing interests and allowing each of us to get on with the business of business. It may not be easy to do, but it can be done and I will show you how. The thrust of my proposal is the creation of a federated network of trust, as an alternative to cumbersome trans-national regulation and as a replacement for the inadequate arrangements we now enjoy. I am not innocently assuming that what I advocate here will happen soon, if at all, but I think there is enough of value in this book to get us started on a collective journey towards a new and better way.

This is a book, not a journalistic piece. This means that while I am following what is going on around the world to clean up the mess we are in, I am not going to provide a blow by blow commentary. However, it is already apparent that politicians, technical experts, academics and commentators are finding it difficult to escape from the shackles of the past. While I see tentative steps being taken in the right direction, I am worried that we will only tinker at the edges, without tackling the nub of the problem, which is that the post-war financial machinery is broken beyond repair and cannot be fixed. We must be as brave in our actions and bold in our thinking as those who created the post Bretton Woods world if we want to leave our children and grandchildren with a solution tailored to meet the needs and expectations of the future. If I achieve nothing else, I would like to think that I have encouraged you to look at the world through the windscreen, rather than the rear vision mirror.

On the issue of how, you will find two appendices to this book. The first is the *Australian Guiding Principles on Extended Performance Management: A Guide to Better Managing, Measuring and Reporting Knowledge Intensive Organizational Resources*. This guide has been prepared by the Society for Knowledge Economics to help fill a gap in the management of intangible assets. We will see later why this is relevant and important to this book. The second appendix is an abridged version of a recent manual on stakeholder management. I have included that to assist readers to best position themselves or their organizations during the years to come.

Introduction

People in the world of finance are sometimes heard suggesting that government should get out of their way, thus allowing those who know best to make the decisions that matter. The events of the last couple of years may still these voices, for a time at least. What we are hearing now, from a broad spectrum of commentators, is that the state should shoulder aside the captains of industry, taking over the reins and driving the economy directly. I beg to differ, from both sides. Those who say that the state should have the levers of power need to remember that the bureaucratic apparatus that runs a state is not designed to support risk taking and entrepreneurship, which are essential ingredients for innovation and economic growth to occur. Those who think the state should get out of their way should remember that the capacity of the financial system to manage risk is built on the guarantees provided by the state, a guarantee built on state power. Paraphrasing Mao Zedong, profits come from the barrel of a gun, since state power ultimately rests on military might.

> *It is only in respect to knowledge that a business can be distinct, can therefore produce something that has a value in the market place.* — Peter Drucker

Without the state, the world of finance would have to revert to using gold and silver as currency. Without the backing of the state, the complex web of twenty-first century finance could come to immediate grinding halt. At best, even if the global financial machinery were to continue to work, without the state investors' appetite for risk would be greatly diminished and those who remain in the game would expect much higher returns, thus taking momentum out of the economy. The Great Recession should have taught us this lesson, if nothing else, given that even the great powers of finance had to humble themselves to secure state guarantees and state funds, to enable them to survive. The state needs the financiers and the entrepreneurs, to keep the economy vital and productive, and they in turn need the state and its machinery, including the machinery of regulation, to keep the economy alive.

In *Compliance and Regulation* I suggested what could and should be done to create a regulatory framework that would be friendly to business, fair to the community, and that would be sustainable. I am not proposing to go over the same ground here.

In this book, I will identify and describe the major waves of change that are coming our way over the next decade or so and then I will provide practical advice on what to do or avoid doing to benefit or suffer least most from what is to come. One of the things we should do, as we emerge from the present crisis, is to get the regulatory environment right in the financial services sector, globally and locally. This is because, as recent events have shown, contemporary capitalism will not work well if the global financial engine is stuttering. In formulating a regulatory framework fit for the twenty-first century, I will emphasize the importance of knowledge capital[1] as a factor in the creation and destruction of value. By knowledge capital I mean capital that is not captured by existing accounting standards, capital that is often labeled as intangible.[2]

> *There are two types of intangibles: hard intangibles (information protected by law, such as trademarks or non-accounting value evidenced by financial transactions such as goodwill); and soft intangibles (knowledge assets — 'what people know', relationship assets — 'who people know', emotional assets — 'motivation levels', and time assets — 'effectiveness levels') . . . Currently, people are aware of hard intangibles and often fail to understand soft intangibles exist. That is even more problematic when 90 percent of intangibles are soft intangibles.*[3]

Just like accounting standards, regulation of financial markets has dealt very poorly with knowledge capital, with the soft intangibles. This may be because regulators and most economists remain strongly influenced by the values of the industrial era, when land, labor and finance were the holy trinity of wealth creation, with maybe a little goodwill thrown in every now and then. Also, regulators have tended to focus on what they can measure easily, on what they can see and understand. Measuring soft intangibles is not easy, although it can be done, as shown by the material at appendix A, the *Australian Guiding Principles on Extended Performance Management*, published by kind permission of the Society for Knowledge Economics (SKE). According to its website, the purpose of the SKE is "to help improve organizational productivity and performance through the better management of knowledge and innovation." The society was founded and the extended principles were prepared in recognition of the fact that "The reality…is that many of the management and measurement tools we depend on to drive organization performance are inadequate in this new environment. Managing a business, government agency or an economy requires new disciplines and measurement systems in this connected economy." This new environment is due to

1 I have settled on this terminology to reflect the point made by Drucker in 1964, though I am aware that others prefer labels such as intangible capital, for example.

2 By that I mean standards and interpretations issued by the International Accounting Standards Board (IASB) and the International Financial Reporting Interpretations Committee (IFRIC). Intangibles are dealt with in IAS 38, a summary of which can be found at http://www.iasplus.com/standard/ias38.htm.

3 "Accounting for the uncountable", by Tamara Plakalo, Fairfax Digital, February 11, 2005, retrieved from http://www.smh.com.au/news/Management-Focus/Accounting-for-the-uncountable/2005/02/14/1108229910079.html.

the emergence of a "new economy", in which knowledge, which increases returns to scale, unlike other types of asset, is changing business fundamentals and providing new opportunities for economic growth and social development.[4]

While we may live in a new economy, our regulatory system, nay our whole economic apparatus has a huge blind spot, because of a continuing fixation with land, labor and money. Until we remedy that shortcoming, we are doomed to be blindsided by relatively small disturbances that fester quietly in the background until they have grown so large that they disrupt the status quo. Humanity learned in the 20th century that disease is best controlled through prevention; we have yet to apply that lesson in the financial services industry, as we continue to bolt the stable doors well after the bulls have gone and the bears—and the crooks—have moved in. Contemporary regulation models are akin to driving while string fixedly into the rear vision mirror, rather than at the road ahead. This reflects dominance by the values of the accounting and auditing culture. By necessity, accountants and auditors are more focused on the past, on hard data, on what can be measured and accounted for. There is nothing wrong with that; it is their proper role. The same can be said of politicians and public servants, who behave just like generals, always ready to fight the next war as if it were the last war—and it never is.

Don't get me wrong, I am not taking a potshot at regulators—I have been one and I know that it is a tough and unrewarding role. Why is this so? When a public servant has to tell someone or some corporation, "no—you can't do that", that public servant is going to win very few friends in the world of business and that public servant will not always be supported by the politicians who made the rules in the first place. Politicians like to play the good cop role, leaving the public servant to be the bad cop. Public servants know this and, fore-armed with this knowledge, they adjust their behavior accordingly. In the beginning, when fresh in the job and backed by an enthusiastic patron or sponsor, they apply the rules, firmly, but fairly. This goes on for a while, but eventually the road of regulation, paved as it is with good intentions, will develop a few bumps; someone important will complain or tough times may suddenly mean that tough regulation gets in the way of business and profits and jobs are at risk—meaning that votes are at risk also. That is when the speed and the keenness to apply the rules will start to wane.

Generally, the toughest stance a regulator will adopt during his or her period of tenure will coincide with the early days of his or her term of office. When the attacks come, as they will, accusing the regulator either of being a patsy of the corporations or a curse on business—and sometimes both accusations are leveled at the same time—the regulator will generally tend to assume a much safer course of action, a line of least resistance. In some cases, the government of the day will have nudged them in that direction, by overruling tough decisions or by cutting resources, sometimes on

4 See www.ske.org.au.

the grounds that the regulator has been so effective that s/he does not need as many teeth or as many heads and arms.

At this point, a regulator may even be praised by all and sundry—except by the odd critic, who will be quickly dismissed as an extremist or a Cassandra—for being level headed and even handed and flexible and responsive. When that time comes, folks, I suggest to you that the regulatory apparatus has ceased to function and that trouble is on its way. The likelihood of trouble is even greater if such events accompany an investment bubble of some sort, when it is most likely that crooked and sharp characters will want to apply their undoubted skills to fleece as many suckers as they can for as long as they are allowed. People like Bernard Madoff or Ken Lay are always happy when the regulator self-regulates itself out of the game, for whatever reason.

Sooner or later, regulators tend to take on the expectations and values of those whom they regulate. No one, not even a saint, always acts entirely in the public interest; that is what it means to be human. Our institutions, just like the individuals who create them, run them and staff them, are fallible—and the degree of fallibility will rise steeply as the tenure of office-holders lengthens, after each re-structure, legislative refresh or new management appointments. Note that I am not saying that all or most public servants feather their own nests, to profit themselves or to profit their cronies. Fortunately, in countries such as Australia, the USA or the UK that is a rare phenomenon. However, individuals inject personal views, biases, or prejudices into the design and implementation of policy, often without being aware they are doing so, thus distorting public policy to accommodate personal, private ends. I have been a public servant for almost four decades and I could not say that I have never done it, even if only unconsciously and in minor ways.

It is the same for organizations. It is a fact that institutions dedicated to serving the public interest will gradually be subverted to serve the private interests of those who work within them, as well as the public interest. Interestingly, this phenomenon will happen without the conscious effort of any individual to make it so. It will happen gradually, invisibly, away from the gaze of the public. Much as barnacles attach themselves to the hull of a ship and quietly, slowly, drag it towards the bottom of the sea, unless they are scraped off regularly, the detritus resulting from the struggle to regulate will drag regulating institutions towards the lowest common denominator. Sooner or later, unless renewed, cleaned out and re-focused, regulators will cease to regulate, providing only a veneer of enforcement, with no teeth or substance. We have seen this recently in the USA in the case of Enron, Bernard Madoff and others.

This is why, as we will see later in the book, regulators need to be truly independent, their activities need to be transparent and accountable, and the politicians who supervise them must be watched closely. Regulators must work to strict, externally imposed standards, with compliance tested by independent and very detached parties, and they must be turned over regularly. By the way, I think this should be done with corporation boards and CEOs also. The logic should not be unfamiliar to you, especially in the USA, because it reflects the check and balance approach used in the US constitution to keep politicians on the right track—the principles of it, though not necessarily the execution. It may not be the perfect system, but, paraphrasing Winston Churchill on the virtues of democracy, while it is the worst system in the world, it is better than all others.

We need someone to watch the watchers and, I am afraid, that cannot be left to politicians alone, for two reasons. First, just like other public servants, politicians end up serving private interests at the expense of the public interest; second, even when a politician is focused on the public interest, it is not possible for him or her to keep the bureaucracy honest—all that politicians can do is to inquire after the event, performing an autopsy on the body politic to ascertain the cause or causes of its demise. There are good reasons why this is so; suffice it to say that the alternative is paralysis by committee.

If you want the public service to be totally ineffective, get the politicians involved in day-to-day decision-making. The alternative I propose is to use standards as the means and process to keep everyone honest while allowing everyone to get his or her job done. Standards provide a consistent framework for monitoring and auditing performance, can be applied across organizational and state boundaries and do not impinge on the independence of corporations or the sovereignty of nations. Also, standards enable competence to be tested objectively: by applying standards, we can actually see whether an institution is capable of doing and is doing what it was established to do. And the same can be done with individuals. We will return to the issue of standards later in the book.

Why regulation matters

Let's be honest: the business of regulation is intrinsically difficult, but it is devilishly difficult when money, power and reputations are at stake and all those ingredients are present in the financial sector. John Kenneth Galbraith, one of the great economic historians of the twentieth century, observed that "The regulation of economic activity is without doubt the most inelegant and unrewarding of public endeavors. Almost everyone is opposed to it in principle; its justification always relies on the unprepossessing case for the lesser evil."[5] I agree with the first part of this proposition, but not the second—I think we can do better than arguing for a lesser evil. Research, experience and judgment combine to tell me that regulation is unavoidable and that an increasingly globalized web of regulation is desirable, to accompany our increasingly globalized way of living and ways of doing business.

5 1997, page 26.

Also, because the responsibility to regulate rests with nation states, the success or failure of global regulation is dependent on the success or failure of its weakest link, its weakest component and that, in a globalized economy, no country or business can make itself invulnerable to shocks to the system that are big enough to affect a significant element or component of that system. As recent events illustrate, the weakest element can be the largest economy in the world, the lone superpower. This should not surprise us. It is more likely to be the largest economy in the world that puts us all in a perilous situation than a lesser power, such as Mexico, Argentina or even the United Kingdom, because our dependence on the former is likely to be much greater than on the latter. And then, the track record of regulation in the USA is not great. Americans have a strong belief in the power of the market, tend to resent government interference and worship entrepreneurs and risk-takers. This is not a good set of indicators when assessing the capacity of a nation to get the balance right between freedom and restriction, which a condition precedent for effective regulation. Looking forward a decade or two, any global accord on how to manage the financial system must take into account the share of risk presented to the system by larger economies, especially those that have a poor track record or inadequate regulatory infrastructure.

> *The regulation of economic activity is without doubt the most inelegant and unrewarding of public endeavors. Almost everyone is opposed to it in principle; its justification always relies on the unprepossessing case for the lesser evil.* — JK Galbraith

We do this in our businesses, when we consider with whom to partner and whom to avoid, or when we make decisions about how much insurance to take out, and how much should be set aside to deal with unforeseen contingencies. But we don't do it in international relations, where nation-states indulge each other with the fiction that each state is independent and sovereign. While the concept of sovereignty makes sense in a legal setting, allowing us to keep our own laws and customs, it makes no sense when we turn to the movement of money across borders. Here each state depends on all others—much as consumers of water depend on the good behavior of all others who are upstream from the point at which they tap the river. Big land users upstream present a much greater risk than individual users, because of their intrinsically greater capacity to pollute. This reality is recognized in law, by placing on land users upstream the responsibility to protect the supply of water to those downstream, whoever they may be.

We need a similar approach in the financial services industry. We need to acknowledge explicitly the collective responsibility of nation-states and of large corporations to keep the flow of money clean and unadulterated, within and across borders. We also need to apportion the responsibility for mitigating risk to the global financial system to those that have the greatest capacity to do harm to that system. Capacity to do harm should be determined by assessing the significance of an economy within the system (scale); the level of competence of that economy in managing its affairs, its creatures (corporations) and its impact on others, through action or omission; and its political and social stability. By my rough calculations, this means that our focus should be primarily on the USA, China, India, Russia, and Brazil, with secondary attention paid to the European Union (EU) and Japan. In the case of the last two, we should actually watch that their natural tendency to over-regulate does not win out, remembering that death from either fever or sclerosis is an equally final and equally unpleasant event. Using this model, the straws blowing in the wind suggest that the next bubble with global impact is most likely to arise in China. This is why.

There are strong wealth imbalances developing in China; the economy, after a relatively brief slowdown, is likely to soon resume its feverish pace; the country's political and regulatory structures are immature and highly prone to cronyism on a large scale, as evidenced by the melamine in milk scandal and its aftermath; the media in China are not independent; and civil society is very weak. Using fire risk terminology, if China's economy were a forest, we would say that it is ready to burn and catastrophically so. Given the amount of capital now vested in Chinese hands and especially given the dependence of the USA on Chinese investors, any bubble bursting in Beijing would have disastrous consequences for the world's economy. More disturbingly still, it is quite likely that an economic crisis in China would usher in political trouble, because of the gap between rich and poor, between country and city and between the east and the west of that vast nation. Nations in economic and political trouble tend to become warlike or, at best, highly unpredictable. We should start building our new risk management engine right now, I suggest, so that we are ready for the next wildfire and, preferably, so that we can start to reduce the risk of fire, right now.

Of course, even without a global approach, it is possible for countries or businesses to reduce the impact of a burst bubble. For example, Australia was left relatively unaffected by the subprime crisis, because its internal regulation of the financial system has made it impossible for any Australian financial institution to become too enmeshed in the business practices that trapped other companies, in other jurisdictions—notably, the USA. However, in the long run financial or economic crises in significant economies cannot be contained by national borders. Even a relatively minor crisis in one continent can, given the right circumstances, quickly become a global crisis, spreading as if by contagion, as if it were influenza or AIDS.[6] We will return to this simile in chapter 6, to help us understand how financial crises start and spread and how they can be managed, drawing on lessons from the discipline of epidemiology.

6 Paul Krugman, in *The Return of Depression Economics and the Crisis of 2008*, provides some good examples of this, as we will see later in the book.

In *Compliance and Regulation* I proposed generic strategies to help people in business to profit from regulation—a much better argument that accepting a lesser evil. Those strategies provide the foundations for this book, addressing the fundamental challenges posed by the need to regulate and to be regulated. While I will recap, briefly, on those challenges and my suggested remedies, in this book I will focus on the other significant challenges we are likely to face in the financial services sector, some of which carry much greater potential for harm—or for good, if tackled wisely—than the subprime crisis and any tendency to over-regulate that might be triggered by that crisis. That tendency is already evident, in actions by government and in the calls from sections of the media, academia and even the world of business for government to step up and assume responsibility for the management of national economies. Given the track record of governments in this area, I think we should look elsewhere for a solution, but I will consider the case for government to have a greater role in economic management, in chapter 6.

One of the reasons for my skepticism about government as the ultimate economic manager is that during the next few decades the pace of change in various aspects of the economy and of society will accelerate, exceeding anything we have experienced to date. The ability of governments, of whatever persuasion and type, to adapt quickly and to respond rapidly to new challenges is remarkably poor, as the climate change debate, discussed in chapter 4, illustrates. We need to harness a broader coalition of thinkers and doers to enable us to deal with what promises to be a challenging and turbulent century, in the financial services industry in particular. This book is about the challenges, people, businesses and the financial services industry will face in the remaining decades of the twenty-first century and the means to deal with those challenges. The challenges are many. First, recent events have shown that we need to rethink and rebuild the architecture that holds together the global financial system. Second, there is the challenge of information and communication technology (ICT), which continues to disrupt economic and social arrangements across the world. Third is the geopolitical change arising from the rapid development of economies such as China and India.

Next is the transformation from a post-industrial to a knowledge economy, with some economies skipping the post-industrial phase to go straight to the latter from an industrial stage of development. We are in the early stages of this transformation now, a process that may last ten years or more, depending on the general state of the global economy, the consequences of climate change and the absence of widespread conflict. Fifth, last and most important, though perhaps not most urgent, is the cluster of challenges referred to as climate change or sometimes as global warming. Of course, there are also the traditional challenges humanity has been facing for millennia, such as war, famine, disease and death, which are likely to be accentuated in a world where potable water is a scarce resource, the global population keeps growing and the expectations of billions seeking a better life are rising. I am not going to address the Horsemen of the Apocalypse directly, but rest assured that I am not forgetting about them, as I write about their new confrères. Actually, the discussion of climate change in chapter 4 will give us an opportunity to re-visit both old and new perceptions of how the age in which we live might end.

Dealing with wicked problems

The word wicked, as I use it here, has a flavor of double entendre. A strong reason for linking up a discussion of climate change and the economy, or more specifically the financial services industry, is that the problems inherent to climate change and to the management of the economy are strangely similar. In both cases we are dealing with complex systems and complex systems give rise to wicked problems. Wicked problems have these defining (and scary) characteristics:[7]

1. *The problem cannot be understood until it has been solved.* The problem is a mixture of interlocking issues and constraints that keep changing and are hard to fix on. Also, people have different views about what the problem is and what may be an acceptable solution. This makes it difficult to define the problem precisely.
2. *Wicked problems have no stopping rule.* It is impossible to define where the problem begins and ends and to determine when it is solved. Simon called this "satisficing", stopping when you have a solution that is "good enough"[8]—however, what is good enough and for whom and who says so?
3. *Solutions to wicked problems are not right or wrong.* They are "better", "worse", "good enough" or "not good enough." With wicked problems, the determination of success cannot be formulaic or prescribed in advance, because there is no agreed definition of the problem. This is why consultants love wicked problems—the potential profits that can be made by providing advice on how to solve such problems is huge!
4. *Every wicked problem is unique.* Just like failed relationships, no two wicked problems are alike. Even with similar subject matter, geographic, cultural or other factors make the problem unique, defined by its specific circumstances and captured within its own specific timeframe. Thus, transferring solutions across geographic, cultural or historical boundaries or across time is a risky enterprise. Even if a solution has worked somewhere else or at some time in the past, we can take no comfort in it here and now. This is where consultancy firms, especially large transnationals, let their clients down, by

7 H Rittel and M Webber (1973) "Dilemmas in a General Theory of Planning" pp 155-169, *Policy Sciences*, Vol. 4, Elsevier Scientific Publishing Company Inc., Amsterdam.
8 HA Simon (1969) *The Sciences of the Artificial*, Second Edition, MIT Press, Cambridge, Mass.

re-packaging solutions across borders, cultures and time, as if they were selling a car or ice-cream.

5. Rittel says that *every solution to a wicked problem is a "one-shot operation", it cannot be iterative.* I disagree. Managing wicked problems is best done iteratively; we can take steps in what we think is the right direction, quickly evaluate the responses we get and adjust our course as we go. This is what Stephan H. Haeckel called the sense and respond model. Haeckel says that when unpredictability is a given, companies must anticipate, adapt and respond to continually changing customer needs by fostering the capability to sense and interpret changes faster and better than others do.[9] I agree with him and I suggest that when faced with a wicked problem, adaptability and responsiveness are essential.
6. *Wicked problems have no alternative solutions.* There are no off the shelf, generic solution to a wicked problem. Creativity and judgment are required in design and execution of a solution that will have to be tailor made, to suit the unique circumstances of each problem. However, a general approach to dealing with wicked problems can be formulated and applied across different circumstances (see 5).

Wicked problems and Homo Economicus

Now that we know what a wicked problem is, let us deal with a most wicked problem indeed, the myth of *Homo Economicus*, the basis for the assumption that human beings are rational and will always act rationally, with the objective of maximizing the return they get from their actions. It is a wicked problem in the alternative meaning of the word, because relying on this unrealistic assumption undermines our ability to deal with reality, which is difficult enough as it is. In the world of economics, the economy behaves according to relatively simple laws, which can be applied to define and solve problems, using complex mathematics. In the real world, the economy behaves like the complex system it is and the humans within it are the source of that complexity. A complex system behaves in ways that cannot be explained by studying its component parts. The actions of a complex system are inherently unpredictable, beyond a very limited period of time, and almost impossible to replicate exactly. Understanding a complex system is a wicked problem, in the sense discussed just above.

Allow me to illustrate. A combustion engine can be taken apart, analyzed, understood and put together again—and, if all the parts are re-assembled correctly, it will work. A combustion engine is a complicated system, having many parts, but it is not complex. Any competent mechanic or engineer could deduce the function of such an engine and how it works by reference to a few components only. Also, what a

9 *Adaptive Enterprise: Creating and Leading Sense-And-Respond Organizations* (1999), Harvard Business Press.

combustion engine does is both predictable and amenable to precise replication. On the other hand, one cannot take a human being apart and then re-construct the body and bring it back to life. We cannot even do this with a mouse or a worm, because they are also complex systems, though, a worm, for example, is not that complicated. A complex system has meaning beyond the mere sum of its parts and understanding any complex system is a wicked problem indeed. Mapping the human genome is not the same as taking an engine apart. Having the map of an organism's DNA does not enable us to replicate it. Nor does it enable us to predict precisely what it would do if we were able to. Remember Dr Frankenstein and his monster? Or what about Dolly, the first cloned sheep? Scientists were stunned when it died so young, as if its ageing process had been greatly accelerated. Whether the cloning process caused Dolly to die earlier than average or not is in doubt, but the fact is that those who cloned her did not expect it.

It is hard enough to map and understand the DNA of a single organism. The challenge assumes an entirely different magnitude when we try to map and understand a system of global scale, such as the weather. It is even more difficult to understand climate. Climate encompasses the temperature, humidity, rainfall and other meteorological factors in a given region over long periods of time, whereas the weather is merely what is going on now in a particular locality. The climate itself is a manifestation of a larger complex system, the Earth's biosphere, which, according to Wikipedia, is "the global ecological system integrating all living beings and their relationships, including their interaction with the elements of the lithosphere, hydrosphere, and atmosphere... postulated to have evolved...at least some 3.5 billion years ago".[10]

The financial system and the economy, despite the best efforts of economists to persuade us otherwise, are also complex entities, not amenable to disassembly and re-assembly—and hard to predict or replicate. This is why economics is not a science, it is a craft. Unfortunately, most of its practitioners are social scientists who pretend they are physicists, making extensive use of mathematical incantations to cover up their lack of understanding of what is actually going on and why. This is because economists assume that the economy is governed by something called "economic laws". Wrong. The economy is a specialized application of the same rules that govern the rest of human society and their laws, insofar as there are any such things, derive from sociology, psychology, biology and physics.

There is nothing fundamental in economics that cannot be explained by reference to one or more of those disciplines. I should say here that I am not comfortable using the term "law", because a law is a set of rules made and enforced by institutions—law is normative. In science, a law is at best descriptive—it is never normative. The laws of physics, for example, are generalizations based on empirical observations—they are reliable hypotheses of how the universe is thought to work. In economics not even

10 From http://en.wikipedia.org/wiki/Biosphere, retrieved on 19 February 2009.

this level of reliability is possible, which is why economists have resorted to using the term "natural laws". By using the adjective natural, they are claiming that their so-called laws are like gravity, an intrinsic characteristic of the physical world. Again, wrong! The natural laws of economics are unproven and usually unprovable assumptions about how the world works. Because they cannot be proved or disproved, they are an act of faith, not a product of science.

Let us consider two of these laws, to illustrate my point, two laws that are fundamental to the whole edifice of economics: the law of economizing and the law of economic rationality. [11] Taken together, these state that people tend to economize, maximizing gains for a given cost, and minimizing costs for a given gain, and that human action is economically rational if one's preferences are consistent and if one economizes. In simpler terms, this means that people are rational beings, who always make the optimum economic choice. Do you know anyone who is like that? I don't and I think there are none.

The reason for that is that people are not rational beings and that is not an assertion, it is a generalization based on empirical observations, it is science. To their credit, some economists recognize this fallacy at the core of their discipline. Paul Ormerod, for example, has stated in plain terms that the idea that economics is based on Rational (Wo)man or Homo Economicus is not based in reality and has observed that most of the Nobel prizes for economics in the twenty-first century have gone to economists working beyond rationality.[12] Actually, in the eighteenth century the father of classical economics, Adam Smith, was well aware, as he was writing books such as *The Theory of Moral Sentiments and The Wealth of Nations*, of the power of the human mind and of the passions of the crowd. In the twentieth century, John Maynard Keynes coined the concept he described as animal spirits, to describe the creative power of confidence. According to Keynes, animal spirits are a particular sort of confidence he thought of as "naive optimism", meaning that "the thought of ultimate loss which often overtakes pioneers, as experience undoubtedly tells us and them, is put aside as a healthy man puts aside the expectation of death". Keynes also coined the term "casino capitalism", to describe the somewhat reckless approach some take to the "game" of investment.

> *If economists could manage to get themselves thought of as humble, competent people on a level with dentists, that would be splendid.*
> *John Maynard Keynes*

11 I am relying on a list published at http://www.progress.org/2004/fold379.htm, retrieved on 27 March 2009.
12 See the bibliography for suggested reading.

The seminal thinker on this issue in economics is Herbert Simon, who developed a behavioral theory based on "bounded rationality". The theory is simple. People face uncertainty about the future and costs in acquiring information in the present (I would add that information is also imperfect and often not available). This limits the extent to which people can make rational decisions. What we do, according to Simon, is to exercise "bounded rationality", setting an aspiration level which, if achieved, will be enough to "satisfice" us, which will be almost certainly short of the theoretical optimum towards which *Homo Economicus* is supposed to strive. Of course, a first year student in psychology could tell you that, as could any parent or manager or, indeed, anyone at all out there in the real world.[13] It is only in the closeted world of academia or a boardroom or a trading room that otherwise intelligent people delude themselves otherwise. In *The Great Crash 1929*, Galbraith provides several example of this delusion at work. Here is one that illustrates the point.

> *It was a golden age for professors. The American Founders Group, an awe-inspiring family of investment trusts, had as a director Professor Edwin W. Kemmerer, the famous Princeton money expert...That economists were not yet functioning with perfect foresight is perhaps suggested by the subsequent history of the enterprise. United Founders, the largest company in the group, suffered a great contraction in its assets of $301,385,504 by the end of 1935, and its stock dropped from a high of over $75 share in 1929 to a little under 75 cents.*[14]

And here is another example provided by Galbraith, for good measure (and because I find these vignettes amusing).

> *In a statement that achieved minor notoriety, Lawrence of Princeton said that "the consensus of judgment of the millions whose valuations function on that admirable market, the Stock Exchange, is that stocks are not at present over-valued." He added: "Where is that group of men with the all-embracing wisdom which will entitle them to veto the judgment of this intelligent minority?"*[15]

I am sure we can all point to contemporary versions of these studies in hubris. My recollection of 2005 and 2006 is that journalists, commentators and (most) economists were falling over themselves in their rush to tell us that the business cycle, the endless run of boom and bust, had finally been brought to an end and that the stock market would continue to rise forever. I am also sure that in our heart of hearts we all thought they might be right—or at least wished it were so. I know I did, in my weaker moments, when my brain fell prey to my heart. This is an example of how our rational minds are

13 See the excellent article on Homo Economicus on Wikipedia, at http://en.wikipedia.org/wiki/Homo_economicus, which I consulted on 27 March 2009.

14 From page 55.

15 From page 70.

affected by our emotions, our desires, our wants. In this, economists, bankers, politicians and journalists are no different from the rest of us. However exalted our position or our intellect or our understanding of the intricacies of the market, we remain human, moved by a mix of genetics, emotions and brainpower and always missing much of the information and understanding we really need to make difficult decisions in difficult circumstances. This is what Simon meant when he spoke of bounded rationality.

Why human beings are not rational

The concept of bounded rationality has been validated by extensive empirical research. For example, as Michael Shermer explains, humans are irrationally loss averse.[16] "Thousands of experiments in behavioral economics since Daniel Kahneman and Amos Tversky founded the field with their seminal 1979 paper, 'Prospect Theory: An Analysis of Decision under Risk', have demonstrated that most of us are highly loss averse. Specifically, most people will reject the prospect of a 50—50 probability of gaining or losing money, unless the amount to be gained is at least double the amount to be lost. That is, people feel worse about the pain of a loss than they feel better about the pleasure of a gain. Twice as badly, in fact." In the same article from which I have taken these words, Shermer recounts that we even have hard evidence of how the brain does this. Using a type of magnetic resonance imaging, researchers at California University, Los Angeles, found that, as the potential for gains by study participants rose, activity in the mesolimbic and mesocortical dopamine systems increased. These are areas of the brain that act as our inbuilt reward system. They also found that, as the potential for loss increased, activity in these same reward-sensitive areas decreased.[17] Far from being prone to making rational, value-maximizing decisions, it seems that humans may be wired to avoid loss, but it gets even more interesting.

Kahneman and Tversky found that when given a choice between a certain return of $1000 and a fifty percent chance of a return of $2500, people were more likely to choose the former. However, they also found that people, when offered a certain loss of $1000 versus a fifty percent chance of no loss or a $2500 loss tend to choose the latter, which is a risky choice. In both cases people did not behave as *Homo Economicus* is supposed to behave.[18] By the way, Kahneman and Tversky, despite being awarded a Nobel Prize in Economics in 2002, are not economists; they are psychologists. This should not surprise us, really, because psychology is the discipline that actually studies human behavior, whereas economics focuses on the mathematical fluff in its own

16 "The Prospects for Homo economicus", *Scientific American*, July 2007.

17 Dopamine has many functions in the brain, including important roles in behavior and cognition, motor activity, motivation and reward, inhibition of prolactin production (involved in lactation), sleep, mood, attention, and learning, see http://en.wikipedia.org/wiki/Dopamine.

18 D Kahneman and A Tversky (1979), "Prospect theory: An analysis of decisions under risk", *Econometrica*, 47, 313-327.

metaphorical navel.[19] So, let us forget about *Homo Economicus* and let us concentrate instead on *Homo Sapiens* and the complex social systems in which we live and work, of which the economy is one.

In the economy, the behavior of individuals and of organizations is driven and shaped by a mix of factors, some of which may be physiological, as we have just seen, or a mix of psychology and physiology. Other factors result from interactions between psychological (or individual) and social (or group) processes. This means that, sometimes, our innate tendency towards risk aversion gets turned off by another of our human predilections, our desire to be one of a crowd. Humans, despite Margaret Thatcher's views to the contrary, are social animals. With rare exceptions, we like to be in a herd, because the herd provides protection and opportunities for interactions with others. These are good things, in most circumstances, but our desire to be part of a crowd can also produce nefarious effects.

Gustave le Bon wrote about the psychology of the crowd in an eponymous book in the late nineteenth century. In that book he observed, "In its ordinary sense the word 'crowd' means a gathering of individuals of whatever nationality, profession, or sex, and whatever be the chances that have brought them together. From the psychological point of view the expression "crowd" assumes quite a different signification. Under certain given circumstances, and only under those circumstances, an agglomeration of men presents new characteristics very different from those of the individuals composing it. The sentiments and ideas of all the persons in the gathering take one and the same direction, and their conscious personality vanishes. A collective mind is formed, doubtless transitory, but presenting very clearly defined characteristics. The gathering has thus become what, in the absence of a better expression, I will call an organized crowd, or, if the term is considered preferable, a psychological crowd. It forms a single being, and is subjected to the law of the mental unity of crowds. "[20]

This is how riots, lynchings, witch hunts and teenage crazes can all be explained, as can rave dancing and Adolph Hitler's charisma. It also explains why company boards and governments can enter a world where the world is left behind and a new reality is created, a reality that then leads the group to behave in ways that, after the event, seem totally detached from the reality of the marketplace or of the electorate. It has been argued that the presidency of the younger George Bush was afflicted by "the law of the mental unity of crowds"; for eight years, it may be that the USA was run by groupthink. Groupthink was also a feature of the Nixon White House in its dying days and is generally evident in dictatorships, of the right and left, often extremely so, because it is enforced by the power of the state. Contemporary news reports also suggest that groupthink is contributing to the destruction of the prime

19 Declaring my bias here, I will confess that my first degree is in psychology.

20 At pages 2-3, from an online version of the book published by the Electronic Text Center, University of Virginia Library, retrieved on 8 April 2009.

ministership of Gordon Brown in the UK. I think we need to know a bit more about groupthink and how it affects behavior in the markets.

Groupthink, genes and markets

Groupthink is a concept put forward by Irving Janis to explain faulty decision-making in and by a group. The suggestion is that people caught up in groupthink do not consider all alternatives and focus on achieving unanimity at the expense of quality decisions.[21] The phenomenon of groupthink can operate on a macro, as well as a micro scale. JK Galbraith hit the nail on the head when he wrote this about the causes of the 1929 crash, "Far more important than rate of interest and the supply of credit is the mood. Speculation on a large scale requires a pervasive sense of confidence and optimism and conviction that ordinary people were meant to be rich."[22] This is the same sort of large scale crowd behavior that has driven many a gold rush. This is how a California "forty-niner", Mr. S. Shufelt described his reasons for joining the rush, "I have left those that I love as my own life behind and risked everything and endured many hardships to get here. I want to make enough to live easier and do some good with, before I return."[23] Mr. Shufelt, like tens of thousands of others who rushed to dig California gold in the mid-nineteenth century had caught "gold fever" and, like most who suffered from that ailment, he did not become a rich man, just as most people who get caught up in investment bubbles do not get rich, though a few usually do.

How is it that bubble and gold fevers catch on and spread across nations, oceans and language divides? Again, Le Bon described a mechanism that would enable this to happen, when he wrote "The second cause, which is contagion, also intervenes to determine the manifestation in crowds of their special characteristics, and at the same time the trend they are to take. Contagion is a phenomenon of which it is easy to establish the presence, but that it is not easy to explain. It must be classed among those phenomena of a hypnotic order, which we shall shortly study. In a crowd every sentiment and act is contagious, and contagious to such a degree that an individual readily sacrifices his personal interest to the collective interest. This is an aptitude very contrary to his nature, and of which a man is scarcely capable, except when he makes part of a crowd."[24] Of course, he was writing about a physical crowd, but the same process can occur within a virtual crowd, even one so large as to span the whole globe. The mechanism that underpins crowd behavior on this macro scale was described by Richard Dawkins.

Richard Dawkins is a British evolutionary biologist and science author. In the book *The Selfish Gene* (1976), Dawkins advanced a gene-centered view of evolution.

21 *Victims of groupthink*, Houghton Mifflin, 1972.
22 *The Great crash 1929*, at page 169.
23 From http://www.eyewitnesstohistory.com/californiagoldrush.htm, retrieved on 8 April 2009.
24 Op. cit., at page 10.

Wikipedia explains the concept of the selfish gene thus, "Dawkins coined the term selfish gene as a way of expressing the gene-centered view of evolution, which holds that evolution is best viewed as acting on genes and that selection at the level of organisms or populations almost never overrides selection based on genes. An organism is expected to evolve to maximize its inclusive fitness—the number of copies of its genes passed on globally (rather than by a particular individual). As a result, populations will tend towards an evolutionarily stable strategy."[25] This view aligns with the broad principles of Darwinian evolution, since it relies on mutations and natural selection, but it challenges Darwin by postulating that evolution occurs at the level of the gene, demoting the organism, we humans for example, to the role of carrier and host. To me this is replay of the nature versus nurture debate, albeit on a purely biological plane this time. I am not keen on arguments that require us to choose between diametrically opposed positions. I prefer synthesis, finding what truth there is in both and going on from there. Because of that, I think that evolution occurs at several levels; it occurs at the level of the gene, of the organism, at the social level and, perhaps, even at the level of the biosphere, the Earth as a whole, if James Lovelock's Gaia hypothesis holds true.

Anyway, the selfish gene is not directly pertinent to our purpose here. But something else is. In the same book that gave us the notion of the selfish gene, Dawkins introduced us to the concept of the "meme". This how Dawkins explains what a meme is and how it works. "Examples of memes are tunes, ideas, catch-phrases, clothes fashions, ways of making pots or of building arches. Just as genes propagate themselves in the gene pool by leaping from body to body via sperms or eggs, so memes propagate themselves in the meme pool by leaping from brain to brain via a process which, in the broad sense, can be called imitation. If a scientist hears, or reads about, a good idea, he passed it on to his colleagues and students.. He mentions it in his articles and his lectures. If the idea catches on, it can be said to propagate itself, spreading from brain to brain. As my colleague N.K. Humphrey neatly summed up an earlier draft of this chapter: "... memes should be regarded as living structures, not just metaphorically but technically... When you plant a fertile meme in my mind you literally parasitize my brain, turning it into a vehicle for the meme's propagation in just the way that a virus may parasitize the genetic mechanism of a host cell. And this isn't just a way of talking—the meme for, say, "belief in life after death" is actually realized physically, millions of times over, as a structure in the nervous systems of individual men the world over."[26]

Most of us would be familiar with the terminology used in modern genetics. We know that a gene is a component of DNA and that DNA is a chemical information database, the blueprint of life. Each gene, of which DNA has many, contains a

25 Retrieved from http://en.wikipedia.org/wiki/The_Selfish_Gene, on 8 April 2009.
26 From chapter 11.

particular set of instructions, usually coding for a specific protein. Memes are the cultural equivalent of genes, because they carry within them humanity's ideas and knowledge. In fact, human evolution is best understood as a process of co-evolution between genes and memes. Memes, sometimes referred to as viruses of the mind, are not intrinsically good or benign. A meme for racism, for example, can infect and affect the mind just as the influenza virus can infect and affect a person's respiratory system, with unpleasant results in both cases, though the meme infection may be much more persistent than the influenza infection. Memes are spread by direct or indirect contact. Have you ever wondered how crazes spread across the world, for hula hoops or a musical group or Twittering or investing in a particular stock? Ask anyone in advertising about the hottest new concept in the business and they will talk to you about viral advertising, marketing on a peer to peer basis. The World Wide Web provides memes with a wonderful mechanism for transmission, as repressive regimes like China or North Korea know all too well. Dictators lock down access to the Web so that any infective external idea is (hopefully) kept out. However, the Web is only the latest vehicle memes have adapted to their purposes.

Gold rushes, bubbles and memes

In the nineteenth century, the meme for gold fever spread by voice, by telegraph and by newspaper, at relatively slow speeds, but even then, it did not take long for the fever to engulf the world, causing thousands of people to abandon countries, families and jobs to chase a pot of gold at the end of the rainbow in a faraway place. Today, memes can spread within days or even hours, as evidenced by the various email scams that seek to push up or down a particular stock, to benefit the scammers of course. The process is helped along by what Malcolm Gladwell called the "Law of the Few", which he described in his first best-seller, *The Tipping Point: How Little Things Can Make a Big Difference*, published in 2000. According to Gladwell, "The success of any kind of social epidemic is heavily dependent on the involvement of people with a particular and rare set of social skills."[27]

These are the people Gladwell describes as the mavens, connectors and salesmen. Mavens accumulate knowledge, especially about the marketplace, and know how to share it with others. Connectors specialize in linking us up with what is going on in the world; they are people who are excellent at striking up friendships and acquaintances and who build up large and often influential networks. Salesmen are persuaders, people with powerful negotiation and interpersonal skills, sometimes endowed with charisma. Salesmen can lead people towards places to which they might otherwise not go.

27 At page 33.

I am sure we have all met these three types; hey you might be one of them yourself. Some rare individuals can even bring together two or more of these sets of abilities. Bernard Madoff, for example, strikes me as someone who had or claimed to have specialized knowledge of the marketplace, which he used within his extensive network to lead people to places they might otherwise ignored or chosen to avoid. Some of these people would have brought others with them, thus adding to Madoff's circle of influence and to the scale of the Ponzi scheme he had concocted.

> *... a Newsweek article identified Madoff's scheme as "an affinity Ponzi". Madoff was a "master marketer," and his fund was considered exclusive, giving the appearance of a "velvet rope." Some Madoff investors were wary of removing their money from his fund, in case they could not get back in later. One New York real estate investor said she "literally begged" Madoff to take her money, and he refused. (From Wikipedia)*

To sum up, just as finding a nugget or a few grains of gold in a pan can eventually lead to a gold fever that brings tens of thousands of people across continents and that reshapes the fate of cities, regions or even whole countries, finding a specialized vein of investment potential can lead to a bubble spanning a whole economy and, if the bubble occurs in the right (or is it wrong?) place, infecting the whole world with financial poison.

The specialized knowledge of a few spreads to many, creates its own momentum, as Le Bon described, and takes on a life of its own, fed by the belief that on this occasion wealth can be created for and had by all who have the will to jump in and take part. What we have now is a self-fulfilling prophecy and it is worth noting here that even in normal times, almost sixty per cent of the aggregate value of the US stock market is based on investors' perceptions of future value.[28]

Remember the Kahneman and Tversky experiments? In the right context, people will take irrational risks, and the seeming safety inherent to being part of a herd presents just such a context. "Let them eat cake", Marie-Antoinette is supposed to have said; well, in an investment bubble there is cake for all or so it seems or, to modernize the tale, donuts for all, perhaps. However, at some point a few break from the crowd, perhaps for reasons completely unrelated to events in the market, such as a change in personal circumstances, or because they smell danger in the wind. Whatever the reason, they desert the herd and reveal the hole at the center of the donut, at which point the herd rediscovers its aversion to risk and flees, swiftly and totally. There you have it, an investment bubble, inflated and deflated by the herd instinct of humans;

28 *Future Value. The $7 Trillion Challenge*, by John J. Ballow, Robert J. Thomas and Göran Roos, paper published by Accenture in 2004, see www.accenture.com.

a complex process in a complex system can be explained by simple principles, if one knows where to look.

Speaking of looking, the whole process of bubble forming and deflation is greatly helped by the lack of visibility into the financial system. Using the argument that what goes on in the financial system is of a private commercial nature, those outside the system, including regulators, have very limited opportunities to see what goes on, until it is too late. Phenomena like crowd behavior and groupthink are facilitated by opaque organizational arrangements and relationships not open to scrutiny and we have already seen how secrecy can aid and abet financial skulduggery. This is why I believe that the financial sector should be treated as if were a utility sector or a producer of food. Money is as essential to our survival and well being as is electricity or food and should be regulated accordingly. This must include abandoning the convenient pretence—convenient for the few on the inside, that is— that what goes on in the world of finance is entirely private. What consenting adults do in the privacy of the boardroom or the smoking room of their favorite club ceases to be private when it affects the rest of us.

If the creators of the securities that caused the subprime crisis had been exposed to the same sort of scrutiny as a manufacturer of dog food, let alone the sort of scrutiny that a pharmaceutical company undergoes, the toxic debt would not have gone to market. We require manufacturers of food to behave according to standards, with compliance backed up by legal sanctions and by open scrutiny of the manufacturing and distribution processes. We also do it with people who run casinos, where people put their money at risk voluntarily. We should do the same with financial institutions. After all, we have no choice to engage with these institutions or not, while gambling in a casino is entirely optional, and the risk generated for each of us and for whole societies in and by the financial markets is substantially greater. I will have more to say on this in chapter 6.

Understanding complex systems

The weather is a complex system, as is the economy, but it is easier to forecast the weather a few days ahead with reasonable accuracy than it is to forecast currency movements over the same period. That is because we have some science to guide us in our efforts to understand climate and weather, much more than we have to enable us to understand the economy. However, understanding the principles that drive one can certainly help us to understand the other. It should not surprise us, for example, that both the weather and the stock market can be studied and explained by charting. Charting or technical analysis is a method used by professional traders to evaluate how and when to trade into and out of the financial markets. It relies on collecting data from the market and then using various techniques to identify trends in the markets, short, medium and long term. Love it or hate it, it is the closest thing to science in the financial world, because it relies on data about the market and uses techniques that allow for testing of validity and reliability. However, science sometimes goes out of the window when experts interpret what the charts display—as it does in the realm of long term weather forecasting.

When we understand that we are dealing with complex systems, which are inherently unpredictable, it is no surprise that economic modeling of climate change is so difficult, as we will see later. What the poor souls doing this work are trying to do is to model the interactions over a long period of time of two complex systems, when we lack the tools to understand either one, on its own. When we realize that we haven't a clue as to what stock markets or currencies are going to do, when and why, it is hard to avoid the conclusion that economic modeling of climate change is akin to trying to see the future by reading the entrails of animals.[29] If an organization is a complex, adaptive (or chaotic) system and knowledge of initial conditions is necessarily less than complete, which is inevitably the case, the behavior of that organization is inherently unpredictable.[30]

I should say that words like chaos and chaotic do not mean untidy and messy, as in a teenager's bedroom. Rather, they mean complex, unpredictable and sometimes unfathomable, like the trading floor in a stock exchange before computers took over—or the lottery we know as the currency market or the economy itself. Science tells us that the level of complexity of a system is related to the complexity of the model needed to predict accurately the behavior of the system.[31] According to Lorenz, for example, the weather is a system so complex that it can be modeled only by a duplicate of itself and similar arguments have been advanced about the human brain and the universe.[32] I think we could say the same about the economy, could we not? That means that the economy and the Earth's climate are awfully complex and that anyone who pretends to be able to forecast accurately how each will affect the other is kidding us. However, this is not to say that we cannot make educated guesses about what is or is not likely to happen, much as we do now with long-term weather predictions or with stock charting. On the topic of charting, this is a (small) part of what a blogger and chart enthusiast published on 23 May 2006.[33]

29 We have seen, thanks to Paul Krugman and JK Galbraith, how even a collection of great mathematical minds and a great collection of Harvard economists can get the market very badly wrong, a few decades apart, proving that people like Warren Buffett are rare indeed.

30 Stacey 1991; Wheatley 1994; Gregersen and Sailer 1993; and Cartwright 1991.

31 Prigogine and Stengers 1985.

32 Penrose 1989, 1995; Tipler 1995.

33 From http://www.stock-market-crash.net/blog.htm, retrieved on 7 February 2009.

A Confluence of Bearish Catalysts

In my first Dow 11,400 blog post, I described several fundamental reasons why we might see a severe correction, upon a false breakout in the Dow. Now that a false breakout has occurred, I'd like to revisit this bearish scenario and publish a more detailed list explaining several catalysts for a further drop in stock prices.

1) The Dow's rejection of the 11,400 resistance is highly bearish, as the failure to breach this level resulted in the 2000-2002 bear market. 11,400 is a psychological barrier, and the failure to break shows the underlying weakness of this market. Such a weak market is vulnerable to dramatic drops upon even the slightest hint of negative news.

The current Dow MAY be experiencing a similar pattern to its sideways pattern that lasted from the mid-1960's until 1982, as the Dow repeatedly attempted to breach the 1,000 level, only to result in four different bear markets. A 20-year stagnation ensued as the Dow stayed flat.

Barry Ritholz, of The Big Picture Blog, created a post c*omparing the present with 1973-74 cycle*, using a chart to show that today's Dow is following the 1970's Dow's pattern with a 60 percent correlation. If the comparison holds true, 2006 is now equivalent to 1973, a year that marked the start of a bear market that finally ended in 1975, with a 40 percent loss. Lets hope we don't see a repeat of that action, as it would imply the Dow hitting 6,700. Make sure you pay Barry a visit, as his analysis is extremely cogent and insightful.

2) We're late into the interest rate cycle, with the Fed having lifted the benchmark lending rate 16 times since June 2004. Bull markets have tendency to start right after the Fed has a series of rate cuts, while many bear markets have started after a series of rate hikes, causing a slowdown in business conditions. Additionally, during periods of monetary tightening, the Fed has tended to overshoot and tighten too much, often resulting in hard landings or recessions.

When I first read these words, the US market had not got down to 6,700, but I observed to myself that it is worth remembering that the 1929 Crash was not the end of the downhill run for stocks. As I write this, on 10 March 2009, the Dow is at 6585, with a fifty-two week low of 6469.95.[34] If you study the graph at figure 1, however, you will

34 From http://money.cnn.com/data/markets/, retrieved on 10 March 2009, and http://www.djindexes.com/, retrieved on 12 march 2009.

see that we have hit this point much later than the unknown chartist seems to have suggested. Please note the point about the Fed, interest rates and recessions, because we will come back to this later, as we discuss the lessons we should learn from this crash and this recession and previous ones, lessons we should apply in managing the economy.[35]

Figure 1: Comparison with the 1973-74 cycle[36]

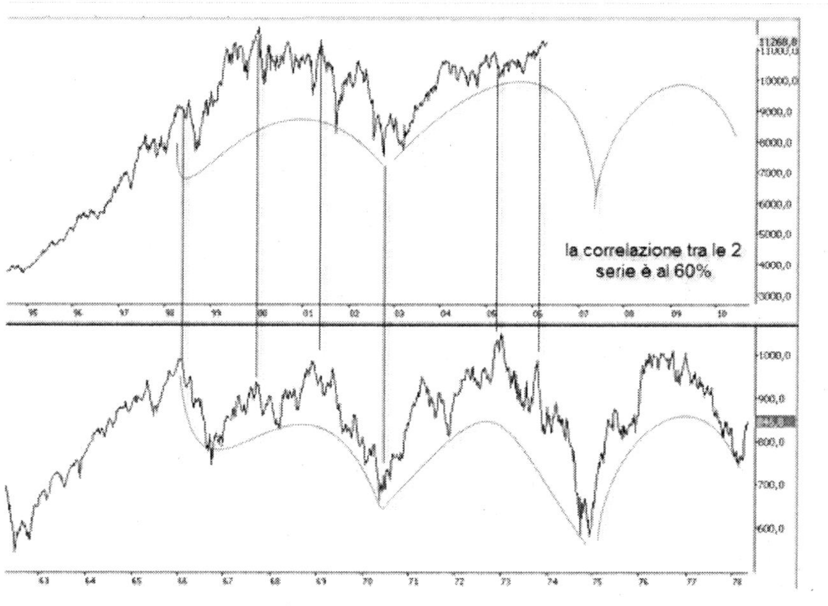

Bubbles and intangibles

I often quote Drucker on the importance of knowledge in the world of business and I make reference to the *knowledge economy*. I use that term to describe the emerging state of economic development in advanced economies, which differs from the condition we have been in since the Industrial Revolution in Great Britain in the eighteenth century, known as the industrial economy.[37] A tangible way of examining the transition that developed economies have undergone is provided by the SKE in a report titled *Intangible Drivers of Organizational Productivity and Prosperity*, published in 2006.[38] On the home page of its website, the SKE states that,

35 As I write this, I also note that the markets have gone up ten percent in a week in the US. Is this a bear market rally or was 6500 the bottom? Time will tell.

36 From h ttp://money.cnn.com/data/markets/, retrieved on 10 March 2009.

37 Sometimes you will see that economists and authors refer to our present state as post-industrial. While this is an accurate observation, since we are now past the industrial era, it is not very helpful terminology, because it tells us nothing about the differences between now and the past. The term knowledge economy, in my opinion, makes good that deficiency.

38 I am proud to be one of the founders of the society.

> *Over the last three decades, the world has witnessed historically unprecedented levels of economic liberalization resulting in the increased flow of people, goods, capital and money between nations, markets and economic spheres. This seemingly irreversible process has simultaneously slowed down and facilitated economic growth and productivity in different parts of the globe, changing the nature of societies, their labor markets and national economies themselves. The impact of the newly globalised and technology-driven economy on developed societies has been profound. No longer locality-dependent, its manufacturing bases have steadily moved to cheaper labor markets leaving developed nations to focus on the development of knowledge-intensive economic structures.*[39]

> *The average duration of a soap bubble is known. It's about 26 seconds. Then the surface tension becomes too great and it begins to burst. For speculative crazes, it's about 18 months.—Peter Drucker*

The process of transformation is shown at table 1.[40] The SKE argues that transformation has been driven by "the growth in service-based industries in which intangible resources, be they *relational*, *structural* or *human*, constitute the main part of the value creation process". The SKE quotes figures from the World Bank that attribute (in 2005) sixty-eight percent of global GDP to service-based industries, up from sixty-one percent in 1990; manufacturing had lost share, from thirty-four to twenty-eight percent, as had agriculture, from five to four percent.

The concept of intangible asset is covered by the International Financial Reporting Standards (IFRS). The IFRS are standards and interpretations adopted by the International Accounting Standards Board (IASB), which is an independent, privately-funded standards body based in London. The IFRS are generally accepted as the model for accounting in business and in government across the OECD and beyond.

According to the IFRS, an intangible asset is a "nonmonetary asset without physical substance." To be recognized on the balance sheet, an intangible asset must be identifiable, controllable, reliably measurable and provide future economic benefits (such as revenues or reduced future costs). An intangible asset is identifiable when it is separable (capable of being separated and sold, transferred, licensed, rented, or exchanged, either individually or as part of a package; or arises from contractual or other legal rights, regardless of whether those rights are transferable or separable from the entity or from other rights and obligations. This is a limited and limiting view of intangible assets as a category. Later in the book I will propose that the IFRS should be

39 From http://www.ske.org.au/, retrieved on 31 January 2009.
40 See http://www.ske.org.au/downloads/Australian-Guiding-Principles.pdf.This report was commissioned by the (then) Australian Government Department of Finance and Administration.

changed and explain why we must change them. For now, it is sufficient to say that the IFRS, because they do not account adequately for intangible assets, distort investment decisions and are a negative influence on the global economy.

Table 1: Economic transformations

	Economic activity	Factors of economic production
Agricultural economy (Pre-1800)	Harvesting	Land Land owners and workers
Industrial economy (eighteenth to twentieth century)	Manufacturing	Labor Machinery Raw material
Knowledge economy (twentieth century and onwards)	Mediation of knowledge and services	Relational capital Structural capital Human capital

The SKE report also cites a study conducted by Accenture in 2003, which sought the views of executives from twenty-seven countries and nineteen industries on what they considered to be the drivers of wealth creation. Forty-nine percent of those surveyed considered intangible resources to be the most important factor in the creation of shareholder value; only twenty-five percent of executives surveyed said that they relied primarily on tangible assets for shareholder value creation.[41] Figure 2 shows how the value drivers in the stock market changed in the last quarter of the twentieth century, as our reliance on tangible assets for value creation morphed into reliance on intangible assets.

It seems that increasingly our jobs, our wealth and our lives are firmly rooted in the creation and exploitation of information, which is effected through the management of knowledge, rather than agriculture or manufacturing (see table 1). In the USA, according to *America.gov*, services produced by the private sector accounted for 67.8 percent of US gross domestic product in 2006, while federal, state, and local government accounted for 12.4 percent, adding up to about eighty percent. Manufacturing contributed 12.1 percent, construction 4.9 percent; oil and gas drilling and other mining, added up to 1.9 percent; and agriculture was less than one percent.[42] A similar picture emerges when considering employment data. For example, the proportion of manufacturing jobs was 10.7 percent in 2005, while service industries accounted for 83.4 percent of

41 The original source is "A New Paradigm for Managing Shareholder Value", Accenture Institute for High Business Performance, July 2004.

42 From http://www.america.gov/st/econ-english/2008/April/20080415222038eaifas0.9101831.html, retrieved on 14 March 2009.

nonfarm employment in the same year.[43] What is true of the USA is true of all developed economies, with differences only at the margins. We need the food our farmers grow and the goods our manufacturers make with the raw materials produced by the miners, but our wealth, our workplaces and our societies depend on services rendered.

Figure 2: Changing asset base for the S&P 500

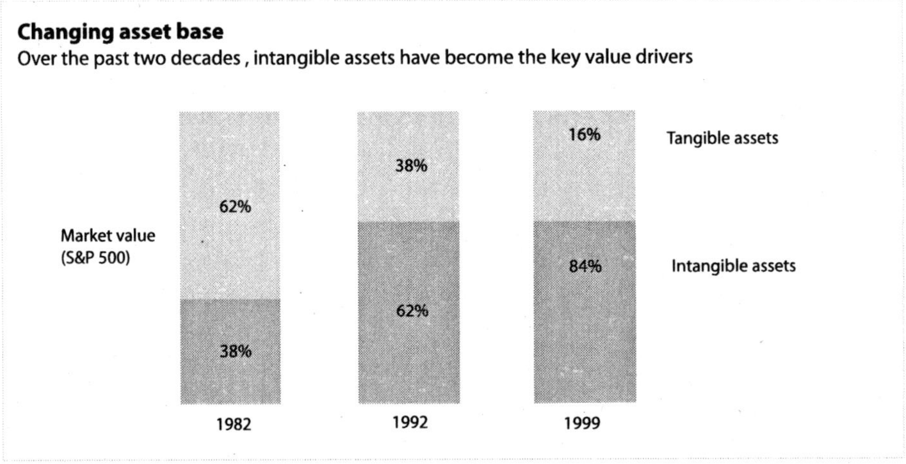

Source: Juergen H Daum: Intangible Assets and Value Creation, John Wiley & Sons, 2002

The value produced by service industries is made up of several factors, but the dominant factors are knowhow (or knowledge) and information. The quality of food in a restaurant or of service in a bank or the success of government policy, all depend on the knowhow of the workers involved in the process and on the quality of information flows. Both elements, knowhow and information are essential. For example, a competent waiter who does not understand the language of a customer is more likely to give poor service. On the other hand, an incompetent waiter who is fluent in the language of his or her customers is also more likely to give poor service. Knowhow is also a factor in farming and manufacturing, of course, as is information, but they are not dominant factors, often playing second fiddle to capital and capital goods, such as machinery and raw materials, or are dependent on the quality of the land and the vagaries of climate. Because of the twin requirements of knowhow and information, service industries are the natural home of knowledge workers. According to Peter Drucker, "The terms "knowledge industries", "knowledge work" and "knowledge worker" are only 40 years old. They were coined around 1960, simultaneously but independently; the first by a Princeton economist, Fritz Machlup, the second and third by this writer."[44] Knowledge

43 From "The American Workplace - The Shift To A Service Economy", at http://jobs.stateuniversity.com/pages/16/American-Workplace-SHIFT-SERVICE-ECONOMY.html, retrieved on 14 March 2009.

44 *The Economist*, "The Next Workforce. Knowledge workers are the new capitalists", by Peter F. Drucker, November 1, 2001, from http://www.druckerinstitute.com/whydrucker/why_articles_nextworkforce.html, retrieved on 14 March 2009.

workers make their living primarily by thinking, rather than doing, which means that not all who work in an office are knowledge workers and not all knowledge workers are to be found in office buildings.

In economies like these and most others in the OECD, between three and four of ten workers are knowledge workers. And, of course, the financial services industry is the knowledge industry par excellence. The value of trading in the stock exchange in New York in 2008 exceeded the US GDP for that year–and nothing physical was transacted, since even share registries these days are computerized. This is why the discussion later in the book, concerning new generations and new ways of working, is very important. In the words of Michael Krokenberger, the twenty-first century will require us to build a "cool, light and dry economy", based on "innovation, knowledge, doing more with less, value adding, being clever".[45]

Why is this important? Our wealth is not now due to the land, to machinery or even to the physical efforts of workers, the traditional elements of capital. Intellectual, relational and other forms of intangible capital matter far more. Well, as we will see in chapter 2, my thesis is that bubbles are built on—well perhaps I should say inflated by—capital that is not physical or tangible. The antonym of tangible is intangible, but because I am uncomfortable with the term intangible capital, I prefer to speak of knowledge capital. This thesis finds its proof at times when capitalism looks to be on very shaky ground, when an investment bubble bursts and stock markets and economies crash. When a bubble deflates, the same factories, houses, roads, ports, markets, workers and financial institutions are there that were present the day before the bubble burst. And yet, large and sometimes huge amounts of wealth, of capital, have been almost instantly destroyed by the burst and by what follows the deflation of the bubble. In a sense, this is what the inventor and then the proponents of Douglas Social Credit have argued for decades.

Social Credit is an economic and moral philosophy developed on and from the writings of CH Douglas, an English engineer and self-taught economist and philosopher. In 1920, Douglas published two books that have provided the intellectual wellspring for Social Credit; the books were titled *Economic Democracy* and *Credit-Power and Democracy*. Social Credit has been influential, to varying degrees, in Canada, Australia and New Zealand, in particular, even assuming the responsibility of government in the Canadian provinces of Alberta and British Columbia—in the latter, from 1952 to 1991. The official Social Credit website describes the movement's philosophy as follows.[46]

Social Credit campaigns for optimum economic and political freedom for each individual by ensuring (a) consumer control over production—economic democracy; (b) voter control over policy—political democracy. Social Credit stands against the political party system, the existing financial system, and against all concentration

45 *The Bulletin*, 30 April 2002, p. 26.
46 From http://198.66.229.35/about.php, retrieved on 16 February 2009.

of power over individuals, whether economic or political. "A phrase such as 'there is no money in the country with which to do such and such' means absolutely nothing unless we are also saying 'the goods and services required to do this thing do not exist and cannot be produced, therefore it is useless to create the money equivalent of them'. For instance, it is simply childish to say that a country has no money for social betterment or for any other purpose when it has the skill, the men and materials to create that betterment. The banks or the Treasury can create the money in five minutes, and are doing it every day...' C. H. Douglas, founder of Social Credit in "Control and Distribution of Production" (2nd edn) (1934).

I am not a proponent of the Social Credit philosophy, mainly because it reminds me of the endless claims made by some that they have built a perpetual motion machine, but I do believe that Douglas was on the right track when he argued that wealth in a twentieth century economy—and it is ever more so in the twenty-first century—is due to factors other than the traditional ones of capital, land, labor and finance. Douglas argued that our wealth was due to our collective cultural inheritance, to intellectual, social, cultural and moral capital. Because of that, my argument is that if we want to develop the means to manage bubbles and their consequences for our collective and individual wealth and well being, we need to understand the importance of intangible capital and we need to be conscious that our ability to produce sustainable wealth rests on our skill in managing intangible capital, including the planet's environment, our biosphere. Thus, my argument for a green agenda, later in the book, is based on enlightened self-interest, not on ideology. Our future and the future of our children and their children can be assured only if we learn to manage the environment as well as we manage machinery and as well as we should manage the land and people.

One more thing; as the proportion of our wealth created by intangibles grows, and as our collective wealth grows, bubbles may become more likely. This is because more and more money is going to be available for us to realize our dreams, such as owning a McMansion, citing a recent example, or whatever may represent the epitome of success for succeeding generations. And because more and more clever people will seek to make a profit for themselves and their shareholders by finding new and creative ways to help us realize our dreams. While anything electronic is going to keep becoming cheaper and cheaper, at least for the foreseeable future that is not the case with anything solid and hard, like housing or real estate in general. More and more money will be chasing a relatively static stock of desirable goods with more and more ways being devised to help more and more of us to secure what we want. Picture this happening in a world where the climate may be greatly reducing the availability of desirable real estate, as the seas rise and potable water becomes ever scarcer, and a bubble based on acquiring apartments in northern Canada or Siberia is not as strange a prospect as you might think. I think that climate change is going to produce much more economic activity and much more systemic instability, making the challenge of managing national economies and the global economy much harder than it has ever been. This means that we need to deepen and broaden our understanding of the interaction between the economy, society and the climate. Focusing on any one of those elements in isolation will doom us to failure, as we blindly grasp the elephant's tail and assume we have it all.

To get the whole elephant, we need to understand how our biology, our psychology and the environment in which we live have shaped and are shaping us and we need to acquire the means to become a partner in that process, rather than a mere construct of it. Understanding the process of natural selection that shapes our economy, as much as it shapes our biology and the biosphere in which we live, is the first step in that direction. In the economic realm, natural selection generates a powerful drive to compete. It is competition that spurs innovation and weeds out failure, just as competition in the jungle rewards organisms that fit prevailing conditions and eliminates those that do not. However, unbridled competition can produce painful and unnecessary collateral damage and can take us to undesirable places. Competition needs to be balanced by participation and collaboration. In a networked and crowded world, we must know when to compete, so that we can win alone, and when to collaborate, so that we can survive together. We need a process of co-evolution, benefiting all participants sustainably, and not evolution that is red in tooth and claw.

Read my lips, it's all about competitiveness

Because of this, the aim in developed countries should be to promote both competitiveness and participation in the global economy. This encompasses both social and economic objectives. There is a strong synergy between economic objectives (competitiveness) and social objectives (participation), because a sophisticated demand side is crucial to the development of an innovative indigenous knowledge economy. As more people go online, the network externalities inherent in the technology grow, as do the chances of achieving a critical mass of online activity. Greater cultural receptivity to technology and its uses is likely to engender both greater demand and greater capacity, in a virtuous cycle. Our wealth, security and success in the twenty-first century will depend on the brainpower and brain output of knowledge workers, many of whom are barely out of nappies and whose view of the world is likely to differ from mine and from older generations in general, including baby-boomers of whom I am one.

In a world where services is the name of the game and the objective is continuing and sustainable economic growth and increasing community connectivity, the emphasis must shift to the demand side, to focus on the needs of users of the technology, rather than the suppliers. The impending doom of companies such as

General Motors, whose ethos has always been build it and it will sell, is an indication of what we must not do. The main challenge for industry and government alike is to identify value propositions for users. New products and services need to be tailored to the community and be compatible with users' lifestyles. Technology must integrate itself into the cultural and social fabric of the nation—or nations, adding to the magnitude of the challenge—and at the same time immerse people in it. This kind of top down and bottom up integration is not easy to achieve. However, the development and widespread adoption of compelling applications in fields such as health, education, community development and entertainment can drive the further development of the knowledge economy and, in turn, create a virtuous economic development and growth cycle.

To achieve this, application providers need to go beyond digitization—putting stuff online—and automation of existing services; we must develop and exploit new capabilities. There is a need to move beyond applications and content generated for the high user audience of young people aged thirteen—twenty-five years, for example, those working in the high tech sector and white collar workers in ICT intensive industries. For this to happen, it will be necessary to tap in to the needs and lifestyle expectations of retirees—a fast growing group with an interest in leisure and quality of lifestyle and recognize the trends in consumer demand towards greater customization and interactivity, giving communities the skills and tools to directly participate by making their own content. After all, what is relevant for most of us is what's happening in our local community. This level of online adoption would embed the technology into the day-to-day lives of families and communities—and businesses, large and small. We will return to these themes in chapter 2.

Understanding and measuring competitiveness

> *Innovation...requires hard, focused, purposeful work.* — *Peter Drucker*

In this book we will spend some time discussing competitiveness. What is competitiveness? There are differing views, but I rely on the definition by the World Economic Forum, which tells us that "A nation's level of competitiveness reflects the extent to which it is able to provide rising prosperity to its citizens." The focus is on "sustained economic growth and long-term prosperity".[47] This perspective is derived from Michael Porter's *The Competitive Advantage of Nations*, where Porter explains,

> *The principal economic goal of a nation is to produce a high and rising standard of living for its citizens. The ability to do so depends not on the amorphous notion of "competitiveness" but on the productivity with which a nation's resources…are employed. Productivity is the value of the output produced by a unit of labor or capital.*

47 *The Global Competitiveness Report 2008-2009*, page 3.

> *It depends on both the quality and features of products (which determine the prices they can command) and the efficiency with which they are produced.*[48]

Porter is the Bishop William Lawrence University Professor at Harvard Business School and is the head of the Institute for Strategy and Competitiveness, which studies competition and its implications for company strategy and the competitiveness of nations, regions and cities. The proposition that productivity is central to competitiveness at both the firm and the macro levels is central to Porter's work and it has much to commend it. Productivity is a reliable indicator of economic success, as the long-running competitiveness series of indices produced by the World Economic Forum (WEF) makes plain. On its website, the WEF defines itself as

> *...an independent, international organization incorporated as a Swiss not-for-profit foundation. We are striving towards a world-class corporate governance system where values are as important a basis as rules. Our motto is 'entrepreneurship in the global public interest'. We believe that economic progress without social development is not sustainable, while social development without economic progress is not feasible. Our vision for the World Economic Forum is threefold. It aims to be: the foremost organization which builds and energizes leading global communities; the creative force shaping global, regional and industry strategies; the catalyst of choice for its communities when undertaking global initiatives to improve the state the world.*[49]

The WEF began life in 1971 as the European Management Forum, formed by a group of European business leaders under the patronage of the European Commission and supported by European industrial associations. It assumed its present name in 1987 and its showpiece, its star attraction is the annual forum held in Davos, Switzerland. The purpose of the WEF and of the annual meeting specifically is to bring together "leaders in business, politics and society to address the issues affecting our world". Attendance is by invitation only. These are statistics published by the WEF for the 2009 event. During the five-day Meeting, about 2,500 participants from ninety-six countries will attend. Around fifty-six percent are business leaders, representing the one thousand most significant companies from around the world, spanning all sectors of the economy. Other participants include 250 public figures, with forty-one heads of state or government, sixty ministers, thirty heads or senior officials of international organizations and ten ambassadors. In addition, there are 510 participants from civil society, including fifty heads or representatives of non-governmental organizations, 225 media leaders, 215 leaders from academic institutions and think tanks, ten religious leaders of different faiths and ten trade union leaders.[50]

The focus of the meeting shifts from year to year and the theme of the 2009

48 From the Palgrave 1998 edition, at page 6.
49 From http://www.weforum.org/en/about/Our%20Organization/index.htm, retrieved on 25 January 2009.
50 Ibid.

event is "Shaping the Post-Crisis World". Werner Wenning, Chairman of the Board of Management of Bayer AG and Co-Chair of the meeting is quoted as saying, "Davos has often provided a major stimulus in the past, and in January 2009 it should again send out clear signals: that risks must be more carefully managed and that we must apply common principles to establish a business ethic based on sustainability."[51] The 2009 WEF produced a raft of outcomes, most of which can be characterized as either aspirational or as talkfests. The only action I single out as potentially useful is this one: "Convening key trade ministers from 17 economies plus the 27-member EU to deter 'beggar-thy-neighbor' policies that would set the world back into a protectionist spiral reminiscent of the 1930s."[52]

As with any epidemic, the natural tendency is to pull up the draw bridges and to take care of one's own, but when dealing with an economic malaise, protectionism and anti-trade behavior spells disaster for all. As previous retreats from globalization have shown, when international trade becomes an evil, much greater evils follow, including large-scale unemployment and, often enough for us to be concerned, war. Also, trade barriers reduce national competitiveness and productivity, whether self-imposed, as was generally the case after World War 1, or imposed by others. For an example of the latter, examine the situation of Cuba, which has been subjected by the USA to an economic blockade for almost half a century. The Cuban economy is a basket case, though it need not be. Cuba's situation is so dire that it is ignored in the Global Competitiveness Report.

The Global Competitiveness Report is a product of the WEF, which it claims to be "the most comprehensive and authoritative assessment of the comparative strengths and weaknesses of national economies, used by governments, academics and business leaders." The Report was first published in 1979 and now covers 134 economies. The Report brings together business and academic perspectives and seeks to rate economies on their competitiveness, as well as providing guidance on how to increase and sustain competitiveness. The platform on which the ratings are compiled is a pair of indices, which assess business competitiveness (BCI) and growth competitiveness (GCI). Each index is made up of several components, which address what the WEF calls the *twelve pillars of economic competitiveness* (see table 3).[53]

51 From http://www.weforum.org/en/events/AnnualMeeting2009/index.htm, retrieved on 25 January 2009.

52 From the complete list of outcomes, at http://www.weforum.org/pdf/AM_2009/DavosOutcomes.pdf, retrieved on 12 March 2009.

53 From chapter 1.1, page 7 of the report.

Table 2: The 12 Pillars of Competitiveness

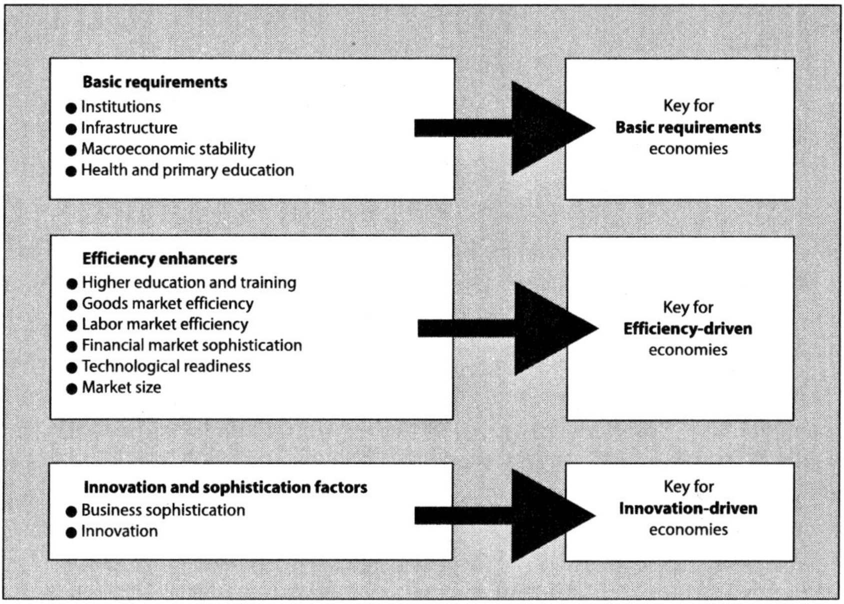

The pillars are: *institutions*, covering governmental elements and, increasingly, private elements, given recent failures of governance; *infrastructure*, which covers transport, utilities and so on; *macroeconomic stability*, which assesses the reliability and continuity of the environment within which business has to operate; *health* and *primary education*, which is self-explanatory, as is *higher education* and *training*; *goods market efficiency*, which assesses how efficiently the market can meet consumer and business demand and expectations; *labor market efficiency*, which focuses on the flexibility and mobility of the workforce; *financial market sophistication*, which needs no explanation; *technological readiness*, with most attention given to ICT; *market size*; *business sophistication*, which "concerns the quality of a country's overall business networks as well as the quality of individual firms' operations and strategies; and *innovation*, which is narrowly defined as technological innovation. In a practical sense, the BCI and GCI together, resting on their twelve pillars, make up a balanced scorecard at the macro or whole of economy (or country) level.

In my view, the twelve pillars are no longer the crucial elements that sustain productivity and, in turn, competitiveness and, in any case, twelve pillars is a few too many. Such a complex catalog of success factors clouds the essential elements on which nations and individual enterprises should focus. In chapter 6, I will propose my own scorecard, which differs from this one in terms of its constituent elements and, more importantly, is simpler.

The BCI includes a rating for the overall environment in the country and a rating for company operations and strategy. The GCI includes ratings for technology, public institutions and the macroeconomic environment. The GCI analyses the potential of an economy to attain sustained economic growth over the medium and long term. The index is founded on three central components: the macroeconomic environment, the quality of public institutions, and technology. The BCI, formerly the Microeconomic Competitiveness Index, identifies the factors that underpin high current productivity and economic performance, as measured by the level of GDP per person. It reflects microeconomic fundamentals, with one sub-index that focuses on company sophistication and another on the quality of the business environment.

In the latest version of this survey, the United States tops the rankings, with Switzerland in second position, followed by Denmark, Sweden and Singapore. European economies continue to prevail in the top ten, with Finland, Germany and the Netherlands following suit. The United Kingdom, while remaining very competitive, has dropped by three places and out of the top ten, which the World Economic Forum attributes to a weakening of its financial markets.[54] The last observation is pertinent and interesting, because the UK seems now likely to be one of the worst afflicted developed economies, as the financial crisis sparked by the subprime debacle plays out. I wonder where the UK will rank in this list when the next one is compiled.

54 The Global Competitiveness Report 2008-2009, from http://www.weforum.org/en/initiatives/gcp/Global%20Competitiveness%20Report/index.htm, retrieved on 25 January 2009.

CHAPTER 1

Foundations

For history is like a nymph glimpsed bathing between leaves: the more you shift perspective, the more is revealed. If you want to see her whole you have to dodge and slip between many different viewpoints. — Felipe Fernández-Armesto.

How to use this book

This chapter provides the context and the foundations of the book, presenting the great ideas on which my own views depend. The next four chapters of the book deal with the waves of change that are the theme of the book, the aftermath of the financial crisis, the impact of information and communication technology, the impact of climate change and the rise of the green movement, and the continuing process of inter-generational change. In each of chapters 2 to 5, practical recommendations relevant to the financial services industry are offered. In chapter 6 we tie the discussion together and further suggestions are made for the benefit of both the industry and regulators.

In chapter 7, which concludes the book, I provide hints and tips for those who make a living in and from the financial services industry. I include hints on how to avoid getting caught up in a bubble or in a dodgy Madoff-like scheme; indicators of an inflating bubble and strategies that you can use to benefit through this process—without pumping more air into the bubble; and strategies to use when a bubble has burst.

To help make sense of the words in these many pages, I have devised a matrix (table 2) that places current events—and future events about which I speculate—in their proper context, the context of history. It is a condensed view of human history, starting in recent pre-history and ending in proximate future-story. Like all history, my-story may tell you more about the writer than about the subject matter, but, if used wisely, this table can help you to understand where we are, where we have been and where we are likely to go—and why. There is evidence to back up the broad characterizations in the table. For example, it is not hard to see how much we all fear being marginalized—and how much we fear those who are marginalized.

That is not unexpected in a society where there are large differences between rich and poor, where information is power and where the "other" is always there to threaten us—the end of the Cold War left us with one superpower and no "other" against which that superpower could test itself, no "other" to be used as an excuse to spend money on weapons, security and to advance the interests of what Dwight Eisenhower called the military-industrial complex. A new "other" has emerged, in the guise of terrorism, fundamentalist Islamic terrorism, to be precise, which, just as the Soviet Empire, is seen as a threat to Western values and Western civilization and must be fought at any cost and anywhere.

We will return to this table and what it means later in the book, when the story is closer to its denouement. For the moment it is sufficient to know that we are in the final throes of the post-industrial era and we are moving towards or perhaps stumbling into the knowledge era.

Table 1.1: A condensed view of human history

Type of economy	Hunter/ gatherer (the last 1 million years)	Agricultural (the last 10,000 years)	Industrial (yesterday)	Post-industrial (today)	Knowledge (tomorrow)
Salient characteristics					
Settlement mode (how do we live)	Nomadic	Rural	Urban	Suburban	Metropolitan
Social orientation (how do we define ourselves)	Tribe	Extended family	Work	Self	Cluster
Ethical orientation (how is morality defined)	Fate (animistic)	Duties (religious)	Rights (ideological)	Mutual obligations (economic)	Self-actualization (spiritual)
Political system (continuum)	Charismatic… despotic	Collectivist… Despotic	Democratic… authoritarian	Oligarchic… Democratic	Anarchic… corporatist
Economic orientation (how do we create value)	Autarchic	Exchange	Mercantilist	Globalized	Eclectic
Value orientation (what do we value)	Survival	Community	Prosperity	Information	Understanding
Nemesis (what do we fear)	Death	Exclusion	Poverty	Marginalization and the marginalized	Being ignored
Apotheosis (to what do we aspire)	Continuity	Heaven	Wealth	Relevance	Nirvana

Glimpses of the nymph: the untruth of history

Because history and historians give us only glimpses of the truth, I will provide enough glimpses to help us to see the nymph of truth entire—with the caution that you may have to use your own imagination to fill in the inevitable blanks. My choice of sources is eclectic, so as to give us the best chance to home in on the truth and I have included a non-historian, so that the perspective provided by the lens of the social sciences can be complemented by the lens of science. Let us start in the nineteenth century, the period during which the foundations of the twentieth century were built. We will start with Karl Marx, who was perhaps the most influential thinker of an era that produced many strong influences. Marx taught us that history has deep patterns and that identifying and understanding these patterns and their causes can help us to understand where and why the future might take us. In chapter 1 of *The Eighteenth Brumaire of Louis Bonaparte*, Marx observed, "Men make their own history, but they do not make it as they please; they do not make it under self-selected circumstances, but under circumstances existing already, given and transmitted from the past. The tradition of all dead generations weighs like an Alp on the brains of the living...".

Marx (aided by Friedrich Engels), developed a theory of history that led him to conclude that the demise of capitalism and the triumph of the proletariat (in the form of communism) was inevitable, an outcome pre-determined by history. In 1844, Marx wrote, "Communism is the riddle of history solved, and it knows itself to be this solution…" and "The entire movement of history (is) simply communism's actual act of genesis…".[1] Marx was theorizing prospectively, extrapolating the future from what he saw as the inevitable result of the past. Francis Fukuyama, pondering on the events of the relatively recent past, reached quite a different conclusion, hailing the global triumph of capitalism—or, as he puts it, "Western liberal democracy"— in a book titled *The End of History and the Last Man*:

> *What we may be witnessing is not just the end of the Cold War, or the passing of a particular period of post-war history, but the end of history as such... That is, the end point of mankind's ideological evolution and the universalization of Western liberal democracy as the final form of human government.*

This conclusion is built on three premises:

- most governments in the world are now democratic and alternative forms of government are becoming discredited;
- the end of the human desire to gain supremacy over others; and
- the universality of the market as the means to create and distribute wealth.

1 In Private Property and Communism, from http://www.marxists.org/archive/marx/works/1844/manuscripts/comm.htm#44CC4, retrieved on 8 February 2009.

All the ancient histories, as one of our wits say, are just fables that have been agreed upon. — Voltaire

Very few things happen at the right time, and the rest do not happen at all: the conscientious historian will correct these defects. — Herodotus

History is a vast early warning system. — Norman Cousins

Fukuyama relied on organizations such as Freedom House to argue for the victory of democracy. The most recent report from Freedom House[2] divides the world into:

- Free: 3,028.2 million (forty-six percent of the world's population) live in ninety of the states.[3]
- Partly free: 1,185.3 million (eighteen percent of the world's population) live in sixty of the states.
- Not free: 2,391.4 million (thirty-six percent of the world's population) live in forty-three of the states.

At best I would call this a draw, rather than a win for democracy, noting that of the 121 "electoral democracies" in the world, as counted by Freedom House, some are democracies in name only, such as Mongolia, for example.[4] I fail to see how Mongolia is more democratic than Russia, as Freedom House would have it. In the same report, Freedom House also has observed that there has been "A resurgence of pragmatic, market-oriented, or energy-rich dictatorships. Most visibly in Russia and China, but also in other parts of the world, governments are trying to harness the power of the marketplace while maintaining closed political systems."

On this evidence, I would say that the first of Fukuyama's premises is shaky indeed. As for the second, human nature has not changed, as we will see later. We are not living in a New Jerusalem or in Marx's private-property free communist utopia. As the more than forty wars and conflicts afflicting the world in 2008 illustrate, the desire to gain supremacy over others is alive and well.[5] This leaves only the third premise standing,

2 Its website describes Freedom House as "a non-profit, nonpartisan organization…a clear voice for democracy and freedom around the world".

3 From http://www.freedomhouse.org/template.cfm?page=130&year=2008, retrieved on 11 January 2009.

4 See "Stabilized Democracy in Mongolia in 2005", by Jeong-jin Lee, Policy Forum Online 05-91A: November 10th, 2005, retrieved from http://www.nautilus.org/fora/security/0591Lee.html on 7 April 2009.

5 "The United Nations defines "major wars" as military conflicts inflicting 1,000 battlefield deaths per year. In 1965, there were 10 major wars under way. The new millennium began with much of the world consumed in armed conflict or cultivating an uncertain peace. As of mid-2005, there were eight Major Wars under way [down from 15 at the end of 2003], with as many as two dozen "lesser" conflicts ongoing with varying degrees of intensity" (from http://www.globalsecurity.org/military/world/war/index.html, retrieved on 8 February 2009).

the universality of the market. As Freedom House has observed, and China is the exemplar in this case, having a market economy is quite compatible with authoritarian, non-democratic forms of government. I regret to say that Fukuyama's celebration of the triumph of Western liberal democracy may have been a little premature.

> *In short, both organic and human history involve the playing of ever-more-numerous, ever-larger, and ever-more-elaborate non-zero-sum games.*—Robert Wright

If history has not ended, what is going on?

In a famous essay, Samuel P Huntington, who died recently, postulated the clash of civilizations as the primary source of conflict in the post-Cold War world. He argued that cultural and religious identities, suppressed by the Superpowers during the Cold War, had resumed their role as the drivers of intra and inter-national strife and war. Where Fukuyama saw the triumph of Western civilization, Huntington saw the delayed continuation of the conflict between Christianity and Islam that occupied much of the Middle Ages and early Renaissance. In the 1993 essay, the theme of which later grew to occupy a book, *The Clash of Civilizations and the Remaking of World Order*, Huntington wrote:

> *It is my hypothesis that the fundamental source of conflict in this new world will not be primarily ideological or primarily economic. The great divisions among humankind and the dominating source of conflict will be cultural. Nation states will remain the most powerful actors in world affairs, but the principal conflicts of global politics will occur between nations and groups of different civilizations. The clash of civilizations will dominate global politics. The fault lines between civilizations will be the battle lines of the future.*[6]

It seems to me that while seeking to define a post-Cold War world, Huntington's mind was firmly mired in a Cold War-like perception of geopolitical reality, postulated on two dominant players calling the shots and using proxies to fight each other. The evidence does not support this. Going back to the forty or so conflicts in the world in 2008, about half were in Africa and involved no one but Africans—often in the form of inter-tribal strife. Of the other half, aside from Iraq and Afghanistan, only a handful involved Western nations, including Israel under that rubric. Looking at the facts, one should conclude that the principal conflicts of global politics are rooted in geography and ethnicity, and not in a supposed clash of civilizations, noting that this concept of

6 "The Clash of Civilizations?", *Foreign Affairs*, Summer 1993.

civilization, at least as Huntington used it, is a curious thing indeed.

Huntington divided the world into "major" civilizations, identifying seven or eight such: Western, Latin American, Islamic, Sinic or Chinese, Hindu, Orthodox, Japanese, and African. I think this is a strange use of the term, civilization. The *Oxford English Dictionary* defines civilization as "the action or process of civilizing or of being civilized; a developed or advanced state of human society." Being civilized refers to being part of a complex, settled society, where cities are the core of the culture of that society. It means not being a barbarian or a primitive; it means being refined, enjoying good food, good manners, art, music and so on. It means that the political system is structured as a state, that there are hierarchies and a culture with traits peculiar to that society.

If this is the case, lumping together European and North American societies under the label of the West, while leaving out Latin America, is peculiar, hard to justify—and what about countries such as South Africa? South Africa is a liberal democracy, has legal and political institutions that are derived from and remain similar to those found in Europe, and is primarily a Christian nation. Yes, it was once an authoritarian state, but so were Spain, Greece and Portugal, for example. Would it be bad of me to suggest that South Africa is not deemed by Huntington to be part of the West because its population is mainly black and because it is located at the bottom of Africa? Surely, since Australia and New Zealand are part of the West, it cannot be that geography is a factor, as they are more distant from Europe and the USA than South Africa is...which leaves only race as a factor...or leads me to conclude that Huntington's so-called civilizations are merely an arbitrary way to justify a theory that appears to have little or no foundation in fact.

> *For the history of civilizations is a path picked among ruins.*—Felipe Fernández-Armesto

It may be that the events of 9/11 (and what followed) led Huntington to believe that al Qaeda and the Taliban were the vanguards of a global Muslim crusade against the West. It may be that having reached this conclusion, he sought to place it in a context he understood, because, as GN Clark said, "Truth is the same thing to the understanding as music to the ear or beauty to the eye".[7] The problem is that the tune Huntington composed with the notes he was given is a cacophony, rather than a symphony, it is a mélange of opinions, rather than a hypothesis rooted to factual foundations. Yet, after 9/11, it was claimed that Huntington's view of the world was correct, because the attacks by the West[8] on New York and the subsequent invasions of Afghanistan

7 As quoted by Felipe Fernández-Armesto in *Truth: A History and a Guide for the Perplexed.*

8 It is worth pointing out that the Coalition of the Willing that invaded Iraq was essentially a US/UK military force, while the attack on the Taliban in Afghanistan was a broader effort, which, in Huntington's terms, was cross-civilizational, rather than merely Western.

and Iraq were wars of values, clashes between the West and Islam. While this thesis is attractively simple, it is fundamentally flawed, a sophisticated version of the Orientalist fallacy exposed long ago by writers Edward Said. As Said observed:

> *The depictions of "the Arab" as irrational, menacing, untrustworthy, anti-Western, dishonest, and—perhaps most importantly—prototypical, are ideas into which Orientalist scholarship has evolved. These notions are trusted as foundations for both ideologies and policies developed by the Occident. Said writes: "The hold these instruments have on the mind is increased by the institutions built around them. For every Orientalist, quite literally, there is a support system of staggering power, considering the ephemerality of the myths that Orientalism propagates. The system now culminates into the very institutions of the state. To write about the Arab Oriental world, therefore, is to write with the authority of a nation, and not with the affirmation of a strident ideology but with the unquestioning certainty of absolute truth backed by absolute force."*[9]

Civilizations do not clash, nor do they fight wars; nations do, tribes do, people do. Most of the wars of the eighteenth, nineteenth and twentieth centuries were fought by people and nations that saw themselves as part of the West. While the two great wars of the twentieth century were classed as world wars, because of their geographic scope, the central clash of values in each case was shaped and fought by nations of the west, Britain, France and Germany in the first and the Atlantic Alliance led by the USA and Germany in the second—and that the principal battlefield was Europe. It is no surprise to me that since Europe has embraced the path of peaceful union, the world has seen no more global wars. To place al Qaeda and its ilk in the same class as Adolf Hitler or even in the role of Stalin in the Cold War is wrong and reflects a desire on the part of some to manufacture yet another excuse to cover up grand policy failures at home and to justify adventurism in international affairs that aggrandizes leaders and nations and cheapens the blood that was shed by millions who fought real tyrants and enemies of civilization.

It is all a matter of perspective

The division of the world into civilizations, with the primary struggle between the West and the Muslims, is no more a viable and credible hypothesis than was the domino theory of the 1960s or the fear of Russian invasion that was endemic in the nineteenth century, affecting countries as far removed from Czarist Russia as Australia. In each case, what we have is a political belief (or ideology) masquerading as historical truth. This is not surprising, because history is not truth, if truth is an objective, factual account of what happened and why. History is a post-hoc interpretation of events, usually written

9 From *Orientalism*, by Edward Said.

by the victors. History is an opinion-based story of the world, with facts cited selectively to support a particular interpretation. This means that relying on one history or one historian is a risky thing to do, if we want to apply lessons from the past (or present) to prepare ourselves for the future.

By studying the historical perspectives that Marx, Fukuyama and Huntington (and others) have formulated, I have learnt that the fundamental human condition is hard to escape. Genetics and millennia of culture weigh on us and shape our thoughts, feelings, dreams and lives. I have also learnt that each of these men made a fundamental error. The cause of the error is this: each of these men was brought up in a world where the Darwinian world view was accepted as the dominant paradigm, not just in the natural sciences, but, in a diluted form, across the whole realm of scientific though, hard, soft and in-between, including history, sociology and economics. Note that I am not saying that Marx, Fukuyama and Huntington were consciously practicing social Darwinism, the belief that the strongest or fittest individual or state will win out in the end over the weaker and the less fit.

However, as any educated person would, then and now, they unconsciously accepted the premise that history is but an application of Darwinism in the realm of human events. Why is this an error? As we will see later, it is an error because evolution is not synonymous with progress, with improvement; evolution is not a long, tedious journey culminating with humanity as its final product. Darwin never argued that this was so, by the way, just as he never said or wrote that natural selection is about the survival of the fittest—Darwin told us that evolution is about the survival of the fit.

This may seem like a quibble, but it is not. If the Earth of the future were characterized by conditions that do not allow for human survival, we would disappear and some other species would take over. Most likely, that species would not be as intelligent, cultured or technological as our own. Putting any modesty on behalf our species aside for a moment, we humans may well be the fittest animals that have ever lived, if intelligence is the measure of fitness, but being the fittest offers no guarantees of long-term survival for our species. It is the same with our present mode of political and economic organization. What we have now, our civilization, may well be the best that has ever been—but that does not guarantee the survival of capitalism or of democracy. On the other hand, glancing at the silver lining of this particular cloud, there is no certainty that capitalism and democracy will not continue to evolve and survive, a process that, in a modest way, this book seeks to assist.

The evolution of human society

Marx believed—and put together a powerful case to support his belief—that history is the story of the inevitable rise of the proletariat, as capitalism is eventually brought undone by contradictions it cannot resolve, ushering in, after an in-between era of socialist tribulations, the era of communism, which, for the uninitiated, is like a Christian state without Christ—or any god at all. From each according to his (or her) skills and to each according to his (or her) needs, which would no longer be essentially materialistic, but spiritual, befitting the communist heaven on Earth that Marx had foreseen. We are still living in a world shaped by this ideology and by its antagonists, including the various Judeo-Christian religions, as each ideology has fought for hearts and minds through promises of relief from this vale of tears, in various forms. On the basis of a carefully constructed argument, Fukuyama postulated that capitalism, having succeeded in resolving its inherent contradictions (or at least succeeding in managing them), had at the end of the twentieth century transcended the course of history as defined by Marx and by those who wrote alternative histories that sought to refute Marx. Thus, for Fukuyama, history had ended and ideology had ceased to be a fundamental driver of change.

Huntington took an alternative, though parallel position, taking Fukuyama head on, arguing that, ideology is dead, if ideology is taken to be including, Nazism, Communism or capitalism), but an older form of ideology had resumed its dominant place in shaping history, because of the end of the Cold War and the weakening of nation-states. In Huntington's world view, the old battles between capitalism and communism would be replaced by battles between western values and Islamic values, for example, or between Sinic (Chinese) and Indian values, and so on, though for Huntington the fundamental divide of the twenty-first century would be between the western and Muslim "civilizations".

The apotheosis of this view of the world could be seen in the shape and character of the presidency of George W. Bush and in the pronouncements of lesser lights such as (former) British Prime Minister Tony Blair or from the lips of vaudeville politicians like Italian Prime Minister Silvio Berlusconi, and could be discerned in various forms through the first decade of the twenty-first century in literature, popular culture and in the words of Polish and German popes of the Roman Catholic Church, for example. In particular, the events of 9/11 and what followed have been taken by many as proof that Huntington was right. The belief in Manichaeism, the ever present battle between the equal powers of good and evil, is deep inside us, despite the best efforts of Christian churches to establish God as an omnipotent being, with power over evil. I beg to differ—Huntington's thesis is wrong.

It is still all about bread and circuses—and the occasional war

In *Civilizations*, Fernández-Armesto says that "to understand man properly, you have to see him in the context of the rest of nature" and that "All history is…in a sense, historical ecology."[10] Our history, including the history that has yet to be, is about how we have survived and thrived by exploiting the resources we have found around us and by competing with each other, in various ways, some lethal and some not. Since the first human tribes roamed the Earth, we have been driven first and foremost by personal and group survival, striving to keep the others (and there is always *others*) at bay and preferably subject to our power. The forces that shape geo-political events today are the same as they have always been, a mélange of the macro and of the micro, of national survival and personal ambition. We are what we are as a result of millennia of complex game-playing, by individuals, groups and nation, with the ultimate prize at stake: survival. My thesis is that the drive to survive has always been the master of our fate and that the nation-state, which is its creature and chief agent, is not withering away, though it may be changing its form. Culture, like religion or ideology is nothing more than a garb worn to deceive and to distract, while the real business of the exercise of power goes on in the background. There are auxiliary forces, such as individual greed or ambition and the desire for wealth and prestige—do you actually think that cathedrals and temples are built for the gods, rather than the priests or the communities that bask in their reflected glory, or that banks need to have such lavish and enormous headquarters?

There is also game-playing—because we all like to play games, whether we understand it or not—which is the last, but not always the least factor. Where there are complex systems, there will be complex games, which occasionally can take on a life of their own. Remember the 1962 Cuba crisis, for example? That is a classic example of a runaway game, as was the 1983 near global holocaust portrayed in a recent movie. It seems that in 1983 nuclear war was close than at any time since the Cuban Missile Crisis. The USSR was convinced NATO was about to launch World War III and was preparing a strike of its own. Ronald Reagan and his advisers may have thought they were playing a long game of bluff to send the USSR broke, casting Moscow as the "evil empire", but the game looked quite different from the other side—it looked like a game of survival, with the USA as the evil empire, armed to the teeth and ready to fire first. So, when NATO carried out a huge military exercise called "Able Archer", or "Able Archer 83", designed to simulate the use of nuclear weapons in an assault against the Soviet Union, and to test command and control procedures, the Soviets saw a cover for a real first strike by NATO. Such a perspective was not unreasonable, particularly when NATO escalated its military alert levels to the point at which NATO nuclear weapons are ready for launch. Fortunately, the game eventually played itself out to a benign end, but it could easily have been otherwise.

Survival, greed, ambition and gaming, operate at different levels within society and sometimes individuals come along who are so powerful that for a moment in time they can distort the fabric of history or so it seems. In 1942, the Japanese military

10 *Civilizations. Culture, Ambition, and the Transformation of Nature*, pages 15-16.

hierarchy tried to game the USA, attacking Hawaii to take out the American Pacific Fleet and to suggest to the Americans that they should allow Japan to carve out an empire in Asia, leaving the USA to dominate the Americas and the Germans to do likewise in Europe. Unfortunately for the Japanese people, the Americans decided to play a very different game, with the outcome we all know, perhaps because of the influence of powerful individuals, such as Roosevelt and Churchill, who was perhaps the master-gamer of the twentieth century. My hypothesis is that any event or era in history for which there is adequate documentation can be explained by reference to this simple rubric of motivations, rather than to a complex theory built on shifting foundations—Ockham's razor at work.[11]

A current example, as explained by Stephan Faris in *Forecast*, is the tragedy of Darfur, in Sudan. Over the last two decades, millions of people have been displaced from their homes and lands and hundreds of thousands have died, been tortured or raped or suffered all three. Prima facie, the sides in the conflict in Darfur are determined by ethnic and cultural divides, because the opposing sides are white Arab nomads and black farmers, differing in race, culture and lifestyle. However, despite some reports to the contrary, both nomads and farmers are prevalently Muslim, which means that the cultural divide between them is limited to lifestyle, mirroring the divide between ranchers and farmers in the American west in the nineteenth and early twentieth centuries. I do not recall anyone ever describing those events as a conflict of cultures, do you? Whatever happened between ranchers and farmers in the USA was due to one thing only—both sides wanted the same bit of land or the same body of water.

It is no different in Darfur. Despite their differences, Faris explains, until climate change in Sudan intervened, these people, black and white, famer and nomad, had lived peacefully together for countless generations, sharing the land through arrangements established by long-held traditions and customs. The black/white and nomad/farmer divisions erupted into conflict only when the land they had shared for so long failed them, because of protracted drought. This has caused harsh competition between farmers and nomads, which has been exploited and made worse by the Sudanese regime for its own political purposes. The cause of the conflict is competition for scarce resources; it is economics that is killing people in Darfur, not religion or race or any difference in culture or values.

A similar explanation can be constructed for conflicts in contemporary Africa, in twentieth century Europe or any other era in human history. While religion, values, culture, race will often be advanced as causes of war, closer analysis will almost always demonstrate conflict arose from causes related to competition for scarce resources, ranging from land, to water, to gold and even people, where slavery is legal. Yes, values

11 William of Ockham was a fourteenth century friar and philosopher. Among other things, he formulated a principle stating that the explanation of any phenomenon should make as few assumptions as possible, eliminating those that make no difference in the observable predictions of the explanatory hypothesis or theory. This is known as Ockham's razor.

sometimes differ between combatants and sometimes civilization is put at risk during a war, but Hitler made war to acquire land and a cheap workforce, just as the South fought the North for five bitter years of civil war to protect its economic base—the abolition of slavery was an economic casus belli, not a moral one, as Abraham Lincoln himself made clear in 1862.[12] As I said earlier, people have commented that the post 9/11 conflicts in Afghanistan and Iraq have confirmed that Huntington was right, because they were examples of a clash of civilizations, Judeo-Christian and Muslim. The way I see it is that a western coalition, mainly Christian, has installed a Muslim, predominantly Shiite, government in Iraq, which, when US troops leave, will cozy up to its Shiite neighbor, Iran. This it will do, not because of religion, but to avoid another Iran-Iraq war, like the one that killed millions in the 1980s. By the way, I wonder how Huntington fits that war in his theory?

The explanation I prefer is that the war was an episode in a struggle for regional supremacy that has gone on for thousands of years, originally driven by the desire to acquire fertile land and water and now by oil and water. As the planet warms up, water will again be the source of many conflicts and in this dry region more than elsewhere, I think. In a later chapter, we will examine several scenarios, courtesy of Gwynne Dyer, that envisage the world at war over food, water and energy.

On with the story: building on big ideas

This book tells of a connected series of happenings, some historical, some related to the present day and some that are speculative, as they concern the future. In other words, this book tells a story, so let us start as any good story should start. Once upon a time, there was a dark and stormy century, full of vague but huge threats—terrorism, global warming, pandemics—with rising giants—China, India—declining giants—the United States of America, the European Union —and many beleaguered small to medium size economies, striving to secure a place in a cut-throat, globalized economy, where size did matter. In this world, after a long period of relative stability, there came a great financial crisis, perhaps the worst since the Great Depression, and people, many for the first time, felt the cold winds of recession and deflation—and panic.

12 Lincoln stated in 1862 that, "I would save the Union. I would save it the shortest way under the Constitution. The sooner the national authority can be restored; the nearer the Union will be "the Union as it was...My paramount object in this struggle is to save the Union, and is not either to save or to destroy slavery. If I could save the Union without freeing any slave I would do it, and if I could save it by freeing all the slaves I would do it; and if I could save it by freeing some and leaving others alone I would also do that. What I do about slavery, and the colored race, I do because I believe it helps to save the Union; and what I forbear, I forbear because I do not believe it would help to save the Union. I shall do less whenever I shall believe what I am doing hurts the cause, and I shall do more whenever I shall believe doing more will help the cause. I shall try to correct errors when shown to be errors; and I shall adopt new views so fast as they shall appear to be true views. I have here stated my purpose according to my view of official duty; and I intend no modification of my oft-expressed personal wish that all men everywhere could be free." From "Letter to Horace Greeley", http://showcase.netins.net/web/creative/lincoln/speeches/greeley.htm, retrieved on 7 February 2009.

I know nothing except the fact of my ignorance. — Socrates

This may sound familiar to you—and it should. This story is set in the twenty-first century and you are right in the thick of it, together with your fellow readers—of whom I hope there are many. In fact, you are not merely reading this story, you are writing it, shaping events and creating the future as you go. In that future, after this crisis has gone and the bulls have had another run, your children and your children's children will themselves experience the highs of investment bubbles and the pain of bubbles bursting. I suggest that reading this story and applying what you learn from it—and passing it on to the next generation—will be well worth your time and money. The origin of this book is a series of great ideas—other people's ideas, seven in total—brought together in a spirit of consilience, which itself is the first big idea, to which we will turn in a moment.

Because, like Socrates, I am wise enough to know the limits of my knowledge and understanding of these complex matters, I will also review the work of others whose thinking may help us to make sense of it all, mostly economists, but not all. I will consider, in no particular order, the work of Paul Ormerod, John Maynard Keynes, Mark Moore, Milton Friedman, Paul Krugman, George Soros, Thomas Friedman, John Kenneth Galbraith—and others, as we will see later. The selection has been based on the principle of consilience. You will also see that I draw on the experience of other industries in dealing with similar problems. When I do that, I am not borrowing solutions, because that would be risky, given the peculiarities of each industry, rather I draw out principles that are then used to shape solutions that fit the circumstances of the financial services industry. This is another example of consilience.

The first great idea: consilience

Consilience is a term that describes the desire to synthesize the many branches of human knowledge that have grown from the original seeds of knowledge cultivated by the earliest humans. The concept comes from the work of one of the chief architects of sociobiology, EO Wilson. Consilience occurs when explanations of two or more different kinds of phenomena are discovered separately, but unexpectedly lead scientists to the same underlying cause. Consilience encourages scholars to bridge the many gaps between and within the sciences, hard and soft, and the arts. No such gaps should exist, Wilson maintains, arguing that the sciences, humanities, and arts have a common goal: to give understanding a purpose, to lend to us all "a conviction, far deeper than a mere working proposition, that the world is orderly and can be explained by a small number of natural laws."[13] This book is an exercise in consilience and so allow me to introduce two great ideas that have generally been seen as antagonistic, though not by the protagonists. These great ideas here have been competitors in the realm of

13 *Consilience: The Unity of Knowledge*, New York, Random House 1999.

evolutionary biology, though now Lamarck's theory is considered to be wrong. Why am I discussing evolutionary biology? As we will see later, there is much that business has to learn from the theory and reality of evolution, starting with the notion of the survival of the fit—not the fittest, the fit.

The origins: Darwin and Lamarck

While they have been competing ideas in the field of evolutionary biology , but in the realm of cultural evolution, as we will see, Darwin and Lamarck's great ideas sit well together[14] Darwin's great idea was that biological evolution takes place through natural selection. Lamarck's great idea was that biological evolution could also occur through the direct inheritance of acquired characteristics, echoing Fernández-Armesto's concept of historical ecology. Allow me to make the difference clearer. According to Darwin, if a species—such as the koala bear or the panda, for example—is reliant on a diet of leaves from a particular plant and that plant becomes scarce or disappears, then the koala or panda will die out, will become extinct, unless any of their number, perhaps because of a genetic mutation, can manage to eat some other plant, which the rest of their fellows could not do. In this case, the genetic material was altered—and the animal's behavior was consequently altered—before the environment changed so as to make that mutation valuable. The behavior followed the genes. This is how evolution works, according to Darwin—this is the orthodox or dominant view.

Jean-Baptiste Lamarck was born in France in 1744; he was a biologist and author of *Flore français (French Flora)*, published in 1773 and *Philosophie zoologique (Zoology)*, published in 1809. Lamarck was the dominant thinker on biological evolution before Charles Darwin came on to the scene. His study of invertebrates in *Histoire des animaux sans vertèbres (Natural History of Invertebrate Animals)*, published in 1822, led to the conviction that species evolve through the hereditary transmission of acquired traits, by means of which each species perfects its adaptation to its environment. For example, Lamarck maintained that the giraffe developed a long neck by stretching to reach tall trees, and then passed this characteristic to its offspring.

Returning to our example of a species faced with starvation because of a dramatic change in the availability of its food source, Lamarck would have argued that if a particular Koala or Panda, faced with a shortage of food, were to develop a taste for some other plant, thus enabling that animal to survive, then that preference would become embedded in its genetic line and would be passed on to its offspring. In this case, the genes would have followed the change in behavior. The contemporary view

14 It is worth noting that epigenetic research may eventually give Lamarck the last laugh. Epigenetics is the study of influences other than DNA that shape the development of an organism—and the environment is a big factor here. For example, recent Australian research suggests that fat people reprogram controls over their DNA and pass on fatness and disease to their children and to future generations (see http://www.news.com.au/heraldsun/story/0,21985,24919451-661,00.html) .

is that this is not possible, though there are some scientists who believe otherwise.[15] Almost immediately after the publication of *On the Origin of Species* in 1859, Charles Darwin's theory of natural selection replaced Lamarck's theory of inheritance of acquired characteristics. Darwin's theory holds that individual variability means that some organisms have a slight advantage over others in their particular ecological niche. That advantage, such as a longer neck when vegetation on or close to the ground is scarce, will allow the organism to be a better competitor in the "struggle for existence". The favored organism will produce more offspring, which in turn will inherit the advantageous qualities, such as a longer neck. Through many generations, this process will produce an animal with a very long neck that is well adapted to grazing on trees, such as a giraffe. That is how biological evolution works.

This theory, by way of metaphor, can also be applied in the realm of human social behavior, in business, for example. In a highly dynamic business environment, an enterprise that is flexible, adaptable and responsive to the demands of the market is more likely to survive and to grow than an enterprise that is limited in its capacity to respond, which is more likely do "die", especially if the business environment hits a particularly turbulent period. However, my argument is that this happens by means of a process akin to Lamarck's hereditary transmission of acquired traits, rather than a simple Darwinian weeding out—we will see later how this works. For now, Let us leave biology, to travel into the realm of the dismal science, economics, where we find our fourth great idea.

Adam Smith, champion of competition

The next great idea is that the market, if left to itself, will tend to revert to a new equilibrium, a new state of balance, after any significant shock it suffers. Or, to put it another way, the economy of a nation-state or of the planet as a whole is a homeostatic entity, capable of sustaining itself in a dynamic environment. That idea comes from Adam Smith. Smith, in *An Inquiry into the Nature and Causes of the Wealth of Nations*, written in 1776, considered that such phenomena as the division of labor were a necessary consequence of certain characteristics inherent to the psychological or social characteristics of human beings. His work is often misunderstood and maligned, for the wrong reasons. Before I read what Smith wrote, rather than what others thought about it, I thought that Adam Smith was a champion of laissez-faire economics and of unbridled market forces. I was wrong. Yes, perhaps Smith's belief in the benevolent results that would flow from the actions of "the invisible hand" was misplaced, because the invisible hand, like evolution, is a blind force that does not necessarily result in progress, *if progress is defined as improvement.* In Smith's world view, as in Darwin's,

15 See *Lamarck's Signature*, by EJ Steele, RA Lindley and RV Blanden, Allen & Unwin, Sydney, 1998, where the authors argue that developments in molecular genetics have restored credibility to Lamarck's theory of hereditary transmission.

evolution is not an uninterrupted progress towards higher forms, however defined; indeed, evolution may result in extinction or in reversion to an earlier (or "lower") state, if that is what the environment and chance (or complexity and chaos) combine to produce.

A classic example in the field of technology is the success of VHS over Betamax technology in the manufacture of video cassette recorders. Betamax was technically superior, but VHS was better suited to the commercial environment in which both products had to survive.[16] Many would say the same about Apple Macs and Windows personal computers or, with the wisdom of hindsight, our grandchildren may say the same about cars powered by internal combustion. In the realm of biology, many species have disappeared from the face of the Earth; some, like dinosaurs, for example, disappeared after a very long period of dominance over the planet's ecology, a period at least fifty times as long as the time that humans have been on the Earth. For any species, the culmination of evolutionary progress may be extinction.

In the arena of competing nation states, the dramatic collapse of the Eastern European command economies is another example of extinction, in some cases, of reversion in other cases, and of improvement in others. East Germany disappeared altogether, merged, though not fully integrated, into a reunified Germany. The Russian economy took many years to return to pre-Yeltsin production levels. Countries like Poland or Hungary are faring much better as capitalist economies than they did as command economies—and their growth curve has been rapid. The unifying theme is that each of these entities has had to adapt to changing environments, with very differing outcomes, despite shared conditions and common circumstances. It is ever thus for organizations engaged in the world of business, as an analysis of the *Fortune 500* lists for the last few decades will illustrate—only a few survive across more than a decade or two. Those that survive, do so because they put into practice the next big idea, non-zero, to remain sustainable businesses despite repeated attempts by the invisible hand to wipe them from the marketplace.

Zero and non-zero

Economics helps us to understand how people deal with wants and needs in an environment where resources are scarce or perceived to be scarce, harking back to the psychological dimension. I prefer this formulation because it makes it clear that when money is involved, human behavior is driven by a complex equation, involving a mixture of need and greed that is shaped by the perceptions of others, as well as our own. In truth, because of this mixture of psychology, sociology and greed, the economy is a wicked problem. By that I mean two things, understanding and managing the economy is a difficult challenge and, more importantly, that it is a wicked problem. As

16 It was all about recording time, perhaps. A VHS recorder could store four hours of television on a tape, perfect for recording the evening prime time schedule or afternoon football games.

we saw earlier, a wicked problem is a problem that cannot be easily defined, requires complex judgments, has no clear stopping rules—it is not clear when the problem is fixed—has better or worse solutions, not right and wrong ones, has no objective measure of success, requires iteration, and has strong moral, political or professional dimensions—or occasionally, as in this case, all three. In short, wicked problems cannot be solved, they can only be managed, and, first they must be understood. A bit like people really; we can be managed or even led, if we are understood by those who seek to manage or to lead, but who can solve the mysteries embedded in each of us?

As is the case with people, to understand a wicked problem, we need to deal in perceptions, as much as we need to tackle the substance of the problem. We need both culture and psychology, because how we perceive is a product of who we are and where we are. So, economics can help us to understand why people behave in certain ways when engaging with others over the allocation and use of scarce resources, like money, for example. This means that we now have the tools to understand who does what to whom and why, but we cannot yet tell us how this complex multi-player game plays out—and there are many ways the game can be played. To do this, we need to understand game theory.

Game theory is the systematic study of behavior in situations involving interdependencies. It is also known as "multi-person decision theory" or "the analysis of conflict". Game theory enables the examination of a situation in which a player in a game is affected by what others may do and what s/he may do in turn. The outcome of the game depends on everyone's decisions and how those decisions are perceived by participants. The relevance of game theory to planning is that, in an environment where there is competition—for resources, markets or anything else—each organization is dependent on what other organizations do. The roots of game theory are to be found in the work by John von Neumann and Oskar Morgenstern, who defined two types of games: in rule-based (or cooperative) games, players interact according to specific "rules of engagement", which are generally explicit; in the second type (non-cooperative games), players interact without explicit rules, although they may still abide by implicit "rules" or understandings.

Game theory has found many applications, particularly in economic theory, but has also been used in analyzing situations where strategy, competition and decision-making are problematic. Commercial organizations are caught up in both rule-based and non-rule-based games. For example, while there may be a contract regulating the relationship between a supplier and a purchaser, there will be aspects of that relationship that are not governed by the terms of the contract and where the parties will have to improvise. This can be complicated by interactions with others that are not parties to the contract at all. Non-commercial organizations, such as public sector agencies, find themselves in similar situations also. Indeed, one of the fields where game theory is a useful tool is in the realm of politics, which impinges significantly on public sector activity, but is also relevant in the corporate world.

Game theory has a specialized application in detection and enforcement of crime, as illustrated by the prisoner's dilemma. You will see, I think, that a clever regulator could use this game to its advantage in dealing with cartel behavior, for example. Company X and Company Y are suspected of having conspired to fix prices unlawfully, which is actually very hard to prove. The CEO of each company is interviewed, separately, and is told that in such cases a whistleblower may be let off with a minimum or even no penalty. The choice for each CEO is simple. If you confess and the other guy remains silent I use your testimony to ensure that your accomplice does serious time, as a deterrent to others. Likewise, if the other CEO confesses while you remain silent, you will do the time. Each CEO would know that if they both remain silent, it is unlikely that any charges will stick, but they also know that, at one stroke, by speaking out a company could both get off with little or no legal baggage and inflict damage on what is, after all, a competitor and, most likely, a dangerous competitor. Quite a dilemma is it not?

Such a case came to light in 2007, involving many of the world's leading airlines. As reported in *Business Day* on 8 December 2007, Qantas, in return for becoming the third international airline (after Korean Air and British Airways) to enter into a plea deal with the US Government, received a relatively light $US61 million fine and its senior executives were told that they would not face any further (and personal) attention by regulators. Qantas also agreed to help the US Justice Department to investigate the many other airlines thought to have been involved in the illegal cartel. Without this Damascene conversion to the path of truth and light, Qantas could have been fined several hundred million dollars by the US Department of Justice, if it had been found guilty.

The "dilemma" faced by the "prisoners" in this example is that, whatever the other does, each is better off confessing than remaining silent. However, in most cases, the outcome obtained when both confess is worse for each than the outcome they would have obtained had they all remained silent. Game theory is more than just theory, in the business world, as we have seen from these examples of zero sum games. They are called zero sum games because there at least as many losers as there are winners and usually there are more. Zero sum games are value destroying games or, at best, value preserving games and, I would argue, earlier models of regulation in the financial sector were zero sum games. The best result one could get for the system as a whole was to limit the damage caused by non complying parties. I prefer non-zero games and so should you, because non-zero games create value, rather than destroying it.

In non-zero-sum there is no single or best solution preferable to all others and the outcome of these games is much harder and often impossible to predict. Non-zero sum games are wicked problems, with both competitive and cooperative elements, recognizing that those engaged in such a game have a range of interests, some of which are complementary and some of which are in conflict. Is this not like the real world of business, where your competitors are sometimes also your partners or collaborators? A good example in the banking sector is check clearance. In Australia, as in most if not all countries, banks have cooperated to develop and adopt systems to allow faster clearance of checks. Since 1999, Australian banks have adopted a technology solution that cut the normal clearance time by two working days. Before April 1999, processing had generally required five working days before a customer had access to cleared funds from a check. Checks are a paper-based system of payment that existed long before electronic computers were invented. The check had its origins in the ancient banking system, in which bankers would issue orders, at the request of customers, to pay money to identified payees.

This was known as a bill of exchange. Bills of exchange facilitated trade by eliminating the need for merchants to carry large quantities of currency (e.g. gold) to purchase goods and services. A check had to be transported physically to the paying bank before processing could begin. If the check was dishonored, it was returned physically to the originating bank. Check particulars are now transmitted electronically and processing can start before the check arrives at the paying bank. This speeds up the clearance process, giving customers faster access to their money. If a customer deposits a check on Monday, funds would normally be available on Thursday at the latest, instead of the following Monday. Some of us would say this is still too long a time for the bank to benefit by holding our money and investing it in the short term money market, but it is better than what we had before.

The banks have collaborated in this initiative and others like it because if they did not, the system would not work, because there is no competitive advantage in check processing and because by cooperating the cost of change for each bank is lessened. There is a lot of upside in cooperation and no downside. The prisoner's dilemma in its pure form is a non-zero game because its outcome is not predictable and it is possible to solve the game so that the outcome for the parties is better than zero. This is because if both parties stay silent, they both get off. I disagree, because in this case, society is the loser and the party game of prisoner's dilemma does not reflect that reality. I prefer games where the end result is more than zero for individuals (or organizations) and for society and that should be the objective of good regulation. As Robert Wright observed,

> *Indeed, in highly non-zero-sum games the players' interests overlap entirely. In 1970, when the three Apollo 13 astronauts were trying to Figure out how to get their stranded spaceship back to earth, they were playing an utterly non-zero-sum game, because the outcome would be either equally good for all of them or equally bad. (It was equally good.)*[17]

17 *Non-zero. The Logic of Human Destiny.*

It was good for them, good for NASA and good for us all, in the end, and good for Ron Howard, who, in 1995, made one of the better space movies using Apollo 13 as the basis for the story told in the film. If you should want to explore the elements of the game as they played out in 1970, the film provides a reliable guide, according to those who went through the experience in real life. Conversations and exchanges between ground control and the astronauts were taken word for word from actual transcripts and recordings, though the famous line "Houston, we have a problem", is a paraphrase of the original.[18] The founders (or may be the codifiers?) of game theory, von Neumann and Morgenstern, suggested that there are two fundamental categories of games that humans play: "zero-sum" games and "non-zero-sum" games. In zero-sum games, the fortunes of the players are inversely related, whereas in non-zero sum games, there is a positive relationship between the fortunes of the players. In non-zero sum games, one plus one can and does produce three, or more—amounting to what Marx and Engels called surplus value. Robert Wright's big idea is that the non-zero-sum dynamic "has crucially shaped the unfolding of life on earth so far".

> *Non-zero-sumness, I'll argue, is something whose ongoing growth and ongoing fulfillment define the arrow of the history of life, from the primordial soup to the World Wide Web.*

Wright's idea is close to what an amalgam of Darwin, Lamarck and Smith would produce. Natural selection working with cultural selection produced what Wright calls an "invisible brain"—a manifestation of which is Smith's invisible hand. The interaction of humans, facilitated by proximity and increasing ease and speed of communication, gradually produced

> *...giant regional brains... And the driving force wasn't periodic environmental "stress" but a more constant force: human vanity, powered by the status competition that is part of all known societies and seems to be innate.*
>
> *The fitful but relentless tendency of invisible social brains to hook up with each other, and eventually submerge themselves into a larger brain, is a central theme of history. The culmination of that process— the construction of a single, planetary brain—is what we are witnessing today, with all its disruptive yet ultimately integrative effects...*

Wright's big idea is that humanity's future will be created by us all, interacting as a collective, invisible brain, for good or for ill, much as Smith viewed the economy (the market) as a creation of us all, interacting as a collective, invisible "hand". Wright argues cogently that the arrow of our destiny is likely to produce a creative, democratic, free

18 The transcripts of the original mission can be found at http://www.hq.nasa.gov/alsj/a13/AS13_TEC.PDF.

future for us, though other, less pleasant scenarios remain possible, if we make the wrong choices. Fukuyama, in his latest book, *State-Building: Governance and World Order in the Twenty-first Century*, illustrates some of the less pleasant scenarios. Fukuyama sees the state as the principal vehicle for a successful human future and his prognosis is not good. He foresees the proliferation of weak, failing states and argues that outside actors have little ability to help countries strengthen their state capacity, sometimes pursuing policies that actually weaken political institutions.

Fukuyama suggests that, in some of the most severe cases, the only option is a return to a neo-colonial or mandate system. We have seen examples of this in recent years, in the Solomon Islands, Iraq, and Afghanistan. I am mentioning Fukuyama here as a portent of what could be, if our big brain gets it wrong—not as a purveyor of a great idea—and we will return to Fukuyama's work in chapter 6. The sixth big idea on which this book is founded is provided by Robert Putnam and it focuses on the social aspects of economics, without which the latter is just a bunch of unprovable theories and indigestible mathematical equations.

Bowling alone: Putnam's big idea

Putnam's big idea is that civil society is a generator of order and creator of social capital—another invisible brain working as a force for good. Putman establishes, to my satisfaction anyway, that there is a strong positive correlation between the size, scope and health of civil society and a state's political and economic health.

> *Whereas physical capital refers to physical objects and human capital refers to the properties of individuals, social capital refers to connections among individuals—social networks and the norms of reciprocity and trustworthiness that arise from them. In that sense social capital is closely related to what some have called "civic virtue." The difference is that "social capital" calls attention to the fact that civic virtue is most powerful when embedded in a sense network of reciprocal social relations. A society of many virtuous but isolated individuals is not necessarily rich in social capital.*[19]

By correlation I mean that where civil society is healthy, the state and the economy also tend to be healthy. It is not clear which of these elements causes what or whether they are all consequences of a fundamental cause that is not obvious to me—but that is not important, if one takes a pragmatic, Machiavellian stance. What is important, if we want a stable society, a sound economy and robust state, is to ensure that we have a thriving civil society. Putnam describes four components of civil society, civic engagement, political equality, solidarity, trust and tolerance and a strong associational life. This is the practical dimension of Putnam's big idea. These components are phenomena amenable

19 2000, 19.

to description, measurement, experimentation and intervention. In other words, here we have some of the fundamental elements of a normative theory of government that may be translated into practice, into action. Shortly we will see how that could be (or is it should be?) done, but first let us consider our last big idea, the principles that underpin epidemiology…and perhaps many other things too.

Epidemiology: understanding systems in crisis

I write this, the latest scare is abroad, metaphorically and actually, in the form of the so-called swine flu. Epidemiologists tell us that we are at risk of a global swine flu pandemic, with many deaths in prospect. How do they know? Epidemiology is the study of factors affecting the health and illness of populations and provides the foundations for public health programs. Epidemiologists study, describe and analyze disease patterns in human populations, with the intent of identifying the causes of diseases and also to alert us to the possible outbreak of disease. This work provides data and insights that enable the management, evaluation and planning of services for the prevention, control and treatment of disease. Epidemiology is multi-disciplinary, combining medicine, physical and psychological, health sciences, social sciences and political economy. It makes extensive use of statistics. Epidemiology has gradually transformed how we identify, understand, treat and prevent disease. Generally speaking, epidemiologists are good guys, however painful it might be sometimes to follow the restrictions and controls politicians place on us as a result of the advice provided by epidemiologists.

In the Middle Ages, disease was thought to be an affliction of the body caused by malignant influences that caused an "imbalance of humors", which, in turn caused an excess of blood, which is what gave rise to observed symptoms. If the problem was too much blood, the remedy was obvious, remove some of the blood from the patient's body. Bloodletting was a treatment for many diseases. When a large quantity of blood was required, the appropriate vein was cut. If only a small amount was to be removed, a leech would be used. If removing a small amount did not work, more blood was removed. We have no evidence on the efficacy of this form of therapy at the time, but modern science tells us that the chances of the patient being cured by removing blood would not be great, in most cases.

The underlying logic of the bloodletting approach is that the system is fundamentally healthy and that restoring health requires the restoration of the balance that keeps it healthy. That can be achieved by detecting the bad influence and removing it. This metaphor aligns well with the view that society is inherently healthy, but prone to being unbalanced by individuals who embark on a life of crime. Remove the criminals, remove the crime, thus restoring the natural balance. This is the type of thinking that led Britain in the eighteenth and nineteenth centuries to remove its criminals from within its borders, first to the American colonies and then, after the

American War of Independence, to what would eventually become Australia.

As the centuries pass, how we understand and treat disease has changed. Scientists, such as John Snow, gradually contributed to the development of the modern view of disease, which is predicated primarily on the transmission of disease by bacteria or viruses, which is called "germ theory". John Snow's story is well told in his own words in *On the Mode of Communication of Cholera*, first published in 1849, with the definitive edition published in 1854. The optimal treatment for diseases caused by viruses or bacteria is generally a drug or medicine or by vaccination. This metaphor aligns with the view that criminals are sick or otherwise disturbed individuals, who need to be identified and treated or corrected. This is the type of thinking that gave us prisons as correctional institutions, places where while incarcerated, prisoners would be offered training, education and rehabilitation, as a cure for their criminal tendencies.

The general view is that modern medicine, through drugs and vaccines, complemented by surgery, has made us healthier and given us longer lives than in previous centuries. Research tells us that this is not so, just as research tells us that incarcerating people does not give us lower rates of crime. The biggest contributor to a healthy society is the state of its environment, its water supply, its food supply, its air and its workplaces. All the drugs and all the wonderful surgical techniques we read about can make a significant difference to individuals, but they have relatively little impact on the health of a population. Improving diet, reducing the incidence of smoking or encouraging people to practice safe sex are far more significant lifesavers. That is why the modern approach to public health is concerned with determinants of health across a population, rather than what happens at the level of the individual.

Criminology has reached a similar conclusion, but the results it is producing do not match those achieved in public health. A case in point is the £400 million cross-government commitment to reducing crime made by the British Government in 1999, *"the biggest single investment in an evidence-based approach to crime reduction which has ever taken place in any country"*. This was the Crime Reduction Program (CRP), which had three goals: reducing crime, mainstreaming knowledge of best practice, and cost-effective crime reduction. The CRP was made up of twenty linked crime reduction initiatives, delivered at the local level through "Crime and Disorder Reduction Partnerships". The CRP was not as much of a success as was hoped and, interestingly, the ensuing recommendations amounted to doing more of it, but doing it better—a bit like doing more bloodletting, but doing it better, perhaps?[20]

Why is all this relevant to understanding the financial services industry? The trends we see in regulation are not isolated from other trends in areas of human activity that involve similar elements. This means that what we learn in these related domains can be shared, with appropriate caution (revisit the discussion of wicked problems, please).

20 Home Office Research Study 281, "Investing to deliver: reviewing the implementation of the UK Crime Reduction Programme", Peter Homel, Sandra Nutley, Barry Webb and Nick Tilley, Home Office Research, Development and Statistics Directorate, December 2004.

It also means that policy-makers might find it useful if those domains were to share research, resources and intellectual horsepower, all of which are scarce and expensive commodities. Unfortunately, bureaucracies, like universities, tend to compartmentalize their knowledge, to protect turf and to advance careers. So, those of you who want to be active players in the regulation game would do well to keep an eye on what goes on elsewhere, because events in related domains may act as lead indicators for what might happen in your world or give you ideas about what ought to happen. Then you can facilitate it happening, if you wish, or take steps to stop of modify a trend you do not like.

What is it that is happening or about to happen? In brief, as with health, the focus of regulation is shifting on to the population, rather than on the errant individual or the aberrant business. The assumption is that hardening the economic system, making it less vulnerable to wrongdoing and more likely to lead to compliance, is the way to go. Good governance is achieved by embedding the rules into the fabric of the financial system and encouraging business enterprises to reflect internally the values the system has embraced.

A concomitant development—I use that adjective because I do not know here which is cause and which is effect and it really does not matter—is the increasing drive towards standardization. One might debate whether this demand is itself driven by a systemic requirement to control or limit the degree of variation in the system or whether the cause is something more prosaic, such as the efficiency that can be derived by constructing routines based around standards. Whatever the case may be, embedding the rules into everyday procedures through standardization is, in my view, the future of regulation. We will discuss later, in chapter 6, what might mean for the financial services industry in particular.

In chapter 7, when we discuss indicators that point to bubbles and the bursting of bubbles, I will make use of what I have learnt from epidemiology and, in particular, from criteria the discipline has developed to test causation, that is, to see if something caused something else, rather than being merely correlated or associated to it. For example, does short-selling of stocks have anything to do with a crash in the stock-market? Do excessive salaries paid to CEOs cause the economy to go into freefall? Do income tax reductions stimulate demand? Does inadequate regulatory supervision cause fraud in the marketplace? Taking the first example, there is no question that short-selling is associated with (correlated) with a falling stock market; it is hardly likely to happen in a rising market, after all. However, this association does not imply causation or, at least, it does not imply necessarily that short-sellers cause the market to fall, anymore than the *untori* caused the plague in Milan.

The lack of certainty about cause and effect and the public tendency, fed by the media, to demand that someone be blamed for their misfortunes make life difficult for those in government, be they politicians or public servants. The former are usually anxious to be seen to be doing something and to avoid being assigned the blame for whatever went wrong. The latter are ill-equipped to advise their political masters, because, in turn, they too rely on economics and economists to shed light on what is going on and why—the blind leading the blind down a blind alley. Usually this means that good sense and good policy are in scarce supply and that scapegoating is turned into an art. Like a magician on the stage, the government will focus the attention of the public on a distracting item, person or event, thus keeping the masses relatively quiet and peaceful, while the real action goes on somewhere else. It is a rare politician—and Barack Obama may turn out to be such a one—who has the fortitude and the intellect to govern as a government should, to provide a stable, reliable, set of rules within which we can go about our business freely and without fear, whether the circumstances be foul or fair.

The purpose of government

Stripping aside the rhetoric and bombast of politics, the purpose of government is to provide peace, order and good government. This is a tall order, in a complex, difficult world, because it means that a government must:

- provide a governance framework that is inclusive, free of corruption and capable of adapting to changing social, moral and cultural expectations;
- manage that framework accountably, without wrapping itself up in so much red tape that nothing ever happens—a hospital without patients while it might be a bureaucrat's dream, is not much use to anyone;
- enable civil society to develop and thrive, to both complement and challenge government, thus keeping it honest to itself;
- enable the economy to develop and grow sustainably;
- safeguard individual rights, within a framework of mutual obligations;
- protect and manage the commons[21] so that they are sustainable and sustaining of the whole.

Each of these on its own presents us with a wicked problem; taken together, this set of basic functions of government is a wicked problem indeed. To illustrate how these elements fit together, Figure 3, taken from my earlier book, *Compliance and Regulation in the International Financial Services Industry*, presents a model of a successful society, adapting a model of personal needs created by Abraham Maslow.[22] In Maslow's model, the higher needs in this hierarchy become relevant as a motivator of behavior only

21 My definition of the commons is an element of physical, intellectual or virtual property for which no single individual, corporation or state is responsible. The definition includes traditional village commons, open source software, religion and spirituality, office kitchens and outer space, by way of providing examples.
22 "A Theory of Human Motivation", *Psychological Review* 50 (1943):370-96.

when the lower needs are satisfied. Once an individual has moved upwards to the next level, needs in the lower level will no longer be a priority. I think this model is applicable at the societal level as well. At the bottom of the pyramid, we can see that society needs to be protected from external and internal threats, like foreign enemies or terrorists. Then, society needs an adequate supply of food, clean water and clean air, to meet the physiological needs of its constituent elements.

When those needs are satisfied, then psychological needs—or, more appropriately, wants—become motivators. This is the role of the economy. At the next layer up, we find good governance, and then we rise up to the level of civil society, with the spiritual layer next and last, where the pursuit of happiness promised by the US founding fathers finds a home. To influence a level, we must work at the level above it. For example, to push and prod society towards economic arrangements that are appropriate to the times, we must provide good governance. To move society towards a different direction, we must engage with people on and about fundamental values. The model works in reverse also. It is difficult to provide good governance without solid economic foundations and it is not possible to appeal to us to act on the basis of values if our civil society is weak or non-existent. How these elements fit together in a cycle, rather than as a static pyramid, is shown in Figure 4.

Figure 3: Hierarchy of needs to be satisfied by the state

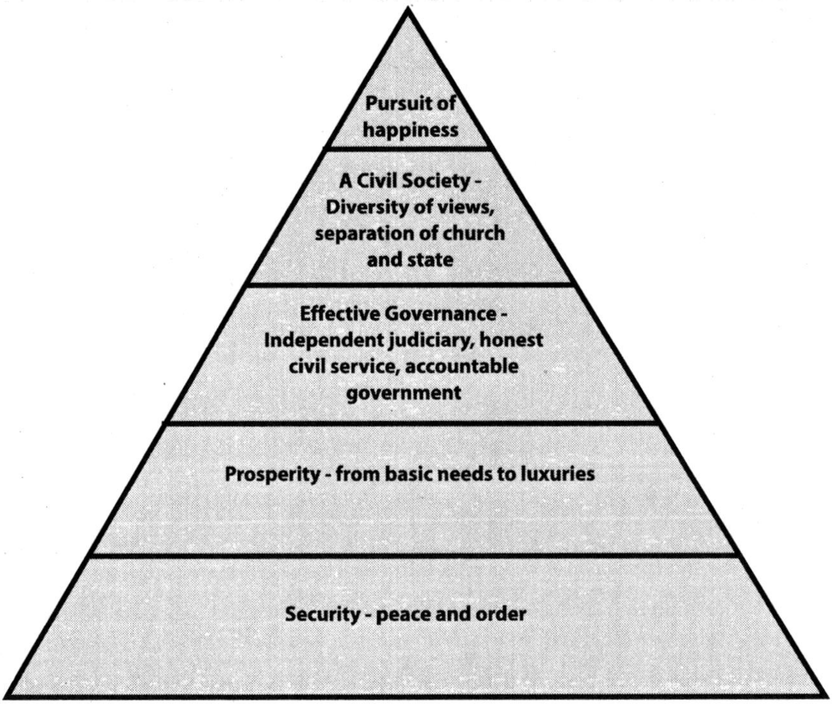

As in Maslow's theory about individuals, we will find that once a satisfactory level of prosperity is achieved through a functioning economy, society will tend to focus on higher layers as priorities for criticism, for dissatisfaction, driven by a desire to remedy real and perceived flaws. Security is self-explanatory; it is about protecting the borders from enemies and maintaining order internally. Governance is about making the right decisions, the right way. Effective governance requires a functioning political system, an effective civil service, a strong civil society, including independent media, an independent judiciary, and rules appropriate to the prevailing social, economic and cultural conditions.

The rules, the body of regulation, is the capstone, if you like, that keeps this complex structure steady, creating the level of predictability and stability that both society and the economy require as a condition precedent to prosperity and development. Governance creates trust between the governors and the governed, giving the state the legitimacy it needs to use state power to achieve public ends. Without good governance there is no trust and when there is no trust, good governance becomes impossible and the state becomes unviable, as witnessed by events in failed states like Zimbabwe or the Solomon Islands. You may notice that I have not mentioned democracy in this discussion. That is because democracy, at least as we understand in the West, is not an essential element of a successful state, though it may be a very desirable one. It is possible to have good governance without what we in the West understand democracy to mean.

Figure 4: The elements of a sound state, a circle of virtue

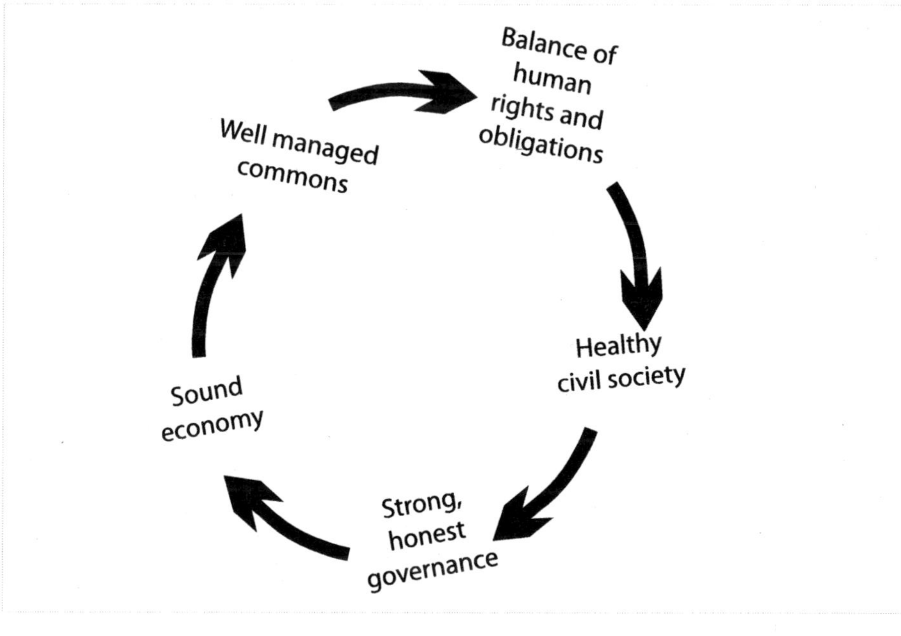

An independent judiciary, a strong civil society and an effective bureaucracy are far more important to social stability and economic development than the application of Jeffersonian, Hamiltonian or Westminster principles. The examples of Singapore and my native homeland, Italy, come to mind. Singapore is not a democracy, as Americans or Australians understand the term. Yet, it is a stable, secure, prosperous state, with no indication of incipient revolt among its citizens against its institutions or its values. Italy, on the other hand, is a prosperous, stable state despite the continuing failure of its democratic institutions in the six decades since the Second World War. Singapore has effective governance despite its lack of democratic zeal, while Italy has effective governance despite its attachment to democratic values.

Of course, governance is not sufficient in and by itself to support a modern state. A modern state requires many things, such as human and financial capital, a secure environment, internally and externally, access to dependable and sustainable resources, such as food, water, clean air, and raw materials, and quality health and education infrastructure. It also needs connectivity, physical and virtual, in the form of road, rail and air transport networks, and ubiquitous high speed broadband. Last, but certainly not least, it must have an effective and efficient financial system, capable of supporting economic, social and cultural life at a standard sufficient to satisfy at least the majority of the population. These are represented in figure 3 as a virtuous cycle, with all elements required so that individuals, businesses and communities can build the future they want.

What follows is not fiction, although some of the details may be speculative. It will work best for you if you use both your knowledge and your imagination, to "encircle the world", as Einstein exhorts us to do. Just as you do when you are reading a good novel or listening to a great yarn. Let the story do the hard work for you—just keep your mind open. It is a positive story, full of challenges overcome, ambitions realized, hard work rewarded, though there are disappointments also, for those who do not or cannot see a way forward in very difficult times. The future I have in mind realizes the promises of the technologists, rather than the fears of the deep ecologists. It extracts the best from capitalism, rather than ameliorating its worst effects.

The chief ingredients of my recipe for success are connectivity, interoperability, predictability and security. Connectivity to enable speed and ease of connection, to create a space for entrepreneurship and the ingredients for social cohesion. Interoperability to cut costs, to generate synergy and to accelerate the process that brings innovations to market. Predictability and security to give individuals, families and communities the confidence, to plan, to invest, to take calculated risks. This is what is needed to have peace, order and good government, noting that the same few ingredients can be mixed in many different ways that would deliver the desired result. These are the areas where government should focus all its efforts, to generate economic and social capital and to enhance competitiveness in a globalized economy.

This may require a rethinking of how government infrastructure is used and in areas of public policy, such as education and training and taxation. What government should do is to create an environment within which opportunities for business are many and flourishing.

Crafting opportunities

The strategic elements outlined above must be oriented towards areas of opportunity, in Drucker's terms, so that the greatest result is derived from the effort expended. Areas of opportunity are most likely to be found where disruptive trends exist. A disruptive trend is a pattern of events with the potential to transform (transform = make a thorough or dramatic change in the form, appearance, character) society, the economy or a significant subset of these. For example, the shift to human labor in factories from human labor on land—as the dominant form of work—was a disruptive trend, as was the later shift to machine assisted human labor in factories in the eighteenth and nineteenth centuries. The emerging shift from machine assisted human labor to machine labor in manufacturing is another disruptive trend, as is the incipient shift from machine assisted labor to machine labor in the white-collar industries. Another, long-running trend is urbanization, which in the West reached a disruptive phase in the eighteenth century and may be presenting us with another disruptive phase within a generation. These disruptive trends may be accompanied by another, linked to the changes in the dominant factor of production: from land to capital and now to knowledge? It may be that, even beyond the search for a theory of everything in physics, the sciences as a whole, hard and soft, are beginning to converge in method, purpose and character (vide bioinformatics, nanotechnology, environmental sciences et al).[23]

It may not be the role of government to define and to provide strategies in response to these (and other) trends. However, the strategic framework for a state as a competitive twenty-first century economy would be grossly deficient if it did not acknowledge such trends and did not point to the need for greater understanding and for research needed to manage them. These trends redefine the economics of an entire industry and invalidate existing business models and can also severely undermine a society's capacity to manage change and to exploit new technologies—if they are left to take their natural course, unobserved and ignored.

As Clayton Christensen notes in his 1997 work *The Innovator's Dilemma*, well-managed firms excel at providing "sustaining technologies". These firms generally follow a predictable path, anticipating the needs of mainstream customers and investing in technologies designed to satisfy those needs. Disruptive technologies create a very different market environment. They fly unseen under the radar, emerging

23 For those who are interested, see http://wilber.shambhala.com/html/books/kosmos/excerptA/intro.cfm/xid,4525113/yid,61816816

with seeming suddenness and great impact, usually a destructive impact to start with. The effect of the large-scale disruptions I have flagged earlier is similar, but on a much grander scale, with negative impacts of much greater magnitude. The collapse of the Soviet Union illustrates this point.[24] Its impact is still being felt across the world and not all effects are obvious. For example, in a profound way the present War on Terror has its roots in the events in the Soviet Union fifteen years ago. And so has the rising tuberculosis epidemic in Europe.

Competiveness=Productivity

The hallmark of success in a globalized economy, especially in a troubled economy, remains competitiveness. Competitiveness depends on productivity—the value of output produced per unit of labor or capital or, to look at it another way, innovation plus process efficiency. The continuing challenge is to grow productivity, but the growth in productivity must be sustainable, factoring in externalities such as environmental degradation. This is true for economies, industries and enterprise, a truth forgotten by companies such as Enron, for example, to the ultimate detriment of many. The objective of Enron's executives, it seems, was not to be productive, to produce value, but to produce wealth for executives and shareholders. This objective was pursued through a sophisticated pea and thimble game, which enabled the company to persuade even sophisticated investors that wealth was being generated on a vast scale, when the truth was more like a corporate Ponzi scheme. It all worked as long as cash kept flowing and Mafia-like silence was the rule. When a thread came undone (or was unpicked, perhaps), the whole tapestry of deceit unraveled, quickly, as everyone sought to rat on everyone else. The Bernard Madoff scandal and Enron are like the bookends of the 2008 financial crisis, marking the beginning of its end and the end of its beginnings, respectively. In both cases, the foundation principles of capitalism were perverted, enslaving capital to serve purely private purposes, rather than corporate objectives. If Stalin was Marxism's ugly face, Bernard Madoff and Kenneth Lay can be seen as the duplicitous face of ugly capitalism.

Because wealth should be a consequence of the exploitation of capital and not its ultimate purpose, our purpose here is to identify the main drivers of productivity in the economy and to lay the foundations for an agenda at the national level, maximizing opportunities and minimizing risk. Significant barriers to progress are discussed under the heading of management of risk. Such an agenda would not be exclusive to government, as government's role is to enable innovation by facilitating collaboration and by acting as a catalyst for positive change. However, it is expected that government would have a leading role in transforming into reality the concepts discussed here. You will see later what I mean by these terms and why our future depends on how well we do in creating

24 See http://news.bbc.co.uk/hi/english/static/in_depth/europe/2001/collapse_of_ussr/default.stm

a connected, interoperable, predictable and secure world. At this point, let me say a bit more about why I have chosen to deal with a serious subject as if it were a story.[25]

Why tell this story?

In *The Symbolic Species*, Terrence Deacon makes a strong case for the fundamental importance of language as a factor distinguishing humans from other animal species. He presents the hypothesis that language and the human brain have co-evolved to make us what we are, dealing a strong blow to both sides of the culture-nurture debate. It may turn out that other species on Earth are capable of developing or using language, but there is no evidence that any species other than *Homo Sapiens* tells stories. The subject matter has varied greatly, from tales of giants, to tales of gods, onto romance, crime and adventure, down to the tales, homilies and diatribes pouring out of the many branches into which knowledge has been split by modern science. The scientists might not be aware that they are engaged in storytelling and might even deny it, fearing it might taint their work with the brush of subjectivity or, worse, with the whiff of fiction. However, it is obvious from a quick perusal of any book by Darwin or Stephen J Gould or Paul Davies or Stephen Weinberg that good science is the telling of a connected series of happenings. Good science writing rises above the realm of data and information to give us access to learning and, sometimes, wisdom.

Stories come from within us and also shape us, as individuals, as communities, as nations and as a species. Stories carry the memes that make us who we are, generally in cooperation, but sometimes in conflict with our genes. In the beginning, stories were painted on cave walls or told kinesthetically, with and through objects and rituals. Then, the spoken word took over. Skilled and highly respected individuals with seemingly prodigious memories roamed the world connecting people and communities through their story telling. More recently, as alphabets were invented and the scribes assumed pre-eminence, stories were written on whatever material technology could supply. The bards were confined to the stage and then to the cinema and TV. The ability to write became commonplace and to be well read became the hallmark of an educated, nay a civilized person. Despite the seeming prevalence of visual media, the printed word remains dominant. We consume almost twenty thousand times as much reading material as people did at the beginning of the printed book, in the Middle Ages. Ten billion books are produced each year around the world.

It may seem that we have had great change, but not much has changed, really, between the time of the scribe and the time of the printing press or of the e-book. Technology has made the written word cheaper to produce and cheaper to consume, but the creative process has remained largely unchanged. This may not be so for

25 For a comprehensive treatment of this topic, see "Learning in the Electronic Age: the Importance of Storytelling", by Patrick Callioni, *International Journal of the Book*, Volume 1, 2003.

much longer. It may be that the very nature of the creative process if being reshaped. A process that has been with us since our time in the caves is perhaps about to evolve into something new. There are straws blowing in the wind that presage that the times are changing, as a late twentieth-century bard used to tell us. With a bit of poetic license one can visualize a world, not too far away in time, when, in the evolutionary journey of human culture, we might be at an evolutionary turning point, a new paradigm. To avoid any tendency to fatalism or any leanings towards historicism, it is worth remembering that evolution may have a broad and general *tendency* to move in the direction of: increasing complexity, but that it does not necessarily result in improvement or betterment, in progress, as the Victorians used to think of it. The coming paradigm is not implicitly going to be better than what we have now, it may not represent progress, if progress means improvement towards some unspoken, yet glorious end.

We have choices to make and we must act and not merely re-act. In this story, on this stage, in this world, pain, death, suffering, joy and success are real and felt as such. They are not mere fictions, idealized ghosts of reality. Storytelling imbues our whole culture and all aspects of our lives, as it did in the age of mythos, before logos consumed us all. Each of us is a player on the stage, but the roles we play are neither fictional nor make believe, as we act out who we truly are and strive for what we could be. This is what it means to be a storyteller and this is why this book tells a story. So, in this story in which we are all players without a script, what is the prime mover, the standard by which our performance will be judged? Well, since I am telling this story, I will indulge myself and my opinions and, in my opinion, what matters most is *competitiveness*. By competitiveness I mean the overall economic performance of the nation, including productivity, the ability to export its goods and services, and the standard of living enjoyed by all—rather than a few. What this means will be made clearer in the next few pages, where the scene for the story is set.

By the way, this story does not have a happy ending, in fact it has no end at all, as we will see. The economy is a complex system and like all complex systems, it will perform best when it teeters on the brink of disaster. What is a complex system? We need to turn to the hard science of physics for an explanation. Werner Heisenberg formulated the classical view of uncertainty. He was a German physicist who expressed the principle according to which the position and momentum of a subatomic particle cannot both be determined precisely at the same time. Measure the position of an electron or any other quantum particle, and, according to Heisenberg, you will disturb its momentum. Measure its momentum, and you will disturb its position. So you can never know both the momentum and the position of a particle at once; one may be measured, but the other may only be estimated. This is a crucial aspect of quantum physics.

It is now accepted in the social sciences that the act of observation carries the potential to affect the phenomenon under observation, though it would be facile to say that this is the same as the quantum conundrum identified by Heisenberg. It is now accepted in the social sciences that the act of observation carries the potential to affect the phenomenon under observation, though it would be facile to say that this is the same as the quantum conundrum identified by Heisenberg. However, it is not facile—and may in fact be wise—to assume that the behavior of human beings or of human social constructs, such as organizations, cannot be predicted precisely, but may only be the subject of approximate judgment, of an estimate or rough calculation.

In other words, knowledge about others necessarily implies the exercise of one's beliefs. In addition, quantum theory and the evolving body of chaos theory have made it plain that complex systems, such as the weather, people or organizations, are sensitive to even tiny variations in "their initial conditions". In other words, dramatically different behavior can arise from very small differences of design.[26] Moving back to the realm of economics, this means that those who observe, comment and advise on economic matters will influence what happens in the economy and that the impact this influence may be unusually strong when the economy is in a state of flux. It also means that even relatively small design errors or omissions in the design of operating rules for the economy can have a disproportionate effect, eventually.

Because it is a complex system, the economy will continue to experience crises, when we consider the origin of the word crisis, it is easy to understand why: a crisis is a crucial or decisive point or situation, a turning point, a point of inflection, where the existing alignment has ceased to be sustainable and a new alignment, a new point of balance must be found—or the system will perish. The economy cannot survive without crises, anymore than human beings can grow and mature without experiencing the willfulness of life or a game of football can be exciting without turning points, moments where the game hangs in the balance and could go either way.

Because there will always be crises and because each crisis will be unique, with its own peculiar history and its own way of unfolding, our focus should be on learning from past crises, because that which does not kill does indeed make a system stronger by forcing it to learn and to adapt; on devising means to perceive as early as possible when a crisis might be upon us; and on developing a greater capacity to manage crises, to minimize the scope, depth and duration; and, lastly, on building into the system greater resilience, flexibility and adaptability. Our focus should not be on excessive executive salaries, fraud and malfeasance or bad decisions by companies or individuals, because those things do not cause a crisis in the financial system or in the economy, just like a fever does not cause influenza, though a patient with the 'flu' will almost always be feverish. Wherever there is illness, death or destruction, real or figurative, there will be opportunists who seek to take advantage from it. Sometimes

26 See Davies and Gribbin 1992.

what these people do may make thinks a little worse and it may even be that what they do or fail to do may trigger an event that, later on when history is written, comes to be seen as the cause of the disaster. However, it is not the trigger of a gun that is responsible for the damage caused by the bullet, is it?

Suggested reading

I have mentioned various books in this chapter that are worth reading and I will not repeat them here, though you will find them in the bibliography at the end of this book. I would like to give honorable mention to a couple more, though. This is because I have cited historians, economists and political activists, but we have not heard from biologists, aside from dead ones, such as Lamarck and Darwin. First, I recommend *The Origins of Virtue*, by Matthew Ridley. In this easy to read book, Ridley explains how many aspects of human culture and of individual behavior can be explained by genetics, without giving in to the temptation of claiming that genes rule the world, as Richard Dawkins asserted in *The Selfish Gene*. As Ridley observes, "Our minds have been built by selfish genes, but they have been built to be social, trustworthy and cooperative."[27] I also suggest you read *Western Civilization in Biological Perspective*, by Stephen Boyden. In particular, I suggest you read chapter 10, which discusses the modern era or, as Boyden refers to it, "Humans in the high energy phase". By reading this chapter, if nothing else, you will round out the perspectives offered by Fukuyama, Huntington et al, as discussed above.

27 At page 249.

CHAPTER 2

Learning from a disaster

In this chapter we will consider the impact of the subprime crisis and of the consequent global financial crisis, and how we can extract value from an apparent disaster. The context for the discussion is globalization. Globalization is usually characterized as an economic phenomenon, involving the increasing interaction, with varying degrees of integration, of national economic systems, especially by means of international trade and capital flows.[1] It is important here to recognize that globalization as we are experiencing it is not only about money. People (and their culture and values) also are increasingly free to move around the world and to set up home wherever a welcoming environment is found. Globalization and modern communication technologies enable capital, knowledge and culture to be shared around the world almost simultaneously, with dramatic effects for all of us.[2] Also, this is not the first time we have been through such a phase and it may be useful to consider earlier waves of globalization, to see what we can learn from the past that can be applied to our understanding of the present and future.

However, before we do that, let us recap on the causes, triggers, symptoms and present state of the global financial crisis in which we are still mired. I will do that with the assistance of some of the economists (and others) I mentioned at the beginning of the book and I will also spend a little time on the previous great financial crisis, the granddaddy of them all, the Great Depression, to see what we can learn from that sad period of the twentieth century. At the end of the chapter I will draw together lessons for the present and for the future, which will then be used in chapter 6 to formulate suggestions and recommendations for those who make a living in the financial services industry and for those who depend on it—which is all of us, really. Unavoidably, there

1 Soros 1998.
2 Handy 1995.

will be much discussion of bubbles and it is a little ironic that I am writing these words at the location of the first great modern investment bubble, Amsterdam, the home of tulip mania. Looking back at that particular series of events, it seems odd to us that people should go crazy about flowers and come close to destroying the economy of the Netherlands as a consequence. A couple of centuries on from now, our descendants may themselves puzzle about their ancestors' crazy hankerings for real estate. It is a universal characteristic of investment bubbles that the craziness of it all is only apparent after the event; at the time, the crazy ones are thought to be the ones who sit it out, who decline to be swept along with the crowd. Later, in the cold light of history, it is all too apparent that the crowd was mad, not wise. Stampedes are never pretty and never end neatly and well for all.

I should say that while the consequences of investment bubbles are usually dire, they can have a silver lining. You see, at least some of the money thy, that flows into an industry as a result of a bubble sometimes finds its way into activities that lead to innovation, to new products or higher productivity or both. Here is an example from the dot.com crash at the beginning of this decade, courtesy of Long Li Yann, from ZDNet Asia.[3]

> *...not all dot-coms were brought down by the bust. Five years after the spectacular crash, a handful weathered the storm. dollarDEX, is one such company. The online wealth management portal was established in Singapore in 1999.*
>
> *Richard Lai, dollarDEX's managing director, said the key to weathering through the crisis was to have a good business plan. The management team was clear about its strategy to go online, and it stuck with the plan. "An online platform makes the most sense for us since, even during that time, the Internet penetration rate was quite high in Singapore," Lai explained. "Also, it was one way to distinguish us from incumbents like the banks and insurance companies. We can then provide 24/7 [customer] service." According to Lai, the boom and the subsequent bust had no effect on the company. "Frankly, the boom did not really figure into our strategy," he said. "We wanted to be profitable as soon as possible and we did so within the first two years. We focused on cash flow, not fund raising. We kept most of the funds raised (US$7.7m) and used them for expansion during the bust."*

It is too early to see whether this kind of experience, which is by no means unique, will be replicated following the Great Recession. There was not much innovation that flowed out of or as a consequence of the Great Depression, I am afraid, which makes me somewhat pessimistic. Companies that survived the Great Depression did so by cutting costs, by expanding beyond their traditional core business or by becoming

3 "From boom to bust and back again", 29 November 2005, retrieved from *http://news.zdnet.co.uk/internet/0,1000000097,39238833,00.htm* on 26 March 2009.

very conservative, even risk averse. The growth rate of US patent applications was considerably lower during the 1930s than in the preceding decade.[4] This statement by Greg Harden, the family's fifth-generation CEO of Harden Furniture (McConnellsville, NY) illustrates the point well.[5]

> *"We simply shrank and reduced expenses", says Harden. The philosophy was "to stay low and not take a bullet to the forehead but not to abandon efforts to promote the brand. You can't shrink yourself to prosperity."*

The evidence is that bubbles are both inevitable and sometimes useful. First and foremost, they are useful because they reset the risk engine that we know as the financial markets. When the economy has run along for a few years without any major crisis, even before a bubble starts to form, the capacity of the financial markets to allocate risk starts to deteriorate. Gradually, more and more risk is placed on shoulders that are not capable of bearing it, as evidenced by the subprime fiasco, for example. This happens quietly, almost invisibly, a bit like metal fatigue in an aircraft, as we will soon see. The bursting of the ensuing bubble resets the risk engine, shifting the load back onto stronger shoulders. Of course, sometimes the pendulum swings too far and a different kind of imbalance results, paralyzing the economy, as happened in the 1930s. Bubbles are useful in another ways also. They serve a function similar to wild fires in the great eucalyptus forests of Australia, where some types of eucalyptus require a forest fire to enable them to reproduce and have evolved to make fires more likely, by constantly shedding bark and limbs, creating a pyre hot enough to activate their seeds. The really interesting things is that most of the eucalyptus trees survive the fire and then go on to breed, while competing species of tree and shrub perish in the fire. By burning the forest, the eucalyptus tree creates an environment most likely to serve its reproductive purposes. A similar cleansing of the marketplace can be seen following investment bubbles also, as evidenced by what is going on in the global car industry, for example, or in the financial sector itself.

The cleansing can produce good results of bad for the economy, depending on the circumstances. In Australia, a small economy, with few players in the industry, the financial crisis has greatly reduced competition, as only the major banks have withstood the cleansing fire. In larger economies, weeding out the weaker specimens may actually produce more vigorous competition in the medium to long term, as enough players survive to support competition and those survivors are stronger for having survived the crisis. A good business can become a great business if a crisis forces it to hone its competitive edge and to reduce its costs. My argument is not that bubbles are inherently bad. They are part and parcel of the ecology of the market, just as fires

4 "Innovation lessons from the 1930s", *The McKinsey Quarterly*, December 2008, retrieved from http://www.mckinseyquarterly.com/Innovation_lessons_from_the_1930s_2266, on 26 march 2009.

5 From "Business Lessons from the Great Depression", *BusinessWeek*, retrieved from http://images.businessweek.com/ss/08/10/1017_depression_lessons/index.htm, on 26 march 2009.

are part of the natural lifecycle of a eucalyptus forest. Rather, I say that neither forest fires nor investment bubbles should catch us unprepared and, really, if we had truly learnt the lessons of the past, we should have been prepared this time. Having suffered the pains of the Great Depression and the warning signs of minor crises during the last two decades, we should have been forewarned and forearmed to deal with the Great Recession. But we were not, we let the herd decide and, as is usually the case, we ended up with a stampede.

The great depression explained

John Kenneth Galbraith wrote *The Great Crash, 1929*, over half a century ago, but I think it remains the best account and provides the most lucid explanation of the crisis that has become the benchmark for all financial crises.[6] Galbraith is considered to be one of the great economists of the twentieth century, though his stature was seen as diminished during the halcyon days of the Chicago School, of monetarism and Thatcherism (and its US counterpart, Reagan's voodoo economics). Now that we are all Keynesians, once again, Galbraith is attracting new admirers. Presciently perhaps, in the introduction to the 1997 edition, Galbraith observed,[7]

> *There is now far more money flowing into the stock markets than there is intelligence to guide it…I am not given to prediction…But there is here a basic and recurrent process. It comes with rising prices…This attracts attention and buyers, which produces the effect of even higher prices. Expectations are thus justified by the very action that sends prices up…Then, for reasons that will endlessly be debated, comes the end. The end is always more sudden than the increase; a balloon that has been puncture does not deflate in an orderly way.*

Galbraith was telling us that the herd was taking over, that we were losing control and merging into a stampeding crowd of unthinking investors—tulips, houses, dodgy investment instruments…we did not care…we bought the lot and asked for more. And we were given more and still we bought, as prices continued to rise. Unlike some unquestioning believers in the infallibility of the market, in 1997 Galbraith could see that bust will always follow boom. There is no genius in that, we all know it, but we did not want to acknowledge that reality, at the time. We thought that our generation had solved the problem, that we had conquered the economy, that we had escaped the endless cycle of boom and bust. Now we remember, now we know that we have not escaped the economic cycle; we are not better economic managers than our grandparents' generation; and we need to understand that wishful thinking cannot

6 The book was first published in 1955; the edition from which I am working was published in 1997, post the Asian crisis.

7 At page xii.

thwart reality. The problem is, how long will this memory, this awareness stick around for this time? And how do we avoid turning our renewed awareness of the reality of boom and bust into endless, bottomless pessimism, as our forbears did in the 1930s? What should we learn from their experience that we can use now? Can the experience of the past make us wiser?

The wisdom of Wile E. Coyote

Here is the first bit of wisdom we should absorb. In *The Great Crash*, Galbraith nonchalantly observes that "...it is in the nature of a speculative boom that almost anything can collapse it."[8] More recently, the man in charge of financial stability at the Bank of England, Andrew Haldane, made similar observations, taking as his starting point the decision to allow Lehman Brothers to fail. In a speech titled "Rethinking the Financial Network", Haldane said (in part) that while the IMF forecasts for world growth have been revised down by more than five percent since the failure of Lehman, the net cost of the credit default swaps that sent the global financial system into a spin was only around US$5 billion. Making a connection with the SARS pandemic fears and their disproportionate impact on the global economy, Haldane remarked that "These similarities (between SARS and Lehman) are striking. An external event strikes. Fear grips the system which, in consequence seizes. The resulting collateral damage is wide and deep. Yet the triggering event is, with hindsight, found to have been rather modest. The flap of a butterfly's wings in New York or Guandong generates a hurricane for the world economy. The dynamics appear chaotic, mathematically and metaphorically."[9] It seems that Haldane has hit on similar themes to the ones I have been exploring in this book and in *Compliance and Regulation*. To wit, the interconnectedness of the global financial system has made it much more vulnerable to tipping points and that we face financial epidemics that are analogous to the plagues of earlier times. Now, when you read this excellent speech by Mr. Haldane, please remember that you read it here first—or at least that I wrote about it first![10]

When I ponder what Galbraith said about the onset of financial crises, when I think on the concept of a tipping point, for some reason the picture that comes to my mind is that of Wile E. Coyote suddenly discovering that he has run out of solid ground, finding himself briefly suspended in mid-air and then suddenly plunging into a great chasm. The unfortunate animal then picks himself up off the ground and goes off to hatch another dastardly, but nonetheless doomed to failure attempt to catch the elusive Road Runner.[11] Having studied the many bubbles that have afflicted the market

8 At page 90.

9 "Rethinking the financial network", Andrew G Haldane, Executive Director, Financial Stability, Bank of England, Speech delivered at the Financial Student Association, Amsterdam, April 2009.

10 I have been blogging on these themes for a few years, most recently on www.openforum.com.au.

11 As Wikipedia (see http://en.wikipedia.org/wiki/Wile_E._Coyote_and_Road_Runner) explains, the cartoon

over the centuries, my conclusion is the same as Galbraith's (and Haldane's it seems). The cause of the deflation is irrelevant, because for every bubble, for every balloon there will be a sharp shock that lets out the air—any sharp shock will do, because what is being pictured is confidence in the hive mind we know as the financial markets; puncturing confidence does not take much effort—we will see later why that is. Every bubble is doomed to burst, just as the Coyote is doomed to fail—but there is always the next bubble, always, and the market, like the Coyote will always get back on its feet and start chasing its quarry again, starting another cycle that will eventually also come to an end. Here another picture comes to mind.

Sticking with the movie theme, while we remain unaware or unwilling to acknowledge the boom and bust cycle, we will be doomed to suffer pointlessly, like the main character in *Groundhog Day*, played by Bill Murray, who was doomed to live the same day over and over again, with no escape route, not even through suicide. While Bill Murray tried to beat the curse, he continued to repeat his old mistakes and remained stuck. It was only when he became aware of how he could turn his plight to his advantage that the curse lifted and he won the girl and embarked on a life that was better than the one he had left behind. I think we are living a version of groundhog day as we continue to believe that we can do what our predecessors have failed to do, that we can beat the curse and ride the stock indices all the way to the sky and beyond.

My assumption is that we can't. You are welcome to prove me wrong and, if you do, I will be pleased to invest every dollar I have and every dollar I can borrow in whatever venture you may propose to me. Until then though, I think that perhaps right now we should be paying more attention to the process that caused the bubble than to the sharp shock—the subprime crisis in our case. Why? Because that is how we can learn how to manage bubbles or at least how to manage the process of inflation so that it causes least damage when the air suddenly escapes, as it will. That is how we can cushion the Coyote's fall down the inevitable precipice, manning the air pumps trying to keep him from encountering solid ground at great speed. When we have done that, we should then ponder what caused him to think that he could walk on air and then we should work on a better and safer means of locomotion! That is our way out of our own version of Groundhog Day.[12]

---

character Wile E. Coyote is endlessly engaged in a quest to catch the Road Runner, with the assistance of devices supplied by the Acme Corporation. The end of the story is always the same, though with different causes and somewhat different scenarios — the coyote ends up "burnt to a crisp, squashed flat, or at the bottom of a canyon (some cartoons show him suffering a combination of these fates)".

12 For those who don't know, *Groundhog Day* is a film from the early 1990s in which Bill Murray plays Phil Connors, a TV weatherman who, while covering the annual Groundhog Day in Punxsutawney (see http://www.groundhog.org/), finds himself repeating the same day over and over again. After going through the classic cycle of anger, denial and so on, he makes radical changes in his life and loves.

Why the stock market is like a railroad track

Now let's leave the world of the movies, to go back to the real world. Have you ever noticed how sand on a dune can pile up gradually, grain by grain, reaching ever greater heights, seemingly forever, and then suddenly, for no apparent reason the tip of the dune breaks up and sand tumbles back to where it came from? Do you know how avalanches occur, as layer of snow piles onto layer of snow until suddenly gravity re-asserts itself and one of more layers slides off the mountain, destroying everything in its path? The only way to test whether an avalanche is imminent and the only way to control avalanches is to place explosives in the areas where they are known to originate. If the snow does not move, an avalanche is unlikely. If it does move, then we have an avalanche occurring in relatively controlled circumstances, with least opportunity for it to cause damage. Are you starting to get the picture?

Or are you familiar with the concept of metal fatigue? Metal fatigue is a process whereby a metal artifact that is subjected to constant loads suddenly and unexpectedly fails, sometimes with catastrophic results, as scholars studying great railroad crashes discovered in the first half of the nineteenth century. The mechanical phenomenon known as metal fatigue is actually the fracturing of the artifact along a fatigue crack. None of the individual stresses or loads applied to the artifact, say a railroad axle, is sufficient in itself to cause the metal to fracture and it is very difficult to predict when sufficient stresses are applied to the axle that might cause it to fracture—complex mathematical equations are required and they are not foolproof. This means that in structural engineering a conservative approach is taken, either designing the use of the artifact to keep the stress below fatigue thresholds or assigning the artifact a finite life, at the end of which it is replaced or asking users to inspect the artifact regularly and closely, with the instruction to replace the item when a discernible crack reaches a certain length. What if markets behave similarly?

I thought that Galbraith's explanation of the 1929 crash and how crashes generally occur resembled the example of the crashing dune, by visualizing the ever-growing amount of money being piled up by buyers and the sudden, unexpected dissolution of the pile, just when it seemed that it could keep on growing forever. The stock market also resembles an avalanche, because we have no reliable way to test its potential to slide, aside from watching what happens when it is hit by a shock. It also resembles the example of metal fatigue, because even during a bull run, a market will suffer shocks, as it did with the Asian crisis in the late 1990s, for example, without crashing. Was the subprime crisis actually that much worse than what happened in the 1997 financial crisis, which some say was caused by policies that distorted incentives within the lender-borrower relationship, which in turn made huge amounts of credit available to risk-takers, who used other people's money to push asset prices to an unsustainable level?[13] What about when Mexico defaulted on its national debt or when Russia did the same a little later? Would Bernard Madoff's colossal Ponzi scheme have brought the market undone if that had not already been achieved by a previous sharp shock? I think there is evidence here for the argument that the nature and character of the sharp shock that punctures the balloon is not of crucial importance, circumstantial evidence perhaps, but then in the realm of economics all evidence is circumstantial.[14]

Having read Galbraith's and other explanations of the causes of the Great Crash of 1929 and of the crisis that followed, which we know as the Great Depression, it seems to me that the 1929 crash was a bit like a combination of the dot.com crash and the Asian financial crisis, with some similarity with our present crisis. Let me put it another way; while bubbles and their denouement may share some underlying characteristics and may be explained by reference to common principles, each event is unique. Let us juxtapose 1929 and now. Just like the dot.com crash, much of the speculative money in the second half of the 1920s went into new technologies, such as the radio and the telephone, for example, and the origins of the bubble were in the USA (and to a lesser extent, in the UK); second, among the causes of the crash there was speculation related to real estate; third, the nature of the speculation was unprecedented in size and type, with new tradable instruments and new investment vehicles at the heart of the problem; fourth, the regulators in the USA were found wanting; fifth, the US dollar remains the number one trading currency in the world; the crash caused a loss of confidence that either precipitated a crash in the real economy or actually caused it; sixth, short-selling was blamed and of course there was a Bernard Madoff type caught out by the crisis—well, several of them actually. There are many similarities, but there are also differences.

The Fed in the USA is now believed to be more competent and better armed than the Fed was in 1929; second, the incoming President of the USA is not an anti-market man, as Herbert Hoover turned out to be; third, many more people have a direct or indirect interest in the stock market than was the case in 1929; fourth, while the US dollar is still number one, this time there is a potential replacement, the Euro; fifth, the USA owes the rest of the world a colossal amount of money; sixth, the nature and character of our economy is now firmly intangible, rather than rooted in the tangible, as it was in the 1920s; seventh, international trade now is freer than it has ever been and it is more likely that globalization will not once again recede, as it has done many times before ; and last, but certainly not least, the folks in the 1930s did not have to deal with climate change, their nemesis was much more tangible and visible, in the form of war—the 1930s was a decade of war, across the whole globe, disconnected conflicts, yes, but certainly as ubiquitous as war was in the 1940s.

13 This is what Paul Krugman argues.

14 In law, circumstantial evidence is evidence that can be relied upon as pointing to the existence of a fact. It differs from direct evidence, which can prove a fact directly. In a court of law, a fact can be proved by circumstantial evidence alone.

A concise view of globalization

I said earlier that globalization is not a new phenomenon. Historians classify globalization into different forms, including "archaic, proto, modern and post-colonial". As AG Hopkins explains in *Globalization in World History*, archaic globalization covers the thousands of years before the emergence of the modern state, including the classical Roman Empire, which created a commercial and political integrated entity that covered most of the world known to classical societies. Proto-globalization is a period related to early forays by European powers and by Islam into Asia and Africa between 1600 and 1800, adventures that provided the foundations on which modern globalization was built. Modern globalization, as we will see shortly, is sometimes referred to as the "colonial era", while post-industrial globalization is what we are living through now.

Without going back too far into history, two previous phases of globalization are worth noting, in that they may help us to understand how things might turn out this time. Starting in the fifteenth century, the great naval and commercial powers of the world at the time, England, Holland, Spain, Portugal and France had created a globalized world. Through the window of history, which is actually a mirror distorted by our own values, rather than a clear view of the past, we now speak of this era as the age of European colonial imperialism. This is because between the fifteenth and twentieth centuries, the great European powers carved up the world among them, in their scramble for gold, spices, sugar, tea, land, and slaves.

As and because they did this, the planet became an integrated engine of production serving the needs and wants of a relatively small portion of the world's population; this was the industrial revolution reshaping the global economy and the global balance of power. For example, Indian cotton grown by cheap indigenous labor, Indian peasants, was taken to England where, thanks to cheap indigenous labor, mainly relocated English peasants, it was used to transform Manchester into the eponymous home of cheap manufactured cloth, benefiting the traders, the manufacturers and the Royal Treasury. But doing little good for the labor force.

Both in India and in Manchester, workers were paid poorly, worked extremely long hours and had no rights. In a sense, they were slaves who got paid, though not much. It was even worse for the laborers in Manchester, because on top of the exploitation they had to suffer, they were also exposed to extremely unsafe working conditions. Fires were common in cotton mills, for example, and death rates were high. The cotton example could be replicated for tea, spices, sugar and many other commodities. The business model was simple: many labored for little recompense—no recompense at all for slaves in the Southern states of the USA and some other places—to benefit the few who owned the factors of production and the capacity to acquire and move large quantities of raw materials and manufactured goods. I call this the first wave of manufacturing globalization, because manufacturing was where value was added and harvested. In the latter phases of this era of globalization, other countries joined in, including Germany, Italy, Russia, Japan and, as a minor partner because of its isolationist policies, the USA.

This first wave of globalization did not end with the onset of World War 1, as some might think. Yes, there was some interruption of normal services while millions died in the war to end all wars, but, in reality, commerce continued through the conflict, including trade across the warring coalitions, facilitated by shady deals among great industrialists and by neutral countries. What happened as a consequence of World War 1 is that the great powers of Europe had to surrender their total control of Global Trading Enterprises Inc., to give way to some new players, chief amongst them the USA. The USA became a global power during and because World War 1, not least because of its role as a financier for the winning side, and, as a global power, it wanted a greater share of the action.

This shift in power relationships gave us the second wave of globalization, which still focused on manufacturing. In this phase, control of land, people and raw materials started to depend less on direct political control, colonialism, and more on indirect economic control. Colonial imperialism gradually morphed into economic imperialism. This was particularly evident in Central and South America, where the USA, through a mixture of gunboat diplomacy, corruption of the local governing classes and the power of the dollar, controlled everything of significance that happened in its continental backyard. This was a model that had worked well for the Roman Empire two thousand years ago and the new American empire of the twentieth century put the lessons of history to work well, sometimes bettering its predecessor.

The second wave of globalization based on manufacturing continued to produce grand profits for a few at the expense of many. It did so until the Great Crash of 1929, with the aid of new technologies, such as long range aircraft and the radio, as well as increasingly sophisticated rail and road networks. The Crash itself did not bring this phase of globalization to an end, but the political consequences of the financial crisis that followed the events of 1929 and 1930-32 did. As countries tried to protect their employment base, higher and higher protectionist barriers were raised, diminishing significantly the extent of international trade, already reduced by the fall in purchasing power for most of the people in the USA and Europe. The crisis exacerbated autarchic tendencies in the European dictatorships, including Germany, Italy, Spain and the Soviet Union, but also in Japan and the USA itself. Even now, as I hear President Obama urging Americans to buy American cars, I hear the echoes of the rallying cries by politicians and demagogues of the 1930s. I would urge President Obama to study again the speeches of Mussolini and Hitler and to eschew from his speeches and exhortations any words or phrases resembling what those two had to say in their efforts to bolster their citizens' desire to purchase goods made at home. Autarky and a fragmented world within which each nation believes it needs no other to survive and thrive, leads to war, as we saw with the outbreak of World War 2. The war did not end globalization, it merely marked its end with an exclamation mark, but it also provided the foundations for a new wave of globalization, which this time would rely on services and knowledge, rather than cheap raw materials and cheap labor.

Our descendants may describe it as a third phase of imperialism, because, as in the first two phases, most of the world still labors for relatively little reward to support the lifestyle of a small portion of the world's population. However, we prefer to think of it as the post-industrial era or as the era of the knowledge economy. Because I am a creature of the present and because this is not a book about ideology or politics, I am more comfortable discussing globalization within the context of the knowledge economy. But there is another reason for taking this route. As we saw earlier, markets live and die because of what goes on in our minds, which is a combustible mixture of emotion and rational thinking. If we want to understand what tips markets over and what causes bubbles to inflate and deflate—indeed, if we want to understand how markets operate and why—we need to understand what goes on in our minds and hearts.

Also, if we want to develop the means to make the business cycle less painful and a little more predictable, we need to develop our capabilities on the rational side of the ledger. For centuries, the animal spirits have ruled the financial world; it is time for the human mind to have a little more say in what goes on. This is why I have chosen to focus on knowledge and the knowledge economy, a topic covered in the next section of the book. Shortly I will explain what I mean by that, but first, here is the recommended reading on the complex topic of globalization, starting with *Globalization in World History*, by Anthony G. Hopkins, published by Norton in 2002, which does elegantly what I did very concisely here, canvassing and explaining previous episodes of globalization. For US, Canadian and UK readers, in particular, I also recommend *Globalization and History: The Evolution of a Nineteenth-Century Atlantic Economy*, by Kevin H. O'Rourke and Jeffrey G. Williamson, published by MIT Press in 1999.

Understanding the knowledge economy

Organizations in the public sector and in the private sector are being challenged by the volume of data and information they are required to manage. The challenge is two-fold. There is a logistic challenge, how do we manage the sheer volume of content that flows through our lives? This book is not about that, though my next book might be, so watch this space! There is also a less obvious challenge, as it is becoming clear that in the modern economy value is created by the wise use of data and information, by managing and exploiting knowledge. Getting down to tin tacks, what is a knowledge economy and what does it look like, you might ask. As well as my own writings and thoughts on the subject, here I will rely on the work of Thurow, Boisot, Schumpeter and Drucker. There is confusion to be had aplenty by discussing data, information and knowledge, terms that are often used as if they were interchangeable, whereas they have quite different meanings.

From data to knowledge

Boisot offers definitions he thought would be helpful, but which I find a bit over-elaborate:

> *We take data to be simply a discernible difference between alternative states of a system. It is made up of low level energy that acts informationally rather than mechanically upon an observer. Information is data that modifies the expectations or the conditional readiness of an observer. The more those expectations are modified, the more informative the data is said to be.*
>
> *Knowledge is the set of expectations that an observer holds with respect to an event. It is a disposition to act in a particular way that has to be inferred from behavior rather than observed directly.*
>
> *... [Knowledge assets] can be thought of as that subset of dispositions to act that is embedded in individuals, groups, all artifacts and that has value adding potential.*[15]

I take a more practical stance, best explained by example. This is a set of *data*: 1.3.54. These numbers could mean anything or nothing, on their own. They could be a telephone number, a combination for a safe, my favorite lotto numbers or the space-time coordinates for the Starship Enterprise in *Star Trek*. However, if I were to tell you that those numbers represent a date, then you have a context within which to interpret the data. Now we have *information* available to us, rather than mere data, as the numbers take on a specific meaning, representing day, month and year, respectively. But we have a new problem now. In Europe, the month follows the day, when a date is given, whereas in the USA, the reverse occurs. However, if you were to know that I was born in Europe and that, as a consequence, I retain elements of European culture and beliefs, and also that this is my date of birth, suddenly you may have more than information. This is because you may assume that, given my belief system, I would prefer to structure dates as the Europeans do. Now you have *knowledge*. You know when and where I was born and a little about my belief system, at least in regard to how dates are written.

As we move from data towards knowledge, the difference at each stage is context. It is context that provides meaning, but there are two types of context. Data has no intrinsic meaning; it needs a logical context. If the logical context is provided—if I tell you that a number sequence represents a date—then you have information. While information has meaning (information = data + logical context), it remains an inert

15 *Knowledge Assets: Securing Competitive Advantage in the Information Economy*, Oxford University Press 1998.

substance, with no inherent power of action, motion, or resistance. Information is of limited use—you cannot do much with a date without knowing what the date means. One must add something else to make information useful and that something is belief (in the form of expectations), derived from experience (or knowledge = information + belief); the experience can be our own or someone else's or a mix, which is usually the case. [16] In our example, the experience was reading words I had written for you that provided you with an insight into my belief system, but that is not all. You contributed to that experience, by interpreting what I am saying and translating it within your own context. If you had no awareness of how Europeans prefer to write dates, reading my words would not have helped you to solve the puzzle, you would still now know what the date means.

So, the creation of knowledge is never passive, it requires your input, and knowledge can exist only in someone's mind, because as soon as knowledge is fixed into cold black ink onto a cold white page, it ceases to be knowledge, it reverts to being information. Ponder on this, if you need to, because it is important. It is important because there can be no knowledge without or outside a human mind—though maybe one day artificial intelligence will void this truth—which means that to make knowledge, you need people. It also means that there is no knowledge without action, even if the action is only reading and thinking. To put it another way, managing knowledge means managing an end to end process that links data, through information and knowledge, to action—or, to put it another way, that managing knowledge is managing people. As Dave Snowden is reported to have said, "People always know more than they can say and always say more than they write down."[17] This is because knowledge exists only in people's heads; once knowledge is reduced to writing or even the spoken word, at best it becomes information, at worst mere data—or even gibberish. If this is true—and I believe it is—then understanding what people believe and why is fundamental to understanding how and why people behave in organizations and in the marketplace, alone or as part of the herd.

Why belief is reality

Beliefs are shaped by expectations. In turn, expectations are constructed by interpreting experience, by attributing meaning to events, which is a process completely subsumed within a human brain—and in the world of art. While we cannot (as yet) modify people's brains, except in the crudest fashion through surgery, It is possible to influence or

16 Some of the theoretical material I have used here has been published earlier by me in a book edited by Hasan and Handzic, titled *Australian Studies in Knowledge Management* (Wollongong: WUP, 2003).

17 Dave Snowden is one of the gurus of knowledge management and his thinking is well-worth our attention, though he and I differ somewhat on our approaches, given that he has said that he rejects and despises "the linear model of Data-Information-Knowledge-Wisdom" (see http://www.kwork.org/Stars/snowden_part1.html, retrieved on 2 January 2009). I suspect that Dave assumes that the model is linear, whereas it is not, as I explain in *Australian Studies in Knowledge Management*—see previous note.

shape belief systems held by people by providing common cognitive and interpretive tools and through the culture of the organization (or society or group and so on). What organizations do (and the people in them) is conditioned by the past and by a view of the organization's reasons for acting (including failure to act) that is inherently risky, that is unreflexive. Reflexivity is a process of reflection on one's own acts or omissions or motivations or feelings that may cause a change of understanding of oneself or of the environment or both.[18] In Buddhism the concept is expressed as mindfulness, which is the continual application of presence of mind. Mindfulness means being aware of one's belief systems, emotions and thinking processes and acting on the basis of that understanding, prepared to reap the consequences of our beliefs being externalized as actions. In other words, you know that what you are doing and why you are doing it, and what is likely to follow. Mindfulness is the opposite of unreflexive thinking and helps us to avoid simplistic interpretations of reality and ritualized responses to the world.[19]

This is a theme picked up by George Soros, in his own peculiar way, in a recent book titled *The New Paradigm for Financial Markets: The Credit Crisis of 2008 and What It Means*. The new paradigm put forward by Soros is this, in his words.

> *...market participants cannot base their decisions on knowledge alone, and their biased perceptions have ways of influencing not only market prices but also the fundamentals that those prices are supposed to reflect. On the one hand they seek to understand their situation. I called this the cognitive function. On the other hand, they try to change the situation. I called this the participating or manipulative function. The two functions work in opposite directions and, under certain circumstances, they can interfere with each other. I called this interference reflexivity.*[20]

As we have just seen, this stuff is not new, George Soros has not uncovered or proposed a new paradigm. In fact, we covered reflexivity in my undergraduate psychology and sociology classes in the 1970s and I dealt with these concepts in *Compliance and Regulation* and in earlier writings.[21] The concept is also not new to economics. As leading Australian economist Nicholas Gruen has pointed out, Keynes wrote about this subject many decades ago.[22] In this book, it seems that, unfortunately, George

18 Reflexivity is a process of reflection on one's own acts or omissions or motivations or feelings that may cause a change of understanding of oneself or of the environment or both. In Buddhism the concept is expressed as mindfulness, which is the continual application of presence of mind. Mindfulness means being aware of one's belief systems, emotions and thinking processes and acting on the basis of that understanding, prepared to reap the consequences of our beliefs being externalised as actions. Mindfulness is the opposite of conditioned thinking and helps us to avoid simplistic interpretations of reality and ritualised responses to the world (Tart 1994).

19 Tart 1994.

20 At page viii.

21 "Creating Value by Managing Knowledge", in *Australian Studies in knowledge management*, University of Wollongong Press, 2003.

22 "Cassandras of the Crisis", *The Monthly*, March 2009.

Soros, in a laudable attempt to be innovative in the field of economics, has jumbled together the notion of reflexivity with the concept of bounded rationality, which we discussed earlier. Nonetheless, what Soros says has value, if understood in its proper context, which is not economics. Let us go back to the fundamentals, which are to be found in the literature of sociology, rather than economics.

William Thomas formulated the Thomas theorem in 1928, suggesting that "the situations that men define as true, become true for them."[23] Sociologist Robert K. Merton elaborated the Thomas principle to postulate the notion we know as the self-fulfilling prophecy.[24] We all know what this means; once a prediction is made people tend to adjust their behavior so that a statement that would have been false may become true or vice-versa. In physics this proposition was expressed by Werner Heisenberg as the "observer effect", because the act of observing has an influence on the phenomenon being observed. This concept was proven by a famous series of observations known as the Hawthorne Studies. These studies were conducted by George Elton Mayo at the Hawthorne Works of the Western Electric company in Chicago, between 1924 and 1927. The focus of his study was whether electric light would keep workers awake, which would be good for productivity, or it made them more tired, reducing productivity.

The conclusions usually drawn from the studies are that the physical conditions in which employees work have little impact on their performance, but the social aspects of working in an organization can make a big positive or negative difference. To round out this argument, we also need to touch on groupthink, which was discussed earlier in the book. To save you turning back to the beginning of the book, the research indicates that groups caught up in groupthink do not consider all alternatives as thoroughly as they should, sometimes not at all, and focus on achieving unanimity at the expense of quality decisions. Keeping the herd together is more important than the task at hand. It seems that here again we humans demonstrate that we are not the rational beings imagined by economists. While we generally see the human species as prone to conflict and division, there are times when we value agreement much more than we should. The drive to conform is very strong in humans, as demonstrated by research conducted across the last few decades. For the sake of brevity, I will focus on one set of studies only, conducted by US psychologist Dr Stanley Milgram in the early 1960s.

Studies in obedience

Milgram's purpose was to find out what makes seemingly normal human beings behave in ways that are considered by most of us to be extremely cruel, heartless and devoid of humanity. The trigger for the studies Milgram conducted was the trial of Adolf Eichmann, held in Israel in 1962. Eichmann was a leading organizer of the mass murder of Jews and others during World War 2. He was found guilty as charged

23 WI Thomas and DS Thomas, *The child in America: Behavior problems and programs*, Knopf, 1928.
24 *Social Theory and Social Structure*, The Free Press, 1949.

and executed in 1962. During the trial it became apparent that Eichmann was not a monster or a psychopath. He was an average guy who was instrumental in doing a great deal of evil. He saw himself as an administrator, serving his country and obeying orders. Having observed the trail, Milgram formulated the hypothesis that if placed in particular roles in particular situations, even ordinary people can commit horrendous acts. The experiments he conducted were to test that hypothesis.

The structure of the experiments was simple. Using volunteers, Milgram found that the hypothesis was strongly supported by the evidence, as explained in this extract from a *Psychology Today* article,[25]

> *(Milgram) found that an average, presumably normal group of New Haven, Connecticut, residents would readily inflict very painful and perhaps even harmful electric shocks on innocent victims. The subjects believed they were part of an experiment supposedly dealing with the relationship between punishment and learning. An experimenter—who used no coercive powers beyond a stern aura of mechanical and vacant-eyed efficiency—instructed participants to shock a learner by pressing a lever on a machine each time the learner made a mistake on a word-matching task. Each subsequent error led to an increase in the intensity of the shock in 15-volt increments, from 15 to 450 volts. In actuality, the shock box was a well-crafted prop and the learner an actor who did not actually get shocked. The result: A majority of the subjects continued to obey to the end—believing they were delivering 450 volt shocks—simply because the experimenter commanded them to. Although subjects were told about the deception afterward, the experience was a very real and powerful one for them during the laboratory hour itself.*

Milgram's findings have since been corroborated by other studies and it seems that as well as being prone to irrational decision making in assessing risk, human beings are likely to be strongly influenced by the situation in which they find themselves, sometimes against their best instincts or even their best interest. The next bit of research I am going to present to you illustrates this point quite well.

Travelling to Abilene...whether we like it or not

In 1974, Jerry Harvey published a paper titled "The Abilene paradox: The Management of agreement". Harvey used an example from his own life, a trip to Abilene, to set the scene for his thesis. Harvey saw the management of agreement as a greater problem than the management of conflict, partly because the existence of the former problem was not recognized. Harvey postulated that this seeming paradox resulted from a

25 "The Man Who Shocked the World", by Thomas Blass, *Psychology Today Magazine*, Mar/Apr 2002.

failure of communication—members of organizations fail to communicate to each other their perceptions of reality and their desires. They do this because of a range of factors, including: (1) action anxiety; (2) negative fantasies; (3) real risk; (4) separation anxiety; and (5) the psychological reversal of risk and certainty.

From what Harvey wrote we may conclude that people in organizations and, as a consequence, the organizations they constitute, are capable of formulating a course of action that does not represent accurately their intention and that they may implement this course of action without being aware of what and why they are doing what they are doing (or unreflexively, the social scientists would say). People in organizations and, as a consequence, the organizations they constitute can unconsciously sabotage the design of a course of action on which the organization may wish to embark and may also unconsciously impair the organization's capacity to implement that course of action. When you think about it, most situations where an organization goes off the beaten track, other than when out and out fraud is involved, are due either to groupthink or to the Abilene paradox.

In some cases, groupthink creates a fertile ground for fraud, because it stops the organization being aware of its own behavior. So, for example, if decision-makers in the financial services industry socialize primarily with each other, at work and after work, they will tend to reinforce beliefs and expectations that are already endemic in that social setting. If the mood of the group is blindly optimistic, the tendency of the group towards agreement will cement that mood in place and the individuals concerned will probably not be aware that this is what has happened. The effects of such a mood on an already over-heated market could push it over the edge and, of course, the reverse is true as well. If the group becomes caught in a pessimistic mood, the slide of the market downhill will accelerate. Also, people will tend to do as they are told, especially if they occupy a role in an organization towards which they feel some loyalty and in situations where the way forward is uncertain.

This means that in companies like Enron, a few bad decisions or a few bad people making decisions can take the whole organization and its thousands of employees on a journey they would not take if they were thinking rationally. This means that people like Madoff can take otherwise intelligent and well-informed people for a ride, for years. This means that the relatively few individuals who make the big decisions in companies, regulating authorities and in the media, can engage in a long-term collective delusion that gradually engulfs all of us in an ever growing bubble of enthusiasm—or despondency, depending on the phase of the cycle.

When dealing with individuals, this kind of behavior is considered to be pathological, it is thought to be a sickness, once known as manic-depression and now as bipolar disorder. People with bipolar disorder experience unusually intense emotional states that occur in distinct periods. An overly joyful or overexcited state is called a manic episode and an extremely sad or hopeless state is called a depressive episode. These episodes usually have no external causes, they are only reflections of processes inside the person's mind. Does that ring a bell for those of you who work in the financial markets? I think that when Alan Greenspan spoke of irrational exuberance in the markets, he was speaking of behavior in the markets that did not correlate with reality and others before and since have made similar observations.[26] Unfortunately, having become aware of this fundamental irrationality of the markets did not, it seems, undo Greenspan's belief in the fundamental wisdom of the markets. May be Greenspan thought of irrational exuberance as a spring fever, a quick and relatively harmless aberration. Alas, it is not so. The markets are afflicted by what I call the Icarus syndrome. The tendency to fly too close to the sun and to then crash is as much a part of the ethos of the markets as it is of part of Greek mythology.

I am not saying that this in and by itself explains what happens when markets go bad, but it is a big piece of the puzzle. Yet, very few in the world of economics and even fewer in the upper echelons of the financial industry understand any of this, it seems. It should be no surprise. I doubt that there are too many MBA or DBA courses where this kind of material is dealt with properly, if at all, and I doubt that boards, accountants, auditors and regulators understand any of it either. If there is a stronger argument to say that finance is too important to be left to financiers I would be surprised. And there is no salvation in economics either, where most economists have forgotten that economics is a creature of sociology and prefer to dazzle each other with pointless mathematical exercises[27] or rely blindly on the dogma of the infallible market.[28]

As Soros suggested, this approach is fraught with danger, for the organization, its members and anyone who is within its sphere of influence. Any human social construct, be it a family, an organization a market or a nation, is driven and shaped by brain and brawn and heart and I am afraid that our capacity to manage and measure is good with the middle element, but very poor with the other two. This is a bit like driving with your eyes closed and with cotton wool stuck in your ears. It will only lead to grief, eventually, though it may be strangely exhilarating for a while. If we think that driving like this is crazy, and it is, why is it that we insist on running the economy that way? Is it because we like the thrill or because we know no other way? And there is another way, as I will now explain.

Managing knowledge 101: Tackling the icarus syndrome

It is estimated that in 1980, the book value of the S&P 500 companies was eighty percent of the total value of market capitalization. As the first decade of the twenty-first century

26 If you are curious about the origins of the phrase, I refer you to an amusing and illuminating online essay by Robert J. Shiller at http://www.irrationalexuberance.com/definition.htm, which I retrieved on 8 May 2009.

27 Physics went through a similar stage in the 15th and 16th centuries, when epicycles were in vogue as the means to make sense of an Earth-centered universe when all the evidence put the Sun at the center of the Solar System.

28 Dogma is authoritative doctrine and may not be disputed or doubted.

is closing, book values account for less than one third of the market capitalization of the S&P 500. Fundamental changes have occurred over the last few decades, redefining how economic value is generated. It is now safe to say that growth is driven primarily by factors other than land and capital. Rather, it is human capital and intellectual capital that matter, together with other intangibles, such as relationships, networks, reputation and environmental factors, such as regulatory frameworks. Yet, economic management and regulatory processes are still firmly grounded in the industrial age and decision-makers failing to take this new reality into account.

We live and work in a world where knowledge is power and ignorance is not bliss. We also live in a world where wealth is created primarily by and through the application of knowledge to extract value from both hard and soft resources. Yet, are trying to manage a knowledge based economy as if it were an industrial economy. We have done very little to teach our children, our managers, our workers and our leaders how to manage the source of our wealth and prosperity. So, it is no surprise that our leaders, managers and enterprises continue to make errors that others have made before us, failing to learn the right lessons from history. Just like Icarus, we fail to pay heed to the experience of those who have come before us and, as a consequence, we are doomed to repeat their mistakes. To avoid the fate of Icarus and that of the blind and deafened driver, we need to learn how to manage knowledge, so that we can tame our emotions, so that we can manage the animal spirits loosed into the marketplace by human nature, so that we can be aware of the perils of irrational exuberance, so that we can fly closer to the sun without melting our wings. We then need to be able to measure the value we create or destroy in the economy and society, fully, not selectively, as accounting standards and economics would have us do.

You may have heard of knowledge management and perhaps you have dismissed it as another fad, together with the learning organization, who moved my cheese and so on. If so, I don't blame you. Avoiding fads is wise, because all you end up doing is making consultants rich and wasting productive time. However, please consider this. If you were a carpenter or a mechanic (as my father was) or a doctor or an accountant, you would be provided, or you would acquire, a set of tools to do your work. These tools would have been developed, over decades and sometimes centuries, to provide the tradesperson or professional with the best available means to get the job done. If one were to suggest to any of these workers that they should just turn up for work and hope for the best, you would be laughed out of the room—and quite right too. However, most of us who manage people or processes in organizations are in precisely that position. We are expected to turn up for work and to succeed in a very complex and mutable environment without the benefit of any tools, save that which we can create for ourselves or can borrow, beg or steal from others.

Is it any wonder that managers (and those whom they manage) make mistakes, become victims of stress, cause failures or allow failures to happen? Is it any wonder that most of us—you too, admit it—feel sometimes at risk of drowning in a deluge of data, information and competing demands for our time and attention? Should we be surprised about the rising concern about the enormous gap that older, experienced workers leave behind when they retire or move on? In fact, it is a tribute to all of you who labor in organizations that so much gets done and that it is generally done well, without an established set of tools. Knowledge management seeks to remedy this deficiency, by equipping is with the tools and skills we need to make best use of the resources available to us to do what we need to do, as the following definition illustrates:

> *The term Knowledge Management (KM) refers to a multi-disciplined approach to achieving organizational objectives by making the best use of knowledge. KM focuses on processes such as acquiring, creating and sharing knowledge and the cultural and technical foundations that support them. The aim is to align knowledge processes with organizational objectives.*[29]

Knowledge management differs from information management and data management because it demands mindfulness; it requires people to manage behavior and the context within which beliefs are actuated and given meaning. It requires to know what we are doing and why, so that, if we are offered a ride to Abilene, we can make a rational decision, rather than merely falling in with the crowd, with the herd. By way of contrast, managing data or information is primarily about managing objects, be they physical or digital—a machine can do that. The broader context for our discussion is provided by Thurow, who argues that the global economy is developing beyond the range of international governance structures and is challenging the form and the raison d'être that has supported nation states over the last couple of centuries. Countries themselves are being changed through economic pressure and the emergence of truly global companies is leading to ever-greater size and greater capacity to challenge national governments.[30]

What does a knowledge economy look like?

It is not only academics who ponder what a knowledge economy might look like. The Organization for Economic Cooperation and Development (OECD), in its 2001 report titled "Towards a Knowledge Based Economy", remarked on the rise of the knowledge economy and emphasized that "the ability to create, distribute and exploit knowledge is increasingly central to competitive advantage, wealth creation and better standards of living" . For our purposes here, I define the knowledge economy as "productive

29 Taken from http://www.knowledge.standards.com.au/KM/INFO/KMINTRO/KMINTRO.HTM, on 7 October 2003.

30 *Creating Wealth: The New Rules for Individuals Companies and Countries in a Knowledge-based Economy*, Nicholas Brearley 1999.

activities based on the acquisition, processing and exchange of information, where the value generated is both tangible and intangible". By tangible value I mean the traditional forms of value, land, capital, plant and so on. By intangible value, I mean "human, structure and relational capital".

The European Guidelines for Intellectual Capital Reporting define these terms:

- relational capital is external relationships with customers, suppliers, partners, etc and their perception of the company.
- structural capital is knowledge that remains within a company at the end of the working day and comprising organizational routines, procedures, systems, databases, documents and so on.
- human capital is knowledge that employees take with them when they leave the business. It includes knowledge, experience, skills, and networking abilities associated with their role.

I would add a fourth type. It is my belief that the organization itself, by its very existence, has intrinsic value that is greater than the sum of its parts or the mere summation of the other types of capital. It may be argued that the concept of brand value captures this point, but an organization is also more than a brand or collection of brands. This last type of value is even harder to measure than the other three. As Thomas Stewart observed in *Intellectual Capital*, with a vivid turn of phrase, "Armies of clerks and banks of computers track physical and financial assets, but those accounting systems cannot cope with brainpower." We will return to the question of accounting for value, but let us first place the discussion in its proper global context.

We live in a world where success often depends on how well we compete at the national and international levels. In most industries, competition is global and that is true for the financial industry more than most, because money now is primarily a digital construct and electrons carrying strings of numbers know no boundaries and can be moved around the world instantaneously and easily. For example, a bank in the Netherlands can compete with a lending institution in Sydney without any physical presence in Australia, using shared infrastructure, standardized processes and a big advertising budget. ING has established a viable business in Australia while using only the online channel to harvest deposits and to make loans. I have credit accounts with Citibank, though there is no branch of that bank within hundreds of miles from where I live, in Canberra. This is the first bit of knowledge we need to grasp: in a globalized economy, we need to run just to stand still, because the ground will be moving under your feet.

Why is the financial system so important? The purpose of the global financial system is simple, to enable the lifeblood of capitalism to do its job, to enable capital to go where it can get the greatest return for its owner. The system does that through a plethora of ever more complex arrangements and devices, financial and technological, though its fundamental character remains the same. The financial system has evolved to enable the safe movement of funds across boundaries, organizational or national and, paraphrasing Shubik, money is a substitute for trust, in the world of trade.[31] Money makes the world go round; the rest is detail, to be dipped into only if and when it helps to shed light on the problem we all have to deal with, which is how to make this system work for us.

To illustrate the significance of the financial sector, in the USA, for example, it provides five percent of private sector employment, but produces 8.1 percent of GDP. The securities industry, although it contains only 0.65 percent of private-sector employment, is responsible for 1.4 percent of US GDP.[32] Similar statistics would be disclosed in any developed economy and the relative importance of the financial sector is translated at the global level. However, these are only indicators of the sector's direct value; its indirect value to the global economy is much greater. Because of what it does and how it does it, the global financial system is a de facto risk engine, moving risk along the value chain, across value chains, and through the whole economy, at local, regional, national and global levels. All of us can benefit from the opportunities the financial system creates and all of us suffer the consequences of the obverse of those opportunities, when risk—risk of loss, of failure, of fraud, of missed opportunities—becomes reality.

Ideally, the risk engine embedded in the financial system would operate as classical economists would like it to, blindly, like Adam Smith's invisible hand, but omnisciently and impartially, using the information available to it to allocate risk where it is best dealt with, placing it in the safest hands or on the strongest shoulders. This is a Newtonian view of the world, with the ever reliable mechanical clock as its metaphor. All we humans need do is to wind up the clock, may be dust it occasionally, and it will do its job, creating order in an otherwise disorderly universe.

Alas, in reality the financial system is fallible, like all human creations. It is not a mechanical clock, nor even an atomic clock, which now keeps perfect time, aligning the macro world of people and planets to the micro world of atoms. Rather than a clock, it is more like any one of us, it is a macro reflection of the micro world of individual human endeavor. Information is always imperfect or incomplete, profit is not always the motive of the actors and the laws of economics have to interact with the even less rational laws of politics, they must accommodate cultural and social reality, the stage on which all human activities are performed. So, rather than a clockwork risk engine, delivering predictable and measurable results, the global financial system is more like

31 Martin Shubik, *Theory of Money and Financial Institutions*, MIT Press 1999.

32 From the Interim Report of the Committee on Capital Markets Regulation, 30 November 2006, by the Committee on Capital Markets Regulation. The Committee on Capital Markets Regulation is an independent, bipartisan committee composed of 22 corporate and financial leaders from the investor community, business, finance, law, accounting, and academia. The report can be found at http://crapo.senate.gov/documents/committee_capmarkets_reg.pdf.

the parlor game where players must find a chair when the music stops. Sooner or later, the music will stop and the player without a chair will be the loser and in a globalized world there are many players.

We discussed globalization earlier. Let us accept that it is beyond the scope of this work to debate whether globalization is a blight or a boon or merely a feature of the environment, like the weather.[33] For our purposes it is sufficient to note that we live in a globalized economy. This may be a cliché, but it is nonetheless a useful descriptor of the current state of the world, economically, socially and culturally. Banking is the most truly capitalist of industries, making money primarily from capital, rather than labor or land. It is also a true twenty-first century industry, because its stock in trade is information, its business model is about relationships and its business platform is heavily dependent on information and communication technologies.

We have also discussed the notion of the knowledge economy and concluded that we live and work in a global knowledge economy that is gradually re-shaping national and international economic reality. The financial services sector is a good example of what the knowledge economy means in practice. Making a living from buying and selling money, credit and debt—and endless derivative manifestations of these age-old commodities—is all about acquiring, processing and exchanging information. In this environment, "while traditional management could be characterized as 'the quest for uncertainty reduction', the new management faces the challenge of uncertainty absorption and will be tested by what he calls the (Schumpeterian) creative destruction of its knowledge assets".[34] What does this mean? Well, you could ask the good people who publish the *Encyclopedia Britannica* or the board of Chrysler or the good folks in Iceland. They know what it means—Darwinian natural selection is constantly at work in the economy and more so when times are tough. Here is a good illustration of this, putting flesh and bone on Schumpeter's theme of creative destruction, which I am re-interpreting here as selective destruction, because the result is not necessarily transformative or creative.

Selective destruction: the case of the car industry

Schumpeter introduced us to the concept of creative destruction in *Capitalism, Socialism and* Democracy, originally published in 1942. Schumpeter believed that capitalism would be destroyed by its successes, because it would generate a large intellectual class that would thrive by attacking the very system of private property and freedom so necessary for the existence of that class. While I am not convinced that history has proved Schumpeter right on this point, it has proven him right on his analysis of how

33 Friedman 1999 and 2008.
34 *Knowledge Assets: Securing Competitive Advantage in the Information Economy*, Oxford University Press 1998.

capitalism works. The following extract from Schumpeter's seminal book tells his story well.[35]

> *The fundamental impulse that sets and keeps the capitalist engine in motion comes from the new consumers, goods, the new methods of production or transportation, the new markets, the new forms of industrial organization that capitalist enterprise creates...The opening up of new markets, foreign or domestic, and the organizational development from the craft shop and factory to such concerns as U.S. Steel illustrate the same process of industrial mutation—if I may use that biological term—that incessantly revolutionizes the economic structure from within, incessantly destroying the old one, incessantly creating a new one. This process of Creative Destruction is the essential fact about capitalism. It is what capitalism consists in and what every capitalist concern has got to live in...Every piece of business strategy acquires its true significance only against the background of that process and within the situation created by it. It must be seen in its role in the perennial gale of creative destruction; it cannot be understood irrespective of it or, in fact, on the hypothesis that there is a perennial lull...*

What is happening in the car industry globally is simple to explain. Increasingly, people want smaller, more environmentally friendly cars. Certain segments of the global industry, notably in the USA, have failed to pay sufficient attention to this trend, which has now accelerated as a result of the combined impact of climate change and the credit crisis—and the sustained poor management over decades of the Detroit carmakers, especially Chrysler and General Motors. As a result, there are major shifts occurring in the industry. A few years ago, Italy's Fiat was moribund and might have been absorbed by General Motors. Now, thanks to clever positioning by Fiat's management, which means that Fiat's range includes several of the top ten most fuel efficient and climate friendly car models in the marketplace, and thanks to the Great Recession and the effects of climate change, Fiat is about to take over Chrysler and perhaps also General Motors' European operations, at a bargain basement price. If these deals go ahead, Fiat may emerge from the Great Recession as one of the world's leading carmakers, second only to Toyota, having achieved the scale its own CEO has deemed to be the minimum for survival in the twenty-first century—about 5.5 million cars per year.[36]

The car industry has seen such dramatic turnarounds before. In 1899 and 1900 electric cars outsold all other types of cars in the USA. There were three hundred manufacturers of electric cars in the USA at that time.[37] The electric vehicle was preferred, often by or for women, because it did not require a hand crank to get started

35 *Capitalism, Socialism and Democracy*, (New York: Harper, 1975, pages 82-85.
36 See "Marchionne's Fiat Revival Assists Chrysler, GM Talks (Update3)", from Bloomberg.com, at http://www.bloomberg.com/apps/news?pid=20601109&sid=arDDVQeenwN4&refer=home, retrieved on 4 May 2009.
37 From http://www.electric-cars-are-for-girls.com/history.html, retrieved on 4 May 2009.

and there were no gear levers to make life complicated. In those days, there were few highways and journeys by car tended to be short and could be accommodated by contemporary battery technology. However, the development of a highway system in the USA and the consequent requirement for longer range driving, which batteries could not support, together with the availability of cheap Texas gasoline, soon put an end to the dominance of electric cars.

Henry Ford seized the moment and put the Model T on the market. The Model T ran on gasoline, was much cheaper than electric cars to purchase and was relatively easy to drive and to repair. Interestingly, Henry Ford is reported to have expressed regret at the demise of the electric car and his own wife, Mrs. Clara Ford, drove an electric car, 1914 Detroit Electric Model 47 Brougham, until the 1930s.[38] The Model T was in tune with the times, the electric car was not. Ironically, the combination of the Great Recession and climate change has created an environment where the Detroit car makers, the spiritual inheritors of the Model T, are very much out of tune with the times this time around and are about to be consigned to the same metaphorical junkyard that welcomed the electric car a century ago.

Because capitalism functions in this way, twisting and turning and sometimes eating its own metaphorical children, contemporary economists such as Paul Ormerod argue that governments should get out of the day to day detail of the marketplace.[39] Ormerod argues that governments should be concerned with identifying fundamental frameworks and with building the national capability to navigate unpredictable and complex, unpredictable futures, because, as we saw earlier, economies are a study in dis-equilibrium, not equilibrium, and governments should act as the chief stabilizing influence, as and when necessary. As Ormerod points out in a recent online essay, orthodox economics resolutely refuses to accept this and stubbornly insists on sticking to its orthodoxy. Here is what Ormerod said, in part, referring to the launch of the new journal of the American Economic Association,[40]

> *Economists are notorious in the public mind for disagreeing with each other. But it turns out that, far from being riven by dissent, the academic profession believes it has reached a broad consensus. Indeed, the first issue carries an article by one of the world's leading macroeconomists, Michael Woodford, entitled "Convergence in Macroeconomics: Elements of the New Synthesis". The first and most important part of the new synthesis is that "it is now widely agreed that macroeconomic analysis should employ models with coherent intertemporal general equilibrium foundations". What does this mean in English?*

38 From http://www.henryfordestate.org/claracar.htm, retrieved on 4 May 2009.
39 See The Death of Economics (1994), *Butterfly Economics* (1998) and *Why Most Things Fail* (2005).
40 From "Have economists gone mad?", *The Atlantic*, 5 March 2009, at http://business.theatlantic.com/2009/03/have_economists_gone_mad.php, retrieved on 4 May 2009.

It means (a) people and firms act in a rational, coherent manner; (b) they assess coolly and rationally the future consequences of decisions they take now; and (c) the key driving force underlying the economy is a tendency for it to revert to equilibrium. Yes, rub your eyes. The evidence is now so overwhelming that none of these statements are true that it is hard to see how they could even have been written.

We have seen earlier that this view of how and why people behave (the *Homo Economicus* view) has been discredited by research. Research also suggests that the organization that is most likely to achieve long term survival will be that which is capable of reconciling the conflicting forces for change and stability can maintain a dynamic fit with its environment.[41] It is the tree than bends to the wind that is most likely to survive the storm—the inflexible, however big and strong, will perish. Think of it this way. If you are a large cuddly animal that survives on a diet made up entirely of plants that are in plentiful supply in the neighborhood, you will have an easy life and you and your progeny will grow fat on the bounty of nature without too much effort. Another animal, one that eats a broad diet of different species of insects that may be hard to catch and not always plentiful, will always have to work hard to survive, much harder than the specialist Panda sitting on his broad backside chomping on bamboo shoots. However, if the bamboo forests suddenly start to disappear because of human encroachment, your high degree of specialization will transform itself into a curse, rather than a boon. Whereas the generalist insectivore may find that the presence of human agriculture is making available a greater supply of insects—and any insect will do. Now, picture Chrysler as the panda and Fiat as the insectivore, and you have got my point. Which are you going to be?

What have we learnt?

To recapitulate, my underpinning assumptions are these. First, regulation is unavoidable; second, an increasingly globalized web of regulation is unavoidable, to accompany our increasingly globalized way of living and ways of doing business; third, because the responsibility to regulate rests with nation states, the success or failure of global regulation is dependent on the success or failure of its weakest link, its weakest component; fourth, in a globalized economy, no country or business can make itself invulnerable to shocks to the system that are big enough to affect a significant element or component of that system. However, it is possible for countries or businesses to reduce the impact of such a shock. For example, Australia has been left relatively unaffected by the subprime crisis because its internal regulation of the financial system has made it impossible for any Australian financial institution to become too enmeshed in the business practices that trapped other companies, in other jurisdictions, notably, the USA.

41 *The Living Company*, by De Geus et al (1997) remains the best source of guidance on this subject.

To continue with my assumptions, the fifth is that because of the weakest link argument, no state can focus only on its own regulatory arrangements; it is essential that the stronger help the weak, to ensure that the weak do not bring down the strong. That is true within industry and industry sectors as well. A bank, for example, cannot rely on its own regulatory moat to protect it from the evils of the world, because it must transact with the rest of the world to survive. It is in the interest of that bank to ensure that its supply and distribution lines are clear and protected, which means that the survival of the bank depends on the health of the system as a whole. Sixth, a state cannot regulate without, at least, the acquiescence of its subjects, especially when those subjects are large, influential components of the economy. This gives the subjects the capacity to negotiate with the state, to influence what the state does and how it does it, alone or in association with others in the same industry. Next to last, the complex, globalized nature of the financial system and its regulation provides many opportunities for companies or groups of companies to influence the nature, form and application of regulation, internationally and within jurisdictions. And last, a financial crisis will always reveal the shortcomings of the regulatory system and will cause perpetrators of fraud and malfeasance to be unmasked.

As the 2007-08 subprime crisis has shown, the risk is not always placed in the safest hands or on the strongest shoulders. Rather, it lands where it will, when the music stops, when the bubble bursts, and people get hurt, economies get hurt, sometimes gravely or even fatally. When the financial system fails, economies fail and grief and loss often follow, sometimes accompanied by war and generalized disorder, as happened in the Weimar republic in Germany, between the World Wars, or in Yeltsin's post-communist Russia. Because the financial system is the engine that keeps capitalism alive, and keeping nation-states from imploding, states have a strong interest in making sure that there are no failures or, at worst, that the damage is limited. For example, in developed economies there is an unspoken compact between the banks and the state: let us regulate your activities, perhaps a bit more than you might like, and we will keep you from failing. The recent example of Northern Rock in the United Kingdom is a case in point. As I wrote *Compliance and Regulation*, the British Government was nationalizing Northern Rock to stop it from going under having failed to arrange for a private rescue, underpinned by the government, to do the trick.[42]

Many other such nationalizations or quasi-nationalizations have taken place, even in the home of the free market, the USA. Such rescues have required tens of billions of dollars, pounds sterling or Euros supplied by taxpayers, in the form of direct loans and guarantees or acquisitions of equity. As we have seen earlier, huge amounts of money are often required to fill gaping holes in the global financial infrastructure that are caused by relatively small shocks and involve relatively small actual or potential losses.

42 Britain nationalizes ailing Northern Rock, from http://www.abc.net.au/news/stories/2008/02/18/2165041.htm.

My hypothesis is that we are regulating to catch the motes of dust floating in the air, rather than the beams that end up poking out the eyes of our financial markets. It is as if we were more concerned with preventing the theft of petty cash from the staff kitchen than we are with making sure that the doors to the bank vaults are locked securely. The thing is, that this is exactly what we humans tend to do. When faced with big complex problems, we tend to pretend they are not there and we spend all our time and energy on the little problems that we can fix easily and quickly. That is how we are, people, and we need to know this and to take specific steps to make good this shortcoming, soon. Later in the book I will suggest how we can do just that, by transforming what and how we regulate. Figure 5 provides an illustration of the direction I suggest we take.

Regulation is not merely another form of government red tape. Regulation is pervasive and is a powerful influence on business, especially in the financial sector. Generally regulation is perceived by business as a hindrance or, at best, as a necessary evil. As rules change or new rules are made, there is a direct impact on the environment in which a business operates and sometimes on the business itself. As businesses struggle to comply with what they perceive as red tape, many see regulation and compliance as a threat to profitability and as a factor that discourages investment and damages competitiveness. These are reasonable human reactions, but we need to recognize that such reactions are based on emotional grounds, rather than rational thinking. Modern society cannot exist without regulation and the international financial markets and associated institutions could not exist without a regulatory framework. Only crooks and cheats prosper in an unregulated or improperly regulated market and the evidence is that properly regulated industries thrive to the advantage of most, rather than a few. History shows how, if not why, this is so.

The development of seemingly arcane devices, such as marine insurance laws, was fundamental to the development of mercantilist economies and to capitalism in general. What is significant here is the time it took for such developments to occur, starting with city authorities, such as Barcelona in 1434,[43] enacting codes or ordinances that would not develop into a form we would recognize until the latter part of the eighteenth century.[44] In the twenty-first century, there is a disjuncture between the revolutionary pace driven by technology and the evolutionary pace of systems of rules. We cannot wait for hundreds of years while the rules evolve to suit our requirements; we cannot even wait decades, largely because of the speed of technological development and its social, economic and cultural consequences. Yet, while time is short, the challenge is ever more complex. The challenge is to balance what government wants, maximum compliance, with what business wants, minimum interference and no unnecessary costs. The consequent trade off for a regulatory system is effectiveness versus transaction costs.

43 Gow W (1917) *Marine Insurance: A Handbook* (4th edition). Macmillan & Co Ltd.: London.

44 G Boi (1999) "The Marine Insurance System in Italy: Its Present, its Future". In *Marine Insurance at the Turn of the Millennium Vol. 1* (M Huybrechts EV Hooydonk and C Dieryck eds). Intersentia: Antwerp.

The manifestation of this trade off in the global financial industry's regulatory framework is the move from rule-based towards principle-based compliance regulation. This trend is occurring while other powerful trends are developing internationally, generating ever greater complexity and unpredictability. Complexity and unpredictability in turn produce uncertainty, which the markets do not like. A fundamental objective for all of us who have a stake in the future (or would like to have one) must be to reduce uncertainty. Because we can do little to reduce complexity, it seems that we must focus on reducing unpredictability. An important step in this direction is to design and implement a regulatory framework that encourages and rewards openness and transparency and punishes secrecy and opaqueness. I will now summarize the material covered in *Compliance and Regulation* to sketch for you how this can be done.

Figure 5: Trends in international regulation

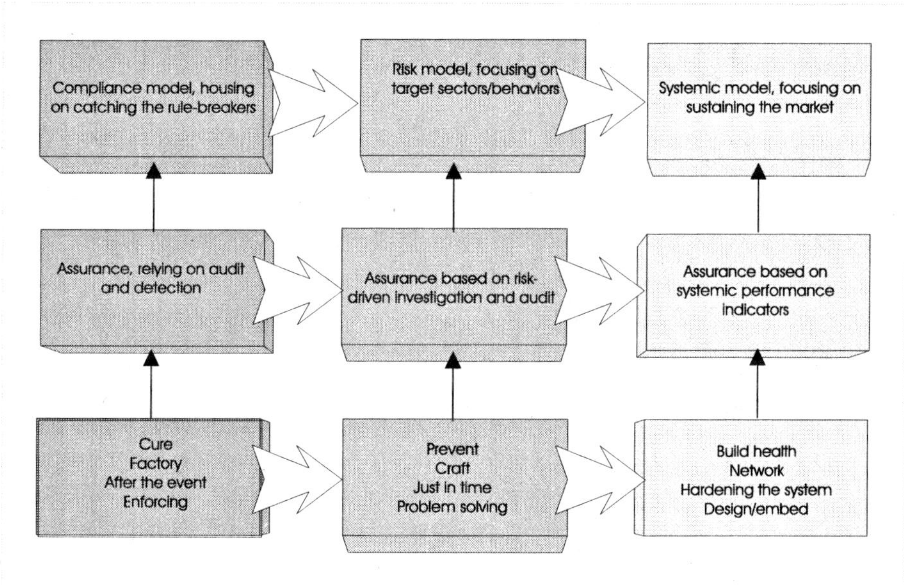

Why regulation should focus on rewarding the good, rather than punishing the bad

Originally, as with any set of rules, the focus was on dealing with the rule-breakers, operating on the assumption that detection and punishment would deter others and would produce general compliance. This was broadly in line with trends in policing and law enforcement generally, as discussed later. The risk based approach in financial regulation aligns surprisingly well with to the development of problem oriented policing (POP). This approach to policing involves the identification and analysis of specific crime problems and seeks to develop response strategies in conjunction with ongoing monitoring. This empirically-based strategy places emphasis on research and analysis as well as crime prevention. It also seeks to engage the broader community to tackle community problems, assuming that this will lead to a reduction of criminal and disorderly behavior. The emerging trend, captured in the last box in figure 4, parallels what is known in law enforcement as intelligence-led policing. What this means is that the system should focus on abating risk, rather than witch-hunting and scapegoating. The *Sarbanes-Oxley Act* of 2002 (SOX) was said to have this intent, but, if so, the intent was not translated adequately into practice. In fact, I think SOX has achieved the reverse, by requiring us to focus on bureaucratic, tick the box mechanisms that distract us from the real game.

Focusing on risk

SOX requires that businesses adopt a definition of internal control in line with industry norms and that they document internal control activities, making evident much that was previously hidden. The assumption is that disclosing a company's internal controls to the market will enable the market to make an informed judgment of how well that company manages risk and how risky an investment it might be. In turn, this should drive the company's management to improve the quality of its controls, to enhance shareholder value and to protect executives from legal and financial retribution. It sound good in theory, but what has happened during the last two years tell us that it has been a monumental failure in practice.

SOX was enacted by the US Congress in response to the Enron and WorldCom financial scandals. The overriding objective of the legislation was to protect shareholders and the general public from accounting errors and fraudulent practices within business enterprises. The act is administered by the Securities and Exchange Commission (SEC), which sets deadlines for compliance and publishes rules on requirements. The consequences for non-compliance are fines, imprisonment, or both. In some organizations, described as best practice in audit circles, responding to SOX has involved appointing a chief risk officer, emulating the process that, in the 1980s and 1990s, resulted in most companies appointing a chief information officer (CIO) and often a chief technology officer as well, with the CIO sometimes at board level, but usually answering to the chief financial officer or the chief operating officer. This trend has weakened a bit of late, with change moving in two directions. Some organizations have accepted that the management of information and communication technologies is of strategic importance and have gradually returned control over ICT assets to the business, to managers. Others, working on the assumption that knowledge, rather than information, is what matters, have appointed chief knowledge officers, who generally sit apart from the technologists and act as a bridge between the business and those managing ICT—as, it must be said, some of the better CIOs have always done.

The argument is that SOX has driven companies to strengthen internal controls and to expand monitoring activities, which could be done only by focusing on understanding and managing risk more effectively. Relying on traditional methods would have been too expensive and intrusive. Also, it was said, the only way to involve the executive layer of management in what amounts to internal regulation is by elevating the regulatory function to the strategic realm, where risk is the common factor. Strategy focuses on managing externally generated risks, while audit and assurance are used to manage internally generated risks and, increasingly, the intersection between external and internal risks.

The evidence is now in and it is plain that SOX is not encouraging a risk-based approach. Rather, it is forcing business to adopt a rigid, black letter approach, mandating standards of corporate governance in legislation. Compliance with this type of regime is expensive, hard to do and not necessarily good for business or for the economy. For example, in 2006, twelve *Fortune 50* CFOs left their jobs, while the year before, companies with $1 billion-plus market caps changed CFOs three times more often than they did in 2002.[45] It is also worth noting that the Interim Report (2006) of the Committee on Capital Markets Regulation found that the US share of initial public offerings (IPOs) on had declined from fifty percent in 2000 to five percent in 2005. In 2005, twenty-four of the biggest IPOs were outside the USA.[46] I am sure that factors other than SOX contributed to these developments, but I am equally sure that SOX was a significant contributor; the evidence speaks for itself.

In the USA, company directors must make an assertion to shareholders that the proper controls over financial reporting are in place and that they are working effectively. That assertion must be based on reasonable evidence, which must be open to scrutiny and therefore has to exist in documented form. The documentation must cover all relevant controls and procedures needed to effect control, must identify the crucial elements of control, evidence that those controls have been tested adequately, and how any shortcomings were or are being addressed. Also, if shortcomings are identified, the documentary evidence must show that they are not significant and explain why that is so. An external auditor has to provide an opinion on the director's declaration and the auditing process, which is long and cumbersome, must itself be documented. All of this is subject to further auditing by the Public Company Accounting Oversight Board. None of this stopped Bernard Madoff, did it?

Of course, this is nothing new to any reader in the USA who is involved in a company, large or small. I am mentioning it here to highlight the burden that falls on

45 "The Truth About CFO Turnover", C.J. Prince, *Chief Executive*, September 2007.
46 See the preceding note.

companies and on directors personally and to lead into the rest of the book, which deals with ways to manage this burden more efficiently and with ways to turn that burden into an advantage. Readers in the USA may also wish to observe that elsewhere, in Australia for example, there has been a less rigid approach in dealing with the issues SOX was designed to address, more in line with a risk management philosophy. The banking sector is globalised. Cross border bank lending is growing as a proportion of all bank lending and the impact of the US subprime crisis on the world is an indicator of the extent of integration of lending across borders. All banks are caught, to a greater or lesser expect, within the same financial web and when the web is disturbed, the ensuing perturbation affects all. International banking groups account for a larger proportion of banking assets worldwide and international profits are of growing importance.

Globalization means that the barriers between different financial markets are coming down and capital can flow easily to locations where it (or its managers) receives the best reward. There is easier access to foreign markets and boundaries between different kinds of financial activity are blurring. Globalization also means that national boundaries offer no protection from international events, wherever they may be. In 2004, according to analyst estimates, cross-border payments represented approximately eight percent of the total volume of commercial payments.[47]

Analysts estimated that the volume of cross-border payments will increase at a compound annual rate of 10.2 percent globally between 2000 and 2010. Securitization is both supply and demand driven. On the supply side, institutions originating credits, typically banks and other mortgage lenders have sought to dispose of parts of their portfolios to free up capital resources for other lending. Legitimate and growing concern exists about the regulatory absence in this area as service firms, unlike banks, are not regulated or supervised by government agencies. On the demand side, insurance companies and pension funds have found themselves with growing inflows of funds needing placements in marketable assets. The increasing complexity of financial instruments is also supply and demand driven. Technological advances in the processing of information (for example, of the development of option pricing theory) have permitted the independent pricing of risk factors that were previously bundled together in the same instrument.

At the same time, the intensification of financial intermediation has given rise to an explosion in the demand for hedging (and position-taking) instruments. The new financial instruments have improved enormously the technology of risk-management, improving the climate for real and financial investment. However, these same instruments, if not properly understood, increase the potential for loss, either from mistakes or deliberate risk taking. Because of globalization, the impact of such losses

47 "The Inefficiencies of Cross-Border Payments: How Current Forces Are Shaping the Future", by Yoon S. Park, PHD & DBA, George Washington University, from http://www.corporate.visa.com/md/dl/documents/downloads/Cross_Border.pdf?topic=gov.

on the stability of the global financial system can be magnified greatly. The competitive climate has got hotter. The focus on shareholder value has induced management to pay more attention to the risk-adjusted rate of return on equity. The good news is that the financial industry is induced to use its capital more efficiently and financial services should become cheaper. The bad news is that the cushion against bad luck or bad judgment is thinner. Franchise values are much smaller, so that an erosion of capital more quickly leads to the threat of failure (and the temptation to take unwarranted risks to stay in business).

The extent of competition may be lessened in the next decade. There is increasing consolidation within the banking sector, which has occurred both nationally and internationally, a process that has been hastened by the financial crisis, as many large players have exited the market, one way or another, as have many smaller players, squeezed out by the high cost of funds. The differentiation among the various elements of the sector is diminishing and this is occurring at the same time as banking has become increasingly focused on derivatives. By the end of 2006 the British Bankers' Association Survey showed the size of the global credit derivatives market to be US$20 trillion, up 300% from 2004 and over 2000% since 2000. All these factors present difficult challenges to national and international regulators.

Why banking in the USA is a disaster area

In the United States of America, business has generally relied on guidance from the Security Exchange Commission (SEC) to ensure compliance. In the USA, banking is regulated at the federal and state level and, prima facie, regulation is fragmented relative to Germany or France, for example, where there is only one regulatory agency. However, within the Euro zone, national regulators have to co-exist with the European Central Bank, creating a situation not dissimilar to the USA. The degree of fragmentation in the USA is nevertheless greater, because unlike Japan and the United Kingdom, where the banking, securities and insurance industries are regulated by the same agency, the USA has separate securities, commodities, and insurance regulatory agencies.

These are separate again from the bank regulatory agencies at the federal and state level. The US regulatory environment for banking is also complex, because a great many policy drivers have created a great many layers of regulation, including safety and soundness related, but also privacy, disclosure, fraud prevention, anti-money laundering, anti-terrorism, anti-usury, and so on. Some of these policy elements, such as usury, are subject to further regulation in some municipalities. Depending on the type of bank and its location, the primary federal regulator could be any one of the following.

The Federal Deposit Insurance Corporation (FDIC) is a government corporation created by the *Glass-Steagall Act* of 1933, as a result of the pandemic of bank failures resulting from the Great Depression. The FDIC guarantees deposits held by commercial banks and provides deposit insurance, which guarantees checking and savings deposits in member banks up to $100,000 per depositor. In February, 2006, President George W. Bush signed the *Federal Deposit Insurance Reform Act* of 2005 (FDIRA) into law. The FDIRA made several significant adjustments to the FDIC arrangements, including merging the Bank Insurance Fund and the Savings Association Insurance Fund into a new fund, the Deposit Insurance Fund (DIF). The FDIC maintains the DIF by levying an insurance premium from relevant financial institutions, based on the balance of insured deposits and the overall risk the financial institution poses to the insurance fund.

The Federal Reserve System (the Fed) is the central banking system of the USA, created in 1913 by the *Federal Reserve Act*. The Fed comprises the Board of Governors of the Federal Reserve System, which is located in Washington, D.C.; and is appointed by the President of the USA; the Federal Open Market Committee (FOMC); twelve regional Federal Reserve Banks, which act as fiscal agents for the US Treasury; private US member banks, which subscribe to required amounts of non-transferable stock in their regional Federal Reserve Banks; and several advisory councils. Since late 2005, Ben Bernanke has been the Chairman of the Board of Governors of the Federal Reserve System.

The Board does not receive funding from Congress and the terms of the seven members of the Board span several presidential and congressional terms. Members of the Board have a great deal of independence, although a member may be removed by the President "for cause." The Board is required to make an annual report of operations to the Speaker of the U.S. House of Representatives. The Board of Governors is responsible for the formulation of monetary policy and supervises and regulates the operations of the Federal Reserve Banks and the US banking system in general.

The FOMC merits particular mention, because it is charged by Congress with the responsibility to oversee open market operations, that is the buying and selling of government securities, and is thereby the principal tool of US national monetary policy. The FOMC sets US interest rates, by specifying the short-term objective for those operations, known as the federal funds rate. The federal funds rate is the rate that commercial banks charge on overnight loans among themselves. This rate is actually determined by the market and is not explicitly mandated by the Fed, but the Fed strives to align the federal funds rate with the targeted rate by adding or subtracting from the money supply through open market operations. An open market operation means buying and selling government securities or other financial instruments. In 2007, the Fed had about $21 billion in assets from Overnight Repurchase agreements, which are the primary asset of choice for the Fed in dealing in the open market.

The Fed sets the discount rate, the interest rate that banks pay the Fed to borrow from it. This rate is generally set close to 100 points above the target federal funds rate, to encourage banks to seek alternative funding before using the discount rate option. The FOMC also directs operations undertaken by the Federal Reserve System in foreign exchange markets, in collaboration with the U.S. Treasury, which has responsibility for formulating US policies regarding the exchange value of the US dollar. The Office of the Comptroller of the Currency (OCC), in Washington, DC, was established by the *National Currency Act* of 1863 and supervises national banks and the federal branches and agencies of foreign banks in the USA. The OCC is a bureau of the United States Department of the Treasury and is headed by the Comptroller of the Currency. It has four district offices, in New York City, Chicago, Dallas and Denver and forty-eight field offices elsewhere in the United States. It also has a London office, to supervise the international activities of national banks.

The OCC ensures the safety and soundness of the national banking system; fosters competition, facilitating new products and services; strives to reduce the regulatory burden; and ensure fair and equal access to financial services to all Americans. The OCC monitors capital, asset quality, management, earnings, liquidity, and sensitivity to market risk, information technology, consumer compliance, and community reinvestment. Relying on intelligence on these elements, the OCC determines whether a bank is operating safely and soundly, meeting all regulatory requirements. The Office of Thrift Supervision (OTS) is an agency of the United States Department of the Treasury and is the primary regulator of federal savings associations (or federal thrifts), including federal savings banks and federal savings and loans. The OTS is also responsible for supervising savings and loan holding companies and some state-chartered institutions. It was established as a bureau of the Department of the Treasury in 1989 as part of the *Financial Institutions Reform, Recovery and Enforcement Act*. OTS supervises holding companies as well as thrift institutions, which means that it oversees firms such as General Electric, Morgan Stanley, and Merrill Lynch.

State-chartered banks are subject to the relevant state regulatory agency, in addition to federal regulation. For example, a California state bank that is not a member of the Federal Reserve System would be regulated by both the California Department of Financial Institutions and the FDIC. Federal banking statutes and regulations can preempt state laws that cover nationally chartered banking institutions and their subsidiaries. Credit Unions are supervised by the National Credit Union Administration. It insures savings in federal and most state-chartered credit unions through the National Credit Union Share Insurance Fund, which is backed by the United States government.

As a final observation on the American way of regulation, the fragmented approach in the USA and the size of its financial sector ensure that the US will continue to be a risk to the global economy. This is illustrated by the response to the 2007-08 subprime crisis. While the Fed was slashing interest rates and the US Congress was voting for billions of dollars of tax rebates, many states, including California, were forced to cut government spending by constitutions that mandate a balanced budget. So, while the Administration and the Fed were pushing hard on the accelerator, state governments were busily pumping the brakes. It does not have to be this way.

Making the system safer through regulation

One of the great myths I would like to bust is that the financial services industry is inherently different from other industries and cannot be understood, managed and regulated as other industries are. This is a lie propagated by those who have an interest in preserving a cloud of mystique around the industry, so that they can continue to profit by charging for access to their special expertise or by cheating and defrauding others—on a grand or petty scale, as the case may be. In this they are aided and abetted by lazy and incompetent regulators (I am giving them the benefit of the doubt here), who seek to explain away their shortcomings by pleading that the industry is too complex and complicated to enable effective regulation to be devised and applied. Allow me to explain why I think this, by examining a few recent events in the industry that have hurt millions around the world, starting with the sub-prime crisis itself.

For anyone who has been hiding under a rock over the last couple of years, this is what the subprime crisis was and what it did—and why. The subprime mortgage crisis was triggered by a dramatic rise in mortgage delinquencies and foreclosures in the USA. The crisis became apparent in 2007 and exposed pervasive weaknesses in financial industry regulation and the global financial system. Senator Chris Dodd, Chairman of the Banking, Housing, and Urban Affairs Committee of the Senate, in February 2007 convened a hearing on predatory lending practices in the mortgage market. The findings from this hearing highlighted that certain financial institutions had targeted minorities, immigrants, the elderly, and other vulnerable individuals, who perhaps thought they would not have been able to borrow in the prime market. Interestingly, in 2006 the *Wall Street Journal* reported that sixty-one percent of borrowers receiving subprime mortgages had credit scores high enough to qualify for prime loans.[48] Up to eighty percent of these loans were secured by adjustable rate mortgages and when US house prices began to decline in 2006-07, refinancing was made more difficult because adjustable-rate mortgages were reset at higher rates. Consequently, mortgage delinquencies soared and securities backed with subprime mortgages, which were often sold on as AAA securities, lost most of their value.

The sub-prime debt had been repackaged by banks and trading houses into attractive-looking investment vehicles, which were acquired by banks, traders, pension funds and hedge funds across the world. When those who had bought these securities found out that their investments had lost most of their value or could not be valued accurately, uncertainty set in, followed by panic, followed by extreme risk averse behavior by banks that previously had lapped up all the risk they could get.

48 Rick Brooks & Ruth Simon, "Subprime Debacle Traps Even Very Credit-Worthy: As Housing Boomed, Industry Pushed Loans To a Broader Market", *Wall Street Journal*, December 3, 2007, at A1.

The banks pulled up their drawbridges and retreated into their corporate keeps, declining to lend to each other and to business. This created a credit crunch, leading to rising cost of money and sometimes drying up the investment well altogether, as is the case in Argentina, for example.[49] Thus the contagion spread from the financial sector to the real economy. You know the result.

Strangely enough, another significant industry has been afflicted by a very similar problem in recent months, though in another part of the world, China. China is now a major exporter of milk products, which are used across the world to manufacture a wide range of foods for human and animal consumption. During 2008, it was revealed that a major Chinese producer had been stretching healthy, wholesome milk powder by adding an industrial waste product, melamine powder—yes, the same stuff from which furniture is made. The reason for doing this is simple: by mixing milk powder with melamine powder, more "milk" powder could be produced and sold, either as powder directly to consumers, to feed babies, for example, or to manufacturers, to include in the production of a wide range of foods sold in many countries, thus extending the damage from China to encompass much of the world. This meant much more profit for the manufacturer of the milk powder and it was made possible by the combination of a greedy producer and less than competent (and perhaps too accommodating) regulatory authorities. Does all this sound familiar to you folks out there in the financial sector? It does to me.

Those organizations that amalgamated and then cut up debt to sell to the world did exactly the same thing as the Chinese manufacturer of milk powder. They took healthy debt—mortgage debt that was likely to be repaid—mixed it up with toxic debt—mortgage debt not likely to be repaid—and then sold the debt on as prime, safe debt, creating untold damage not only in the USA, but to the whole world, in this case. This was done to realize greater profits than was possible by selling the healthy debt on its own and was made possible by incompetent (and perhaps unduly accommodating) regulators. The differences between the subprime crisis and the powdered milk swindle are three. First, what the vendors of the milk powder did was illegal, what the vendors of subprime debt did was legal—strange, is it not? Second, the damage caused by the latter was much greater in scope and depth. For those who would say the toxic milk powder killed or maimed people and that the toxic debt did not, I say, you are wrong. I am prepared to bet that the toxic debt, directly or indirectly, caused death, illness and mental anguish, just as the toxic milk powder did. Third, the subprime problem spread as a contagion across economies and continents, whereas the damage from the contaminated milk was limited to those who consumed it.

What does all this mean? This is what it means to me. First, turning good debt into

49 See http://goliath.ecnext.com/coms2/gi_0199-7334273/Americas-Argentina-Experts-Call-For.html, retrieved on 8 April 2009.

toxic debt should be illegal, just as it is illegal to corrupt milk powder with melamine. Alternatively, if such practices are to be allowed, then the resulting product should be labeled appropriately, so that a prospective buyer can make an informed purchasing decision. Second, if you are buying a financial product—or if you are asked to sell it on behalf of someone else—be it debt or otherwise, test its provenance and if you can't be sure about its state of health, don't touch it. If this were done, it would not be necessary to make the product illegal, anymore than it is necessary to make the sale of old, stinking fish illegal in food stores. I will come back later to the food safety analogy, to propose a new regulatory approach for financial products, but now let us consider another unhealthy offering that has somehow escaped US regulators. Yes, let us speak of Mr Bernard Madoff and his multi-billion dollar Ponzi scheme.

I observed just above that it is not necessary to let people know that fish is too old to be sold as new—covering up the stink and the look of old fish is a bit difficult. However, with other food products, such as minced meat, for example, it is much less difficult. By adding certain chemicals to old minced meat, it can be made to look fresh and new and healthy and appetizing.[50] This practice, like the practice of mixing melamine into milk powder is illegal in any country that has a viable food safety regime, in the same way that Ponzi and other pyramid schemes are proscribed in any developed economy. So, how is it that Bernard Madoff got away with his scheme for so long and with so many? Well, Mr. Madoff in this case was like the X added to minced meat—he made a stinking, unviable unprofitable mess look and smell like a wonderful, safe way to make good profits. After all, how could a Wall Street genius be other than a safe purveyor of wonderful financial merchandise? How could one of us—well, one of them, really, because I am not one of those us, I assure you—cheat us? As it turns out, he did and he did so for years and years, chewing through many billion dollars entrusted to him without creating a single dollar of profit—just lots of expenditures.[51]

What does this mean? What Mr. Madoff did was illegal and the problem was not one that the law can fix. The problem was caused by poor supervision by the regulators and by the gullibility of those who bought into the scheme—P.T. Barnum was right, there is one born every minute. Though in Wall Street, it seems, there must be one born every second, to explain the amounts of money Madoff managed to purloin! My advice is this, for the regulators first and then for the rest of us. The problem with a Ponzi scheme is not where the money is coming from; rather, it is to do with where the money is going. If I were the regulator, I would watch where the money is going. This could be done officially, by asking the fund to account for expenditures and for placements of funds on a regular basis, and unofficially, by tracking large

50 For examples of what food manufacturers can get up to, see page 212 and following of *Violence, inequality, and human freedom*, by P Iadicola and AD Shupe.

51 This makes the Albanian pyramid scheme I discussed in *Compliance and Regulation* look like chicken feed.

transactions to the banking system.[52] Now I expect that some would say, is that not unnecessarily intrusive? Is it unnecessarily intrusive for inspectors to visit regularly places where food is manufactured, to ensure that all is done as it should be? I think not. Why should it be different when money is involved, rather than food, especially when the sums of money in question are large enough to put the financial system itself at risk, as well as placing individual investors at risk.

Information and communication technologies nowadays permit the flows of money to be tracked invisibly, with no visible intrusions—the data can simply be harvested, regularly or ad hoc directly from the network of the company or companies concerned, with no delay or interruption to business in general or in any particular transaction. In the interests of public safety, this should be done, just as it is done in the case of companies that provide other fundamental services, such as food, water, power (think of the nuclear energy generators, for example) and so on. I will return to this point later, but for now let us what an alternative model of regulation could look like and why it would work much better than what we have. I will begin this argument here and conclude it in chapter 6.

A desired future position: a new regulatory paradigm

The argument straightforward and is based on the premises I set out earlier. Regulation is unavoidable and a globalized web of regulation is desirable, because the success or failure of the world's economy, ultimately, is dependent on the success or failure of its weakest link, its weakest component. While it is possible for countries or businesses to reduce the impact of any systemic crisis, no state, no economy can focus only on its own regulatory arrangements and it is necessary that the stronger help the weak, to ensure that the weak do not bring down the strong. Lastly, because regulating financial regulation is not really different from regulating energy, food or public health, we should learn from the experience in other industries, to help us craft a new global consensus on regulation that is in tune with the times and is most likely to work.

We have seen that making rules and focusing on catching the rule-breakers does not work, anymore than it does in any other sector of the economy, including law enforcement. We need something different. We need to focus on prevention and on making the system stronger, to vaccinate it against both stupidity and cupidity. We

52 Media reports today 17 January 2009 (for example, Associated Press at http://www.google.com/hostednews/ap/article/ALeqM5hp_FtaxDqD00vJHWQ6AOZfM6TYHAD95OCLH80), suggest that investigators have found no record of any share placement by Bernard Madoff's organization during its entire existence. If that is so, then the incompetence of the regulators and the ineffectiveness of the regulatory regime in the USA are indeed proven. This finding also establishes that what I am suggesting here is both desirable and feasible.

need to boost compliance, rather than on reducing non-compliance. We need to reward good practice, while we also strive to eliminate systemic flaws. We need to avoid the traditional divide between laissez-faire and strangulation by red tape. How do we do this? We do it by re-shaping the fundamentals of why and how we regulate; tinkering will not suffice, just as more of the same will see us continue to suffer.

We should focus on developing a standards based approach, at both the national and global levels, rather than a traditional regulatory framework. This is so that we can reach the right balance between the needs of the state, of the commons, and of individuals and individual enterprises. Also, this will help us to create a more flexible, responsive system, which means a more resilient system. My proposal is that at the national level regulation should be primarily, but not exclusively built on standards, because there are elements of the present arrangements that work and because change is best when it is gradual. The focus of national regulation should be on each element of the industry, including regulators, but most attention should be paid to those products that are considered to be high risk, either because of their inherent characteristics or because they offer opportunities for fraud and malfeasance or for mere incompetence sufficient to generate significant harm. Note the stress on products, rather than merely on the purveyors of those products.

However, at the international level I am suggesting that the focus should be primarily on regulators. Safeguarding the industry at the enterprise of product level, with some exceptions, as we will see, is best left to national regulators, operating within an international web of standards. However, we need someone to watch those watchers and that is best handled at the supra-national level. Organizations such as the International Standards Organization (ISO), with all its flaws, show that it is possible for industry, government and the community to come together to produce operating rules that enable everyone to get on with their lives and their businesses. ISO is a non-governmental organization that brings together more than 160 national standards organizations. ISO governs a global process that produces international standards for products, services, processes, materials and systems, and for managerial and organizational practice. As its website indicates, the process that produces standards is not rooted in politics and is not tied to the interests of one group or another. The standards are a reflection of global best practice. As the organization itself puts it, "ISO standards avoid having to reinvent the wheel. They distil the latest in expert knowledge and make it available to all. In this way, they propagate new advances and transfer technology, making them an invaluable source of knowledge."[53] The standards are implemented through voluntary compliance processes, supported by a user-pays system.

The downside of the ISO process is that it can be slow and cumbersome and that, while big P politics is not a factor, intra and inter-industry politics are a

53 See http://www.iso.org/iso/isoinbrief_2006-en.pdf, retrieved on 12 May 2009.

factor that influences the development and implementation of standards. These are characteristics that, at times, have both frustrated and infuriated me. However, while the ISO process is by no means perfection exemplified, it provides us with an excellent starting point to help us re-design financial regulation. One of its better qualities is that it prevents any particular individual from having too much power and from being in a position of power for too long. Power is very diffuse in the world of ISO and even behemoths like Microsoft find it difficult to get their way, sometimes.[54]

Within ISO, the balance between the regulators and the regulated is evenly poised, because different people within the process are at times one and at times the other. This is a good thing, because it keeps the system honest. We have also seen that ISO relies on expertise and on a broad range of inputs including users in the process, assuring us that the standards it produces are the product of competence and not connivance. My assumption is that if we succeed in making the regulators both competent and honest, the rest should be relatively easier to handle—and the level of trust in the global market would grow markedly. Also, this way we avoid criticism from the right and from the left, depriving the former of an opportunity to claim that we have taken another step towards a world government and the latter of an opportunity to bemoan first world imperialism. In chapter 6, I will spell out how I think this would work.

Suggested reading

In addition to the references sprinkled through this chapter, I recommend you read *Creating Public Value*, by Mark H Moore. I recommend it because Moore succeeds admirably in explaining how and why public servants and politicians do what they do and why. In particular, I recommend the discussion of the ethical and psychological leadership, in the concluding pages of the book. This quote sums up those challenges well, "Because public executives work for all of us, because we all have different ideas about what would be valuable for them to do, and because we all feel entitled to express those views, an enormous amount of pressure accumulates within their offices. Precisely, because they channel public aspirations, they become lightning rods for social conflict."[55] It is no wonder that the business of regulation is so difficult.

54 For example, see the Wikipedia article on "Office Open XML", at http://en.wikipedia.org/wiki/Office_Open_XML. You will see that Microsoft got its way, eventually, and had its standard approved by the ISO, but it had to make compromises on the way, accepting that it could not secure its position otherwise. I was involved in settling Australia's position on this issue.

55 At pages 305-6.

CHAPTER 3

Why it will not be a good time for technophobes

"The London Stock Exchange suffered its worst breakdown in eight years Monday as a computer problem prevented traders from participating in a worldwide market rally after the American government's takeover of Fannie Mae and Freddie Mac."—The New York Times, September 8, 2008

In this chapter we will consider the impact of technologies, both hard (for example, information and communication technologies) and soft (for example, teleworking). Why are these things important to the financial services industry? A few illustrations will answer this question. First, these days, if one wants to withdraw money from one's bank account, one must generally use a plastic card and a money dispensing machine. The machine will work only if the card is inserted the right way, if the card is valid, if specified sequences of keys are pressed correctly, and if, at the back end of the machine, the right connections are made with the computer that tracks accounts and transactions. Nowadays, it is hard even to imaging how the financial industry, and especially banking, could function without the aid of information and communication technologies (ICT), and technology offers significant opportunities to cut costs and to develop new products and services and new markets. Second, have you seen what happens to the stock market if the computers fail? Third, the proportion of trades on global markets, be they for stocks or for stock (e.g. cattle), that is entirely conducted by electronic means rises every year. Fourth, where would you be without your BlackBerry? Fifth and last, do you have in your home or are acquainted with any teenagers? Enough said, I think.

Now, let us consider what ICT might do for us, to us (and even without us) within a decade or so. Having done that, I will draw out implications specific to the financial services industry and I will offer recommendations for enterprises within that industry—many of which will have more general application. I will also suggest options for further reading.

Humans have always been technological animals, developing and using tools as an extension of their ample brain power and to make up for relatively puny physical bodies. Very few other animals use tools at all and none as well and as extensively as we do. For me, it is impossible to analyze and understand any social or economic concept without understanding the technological foundations on which it rests or in which it is embedded. For example, banking as we know it depends on both hard and soft technologies. By hard technology I mean something physical, like an automatic teller machine or pen and paper. By soft technology I mean the software that drives the hard technologies, whether that software is in a binary form, such as computer code, or in the form of rules, customs and regulations. However, in this chapter we will focus on those technologies that depend on computing power; the rules and regulations are dealt with elsewhere, though here we will discuss the impact of computer power on rules and regulations.

We have a lot of ground to cover, extending from the basic computing that supports corporate and banking activities, for example, to the new media, virtual reality and social networking. We will also discuss the socially disruptive impact of these and other technologies, such as the death of death, the end of privacy—as we have known it—new ways of working and living in cities, new ways to create and measure value, and new models of banking and financing. To cap off the discussion, I will propose a new model of government that may—I stress may—be able to cope with all this change. How is this relevant? The present model of government is straining to keep up with social, technological and cultural change and may not last much longer. Without effective governance of the state, as we have seen, it becomes very difficult to make a buck. As I explained in *Compliance and Regulation*, industries and enterprises should get involved in the process of re-making government and re-structuring regulation, because by being involved you can influence the competitive environment of the future and possibly gain a significant competitive advantage. Having a say in writing the software on which societies and economies run—laws and regulations—can help your business to do business. Abstaining from the process makes you a powerless spectator and you may not like what you end up seeing, though your competitors may!

Information and communication technology trends

We have seen why technology matters. Here we will explore significant trends that emerge from or are greatly influenced by technology, trends that are re-shaping the world, such as the emergence of new communications media, virtual reality, social networking and the (possible) death of privacy. I operate with the assumption that our economic and social well-being depends on striking the right balance between privacy, the control by the individual of information that belongs to that individual, and convenience, the opportunity to transact value with minimum delay and cost. The drive to protect private information is a truism of modern society, though it has not always been so, as we will see later. Because it is a truism, the requirement for privacy is generally unquestioned and unchallenged, though, in practice, it is often abridged or limited. The importance of convenience, however, is poorly understood. My reading of social trends leads me to believe that convenience is fundamental to the modern economy. Let us see why, by reference a so-called law, proposed by Robert Metcalfe.

Metcalfe argued that that the value of a telecommunications network is proportional to the square of the number of users of the system (n^2). This thesis has been generalized to explain the network effects of communication technologies and networks such as the internet, social networking, and the World Wide Web (WWW). An example of the law at work is the telephone. One telephone on its own is not worth anything; in fact, it is a liability, because making that useless object has used up resources that could have been used to do something else. However, two telephones connected to each other are useful and, as we see nowadays, billions of telephones connected to each other are very useful indeed. Starting with Metcalfe's law, I have developed a proposition that may help us to understand how economic value, how profits will be generated in the twenty-first century economy.

I do not rely on the proposition that the value of a network is proportional to the square of the number of users of the system. Rather, in a manner analogous to the theory of money, I say that the value of a network is equivalent to the volume of traffic on that network multiplied by the velocity of that traffic (plus something else, as we will see in a minute). To explain this by way of analogy, the value of a road network is not proportional to the number of access and exit points from the network. Rather, it is the result of an equation that associates the volume of traffic on the network, plus the average speed of vehicles on the network, and the value of what those vehicles are moving using that network. This last element needs to be added to our general equation concerning the value of networks: the value of a network is equivalent to the volume of traffic, multiplied by the average velocity on the network and then multiplied by the value of the information carried on the network. The first two factors are easy to compute, the last is not. It is not easy to compute because it is not possible to know each and every occasion of use and to measure the value generated by all such occasions. We need to find a substitute indicator of value to make the equation usable. We can do that.

The value of the information is not intrinsic to the information; it is a function of the usability and usefulness of the information to the recipient, it is a function of the value of the knowledge acquired or created by using the information, as we have seen earlier. Another analogy may assist here. Water from a tap is not worth much if the user is not sure that the water is potable. That is because the lack of certainty requires that the user assume that it is not, requiring the user to use it for less valuable purposes or to incur the expense of treating the water to be sure that it is potable. The same problem does not arise if the user knows that the water is potable, but how can the user know that? Well, s/he could do her own tests, of course, or s/he could rely on the assurance provided by the utility company that the water is potable. In a society where people trust their utility companies, the latter assumption can be made safely and readily. In societies where people do not trust their utility companies, that assumption is risky. On this basis it can be reasonably argued that a trusted network will produce a higher level of usability and usefulness than a network that is not trusted, meaning that the level of trust associated with a network can be used as a surrogate for use value.

If there is trust in a network, velocity of transactions on that network will also rise, thus increasing again the value of the network. To explain this, let us go back to the road analogy. If I trust the competence of other drivers, of the road designers and builders and the car manufacturers, it is likely that I will able and willing to drive faster than if I do not. What is true on a road, is also true of any other network. If I trust the various components that make up the network, the other users of the network and the operators of the network, I will be prepared to have fewer checks and balances operating in and on the network. In turn, this will free up the movement of data on the network, lifting the speed of traffic on the network. If I do not trust the network, the cost of securing my transaction will go higher. There is an inverse relationship between trust and security. We have already seen that modern society and modern, post-industrial economies, rely on a complex web of legislation and regulation that has evolved over centuries to match the expectations and needs of individuals, businesses and communities. Our daily lives are embedded in rules, determining or at least influencing what we eat and drink, how we move people and goods, how we relate to each other, how we do business, and even regulate life and death. While few of us are involved in the detail of how these rules are made and enforced, very few would be unaware of their existence and none would be free of their impact.

What even fewer people understand is that these rules, the complex and ornate edifice of modern jurisprudence, are themselves embedded, supported and enabled by a shadowy, intangible network of unwritten rules, which have also evolved, over millennia, and that often transcend national and cultural boundaries. These rules are so deep within our psyches and so fundamental to social and economic intercourse that they have become both invisible and unquestioned. What are these rules? First, we tend to expect those whom we know, with whom we have a relationship, to treat us fairly in any transaction and we have an inbuilt tendency to reciprocate. Second, we tend not to trust outsiders, people who are not of our "tribe", which nowadays might mean people from other cities, other countries or even people from another segment of our own company.

Anyone who has worked in a large manufacturing organization will know that engineers do not trust marketing people and vice-versa, just as those who work in branch offices do not trust head office staff, and bureaucrats in the capital city will always dismiss their provincial colleagues as having parochial and narrow views, and so on. As discussed elsewhere in this book, consistency and predictability of behavior can engender trust. If I know you and have always seen you react in a particular way when placed in a given setting, I will rely on you to behave in that particular way when the time comes. So, if I have lent you books on many occasions and had them returned to me on every occasion, I will tend to trust you and lend you another book or maybe even lend you money, if asked. If I do not know you, I have no evidence on which to base my assessment of your level of trustworthiness and, because humans are built that way, I will then tend to take a risk averse approach. Of course, a spotty record as a borrower of books may produce the same result, leading me again to limit the risk to me of any transaction with you.

In general, we are all capable of making reasonably accurate predictions of how others will behave in specific circumstances, adjusting our own behavior to accommodate these expectations. Predictability, reliability and visibility enable us to exercise free will, to go about our business in relative safety. This enables us to trust each other, at least to trust each other enough that the formal, written rules can work. For example, if you did not trust other drivers, you probably would not rely on them stopping at an intersection merely because a colored light on a pole says so. If other drivers did not trust you to stay on your side of the road, merely because a traffic sign says so, our highways would become unusable or very, very dangerous. Believe me, I have been to India and I have seen that this is so! Without trust, there is no law, other than the law of might, of force.

Without trust, society will not work effectively and efficiently. In the old Soviet Empire, the fundamental lack of trust between individuals and the state and between and among individuals crippled both the economy and civil society. The lack of trust among banks resulting from the subprime crisis in the United States inflicted severe damage on the US economy, much more damage than was warranted by the amount of wealth destroyed by that crisis. The lack of trust that permeated the world economy in the late 1920s and in the 1930s gave us the Great Depression, which resulted from fear of the unknown and not from any dramatic change in the underpinnings of the world economy. It seems to me that the importance of trust is growing in our post-industrial, information and knowledge-driven world. Why is this so?

The new commercial reality

I start from the assumption, backed by research and personal experience, that openness and (perceived) fairness are the ingredients that create trust, while secrecy and perceived unfairness tend to destroy trust. In organizations with low trust, communication will be poor, initiative, creativity and morale will be low, and management will tend to resort to command and control methods, which tend to generate lower levels of productivity and are deeply unpopular with Generation Y workers in particular, and knowledge workers in general. Why is this so important now? It is important because, as we have seen earlier, increasingly, economic as well as social value is generated through the creation and manipulation of content. This is not new, have you noticed that the market for stock derivatives now dwarfs the real economy, as well as the stock market itself? That is what I am talking about. To make this work well—with communities and individuals able to gain access to the content they want, at a price they are prepared to pay— we need business people and businesses that drive technology, not the reverse. The means of delivery should not be a concern for the user.

We need service providers selling packages of services tailored for each market, with options tailored for individual preferences within those markets. The same range of services may be delivered by broadband Internet in one location, by digital television in another, through a mobile device in some locations, and by a combination of technologies in yet another. We need regulations governing gambling, adult content and spectrum management, but the rest could be left to the market and to general legislation protecting privacy, intellectual capital and so on. The incipient regulation by stealth of the online entertainment in the USA may well be rued by those who want to grow the market, rather than short-term shareholder profits.[1]

A diverse mix of communications technologies is the key to universal access. It may well be the case, for example, that cable services dominate in large cities where a large proportion of the populace is wired and technology savvy. Meanwhile, retirees in Florida may prefer high definition entertainment programming based on digital broadcasting infrastructure. Sports fans could keep up with their chosen sports by watching multicast subscription television, by cable, satellite or whatever means is best in each area. It may not be enough that many of the above services are currently available via the Internet. For example, Australia has one of the highest internet penetration rates in the world, but Australian Internet take-up rates have slowed and may plateau at around fifty percent, leaving a sizeable proportion of the population without access

1 See http://saveinternetradio.org/

to networked technologies. Service delivery via the ubiquitous cell phone would not be a panacea, but would increase penetration significantly. The objective should be to ensure that people can gain access to products and services through a selection of means appropriate to each community and the individual selects the means of delivery, as well as content. Commercial interests could value add to free government services, providing packages tailored to consumers or the reverse could apply, with commercial interests providing integrated information and service offerings that straddle the private and public sectors. In Australia there is a good example of this, a business portal run by government that also syndicates content to private sector organizations. So, if you are a customer of bank x, you can get all the information and services you need through that bank's website, without having to refer to the government's own website, though many of the services you then receive will be provided by and through government infrastructure, invisibly to you.[2]

To provide another example, a small business may combine e-commerce capability with entertainment for the family and the capacity for narrowcast advertising in the local area. A local government authority may use its service delivery platform to provide services to ratepayers and to service small businesses in the area, in association with a commercial provider that provides access to the "outside world". To sum up, while the challenges before us are great, the possibilities are endless, flowing from an orderly transition from the regulated, technology-focused world of today to a world where the focus is on consumers and on content. The future should belong to the innovators, not the regulators.

The death of death

A combination of ICT and other technologies, such as nanotechnology and genetic manipulation, may enable us to extend human life well beyond its present limits, perhaps to 150 years and even beyond. Moreover, most of this expanded lifespan may be accompanied by a relatively good state of health and mobility. This sounds good, doesn't it? However, leaving aside the social and ethical dimensions of such a development, from a business perspective, especially for the financial sector, I can see that things could get tricky. We have already seen the development of reverse mortgages, which enable older people to draw on equity in their own homes, with the debt to be repaid upon death. In Japan, because of the high cost of real estate, they already have multi-generational mortgages, which shift liability from one generation to the next. Effectively doubling the average lifespan would create the need for entirely new financial products and services, would it not? Let us explore this by way of a hypothetical example.

John and Mary were born in the last decade of the second millennium, in the year 1995. Like most people of their generation, John and Mary stayed at home as

2 See business.gov.au and westpac.com.au, and also australia.gov.au.

long as possible, funded by their parents' resources, and even when they married and left home, to set up a place of their own, they did not see the need to accumulate savings for their old age, which would have eaten up their capacity to travel, to buy and enjoy lots of expensive new technologies, and to fool around in the stock market. Both became professionals, with university degrees, and eventually with two children, while still living in rented accommodation. The Great Recession of 2009 shook them up a bit, but did not really change their approach to saving, though they decided to be more structured in the management of their investments. The only relationship John and Mary had with a bank was to obtain credit cards and the odd personal or car loan and they always shopped around for the best deal they could find at the time of their need. When their children had to go to college, they sold some of their stock holdings and used the proceeds to pay tuition fees and accommodation costs, while still living in rented accommodation.

By now we are in the 2030s and medical science has made tremendous strides, partly because of the additional funding provided by government to support research that would cut the cost of health care and of ageing. The best way to cut these costs was to keep people healthy and mobile, unsurprisingly. John and Mary made best use of all innovations that would help them to say fit, healthy and mobile as they got older. As yet, no relationship with a financial institution was required, like their general approach to life, John and Mary's dealings with the financial world were entirely ad hoc, including the provision of financial advice, because they liked to keep those guys on their toes and changed providers regularly. This process had been greatly facilitated by the banking and financial reforms that followed the Great Recession of 2009 and the green investment bubble and crash of the early 2020s.

Now we are in the 2070s and John and Mary, who have grand and great-grand children by now, but still live in rented accommodation, are still working in their professions and still accumulating capital through investment and, more recently, through buying "golden age bonds". These bonds were introduced by government in recognition of the extended lifespan of citizens and were used to fund new health and other infrastructure. Because of the long-term nature of these bonds, the return on investment was good for John and Mary and they knew that they could accumulate quite a large sum to support them in their second century, by setting aside a relatively small amount each year. They would eventually use the capital to pay for one of the new robotized and automated homes specifically designed for the very old and for limb and organ replacements. They would need quite a bit of money to pay for that, but they had forty or fifty years to build up the required capital. Note: still no relationship with a financial institution.

I could go on, but this is only an illustration and may be a fanciful one at that. No need to belabor the point. The scenario I have sketched here might turn out to be totally wrong, but it serves to show that if the human lifespan were to increase significantly and if people were able to remain active and in the workforce for much longer, what the Baby Boomers have had to achieve in three or four decades, saving for their old age, while supporting their children (and perhaps their aged parents), could perhaps be done in twice that time in future generations. If at present day values, a Baby Boomer has thirty years of earnings at an average of $50,000 per year, that amount is automatically doubled if one has sixty years of earnings, without necessarily doubling outgoings. That is bound to change how people spend, invest, think about money and how much capital they can generate over a lifetime. As I said, this scenario is entirely speculative, but my recommendation is that you get some of your best and brightest (and youngest) people to start thinking about what might happen, if we all start living to an age that challenges Methuselah! If you don't, you can be sure that some of your competitors will.

Quantum computing and beyond

I will not even try to explain what how quantum computing works, beyond pointing you to the excellent article on the subject on Wikipedia. However, trust me when I say that quantum computing could change everything...or change nothing at all, in the end. First, if you work or deal with a bank you will know that while doing business online is convenient, it is also risky, because any password can be cracked if one has access to sufficient computing power. Applications made possible by quantum computing could change that, making online transactions totally secure. This is because with quantum computers we have the capacity to make available to us the electronic equivalent of the German Enigma machine, but with an infinite potential to vary combinations and to vary those combinations on an infinity of occasions. I use the word infinite in the true sense of the word, meaning with no end. This should make electronic transactions impregnable, one would think. Well, maybe, maybe not.

First, quantum computing will do nothing to stop internal fraud, which is still the greatest risk to any financial institution. Also, while the good guys have quantum computers and the bad guys don't, the good guys will stay ahead, but how long is that going to last. Think back to the late 1940s. Only the West had atomic weapons and only the west had thermonuclear (or H) bombs. Also, only the West had the capacity to deliver those weapons at long range, thanks to the contribution made by former Nazi scientists offered a safe haven in the USA and in the UK. The West was safe forever, it seemed, with an unbeatable advantage. Within ten years, the then USSR and then China has already matched the West in nuclear capability and the USSR also in delivery capability. Then we had the balance of terror and everyone was in fear of a global holocaust, needlessly it seems, in hindsight. By now, it seems everyone who wants to shoot a nuclear bomb at long range can buy or steal what is needed to do it and we live in fear again. Fear of terrorists or of rogue governments or of our own over-bellicose presidents and prime ministers. Quantum computing, when it comes, will change many things and your business, especially in the financial sector, will be affected, but do not look upon it as the end of the war between the good guys and the bad guys. It will be merely another and very expensive in the endless tussle between those who have the money and those who want to steal it.

The cloud

The cloud is a term used to describe a mode of computing that enables you to store and manipulate data and to use applications that reside somewhere else, generally outside your own organization. Nothing new here. The World Wide Web is a cloud and we had a cloud back in the 1970s, if you can remember that far back, when we had green screens on our desks and all the action was on a mainframe somewhere, many clicks and miles away. The advent of the personal computer and of network computing changed all that, but not necessarily for the better. I can guarantee that no personal computer in your organization is used beyond ten percent of its hardware potential and that most of the software for which you pay large license fees every year is never used. Also, for security and other reasons, the storage capacity on personal computers is not used, except by those of your employees capable of circumventing company rules and store games or pictures on their hard drive. If you have a thousand personal computers in your organization, your are paying for several terabytes of storage that you are not using, while you are paying for network storage as well. Also, because of the nature of the software market in office applications, your company will almost certainly be obliged de facto to use one brand of software only, brought to you at great cost by uncle Bill and his successors. I know from experience within government that millions of dollars could be saved if there were another way, other than this way. Well, maybe now there is, in the form of the "cloud".

The new version of the cloud is friendlier and more useful than the green screen version. Your staff can sit in front of what looks, sounds, feels and smells like a personal computer, though it will cost you much less to buy and support the type of decisions required for cloud computing. Security is easier to enforce on such devices and there will not be terabytes of wasted storage capacity sitting on people's desks. With the advent of IP telephony, you can make this device perform like a telephone also, which saves you more money and is also good for the environment. The applications people use and the data they need are stored in a virtualized server, which is a mainframe computer in a new form. You will be able to get rid of the requirement to buy or to have access to hundreds of network servers, which are expensive to maintain and are electricity hogs, and also generate a lot of heat, which is not good for either your bottom line or the environment.

Just make sure that your service provider has good back up, business continuity and disaster recovery arrangements in place. If data security is very important to you, as it is in government or in a bank, you may run a cloud of your own inside your own firewall, with the option of insourcing expertise and equipment to do this. Again, the article on Wikipedia on virtualization is worth reading and saves me a little space in this book. When software is changed or upgraded, this is done at a central point, and done only once. But best of all, the introduction of cloud computing services has finally given us the potential to have real competition in the software market. Within two to four years, you should have a choice among several models:

- the traditional personal computing model, with licensed proprietary software for the operating system and for office applications;
- a full cloud model, where staff operate dumb terminals and the data and software are hosted by an external service provider, where the software may be proprietary or open source or a mix;
- a hybrid model, where the software is provided and resides on hosted equipment, but you store the data on equipment you manage (either purchased or leased) and that resides within your own firewall, and again the software may be proprietary or open source or a mix;
- an internal cloud, where the applications and the data reside on your own network and again the software may be proprietary or open source or a mix;
- or your own version of any of the above, to accommodate specific needs, meaning that head office power users may continue to have personal computers, while front office and field staff are supported by cloud computing, for example.

Of course, you will have to make your own assessment of when and if cloud computing is for you. My recommendation is that you have done such an assessment, that is validated by an external party, to keep your IT people honest, and that you review that assessment annually, because in the ICT world things change very quickly.

Dealing with change in a techno world

The examples I have provided here should serve to illustrate my fundamental point. Now, more than ever, standing still in business means death. It may be a cliché, but you do need to run just to keep your place. To me that highlights the importance and usefulness of planning, of thinking strategically, considering:

- new ways of creating and measuring value,
- new ways of working (e.g. teleworking),
- new ways of relating,

- new business models—the digital economy or the new socialism (from each…to each),
- is anything secure?
- possible scenarios

to develop a strategy that suits your business. Every business is different and it is impossible in one book to cover even a representative range of circumstances. So, I have prepared material to get you started on the process of doing it for yourself. This is how I suggest you go about it, to make the best of what the future will bring. This is a task that is difficult enough when the rate and pace of change are low, and an almost impossible task when change is fast, furious and often unpredictable. I say almost impossible, because even in these uncertain times it is not beyond the capacity of the human mind to formulate effective strategies to manage the future. After all, as a species we have been refining our capacity to plan for over a million years now, differentiating ourselves from other species, which can only react to events and cannot anticipate them. To be human is to be a planner.

Planning is a way of managing the future. It is a tool used by individuals, by organizations and by the state. Planning is relevant to all human activities, from personal survival to organizational or national survival. The Chinese military leader Sun Tzu said over 2300 years ago that strategy is

> *... the great work of the organization. In situations of life or death, it is the Tao of survival or extinction. Its study cannot be neglected.*

A modern version of Sun Tzu's definition might be this:

> *A strategy is the pattern or plan that integrates an organization's major goals, policies, and action sequences into a cohesive whole.*

Chandler has provided a widely accepted definition of planning:

> *... the determination of the basic long-range goals and objectives of an enterprise and the adoption of courses of action and the allocation of resources necessary for carrying out these goals.*

I have translated this theoretical formulation into a practical framework, within which strategy has four forms:

1. Strategy is in the mind (of the leader)—the vision of the future.
2. Strategy is a collective plan of action—how the vision is to be realized.
3. Strategy is the deployment of that plan of action—what the organization does to realize the vision.
4. Strategy is the visible effect(s) of the deployment of that plan of action—what is actually achieved (or not).

Relying on the literature, it is possible to formulate a classification of failure that is linked to these forms:

1. Lack of sufficient congruence with corporate objectives—failure of direction.
2. Failure to inform appropriately the process of definition (and redefinition) of corporate objectives—failure of evaluation.
3. Failure to achieve specified goals—failure of execution or implementation.
4. Generation of unintended consequences that have a significant negative impact on the achievement of corporate objectives—failure of analysis.

Making plans and carrying them out is an everyday activity that appears to require little skill; we all do it when we decide what we want to do on the weekend. We set an objective—going to the beach, for example—and we proceed through a series of steps that have that objective in mind. We might even evaluate the outcome, on Monday, when we are back at work. That kind of planning and, perhaps, planning in general, is most often the product of intuition mixed with habit, rather than a formalized procedure. People have an innate ability to build scenarios and to guess or imagine what the future might be like. Neurobiology suggests that this capacity may "hard-wired" into the human brain, closely linked to our abilities to speak and construct language. There is nothing special or "scientific" about the act of planning. A scenario is a story about a possible future; it is not a prediction or even a forecast. Scenario planning uses stories about possible futures to frame and to support strategic planning. Scenarios help us to think about the future, to grasp complexity by focusing on the essential elements of a possible future, allowing us to test our assumptions concerning how various strategic measures might play out when impinged upon by alternative future environments.

To influence its target-audience, scenario analysis needs to involve the preparation of several coherent and plausible alternative plot lines, built around relevant issues, and containing at least some elements of surprise. This provides insights into the alternative future environments in which the implications of current decision-making might be played out. Each scenario is a description of what the future might be like, at a level of detail sufficient to provide insights. It tells one tenable future story, showing logical connections from the past, but embodying changes in patterns and sometimes outright discontinuities. It is commonly built around one key driver, but with interplay from other factors. A scenario is not a prediction, but rather a plausible future. The purpose is not to envision 'what will be', but to perform thought experiments, to tease out dependencies and contingencies, and to encourage readers to perform further thought experiments, based on various assumptions. Here is a scenario on how to go about making decisions on sourcing ICT.

A Guide to Sourcing ICT

Imagine that you are a director on a board, perhaps an independent, non-executive director. Or perhaps you actually are in one of these roles. Either way, this scenario is meant for you, the senior executive, but, for the sake of brevity, we will continue with the example of the director on a company board. It is Friday afternoon, you are looking forward to a golfing week-end and contemplating how to fix your wayward drive, when a large parcel of papers is delivered to you, for next Monday's board meeting. There is only one action item on the agenda: a proposal from the Chief Operating Officer to outsource the company's information technology operations, using a cloud computing model. A proposal opposed by the Chief Information Officer (CIO), who wants to keep those operations in house. You suspect that the CIO is protecting her own job and the jobs of her staff, but you are not sure and, anyway, you would probably do the same if you were in her shoes.

After suppressing a colorful expletive that naturally bubbled up to the surface of your mind, you know you are in trouble. You know nothing about IT or outsourcing or cloud computing. You joined the board only because the fee was good and you were interested in the business. No one ever told you that you would have to make decisions about IT, computers and stuff like that. Yet, you do know that as a director you are responsible for the good governance of the organization and you take your responsibilities seriously. You should not have been surprised. Increasingly boards are being asked to make decisions about outsourcing ICT services and applications—sometimes extending to whole business processes. This is a relatively new phenomenon, as such matters have traditionally been left to CIOs and assorted other technical experts, but it is a phenomenon that is not going away. Company boards, COOs, CEOs, CFOs, business unit managers and business proprietors will find in years to come that they are no longer be able to delegate this responsibility away. As time goes by, the focus on outsourcing is shifting to sourcing: where is the business going to get the services, products, materials and people it needs to deliver ROI to its customers? If you look at it this way, it becomes easier to see why CEOs and boards should concern themselves with such matters.

It's Governance, Stupid

Get the sourcing strategy right and your business will grow or at least hold its own, even in turbulent times. Get it wrong and you may do serious damage to the performance of your business performance—or even sink the ship. Ultimately, this is an issue of governance. The purpose of this scenario is to provide the non-expert director, CEO, CFO, executive manager or business owner with a short guide to the development of a sourcing strategy, focusing on ICT: seven steps to success. The guide is based on personal experience, on research and on a deep understanding of how important ICT is to business, regardless of its size and budget.

On the subject of size, in reading and using the guide, please adapt each step to suit the scale and complexity of your business, applying sound risk management principles. Don't over-engineer. On the other hand, don't skip any of the steps, as each is fundamental to the next and, indeed, to all the others. So, forget about golf for a while and read on.

Step 1. *Determine what kind of business you are.* This used to be described as "determining your core business". That terminology has proved less than helpful, stimulating a lot of academic and consultant hot air and burning holes in corporate wallets—without providing much useful guidance. I suggest a different question: what is it that consumes your resources? Is it moving goods from place to place for other businesses or selling groceries or providing architectural advice to builders, just to give some examples. Notice that you are not being asked: do you run a shop or are you in a professional business or do you run a transport company? For the answer to have meaning, there has to be reasonable specificity implied by the question.

If you are Nordstrom or Marks and Spencer, the answer should be something like, *we sell a broad range of merchandise to the public from multipurpose facilities*. If you are a bank, the answer might be something like, *we manage money on behalf of others and make a profit by buying and selling funds* Or it could be, *we manage risk on behalf of others*. You know your business best; come up with a phrase that uses simple language and that your aged parent would understand. The point is to ascertain what it is that you do that creates value. In retail, it is the activity of selling that creates value. Everything else is a cost centre. In banking, for money to return a profit it must be moving, and quickly, so everything that has to do with moving money (securely) is core business, the rest is peripheral. One would be unwise to outsource the activity that creates value, while one *may* find it useful to outsource anything that is a cost centre. Note that that a choice has to be made even about the latter, which is why the core/non-core debate proved to be sterile. Boards and management must make choices, informed choices. How such choices are made is covered in the next six steps, starting with the step after the next. To give you some notice of what may drive you to outsource or not, you need to ask yourself: what competencies do you rely on to create value for your customers? If the activity covered by a certain cost centre is included under this rubric, it would be risky to your business to outsource it. Notice that a judgment is again required: it may be risky, but, taking all relevant matters into account, it may still be preferable.

Step 2. *Determine your trajectory.* Having determined what you are, the question we ask next is, what do you want to be in the future? Where do you want to take your business? If you are a business concerned with selling groceries to the public from several large sites (otherwise known as supermarkets), do you want to continue as you are for the foreseeable future or do you want to change what you do, perhaps to become a seller of supermarket franchises? If you are a business concerned with lending money to home buyers, do you want to change perhaps to become a provider of commercial credit? This is the thinking process required by this step. The result of this thinking process will feed into steps 4 and 5. Note that a valid answer here may be that you want to keep your options open. This can be accommodated, though you will find that, as with everything in this life, there is a price to be paid for this kind of flexibility.

In summary, at this step there are four possible trajectories: static—you plan to stay as you are; evolutionary—you want to change, but nor radically, relying more or less on the same competencies; radical—you want to transform your business into something quite different, probably requiring a different constellation of competencies; open—for very valid reasons, not through indecision, you want to keep your options open. It is possible to craft a sourcing strategy to accommodate any of these trajectories, but first it is necessary to consider the circumstances in which the business is required to operate.

Step 3. *Understand your environment.* A business should be equipped to deal with its environment, present and projected, and good governance requires that a board or a CEO take steps to map and understand likely future circumstances. In this context, there are only four broad categories that matter and they echo the discussion under the previous heading: steady state—minor or no changes from the present environment; predictable—there is change and it may be significant change, but the nature and pace of the change can be determined with reasonable confidence; turbulent—the environment is likely to be choppy, difficult, even threatening; unstable—the environment is inherently unstable to the point that it may change radically (or not), perhaps with little or no warning.

Occasionally these characteristics may appear in a mixed, hard to define to form. In such a case, treat your future environment as if were unstable. This amounts to sound risk management and will enable (or force) you to keep your options open and to be on your guard. Now that you know what you are, what you want to be and what the world is likely to look like, you are ready to consider what business strategy you ought to be pursuing. You may already know this and be confident of your approach, but I would ask you then to do a quick review of that approach against your findings so far, before moving on to step 5.

Step 4. *Determine your business strategy.* This is what makes your business, your value proposition, unique. This is the reason (or reasons) why your customers choose you from the many options at their disposal. For example, McDonalds attracts adults for one of two reasons: because of its reputation for convenience or because of its reputation as a fun place for kids (or perhaps a blend of these). McDonalds does not attract customers (with few exceptions one suspects) because of the quality of its food. On the other hand, people will travel to a particular destination for no reason other than the reputation of for quality food and service of a certain restaurant. In this latter case, we are not dealing with convenience or fun for kids.

McDonalds and the Tour d'Argent or(…)—substitute your own locus of culinary heaven here—are not competitors. They do not occupy the same ecological niche—or business space—although they are both ostensibly in the "restaurant business". Having said that, it is sometimes possible for businesses that are not direct competitors to cause great damage to each other. For example, Tesco's and the local corner store are not in the same ecological niche. One goes to the former for range and price and to the latter for convenience and customer service. Nor are UBS and the local savings and loans, probably. It should be possible for both to carry on safely in their own business space. However, the mere presence of a giant supermarket in the neighborhood may take away sufficient business from the corner store to make it unviable. This is comparable to the impact humans have on other species. We are not competitors with pandas or with tigers for food. On the other hand, by using portions of the habitat used by these species as cultivated forests and leaving them only with small segments of native forest, we may be causing their extinction.

Coming back to the matter at hand, by now you have identified what your business does, whether you intend to stay in that line of business and what it is that makes your business unique. These are all assets that must be preserved—if not enhanced—by means of a sourcing strategy. Now comes the time to craft such a strategy. You may already have such a strategy, perhaps prompted by someone's call to outsource ICT, usually for the purpose of "cutting costs". If so, please review that strategy now, in the light of your conclusions from steps 1 through to 4, before moving on to step 6.

Step 5. *Craft a sourcing strategy.* The first thing to be said here is that every business should have one, because good governance demands that a CEO or a board secure the assets the business is likely to need in the foreseeable future. Your strategy should be sympathetic to your business: what you do, what you intend to do and how you create value for your customers. Limiting ourselves to ICT, to keep things simple, how important is ICT to what you do, what you intend to do and how you create value for your customers? If you run a small grocery store, not much, one could safely say. If you run a nationwide chain of supermarkets, it is vital to your survival. If you run a bank, however small, you cannot do without it. You cannot run a ***high volume***, logistics dependent, ***24x7*** business without ***solid, reliable*** ICT infrastructure. I have emphasized the key words by emboldening them.

In these circumstances, the ICT sourcing strategy must have key performance indicators (KPIs) that focus on these success criteria: efficient, scalable, reliable, redundant infrastructure—that is price sensitive. The strategy will probably support large investments by the business and/or its ICT supplier(s), because there will be a guarantee of reasonably predictable high volume traffic. Let us consider another example, a ***discrete manufacturing*** concern that creates value for customers by being ***first to market*** with ***innovative*** appliances for home use. Again, the key characteristics of a sound approach for the business are derived by analyzing the underlined words. The business relies on multiple suppliers to support its value chain and is likely to require ICT to manage a complex web of interactions with suppliers and perhaps among suppliers. The business will need access to ICT tools that support innovation, culturally and operationally. Quality, agility, responsiveness and reliability are paramount, price is less important, and the KPIs should reflect these attributes. These are only examples and each board, CEO, business unit manager or business proprietor will have to do this analysis ad hoc, focusing on the unique characteristics of the business, rather than on generalities. However, this is a field where it is possible to acquire quality advice and where there are many instructive case studies available for study and analysis.

Step 6. *What about culture?* This question is important and should arise when considering possible suppliers. In this context culture is defined by shared values, by similarity (or at least compatibility) in how the business and its supplier(s) see the world. It is not so important if one is dealing with commodities. So, cultural fit is of little or no importance in considering where to purchase PCs or fixed telephony or, generally speaking, any hardware or even packaged software (eg Microsoft Office or Lotus Notes). However, if you are purchasing packages of services or outsourcing whole business processes, for example, cultural fit with the supplier is essential—lack of it means that both parties (as well as your customers) will suffer. The concept of culture may seem vague, but it can be made concrete by considering this question: can the supplier meet its ROI targets by helping you meet yours? If the answer is positive, it is likely that there will be a cultural fit. If not, this will provide another, significant risk to be factored into the overall equation. On to the last step, doing it, rather than just talking about it.

Step 7. *Execution.* This is where many grand and not so grand strategies come to grief. It need not be so. There are very good models in the marketplace to guide you and program and project management expertise can be bought or grown (if you have the time). Choose a method that suits your business and the nature and scale of the sourcing strategy and be guided by a professional, dispassionate assessment of risks and opportunities ***and*** by the judgment of your management team—it is a bit late now to have second thoughts about them, is it not?

Wrapping up and moving on

These seven steps will help guide you to understand what is required to devise and execute a successful sourcing strategy, for ICT or for anything else for that matter. However, this guidance is no substitute for your own professional judgment and expertise. Blend these with the ingredients provided here and you will have exercised due diligence and good sense. No one can ask for more. Allow me to conclude by touching on four possible futures that will both be shaped by and will shape how you use ICT in your business. The scenarios depict possible trajectories that reflect important and potentially impactful environmental factors, combined with relevant strategic measures by government.

1. Bottling fog—regulating the online world, but leaving it alive, energetic and challenging. In this world, there will be maximum freedom to make choices to suit particular circumstances, but there may also be a high level of unpredictability and instability, as concomitant of freedom of choice.
2. WIKI government—where proprietary enterprises and proprietary government morph into network enterprises and network government. In this world, the emphasis will be on being connected and anyone or any organization that sits out on its own will be at risk of marginalization, although there may be significant prizes for those who succeed in carving their own way forward.
3. The corporate state, where the organs of the state become vestigial appendages to the corporations. In this world, the corporations will be the primary source of power, as the great Dutch and British mercantile companies of the seventeenth and eighteenth centuries were. Consumerism and faux choice will be the primary characteristics, since the profits will go to those who can keep selling the same stuff to the same people over and over again and keep them happy...bread and circuses worked for Imperial Rome, remember?
4. The grey option, the sclerotic cloud, where government regulates technology and its impact to such an extent that its value is both eroded and trivialized. This is a world where the state is the nanny and people cannot make choices that involve any risk to them, giving us a twenty-first capitalist version of twentieth century communist East Germany. Trabants for all!

Don't make too much of these scenarios. I have put them in to stimulate thought and discussion, to pose questions and not to give answers. Before you start thinking of answers to give or of more questions, I suggest you read at least chapters 4 and 5.

CHAPTER 4

Why the future is best seen through green colored lenses

Too late to save the world.—James Lovelock

Green is not simply a new form of generating electric power. It is a new form of generating national power—period.—David Rothkopf[1]

I don't know about you, but I get the feeling that Messrs Lovelock and Rothkopf feel very strongly about the issue of climate change and environmental politics, respectively. These are definitive, unambiguous statements, full of emotion, a mixture of sorrow, anger and determination, leaving little room for doubt or compromise. These few words capture the essence of this chapter, where we discuss the waves of change likely to flow from the growing belief that the Earth is experiencing global warming induced

1 As quoted by Thomas L. Friedman in *Hot, Flat and Crowded*, page 23.

by human activity. I am not convinced that it is too late to save the world; I am not even sure that the world needs saving, though we humans might need some help, but Lovelock is right if he means that the world as we know it is about to be transformed.

As for Rothkopf, I agree that green issues will be central to twenty-first century politics. By the middle of this century, governments and businesses that have not embraced the emerging green orthodoxy will suffer. The politics of development and growth and the rhetoric of development and growth are about to give way to new forms of politics and to new forms of rhetoric. We will touch on all these points in this chapter, to the level of detail we need to address our major concern here, which is the nature and character of the financial services industry. Because this is not a book about climate change or environmental politics, the depth of analysis of these issues will not be as deep as it could be, but I will point out to you books that cover these topics well.

> *Before we succumb to the oracles of doom, we should formulate a new scientific law: small fluctuations in scientific data produce disproportionate panic in the populace. Climate scares have become like health scares: there is a new one almost every week, and they get less persuasive as they multiply.*—Felipe Fernandez-Armesto

Having got the introduction out of the way, let us start our investigation of the issues in the right place. For our purposes, it is not necessary to conclude whether or not climate change is or is not occurring. All we need to do is to accept that governments around the world, the bulk of the scientific community, most commentators and the general public are all convinced that it is occurring and are shaping courses of action that reflect this belief. As in the stock market, perceptions can shape reality and, some would argue, humans seem to have a penchant for disasters, in life and in the movies. This is a point made well by Richard Overy, a historian who has studied the development across the centuries of end of the world stories. His book, published by Allen Lane, is titled *The Morbid Age*. His message is that we might do better as a species if we were to adopt a somewhat more positive attitude. Well said, but if most people believe that the planet is getting hotter and that deleterious consequences will follow, then societies, communities, businesses and individuals will shape their actions accordingly. Belief drives action—not the other way around. Despite what behaviorist psychologists have concluded from animal experiments, people cannot be conditioned to behave in certain ways in the same way as Pavlov's dog or a rat in a first year psychology experiment at university. Animals do not have belief systems; humans do. Outside the lab, unless the conditioning is constantly re-applied, people will revert to type, acting in accordance with their interpretation of the world, which, in turn, is the result of a mix of genetics, experience and learning, filtered by a complex mélange of emotions. You know what goes through your head when you are faced with a difficult moral or ethical choice or even when you have to choose which type of coffee to have at Starbucks!

Well, believe it or not, everyone is like that. Other people are just as complex and conflicted as you are, though some manage to hide it better than others. This is why if we believe the world is going to pot, we are going to act accordingly. For the sake of clarity, allow me to put my beliefs on the table. I am not entirely convinced that human induced global warming, to use the correct phraseology, is occurring, but I am convinced that we have over exploited our planet and that it is time we stop, because that way takes us to disaster and maybe even oblivion, as I will explain.

As with other chapters, my recommendations for action will focus on the financial services industry and I will suggest options for further reading. The basis for my recommendations is that we are entering a new era, with new rules and that those who want to succeed in this new era had better learn the new rules fast...or preferably participate in creating those new rules.

The climate change juggernaut

It is hard to open a newspaper or magazine or to watch television without being exposed to the raging debate concerning the future of our climate. Between that and the Great Recession, it is hard to find good news these days, isn't it? The quote that starts this chapter represents the pessimistic end of the spectrum. The newspaper article headed by the words "Too late to save the world " went on to say, "Climate change will wipe out most life on Earth by the end of this century and mankind is too late to avert catastrophe, a leading British climate scientist (James Lovelock) says."[2] It can't get much worse than the end of the Earth, which is what awaits us, according to Lovelock, albeit sans a returning Jesus Christ and with no guilt to be placed on anyone other than the human race. Lovelock is not alone in making statements such as these and his views should not be dismissed lightly; he is a serious scientist and has serious science behind him.

However, it is just possible that Lovelock may be wrong, as we will see later in this chapter, when we consider global warming and related issues. I empathize strongly with the quote from Felipe Fernandez-Armesto you can see opposite.[3] Don't worry, I am not going to unleash an avalanche of science or of pessimism, but I also would urge that if you are wearing rose colored glasses, you should now take them off. It is

2 *The Press*, Christchurch (New Zealand), Friday, February 27, 2009, page B1.

3 Taken from an excellent essay published in *The Independent on Sunday* on 26 April 2009, titled "It's been a long, cold, lonely winter but, here comes the Sun. (And yes, it's all right)".

possible that Lovelock may be wrong, but that does not mean that the damage we have done and are doing to the environment is not going to bite back. In countries like mine, Australia, it is arguable that elements of Lovelock's dire forecasts are already manifesting themselves, in the form of contemporaneous fire in the south and flood in the north of the country, just as the global warming Cassandras have predicted.[4]

This is the evidence on climate change, as I understand it

I am basing this part of the book on the orthodoxy of climate change, as represented in three significant and very large reports. First, a series of reports by the Intergovernmental Panel on Climate Change (IPCC), considered to be the most authoritative source of scientific analysis of climate change. The IPCC is an intergovernmental body established in 1988 by the World Meteorological Organization (WMO) and by the United Nations Environment Program (UNEP). According to its website, the IPCC "is a scientific body: the information it provides with its reports is based on scientific evidence and reflects existing viewpoints within the scientific community. The comprehensiveness of the scientific content is achieved through contributions from experts in all regions of the world and all relevant disciplines including, where appropriately documented, industry literature and traditional practices, and a two stage review process by experts and governments. Because of its intergovernmental nature, the IPCC is able to provide scientific technical and socio-economic information in a policy-relevant but policy neutral way to decision makers. When governments accept the IPCC reports and approve their Summary for Policymakers, they acknowledge the legitimacy of their scientific content."[5] I ask you to note two points in particular: the IPCC is a scientific body and it is "policy" neutral—I think they mean politically neutral, rather than policy neutral, because it is not possible, even for science, to be outside the realm of policy. After all, the fact that the IPCC itself exists is a statement of policy: the policy is that climate change matters and must be taken seriously.

In its *Climate Change 2007: Synthesis Report — Summary for Policymakers*, the IPCC presented an "assessment carried out by the three Working Groups of the Intergovernmental Panel on Climate Change (IPCC). It provides an integrated view of climate change as the final part of the IPCC's Fourth Assessment Report (AR4)". These are the (abridged) chief elements of that assessment:

1. Warming of the climate system is unequivocal, as is now evident from observations of increases in global average air and ocean temperatures, widespread melting of snow and ice and rising global average sea level.
2. Changes in atmospheric concentrations of greenhouse gases (GHGs) and aerosols, land cover and solar radiation alter the energy balance of the

4 Cassandra was a Trojan princess, cursed by the god Apollo. The curse was that Cassandra was doomed to tell the truth, but would never be believed.

5 From http://www.ipcc.ch/about/index.htm, retrieved on 12 April 2009.

climate system...Global GHG emissions due to human activities have grown since pre-industrial times, with an increase of 70% between 1970 and 2004...Carbon dioxide (CO2) is the most important anthropogenic GHG. Its annual emissions grew by about 80% between 1970 and 2004. The long-term trend of declining CO2 emissions per unit of energy supplied reversed after 2000. Most of the observed increase in global average temperatures since the mid-twentieth century is very likely due to the observed increase in anthropogenic GHG concentrations. It is likely that there has been significant anthropogenic warming over the past 50 years averaged over each continent (except Antarctica).

3. There is high agreement and much evidence that with current climate change mitigation policies and related sustainable development practices, global GHG emissions will continue to grow over the next few decades. Continued GHG emissions at or above current rates would cause further warming and induce many changes in the global climate system during the twenty-first century that would very likely be larger than those observed during the twentieth century.
4. A wide array of adaptation options is available, but more extensive adaptation than is currently occurring is required to reduce vulnerability to climate change. There are barriers, limits and costs, which are not fully understood.
5. Determining what constitutes "dangerous anthropogenic interference with the climate system" in relation to Article 2 of the UNFCCC involves value judgments. Science can support informed decisions on this issue, including by providing criteria for judging which vulnerabilities might be labeled "key".

To sum up, the world is warming more than we thought it would; we humans are causing the warming, primarily by causing a significant increase in carbon dioxide levels in the atmosphere; things will get worse if we don't do something soon; what we are doing now is not enough, though we are not sure whether doing other things would help or how much it would help; and deciding how much carbon dioxide the atmosphere can support is a decisions politicians should make, with advice from scientists. See, they lose me, right there. Points one to four make sense, if the underpinning data are accepted as valid, but that last point tells me that the scientists are not sure of their ground, they are not actually convinced about the science supporting points one to four.

Why do I say this? Among other things, I am a barrister, a litigator in US English. If I found myself in court and the other side came to me and said something like this...B is happening, A causes B and if levels of A keep rising, B will get worse and we can prove it—because your client controls production of A, we will sue for any damages caused by your client's failure to reduce A to a point where it is not dangerous, which scientists tell us is X—and we can prove that too. Faced with that sort of case, my advice to my client would be to fix the problem and to do it pronto. However, If I were presented with this case instead.... B is happening, A causes B and if levels of A keep rising, B will get worse and we can prove it...because your client controls production of A, we will sue for any damages caused by your client's failure to reduce A to a point where it is not dangerous...but we are not actually sure at what point A becomes dangerous... scientists tell us that there is no conclusive evidence about that...so we will just pick a level and argue for that. The differences between these two scenarios are significant. In the latter scenario, my advice to a client would be to fight and to ask for punitive costs when we win!

The second report on which I rely is *The Stern Review: The Economics of Climate Change* (The Stern Review), which focuses on the economics of climate change. The review was commissioned by the Government of the United Kingdom "as a contribution to assessing the evidence and building understanding of the economics of climate change."[6] That review assessed the dangers arising from climate change as follows.

The dangers

All countries will be affected by climate change, but the poorest countries will suffer earliest and most, and average temperatures could rise by five degrees (Celsius) from pre-industrial levels if climate change goes unchecked. Warming of three or four degrees will result in many millions more people being flooded. By the middle of the century, Stern foreshadows that as many as two hundred million people may be permanently displaced due to rising sea levels, heavier floods and drought. Warming of four degrees or more is likely to seriously affect global food production. Warming of two degrees could leave 15-40% species facing extinction.[7] Before the industrial revolution, the level of greenhouse gases in the atmosphere was 280 parts per million (or ppm) CO^2 equivalent (CO^2e); the current level is 430ppm CO^2e. The level should be limited to 450-550ppm CO^2. According to Stern, any level higher than this would substantially increase risks of very harmful impacts. Anything lower would impose very high adjustment costs in the near term and might not even be feasible. Deforestation is responsible for more emissions than the transport sector. Climate change is the greatest and widest-ranging market failure ever —a statement with which I heartily concur, unlike certain others in this rubric of strong conclusions based on a mixture of science and leaps of faith. On the back of these findings, Stern recommended that governments consider certain actions, summarized below.

6 From the Executive Summary, page 1.
7 The breadth of this estimate suggests to me that the underlying science is a bit rubbery.

Recommended actions

Stern identified three elements of policy required to support an effective response: carbon emissions pricing, technology policy and energy efficiency. The report puts forward a strong case for carbon pricing, leaving open the means to place a price on emissions, through taxation, emissions trading or regulation. The gist of that argument is that turning carbon emissions into a cost of production, rather than an economic externality, will make explicit the full social and environmental costs of failing to curb or eliminate emissions. Stern argued for an international and inter-sectoral approach, building on existing emissions trading schemes, such as that operating across the EU. Stern proposed that technology policy should drive the large-scale development and use of many low-carbon and high-efficiency products.

He urged that support for energy research and development should at least double, while support for the deployment of low-carbon technologies should be increased by up to five times. In a rare moment of timidity, Stern suggested that "International product standards could be introduced". I would have thought that it would be very difficult, if not impossible, to sustain a rapidly growing international effort in this area without standardization. Without standardization, it would take much longer and, according to Stern (and others) time is of the essence in the fight against climate change. Stern went on to recommend that large-scale international pilot programs to explore the best ways to curb deforestation should be started very quickly—again, if the problem is as bad as Stern argues, should we not take immediate steps globally to stop (and reverse) deforestation?

Staying with the policy theme, Stern recommended that climate change be fully integrated into development policy and that rich countries should honor pledges to increase support through overseas development assistance; that international funding should support improved regional information on climate change impacts; and that international funding should go into researching new crop varieties that will be more resilient to drought and flood. The arguments on which these recommendations rest are strongly rooted in economics.

Economic impacts

According to Stern, the benefits of strong, early action considerably outweigh the costs of delayed action or inaction. The report claims that inaction could cost the world at least 5% of GDP each year or as much as 20% of GDP if more dramatic predictions related to climate change come to pass. These numbers put the "Great Recession" in perspective, do they not? On the other hand, Stern says,[8] the cost of

8 These conclusions are broadly supported by a report prepared for the Australian Government by another economist, Professor Ross Garnaut. The report is titled *The Garnaut Climate Change Review: Final Report*. Professor Ross Garnaut is one of Australia's most distinguished and well-known economists. As explained

reducing emissions could be limited to around 1% of global GDP. The economic foundations for this claim are that:

- each (metric) tonne of CO^2 we emit causes damages worth at least $85, but emissions can be cut at a cost of less than $25 a tonne;
- shifting the world onto a low-carbon path could eventually benefit the economy by $2.5 trillion a year;
- by 2050, markets for low-carbon technologies could be worth at least $500 billion a year; and
- what we do now can have only a limited effect on the climate over the next forty or fifty years, but what we do in the next ten to twenty years can have a profound effect on the climate in the second half of the twenty-first century.

What it all means

In *Hot, Flat and Crowded*, Friedman explains that what we are facing is not well described as climate change or global warming. Friedman quotes Hunter Lovins, a climate scientist, who tells us that what we are facing is climate *weirding*. By that he means that global warming is going to give rise to all sorts of unusual phenomena, "hotter heat spells, longer and sharper droughts, more violent storms, and more intense flooding". Climate change or climate weirding means that our environment, the unusually benign environment we have enjoyed for about ten thousand years, is changing. The nature and extent of the change is hard to predict, though the best science we have tells us that the planet will, on average, become warmer, by perhaps x-y degrees centigrade. However, that average masks the fact that some parts of the globe may warm by more than that, while some may actually become cooler.

More importantly, what is happening is that our climate is becoming less stable, less predictable. Picture in your mind's eye a delicately poised object that is held steady by a balance of its own movement, gravity and centrifugal forces, like, say, a spinning top, steadily progressing along the kitchen floor. Then, imagine that a gust of wind buffets the top, not so hard as to totally knock it off balance, thus forcing it to crash, but just enough to interfere with the balance of forces that have kept the top on a steady course across the kitchen floor. What the top is likely to do then is to start wobbling on its axis, thus causing its course to become erratic, less predictable, sometimes coming perilously close to crashing into a wall or tipping over the cat's water bowl. That is

in the report's preface, "The Garnaut Climate Change Review was initiated in April 2007 by the then Leader of the Opposition, Kevin Rudd, and by the Premiers of the six states and the Chief Ministers of the two territories of Australia. It was commissioned by the First Ministers on 30 April 2007. The Commonwealth Government joined the Review in January 2008 after Mr Rudd became Prime Minister of Australia. The Review was required to examine the impacts of climate change on the Australian economy, and to recommend medium- to long-term policies and policy frameworks to improve the prospects of sustainable prosperity."

what is happening to our climate, folks. The steady spin, the gradual progress is being replaced with erratic, unpredictable, scary zigzagging!

We can expect direct changes in our weather, such as more and more powerful hurricanes in hurricane prone areas, more wildfires in vulnerable regions, less rain in dry areas and more rain in tropical areas. We can also expect direct changes in climate, with fertile areas becoming desert, permafrost thawing and allowing agriculture to flourish in what was once a frozen desert, shorter winters and longer summers in England and the disappearance of the in-between seasons, spring and fall, in Mediterranean countries. We can also expect indirect changes in weather and climate, such as growing salinity in rivers and lakes and increases in pest numbers, such as locusts, for example. In turn, our newly erratic climate will give us higher insurance costs; more cross-frontier movements of large numbers of people, voluntary and involuntary; less political stability and new political alliances forming within states and across states; more (and new?) disease around the world, with poorer countries suffering even more than they are now from illness and malnutrition; shifting ethical, moral and religious values; and more conflict, over water, over land, over food, within states and between states. Let us consider each of those not so pleasant items, to understand better what may or is likely to happen and what we can do to prevent the worst from happening or to enable us to deal with whatever comes.

Are we the new Easter Islanders?

The recent tragic forest fires in Australia, which claimed many lives, provide a useful simile to help us understand how crisis develop and manifest themselves in the financial world. Bushfires, as we call them in Australia, occur include the presence of fuel, oxygen and an ignition source; the intensity of the fire and the speed at which it spreads depend on ambient temperature, fuel load, fuel moisture, wind speed and slope angle. The greater the fuel load, the hotter and more intense the fire. Fuel that is concentrated will burn faster than heavily compacted or scattered fuel sources. Of course, however great the load and regardless of how conducive to a fire the environment may be, there will be no fire without ignition. Lightning is the most common igniter of fires, in Australia, while the rest of the fires are accidentally or intentionally ignited by human activity.

Notice that I have avoided saying that lightning or humans cause bushfires.[9] That is because neither lightning nor a match will start a fire in a forest if the conditions are not right, if the fuel load is light or the forest has just been drenched by rain, for example. It is the same with financial or economic wildfires, such as the subprime crisis or the Great Recession itself. A financial crisis will occur only when the fuel is there, in the form

9 If you want to know more about how bushfires start and spread, go to the website of Geoscience Australia, at http://www.ga.gov.au/hazards/bushfire/causes.jsp.MY observations are based on the information provided there.

of an investment bubble, if the environment is accommodating, because regulation is inadequate or enforced poorly and there is a general climate of euphoria that blinds almost everyone to the reality of the situation, and if some factor (or combination of factors), intentional or accidental, provides the spark to ignite the fuel.

This picture of how a disaster is made is evident in a wonderful book by Jared Diamond, titled *Collapse: How Societies Choose to Fail or Succeed.*[10] In that book, Diamond examine why some ancient societies, including the Anasazi of the American Southwest, the Viking colonies of Greenland, and the civilization that once thrived on Easter Island in the Pacific Ocean, have fallen apart. Diamond also provides with challenges faced by modern societies, including my homeland, Australia. Diamond uses the events that brought down these societies as parables illustrating the perils we face in the twenty-first century, primarily due to our impact on the Earth's ecology. The parable I would like to borrow from Diamond concerns Easter Island.

Easter Island is a tiny island in the southeastern Pacific Ocean and is a special territory of Chile. The island is famous for the huge statues (called moai) seen on and near its shores. These statues were erected by the Rapanui people, the indigenous inhabitants of the island. The Rapanui had a strict class system, with a king to whom were attributed god-like powers. Ancestral worship was the dominant character of Rapanui society and, though this is not certain, it is thought that the erection of the moai was a crucial element of the islanders' belief system. In the mid-eighteenth century, a new cult replaced ancestral worship. At that time, it is believed that moai were toppled all over the island. These events took place during the Little Ice Age, which affected the world from 1650 to1850, possibly damaging agriculture and fishing resources on which the Rapanui depended. Whatever happened at that time resulted in the almost total disruption of Rapanui society, which, in turn, disrupted land and fishing management practices, causing great damage to the local ecosystem. Famine, sickness and premature death became endemic on the island.

Jared Diamond argues that the disappearance of the island's palm trees coincided with the decline of its civilization. Archeological evidence established that there was a sudden drop in quantities of fish and bird bones in the relevant period, perhaps because the islanders had lost the means to construct fishing vessels and the birds lost their nesting sites—a result of the new cult. Sediment samples suggest that up to half of the native plants had become extinct and that the vegetation of the island had been drastically altered. Chickens and rats became leading items of diet and there are contested hints that cannibalism occurred, based on human remains associated with cooking sites, especially in caves. As with a bushfire, what Diamond describes is a situation where all the preconditions for a disaster were in place—and the sudden ascent of a new cult was the factor that ignited the pyre. You may have heard of or even

10 If you want to avoid having to read the book, go to the video kindly provided by YouTube at http://video.google.com/videoplay?docid=4271982381147720351.

seen the movie, *The Perfect Storm*, which is based on events that took place in 1991. The film tells the story of a fishing boat that is caught in a great storm, a perfect storm, and is lost with all hands. A perfect storm results from the simultaneous occurrence of weather events that, on their own, would not be nearly as dramatic in their effect. Easter Island was caught up in a perfect storm, hit simultaneously by a constellation of negative events, each of which could have been survived, if on its own, but that proved deadly to a civilization because of their timing and combined impact on an already weakened victim.

Most climate change scenarios, as we will see, paint a picture of our future that is not dissimilar from what happened on Easter Island, though the scale is global, rather than local. Our focus on the cult of economic growth and our reliance on rapidly disappearing natural resources could take us as a species to the same place in which the Rapanui found themselves, the brink of extinction. The impact of climate change could disrupt the political and economic foundations that sustain our civilization, at the same time as it causes a dramatic reduction in the capacity of the planet to sustain us, with catastrophic effects, including famine, disease, war and civil unrest. The difference is that no one is going to come to our rescue, as arguably was the case when European vessels finally reached Easter Island and connected it with the world. Also, we cannot make the modern equivalent of a raft and leave our doomed home, though James Lovelock, among others, argues that we should focus on creating safe havens for humans in areas that will not be too badly affected by climate change, most likely to be found at the polar extremes of the planet and in higher latitudes in what is now Siberia, for example.[11] Safe havens for seeds of plants already exist, in several locations around the world. The best known and perhaps the most recent addition to the world's seed banks is the Svalbard Global Seed Vault, in Norway, a location of which Lovelock would approve, I believe.

The concept of a human safe haven has been explored in science fiction, as well as mooted by scientists. The former have not painted a rosy picture of what a world of safe havens would be like. In the eerily prescient 1973 film, titled *Soylent Green*, global warming and overpopulation have lead to widespread unemployment and poverty. Fruit, vegetables, and meat are rare and expensive. Most of the surviving humans live on processed food rations, including soylent green wafers, made from scarce plankton. Most of the food wafers are red or yellow, made by combining lentil and soya flours, which are much less popular than the green version. Get the movie and watch it, anew or again. It is a cautionary tale of where we might end up if we do not change course, remembering that what Lovelock foresees is worse than the scenario posited in the movie.

Leaving aside science fiction, as I write this, the realization strikes me that if I had been writing this book twenty years ago or even ten years ago, this topic would not have merited a chapter on its own in a book intended for an audience in the financial

11 From the previously cited interview reported in *The Press.*

services industry. Seriously, for those of a certain age—and living outside weather-obsessed Britain—it must seem strange to have so many words written, said, discussed and shouted on the topic of climate. Not so for anyone under the age of twenty, perhaps, because for them global warming represents what the threat of nuclear war meant for the children of the 1950s and 1960s. It is a supervening, all-encompassing issue, next to which any other problem is negligible. However, for any Baby Boomer or anyone older, who has lived through a series of threats to humanity's survival, such as nuclear war and a consequent nuclear winter, famine and pestilence, Y2K, wandering asteroids, and so on, this sustained focus on climate is a bit hard to take. Don't get me wrong, I am not saying that climate change is not important or that Al Gore did not deserve his Nobel Prize.

However, the wall to wall media coverage of climate change has more than a whiff of groupthink accompanying it. This bothers me a great deal—groupthink leads to Nixon's Watergate, to chopping down the last tree on Easter Island, and to wasting billions of dollars on non-existent problems, such as Y2K, mob behavior and final solutions. Those are not good things, so I think it is time to get some perspective into the debate, time to cool things down a little, if you will pardon a small, harmless pun. Because people find the evidence on climate change and its likely impact either totally compelling or frighteningly biased, any attempt to study the issue forces us to take a similarly divergent approach; in effect, we are asked to choose sides, to have faith in the arguments of one side or the other. Two-legged arguments, which is what this is, are as viable and as comfortable as two-legged stools. To give the argument the third leg it needs, I have injected another point of view, that of the skeptic, the position that is most natural to me. When we get to the scenarios, later in this chapter, I will provide advice on what to do, covering the gamut of possibilities, starting with outright denial, continuing through skepticism and going all the way to unquestioning acceptance.

> *I distrust people who claim to know the whole truth and who seek to orchestrate the world in line with that one true truth. I think that's a very dangerous position in the world. It needs to be challenged. It needs to be challenged constantly in all sorts of ways, and that's what I tried to do.*—Salman Rushdie.

Some may think that a skeptic is someone who enjoys being cynical or disbelieves all and sundry, without advancing any alternative argument. Some skeptics are like that and they give the rest of us a bad name. Actually, a skeptic is someone who must see compelling evidence before s/he believes. In other words, a skeptic forms a belief through thought, rather than faith. The doubting Thomas of the Gospels was a skeptic, as were Gautama Buddha, Socrates and Descartes. To illustrate the point, skepticism is what stops me from declaring for atheism, because while I see no compelling evidence of the existence of God, I also see no compelling evidence of God's non-existence and I refuse to be bound to take one position or the other. The evidence on God's existence, as I interpret it, does not allow a conclusion to be reached safely without a leap of faith, for both sides. To be an atheist, I think, requires as big a leap of faith as to be a believer. Therefore, I keep an open mind and continue to sift through evidence that comes my way, adjusting my point of view, if the evidence requires it. For example, I used to think that regulation was a bad thing, an attempt by government to control my freedom and independence. The evidence has now persuaded me otherwise. I approach climate change with the same mindset, trawling for evidence, assessing its probative value and striving to reach a conclusion, if the evidence allows it.

With climate change, I have not, as yet, managed to get to the last stage, to reach a firm conclusion, because, as we will see, I think the evidence is inadequate; any conclusion as to whether or not humans are causing dangerous climate change would be unsafe, on the evidence we have. Others disagree, as is their right, stating with certainty that humanity is either guilty or not guilty as charged, and citing reams of evidence, mainly statistical, to support their conclusion. I think that they have jumped to a conclusion and then found evidence to bolster it, after the event, because the causal connection they claim to see or to deny can neither be proven nor disproven on the evidence we have. I think that those who claim to have reached a firm conclusion on climate change, like James Lovelock, for example, have made a leap of faith to bridge a gap that science has so far left unfilled.

Consider the terminology used to define the sides in the debate, dividing those who deny from those who believe. These are strange terms in a scientific debate, though they are apt terms in a debate on theology, where faith and belief (or their absence) make up the entirety of the argument, on both sides. If the evidence on climate change were truly compelling, belief would not be required—only science. However, as we will see later, science is not up to it, at least not yet. We do not know enough and certainly we do not understand enough in this field to give science the pre-eminence it usually has in our twenty-first century world—hence my skepticism.

Learning from history

In case you want to know what has made me a skeptic, the answer is simple, history. Conjecture about the end of life as we know it has been around a long time and it tends to be most acute at certain times, around major points in time, such as millennial ends and beginnings. For example, at the beginning of the second millennium, some people, though not all, believed that the world would come to an end, because Jesus would be making a return visit to establish the prophesied New Jerusalem. With this belief in mind, any and every event was interpreted as supporting the conclusion that the world had reached its end, that those days were indeed the last days. We now know that those who thought this way were wrong, because we are still here, are we not? But we should not feel smug about that, there is no glory in the wisdom of hindsight. And, who knows, a thousand years from now someone might be writing in a similar vein about our present fears and trepidations. It may be that the world as we know it is not about to end. However, an argument such as this, however, beguiling, does not in itself constitute a valid reason to avoid fixing up the colossal environmental damage we have created over the last century or so.

A bit of cultural perspective may also be enlightening. In the West we tend towards unsophisticated conceptual models, such as millenarianism, as we have seen, or fundamentalist belief systems that echo Jewish Messianic beliefs, such as the biblically prophesied second coming of The Lord or alternative versions, as we find in Christian sects such as Mormonism or the creed of Jehovah's Witnesses. We westerners tend to have an alpha and omega view of history, egotistically tying the fate of the whole universe to the events in our little corner of it, and within the time span marked out by our pitifully short lives. It is the curse of each age to think of itself as special and we of this age are no different. Like those before us, we tend to believe that we live in special times, be they the worst of times or the best of times. At the moment, it seems that we have gone a bit millenarian, albeit belatedly, since the third millennium is no longer new.

News reports seem to produce a new world-ending crisis every week, ranging from climate change, to asteroid strikes, then on to world-shattering volcanic eruptions and an old favorite, a plague of some sort. AIDS, however malevolent, has not been up to the challenge of ending humanity, so we have turned to more mundane diseases, like influenza, to fill the gap. Don't get me wrong, I am neither saying that these are not nasty diseases nor denying that many have suffered because of them. However, the science of statistics tells us that the odds of this generation, among the thousands that have and will live on this planet, being the one to usher in the end of days are very, very poor. Don't bet your house or your business on the likelihood of any of the horses of the Apocalypse ending life as we know it, not just yet.

In defense of the belief that we are special, let me say that this is only human nature at work. By making ourselves the center of the universe, the pivot of history, we try to control that which we can neither understand nor command. Our ancestors did this by sacrificing animals or children to propitiate or appease a particular deity or by dancing naked around stones standing in cold windswept places or by knocking on wood to avoid bad luck. Many of us might do just that even today, without thinking about what we are actually doing—for you Christians out there, knocking on wood is actually a physical manifestation of the vestigial paganism that lives on under the garb of superstition, much of which has actually been incorporated by Christianity into its own ceremonial and quasi-ceremonial repertoire.

The Christmas tree, for example, dates back to Iron Age Britain, where the Druids used evergreen trees during their winter solstice rituals, and used holly and mistletoe as symbols of eternal life, placing evergreen branches over doors to keep away evil spirits, much as we do with Christmas wreaths. Similar practices were common in what is now Germany, where local tribes in pre-Roman and Roman times tied fruit and attached candles to evergreen tree branches, in honor of the god Woden. These tribes considered trees as symbolizing eternal life. Of course, Christmas itself is a continuation of ancient festivals, such as the Roman Saturnalia, and the best evidence tells us that Christ was born during the month of September, perhaps in the year 3BC or may be as early as 6-4BC.[12] I am writing this on the day when Easter is celebrated and it is worth noting that the word Easter comes from the name of the Anglo-Saxon goddess Ēostre, in whose honor great feats used to be held during the month we now know as April. Humans have always celebrated the end of the cold and the return of warmth and of life, as evidenced by flowers in the meadows and new leaves on the trees. In this also, we are neither special nor different from those who have preceded us or from those who will follow. Less economically developed societies, because they remain dependent on the seasons more than we are, understand this better than we do.

In the West we tend to experience and to understand present events with inadequate reference to the past. As a result, we fall into an emotional and logical trap: normality is what we have experienced to date and any deviation from our necessarily limited range of experiences is considered abnormal. So, the way we now see and understand Christmas and Christmas trees is normal and whatever came before was a gradual progression leading to the present state. Because what we have is normal and because we believe in the notion of progress, we think we are the peak of human development. We believe that we are the wisest, most civilized people who have ever lived. I hate to blow away this illusion, but while our technological prowess may be unsurpassed, our capacity to analyze and to understand issues, and to deal with ethical and moral challenges is not superior to that of our ancestors.

In some ways, actually, we have gone backwards. After all, the great philosophers and thinkers who have shaped the Judeo-Christian, Indian, Chinese, Japanese and other cultures are long dead. All we do now is akin to tinkering at the edges, tuning the great ethical engine we call religion to better suit our times, but L. Ron Hubbard aside—joke, folks, joke—the great religions of the world now are those we have always had, at least for the last millennium or even longer. Even what we call humanism is not new, because its origins and principles are to be found in ancient Greece and classical Rome, in the writings of Socrates and Confucius, found also in the thoughts and deeds of the Roman Emperor we know as Julian.[13]

12 See the Wikipedia entry on the Nativity of Jesus, at http://en.wikipedia.org/wiki/Nativity_of_Jesus, retrieved on 18 January 2009.

13 For an excellent discussion of what is and is not humanism, go to http://www.jcn.com/humanism.html, which I perused on 1 March 2009.

The core of humanism is simple to explain. First, people should learn to think for themselves on moral and ethical matters and should not accept unquestioningly what they are told by figures of authority. Second, values and value judgments should be based and understood within the context of our humanity. When we decide what is wrong and what is right, we do so after having assessed whether our choice would promote the maintenance or development of human beings, either individually or as a species, depending on the issue. I would add a third element, which is that we should do what is right because it is right to do so and not because we are promised either heavenly rewards or dire punishments after we die. Thomas Paine said, "My country is the world and my religion is to do good" and this could be the motto for all humanists. I would also add that humanism implies assuming a skeptical position and using the principles of the Socratic Method to get closer to the truth. Using such a method allows us to escape the limitations of the two-legged stool, it allows us to step outside the boundaries of the conventional and the normal, to glimpse reality a little more clearly. Allow me to provide an example of how the world we know, the reality we understand, colors our perceptions of normality. I do this so that we can then discuss what might happen to normality, and why. I will use an example close to the heart of all of us, the family.

Why normality is not normal

Let us ponder what we mean when we say that something is or is not normal, focusing on a subject very close to home, literally. In recent years we have seen what I consider to be an absurd debate about protecting the traditional family, driven by those who believe that any social unit that does not have a father and a mother, lawfully wedded, of course, and with one or more children, is not the norm. This position is predicated on the belief that the nuclear family is the normal social unit, the arrangement that people, if left to their own devices, tend to prefer. This belief is based on a false view of human society, because most social units in the west do not look like this. Let us consider the facts. In Australia, only slightly more than one in three family units is made up of parents with dependent children; an equivalent number is made of couples only. To put this another way, two-thirds of family units in Australia do not fit the traditional notion of a nuclear family.[14]

In the USA, one in two families is a nuclear family.[15] While this is a more traditional picture than we see in Australia, it means that one in every two families does not fit the white picket fence view of the world; it means that nuclear families are not the dominant form of social unit, even in the USA. That is so in most western societies. A scan of human societies over the last two to three thousand years tells us that the type

14 From the Australian Institute of Family Studies, at http://www.aifs.gov.au/institute/info/charts/familystructure/ftype06.html, retrieved on 18 January 2009.

15 From infoplease, at http://www.infoplease.com/ipa/A0880690.html, retrieved on 18 January 2009.

of family unit beloved by the social conservatives is not at all typical and is, using the terminology of statistics, actually abnormal. Yet, much of our public policy continues to be developed and implemented on the mistaken assumption that the nuclear family is what we want and what we need.

Equally, the climate change debate, regardless of which side you take, is predicated on the assumption that our ten thousand year window of unusually benign climate is normal and that it will continue unless the status quo is disturbed in some way, say by raising atmospheric levels of carbon dioxide. If we want a serious debate on climate change, we must first accept that even without any intervention by humans, the present benign conditions are not likely to continue for much longer. The argument should not be about preserving the "normal" status quo; rather, it should be about how we can best manage the Earth's biosphere, how we can do what it is right to do. My argument for action to redress our past ecological errors does not rest on what is or is not normal. My suggested approach is based on the compelling evidence that we cannot continue to exploit the Earth as we have been doing in the developed world for the last few decades, because it is not right, not right for us humans primarily, but also not right because of the effect it is having on the rest of life on Earth. That last point is not made altruistically. It is made because our survival as a species is inextricably linked with life on Earth, with the biosphere.

If everyone on the planet were to enjoy a western lifestyle—like yours or mine—we would need several Earths, several biospheres, to keep us fed, house and amused. Obviously, this is not possible, at least not for the next several decades. Oil may not be at peak yet, we may not be about to run out, just yet, but the supply of oil is finite, as is the supply of coal and of any other mineral resource. Until we can mine the asteroids or the Moon or Mars, what mineral resources we have are contained within Earth's atmosphere. When the last pint of oil is poured into a car and is burnt to propel it, there will be no more oil—just as no trees were left on Easter island after the last tree standing was cut down to build a hut, or to burn in a fire or to provide the last log on which the last gigantic statue to be erected was rolled into place. Except that, if we really wanted to, we humans could grow trees on Easter Island again—but making oil to burn in cars or to make supermarket plastic bags or a life saving prosthetic device is a little trickier, because the energy required to make a pint of oil is greater than the energy produced by burning the oil. It is a little bit like selling goods for less than they are worth. We can do that for a while, relying on our capital reserves, but once those reserves are gone, if you sell something at a price lower than it cost you to make it you will not stay in business for long.

Leaving minerals aside, what about the food and water we need to eat every day? Until we learn how to make food from air or sea water, using nanotechnology or some as yet undreamt of technology, the only food we have is that which we can grow or catch on this one planet we have. We have enough food to feed everyone, just, but if the world's population continues to grow, if we go on burning food to fuel our cars, and if even the mildest scenario for climate change pans out, we will not have nearly enough. Our water situation is even worse, because most water on the planet is salty. Yes, we can take the salt out of the water, but that expensive, financially and in terms of the energy required to do so. The inevitable conclusion, whether we believe in climate change or not, is that we must learn to use the planet's limited resources more efficiently and more wisely, and we must do it soon.

Living in abnormal times

The climate experienced by you and me thus far in our lives and by those who preceded us, insofar as records tell us—and our records don't amount to much if we go back more than two centuries—is not *necessarily* normal. That is if by normal we mean the state to which a system tends to revert, which is what normal means when the word is separated from the emotional connotations that usually accompany it. Normal is not synonymous with good or with preferable, rather it is synonymous with typical, natural, usual or common. Well, if we look over the climatologically history of the Earth, the last ten thousand years have been typical, common or usual, though they may have been natural, at least until two hundred years ago. The scientific and historical evidence align to tell us that the period in which we have been living has been characterized by deeply abnormal climate patterns. The last ten thousand years, the years that have seen humanity become civilized, have been an abnormally benign period climatologically. As for being natural, the climate over the last two hundred years has been increasingly influenced by human activity, to the point where now we are not sure what would happen if we were to remove our influence. Would we continue to enjoy a mild inter-glacial experience? Would we suddenly drop into a new ice age? Would global warming continue unabated? No one knows, we can only speculate.

If we stretch our perspective of the Earth's climate beyond the 11,000 or so years that encompass human prehistory and history (a period known as the Holocene), reaching back just beyond the previous inter-glacial period (see figure x), we can see that the peak of that interglaciation was about where we are now. At the equivalent point in the cycle, the Earth was about to enter a long cooling period that would eventually result in the last glacial era the planet has experienced, so far. During those 150,000 years and even during the Holocene, our time, if you like, the climate has undergone significant oscillations to warmer and cooler points, oscillations that disappear from sight in a diagram that illustrates 150 millennia in a few centimeters.

Studies of climate during this period and of earlier eras make it clear that the climate is a complex system that strives for equilibrium. When it reaches a point of equilibrium, it tends to stay there for a while, because inertia is a powerful force. However, if the equilibrium is disturbed, by one factor or a combination of factors, then the climate will change relatively quickly, in search of a new equilibrium. The best description of how the Earth's climate behaves is expressed by Jonathan Adams and Randy Foote, who have prepared a comprehensive analysis of research on climate. "Such observations show that even without anthropogenic climate modification there is always an axe hanging over our head, in the form of random very large-scale changes in the natural climate system; a possibility that policy makers should perhaps bear in mind with contingency plans and international treaties designed to cope with sudden famines on a greater scale than any experienced in written history. By starting to disturb the system, humans may simply be increasing the likelihood of sudden events which could always occur anyway."[16]

Figure 6: The Earth's climate during the last 150,000 years[17]

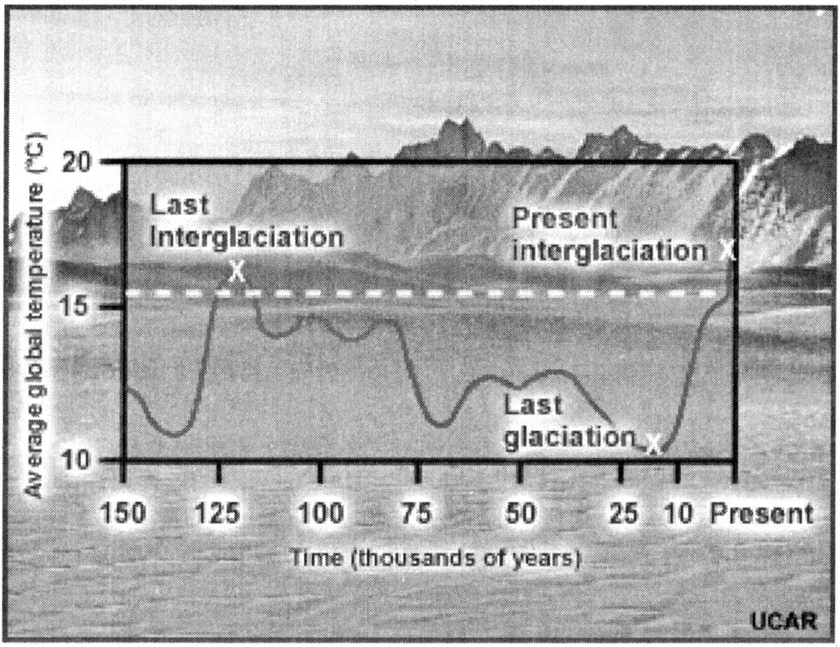

The problem is that we humans tend to think that there was nothing worthwhile before us and there will be nothing at all after us; we are all little Sun Kings and Queens, in our private kingdoms of the mind. And this mental straitjacket binds even great minds, much greater minds than mine. Earlier in the book I discussed theories of history put forward by Karl Marx, Francis Fukuyama, Samuel P. Huntington, and Jared

16 "Sudden Climate Change Through Human History", retrieved from http://dieoff.org/page127.htm, on 16 March 2009.

17 From http://www.ucar.edu/learn/1_4_1.htm, retrieved on 16 March 2009.

Diamond. Marx was a political economist and philosopher; Fukuyama is a historian, as was Huntington; Diamond is a scientist. Each of these significant thinkers has given us useful insights into the human condition and glimpses of our future or at least of possible futures. However, all of them bar one, Diamond, the scientist, have fallen into the trap of assuming that the period in which we live, think and write is somehow extraordinary, different, pivotal, exceptional. I submit that each generation thinks itself to be different, a break from the past, a bridge to the future. This is not how it is. Each generation stands on the back of previous generations and sees a little further and may be perceives things a little differently, and each generation in turn gives a boost to the next, propping its successor on its own shoulders, where our successors may see just a little bit further and perceive things a little differently.

These gradual changes accumulate and over centuries amount to a great deal of change, even transformation. The world in which we live now is very different from the world inhabited by our great-great-grandparents in the nineteenth century, but it is not fundamentally different from the world on the 1990s or 1970s. An individual from those decades magically transported into our times would adapt quickly to mobile telephones, Facebook, Twitter and all the other ephemeral phenomena we think make our times so different. The reverse would also work. However, a trip to the 1890s or 1870s or its reverse to our time would not be so smooth. Life was very different then, culturally, technologically, socially, even politically. Historians should know this, they should have this perspective, but in writing their histories, they forget that each generation, each decade, each era is part of the river of history and seemingly convince themselves that the place from which they observe is not caught up in the flow, as connected to the past as it is to the future. Diamond, the scientist, does not make this mistake; he understands that the human condition is not just universal, at least on this planet, but also permanent.

Crying wolf

The religion we call Hinduism has a more sophisticated conception of history than we do in the west.[18] For a Hindu, just as each of us is doomed to death and reincarnation until personal enlightenment (or awakening) is achieved, humanity as a whole is also tied to a great wheel of perpetual change, which sees civilizations born, thriving, dominant for a time and then doomed to disappear. The causes of that disappearance will change, sometimes it is war, sometimes pestilence, sometimes moral decay and sometimes just plain bad luck, but the result is always the same. We rise from a dark age, thinking we are the first to do so in the history of humanity, we build a

18 Hindu is a Persian term used to refer to the people of what is now northern India and its meaning was broadened by the English to connote anything Indian. The Indians use terms for their religion similar to Taoism. While Tao is the way, Hinduism is eternal law. While it is thought that Hinduism has thousands of gods, it is more correct to say that it is a set of beliefs in one god that has thousands of manifestations. Indian gods are more like Roman Catholic saints than deities as we in the west would conceive.

new civilization, ignorant of echoes of past ones, and then, as hubris sets in, we are plunged into a long dark night, again. Jared Diamond's book, *Collapse*, provides many examples of how and why this happens. I think that while we do not understand that this is how history works, we feel it in our bones, which is why doom and gloom, the fear of the end of days, makes a regular appearance in our midst, in the churches, in the media, in the arts, in the marketplace. To date, the prophets of doom have not been vindicated by events, but just because the boy has cried wolf so many times with no cause, we should not assume that the next wolf scare is not real.

Generally, the prophets of doom take existing conditions, extrapolate them into the future, sometimes to a precise point in time, sometimes not, and then conclude that things just cannot continue as they are. In the relatively recent past, Malthus put forward a credible hypothesis concerning the end of humanity, resting on the premise that geometric population growth would eventually outstrip arithmetic growth rates of food production, with the eventual outcome being a sudden collapse of human population across the globe. In the third quarter of the twentieth century, the Club of Rome put forward a similar hypothesis, which would have had the world in a permanent state of famine well before the beginning of the twenty-first century, had the hypothesis held true. As we know from experience, this did not occur.

In the latter part of the twentieth century there was also much speculation about the probability of the relatively rapid onset of a new global ice age, due to occur over a few decades. The proponents of that view are still around, now suggesting that global warming has held off the next ice age and may actually cancel for good the cycle of freezing and warming that has been a feature of our planet for eons. None of those cries of wolf has yet been accompanied by a real wolf, fortunately for us. In the last decade of the twentieth century we also had the Y2K scare, when it was thought that the world's computers would fail, because of minor design failure concerning dates, and that, as a consequence, society and the global economy would fall apart. It may be that the billions spent in advanced economies as a result of that fear prevented the Y2K wolf from biting, but nothing happened in poor countries that spent little or nothing on the problem, which is interesting, is it not? You see here that a little bit of perspective is already beginning to have an impact on your thinking...well, it certainly has on mine. But as I said, we should not jump to the conclusion that the climate change wolf is another Y2K sheep in disguise.

The great wheel turns[19]

I find it difficult to imagine that anything we humans do, even with the augmented power we derive from technology, will end a cycle of freezing and warming of the

19 The image above is of is a depiction of Lord Shiva as the cosmic dancer, performing his divine dance to destroy a weary universe and to prepare for Lord Brahma to start the process of creation.

Earth that has continued for millions of years. This is made plain by the science. The levels of global warming gases present in the atmosphere now have been experienced by the Earth many times before, but the great cycles continued. The earth has many times been as warm as some of the more extreme climate change projections theorize, and we do not have to go far in the past to find an example, we need only look back a thousand years or so. At the beginning of the second millennium, the Earth was significantly warmer than it is now, and this was no bad thing for humans. For example, those occupying Britain and North America at the time were able to grow Mediterranean crops and the colonization of Greenland was made possible by the warming of the planet. That warm period had nothing to do with anything our ancestors did or did not do. There was very little production of carbon by humans at that time and there were not many people on the planet, relative to now.

Having reviewed the science, it seems to me that, while we can explain *how* cycles of warming and cooling have started and ended, we do not understand *why* they occurred. We do know that the Earth is warmer than it would otherwise be because of the effect of so-called greenhouse gases, including include water vapor, carbon dioxide and methane. These gases are present in the atmosphere and absorb absorbing heat from the Earth's surface, from the atmosphere itself, and from clouds. Without the warming effect of these gases, the Earth would not be a very hospitable place, as the average surface temperature[of 14 °C (57 °F) could be as low as −18 °C (−0.4 °F).[20] While all the attention now seems to be on carbon dioxide (with methane as its partner), the most common greenhouse gas is actually water vapor. The excellent article in Wikipedia on the greenhouse effect, reproduced in part below, makes this obvious, but note the big range attributed to each gas and note also that clouds contribute to the greenhouse effect.[21]

When these gases are ranked by their contribution to the greenhouse effect, the most important are:

- *water vapor, which contributes 36–70%*

20 See http://data.giss.nasa.gov/gistemp/abs_temp.html, retrieved on 29 March 2009, and the Intergovernmental Panel on Climate Change Fourth Assessment Report, Chapter 1: Historical overview of climate change science.

21 See h*ttp://en.wikipedia.org/wiki/Greenhouse_effect#cite_note-IPCC4_ch01*-7, retrieved on 29 March 2009.

- *carbon dioxide, which contributes 9–26%*
- *methane, which contributes 4–9%*
- *ozone, which contributes 3–7%*

The major non-gas contributor to the Earth's greenhouse effect, clouds, also absorb and emit infrared radiation and thus have an effect on radiative properties of the greenhouse gases.

If one were to look at this list starting from first principles, one might conclude that our focus should be on water vapor, not carbon dioxide, and that we should put a lot of effort into reducing the variability in the estimates and to help us understand how clouds affect the picture. The last point is especially relevant because of the expectation that global warming will make wet parts of the globe wetter and dry parts of the globe drier, which might reduce global cloud cover, thus reducing the greenhouse effect. But wait, clouds also help to cool the planet, reflecting the sun's radiation back into space, so reduced cloud cover might make the Earth warmer. Are you confused yet? Oh, and the evidence we have on the connection between gases such as carbon dioxide and the planet's climatic cycles is only circumstantial, because it is based on correlations, not on a hard causal connection.

We do not have proof of a causal connection between the level of carbon dioxide in the atmosphere and global temperatures, though we can postulate one exists because the circumstantial evidence is relatively strong, but not linear. For example, the increase in atmospheric carbon dioxide that has occurred in recent decades has been the same increase that in the past has been associated with average global temperature increases of five degrees centigrade.[22] However, the observed increase in temperature so far has amounted to less than one degree.[23] Global surface temperature increased 0.74 ± 0.18 °centigrade during the one hundred years ending in 2005.[24] The climate change deniers use this kind of observation to accuse the climate change believers of statistical chicanery. Then the same people go on to some chicanery of their own, using even shorter time series than those used by the IPCC, to "prove" that there is no evidence of global warming. The IPCC used a one thousand year timeframe; most of its critics use timeframes of a decade or two.[25] I think we need dig a lot deeper than either side in this debate, because even a one thousand year timeline is short indeed when measured against the Earth's cycles, when timelines amount to millions of years or even billions, especially when we know little and understand less about what actually causes what and when.

---

22 Gwynne Dyer discusses this in *Climate Wars*, page 26.

23 I prefer the term centigrade rather than Celsius.

24 *Summary for Policymakers. Climate Change 2007: The Physical Science Basis. Contribution of Working Group I to the Fourth Assessment Report of the Intergovernmental Panel on Climate Change.*

25 For example, see "The IPCC: on the Run at Last", retrieved from http://www.canadafreepress.com/index.php/article/2352 on 28 February 2009, where the writer supports his argument with a graph of global temperatures from 1979 to 1998.

The hypothesis I put forward is this. The Earth undergoes great cycles, which we understand poorly, cycles that can have beneficial or malefic effects on humanity—I use the word malefic loosely, because, for example, without the recurring Ice Ages, we might not have evolved as quickly or progressed technologically as much as we have. It is more likely than not that nothing we do or do not do will change these cycles, at least not within the parameters of present and likely future technological development. However, there is a risk, however small, that we may cause change that is detrimental to us. In lawyer-speak, we cannot be satisfied beyond reasonable doubt that we are doing no harm. While the probability of harm may be small, the consequences would be catastrophic.

Any sensible analysis by a risk management expert would conclude that the risk we face is very high indeed. That is because risk is computed by combining the likelihood of a given event with its impact should the worst come to pass.[26] The sensible position to take is that if there are even a few chances in a hundred that we are headed towards runaway global warming, the consequences would be o dire that we need to act. However, when we take this approach, our perspective shifts somewhat, to encompass other scenarios. For example, on some calculations, the risk of a global ice age is as great as the risk of damaging global warming, noting that the next ice age is somewhat overdue and that, paradoxically, global warming could cause an ice age in northern Europe while other parts of the planet are comprehensively desertified by heat. This is because if the Greenland ice sheet were to melt, it could cause large quantities of cold water to enter the North Atlantic Ocean. That could change the salinity of the ocean water and stop the Gulf Current, which is what makes Scotland's climate, warmer than the climate in Canada at the same latitude.

This is a proposition put forward by credible scientists, including a paleo-climatologist from the Australian National University, Dr Timothy Barrows.[27] Also, those who argue that global climate is influenced by solar activity have put forward credible evidence that the whole Earth could plunge into an ice age quite soon and quite quickly. For example, in 1999, Nigel Weiss, a Cambridge University physicist, announced that new computer models combining historical patterns of solar activity and human impacts on the climate suggested that the current global warming trend could "paradoxically tip the world into a sudden ice age".[28] It may even be that the sun will save us from global warming, because it seems that sun spot activity is now at such a low level that its effect would offset the warming effect of carbon dioxide. From the middle of the seventeenth century to the early eighteenth, a period known as the

26 For example, see the Australian and New Zealand approach to risk assessment and management, as set out in AS/NZS 4360, published by Standards Australia. It can be purchased from http://www.saiglobal.com.

27 "New northern ice age could send refugees to Australia", by Ashley Hall, ABC News, retrieved from http://www.abc.net.au/news/stories/2007/10/05/2052408.htm on 28 February 2009.

28 "Earth At Risk Of Ice Age, Physicist Says", Clive Cookson, Financial Times, 11 August 1999, retrieved from the United Nations Foundation website, http://www.unwire.org/unwire/19990811/4286_story.asp, on 28 February 2009.

Maunder Minimum, sunspots were extremely rare. There is credible science suggesting that the lack of sunspot activity coincided with the Little Ice Age.[29]

Because of this uncertainty and because of the risk profile presented by any and all these possible futures, our best survival strategy as a species is to plan for the worst and hope for the best. Our best survival strategy is to accept that we must act as a species to manage or at least to influence the natural environment, to shape it, as much as possible, to be friendly to life as we know it. What does that mean in practice? It means that we should limit our impact on the ecological well being of the Earth, because a more complex ecology is a more resilient ecology, better able to adapt and to enable us to adapt to the changes wrought by the turning of the wheel, whether the wheel brings ice or fire. It means that we should invest in the scientific effort we need to make to dispel the confusion that exists at present about why the climate of the Earth does what it does. It means that we should husband carefully the limited natural resources we have.

I do not support the reduction of fossil fuels utilization because I think that it will have an impact on global warming—it may, but to me it is a little like a child bailing out the ocean as the tide retreats. It may indeed reduce the amount of water returned to the ocean, but to what avail? I support efforts to reduce consumption of fossil fuels because it is at the same time an inefficient use of scarce resources and a destroyer of the planet's ecological complexity. I support the development of alternative power sources because we need a sustainable supply of power sufficient to enable the people of the world to enjoy the quality of life that is now reserved for the privileged few in the developed world. I support the re-development of our economy as a low carbon economy because it will enable us to continue to grow our financial and social wealth, while continuing on our present path will result in future generations being poorer than their predecessors. If we are indeed the dominant species on the planet, we should behave as such, we should accept the responsibility inherent to that status.

Managing the planet: Why we must act now

We Baby Boomers have tended to deal with crises, of whatever kind, as if they were a war, using the metaphor of war and the language that goes with it to discuss what we need to do, what we must do about climate change. This is a trait we have inherited from our predecessor generation, the Veterans (see chapter 5), perhaps because, as was the case for them, our collective character was also forged during a war, albeit that ours was cold, while theirs was very hot indeed. The metaphor of war colors our thinking and limits our imagination; it also leads us down blind alleys. The ecological problems we are experiencing are not equivalent to a war. There is no enemy, unless

29 "Sunspots Are Fewest Since 1954, but Significance Is Unclear", by Kenneth Chang, 2 October 2 2008, The New York Times, retrieved from http://www.nytimes.com/2008/10/03/science/space/03sun.html?n=Top/News/Science/Topics/Sun, on 28 February 2009.

we think of ourselves as such. There is no battlefield, there will not be winners or losers; if we lose, there will be only losers. That is why I think it is high time for us to switch to a more apposite peacetime metaphor, that of management or of stewardship. Our challenge is to manage the common air, water and earth we all share, as property in commons, to be stewards of the planet we know as the Earth. If we fail to do so, we will be doomed to repeat the mistake made by our ancestors, once again giving rise to a tragedy of the commons.

You may already be familiar with the allegory of the tragedy of the commons. If so, please skip the next few paragraphs. If not, please read on. The tragedy of the commons is a phenomenon most of us have experienced and, probably, more than once. Remember when you were at college or first left from the parental home and you shared a house with strangers (or friends, it makes no difference) and the shared parts of the house were always a mess that no one ever cleaned up, except perhaps when you brought your first love home or mum and dad made one of their regular (inspection) visits? If you do, you have experienced the tragedy of the commons. Remember reading earlier about Easter Island and how the islanders had irresponsibly cut down every single tree on the island, destroying their natural environment and threatening their very survival? That is another instance of the tragedy of the commons.

Have you watched the endless proceedings of the United Nations or of your own elected representatives on finding a solution to global warming and wondered why an agreement could not be reached even when those arguing believe, in the main, that catastrophe is staring us in the face? Again, what you have been witnessing is a tragedy of the commons, the commons we all share as the planet Earth. The term tragedy of the commons was popularized by Hardin in 1968, when he reflected how in medieval England benefit-maximizing rational individuals intensively grazed their own sheep in the common pasture, harming it and leaving everyone worse off, including themselves, of course. In Hardin's words, this is how the tragedy of the commons unfolded and why:

> *As a rational being, each herdsman seeks to maximize his gain. Explicitly or implicitly, more or less consciously, he asks, "What is the utility to me of adding one more animal to my herd?" This utility has one negative and one positive component.*
>
> - *1. The positive component is a function of the increment of one animal. Since the herdsman receives all the proceeds from the sale of the additional animal, the positive utility is nearly + 1.*
> - *2. The negative component is a function of the additional overgrazing created by one more animal. Since, however, the effects of overgrazing are shared by all the herdsmen, the negative utility for any particular decision -making herdsman is only a fraction of 1.*

Adding together the component partial utilities, the rational herdsman concludes that the only sensible course for him to pursue is to add another animal to his herd. And another... But this is the conclusion reached by each and every rational herdsman sharing a commons. Therein is the tragedy. Each man is locked into a system that compels him to increase his herd without limit—in a world that is limited. Ruin is the destination toward which all men rush, each pursuing his own best interest in a society that believes in the freedom of the commons. Freedom in a commons brings ruin to all.

We may not be the new Easter Islanders, but we still seem to act just as rational herdsmen did in the Middle Ages, because our belief systems are not fundamentally different. Individual rationality can lead to collective disaster. Indeed, freedom in a commons generally brings ruin to all and we have treated our planet just as Hardin's herdsmen treated the village commons, with similar results, but on a much grander scale. That is why the world as we know it must change. We need to think and act as like business owners, not like herdsmen. We need to start managing this planet as if we owned it, because if we do not, we will suffer evil consequences. When I say we should think as business owners, I mean that we should become aware of the fact that we have accumulated a huge environmental overdraft and that the lender may be about to call in the debt. We should act quickly to reduce that overdraft, before we lose the entire business. The case for this position is strong.

The case for action

Allow me to sum up the reasons why we should reduce our impact on the Earth, without invoking global warming. First, as I said, the supply of minerals we need is limited. Even with something relatively common, like coal, at present rates of use it will not last long. According to the World Coal Institute, "At current production levels, proven coal reserves are estimated to last 133 years".[30] However, if the Chinese were to continue to build two new coal fired power stations every week, which is what China was doing in 2007, the consumption of coal will increase and those 133 years will become fewer.[31] The likelihood in years to come of the Chinese needing coal to fuel energy production is high. According to BP, in 2008 China accounted for half of the world's growth in energy requirements.[32] The global economic crisis will slow this down for a while, but by 2011-12, I expect China's economic growth to be back to 2007-08 levels.

With oil, things are less rosy, though there is also less clarity about how much oil is left that can be exploited commercially. There are three recognized types of oil

30 From http://www.worldcoal.org/pages/content/index.asp?PageID=188, retrieved on 11 March 2009.
31 From BBC News, at http://news.bbc.co.uk/2/hi/asia-pacific/6769743.stm, retrieved on 11 March 2009.
32 From the Statistical Review of World Energy 2008, retrieved from http://www.bp.com/sectiongenericarticle.do?categoryId=9023769&contentId=7044915 on 11 March 2009.

reserve, starting with proven reserves, which BP defines as "the estimated quantities of oil which geological and engineering data demonstrate with reasonable certainty to be recoverable in future years from known reservoirs under current economic and operating conditions." The second type is called estimated ultimately recoverable oil, from deposits that are not viable at present, for economic or technical reasons; here we also include oil that is yet to be found, like the oil that may be in the Canadian Arctic, for example. The last type includes oil made from coal, oil shale, oil sands, tar sands, bitumen, heavy and extra heavy oil, deep water oil, polar oil and natural gas condensates. This type is labeled non-conventional. Most of the world's oil is controlled by countries that are members of the Organization of the Petroleum Exporting Countries (OPEC). Data from OPEC about reserves and production are not considered to be reliable. With all these caveats, BP's best estimate (in 2007) is that the world has enough oil for forty years, at present rates of consumption.[33] Forty years is not a long time.

Then, leaving aside global warming and climate change, we must consider that burning oil and coal to produce energy produces very unpleasant pollution, as we saw at the Beijing Olympics in 2008. According to a US organization, Physicians for Social Responsibility, particulate matter released through smokestacks of coal-fired power stations causes 24,000 premature deaths in the USA alone, as well as over three million days of lost production through ill health. Burning coal to produce power also releases large quantities of mercury, placing hundreds of thousands of children at risk of neurological impairment. [34] According to the Australian Government, research has "linked exposure to particle pollution to (several) health problems including respiratory illnesses (such as asthma and bronchitis) and cardiovascular disease. In addition, the chemical components of some particles, particularly combustion products, have been shown to cause cancer. These effects are often more pronounced for vulnerable groups, such as the very young and the elderly. Particle pollution is the major cause of reduced visibility. This can be a serious safety issue on roads and in traffic tunnels and can also affect our enjoyment of the natural landscape."[35]

Next, high impact agriculture, using fertilizers made from non-renewable resources (mostly from oil, which may I remind you, will not last forever), as well as non-organic pesticides and herbicides, is reducing the capacity of arable land to produce food. When combined with over-use and with the impact of periodic droughts, a study in 2000 found that nearly forty percent of the world's agricultural land was seriously degraded, with a significant negative impact on the productivity of about sixteen

33 From http://www.finfacts.ie/irelandbusinessnews/publish/article_1010328.shtml, retrieved on 11 March 2009.

34 From http://www.psr.org/site/DocServer/Coal_Power_Fact_Sheet.pdf?docID=2821, retrieved on 11 March 2009.

35 Air quality fact sheet, Department of the Environment and Heritage 2005, from http://www.environment.gov.au/atmosphere/airquality/publications/particles.html, retrieved on 11 March 2009.

percent of the farmland.[36] Let us record here that there are reliable forecasts that world population will grow to ten billion people in 2040, "requiring food production at least to triple, as a combined result of population growth and dietary changes". That same study suggests that by focusing on producing maximum yields, ten billion people can be fed well. [37] Of course, yield-intensive agriculture requires large quantities of fertilizer and water, both of which will be increasingly hard to get. Hints of what is to come can be seen in India. While India is getting richer every year in economic terms, the food supply has declined from 177 kilograms per person per year in 1991 to 152 kilograms per person per year in 2008. "Economic growth has gone hand in hand with growth in hunger. One million children in India die every year for lack of food."[38]

To balance this, China has not had the same problems. Economic growth, to date, has been accompanied by food security, for the vast majority of Chinese, though at least a portion of that security has been bought from abroad, since China became a net food importer in 2004.[39] China's main problem in agriculture is going to be the lack of water. China does not have enough water to supply all the demand, by cities, by industry, by mining and by farming. The present drought has highlighted this. According to Dr Zhang Quanyi, associate professor of political science at Zhejiang Wanli University, "although China may suffer poor harvests this summer, the people will not go hungry, nor will China make heavy demands on the world's grain supplies. For the time being the country's food security is assured and all such fears may be put to rest."[40] For the time being, but in the future? According to the US Department of Commerce, China has only one-quarter of the global average of water per capita and the forecast population growth to 1.6 billion in the mid-twenty-first century will decrease the per capita availability to 1,760 cubic meters, from 2,200 cubic meters, presaging serious water shortages. What is worse, according to the same report, most water sources in China are seriously polluted.[41]

Then, there is the issue of perceptions. Perceptions are powerful enough to plunge the world into recession all on their own. If people believe that climate change is occurring, they will modify their behavior accordingly. If most people believe that climate change is occurring and that it may have the impact suggested by Lovelock and others, the changes in behavior that are likely to follow spell disaster for the economy, locally and globally. People will react emotionally to oppose anything they see as adding

36 From BBC News, at http://news.bbc.co.uk/2/hi/science/nature/758899.stm, retrieved on 11 March 2009.

37 "Food supply capacity study at global scale", Nutrient Cycling in Agroecosystems, Volume 50, Numbers 1-3, March 1998 , pp. 181-189(9).

38 "The food emergency and food myths. Why Bush is wrong to blame Indians for the rise in food prices", Vandana Shiva, from http://www.grain.org/seedling/?id=552, retrieved on 11 March 2009.

39 From http://www.reuters.com/article/environmentNews/idUSPEK25204120070823, retrieved on 11 March 2009.

40 From http://www.upiasia.com/Society_Culture/2009/02/12/chinas_food_supply_secure_despite_drought/5840/, retrieved on 11 March 2009.

41 Water Supply and Wastewater Treatment Market in China, January 2005, from http://www.icwt.net/China%20Water.pdf, retrieved on 11 March 2009.

fuel to the fire, returning to the bushfire metaphor for the moment. Opportunists will exploit this tendency. We have already seen this develop. You have heard of ethanol, I presume. Ethanol is a type of alcohol, made from vegetable matter through a process of distillation. It can be used as a fuel for internal combustion engines, generally mixed with gasoline, rather than on its own. Because ethanol is made from vegetable matter, it is a renewable fuel, unlike gasoline. Because of this, in countries such as the USA and Australia ethanol has been promoted as a green fuel and drivers have been urged to fill their tanks with a blend of gasoline and ethanol, usually with ten to fifteen percent of each gallon or liter in the form of ethanol.

Sounds good, does it not, as we are replacing ten to fifteen percent of a fossil fuel—a bad fuel, because it comes from non-renewable sources—with a renewable fuel. It sounds good, but it is not. Most of the world's ethanol is made from corn or sugarcane, both of which are foods eaten by humans and the first of which is a staple for millions around the world. This means that when we put ethanol in our cars, we are burning food, food that is going to become increasingly precious as the world's population grows. Also, using corn to produce ethanol is pushing up the price of corn, often beyond the reach of consumers in the developing world that need it for their table, rather than as fuel for their vehicles. There is more and it is worse. Producing ethanol is highly energy intensive, especially when it is made from corn grown through energy intensive agriculture in the USA. If you are using ethanol made from US corn almost as much energy is used to produce it as is saved through its use. And, by the way, ethanol is less efficient than gasoline, which means that if you are buying it because an ethanol blend is cheaper than straight gasoline you will probably end up spending just as much on fuel anyway.

The way I see it, ethanol is more of a hidden way to subsidize farmers in the USA and to make governments look like they are doing something about climate change, than it is a real alternative to gasoline. Oh, and don't get me started on cars that rely on electric batteries for propulsion, such as the *Prius*. A *Boeing 737* is more fuel efficient than a *Prius*[42] *and some gasoline fuelled cars have a smaller ecological footprint than a Prius*, especially when the impact of making and replacing batteries is factored into the equation. Without accounting for the batteries, the *smartfortwo* is better than a *Prius* in terms of greenhouse gas production and a *Fiat 500* is rated about the same as a *Prius*. Two models of the *Fiat 500* are more efficient users of fuel than the *Prius*.[43] If you want to drive a green car, there are better choices than the *Prius*. Better still, take a train, bus or airplane, in that order.

For very sensible, pragmatic reasons, legitimate and reasonable efforts to reduce humanity's impact on the planet's ecology should be supported. I do not recommend

42 See "More Fuel Efficient: Prius or Airplane?", retrieved from http://ddimick.typepad.com/dennis_dimicks_blog/2009/02/more-fuel-efficient-prius-or-airplane.html, on 16 March 2009.

43 See the Green Vehicle Guide provided by the Australian Government at ***http://www.greenvehicleguide.gov.au*** .

this position because I think global warming caused by humans will destroy the Earth. To believe that we can destroy or even damage the planet terminally is hubris on a grand scale, matched only by the hubris of those who deny the damage we have actually done. The planet and its deep ecological cycles will live on for a few billion years more than the several billion it has already enjoyed, whatever we do or do not do. However, we may well destroy ourselves or at least our present civilization, if we do not take steps now to reduce our demand on the planet's resources and to lessen the chances of a climate shock. The last reason is perhaps the most important. If our political and scientific creativity and billions of dollars are thrown at the climate change problem, we will have missed a grand opportunity to transform our relationship with our home planet. In my opinion, and I will explain why, we must do more than alternate between the role of wanton destroyers of ecological value and firefighters, striving to turn down global temperatures. The present crisis has made it obvious that the role of humanity now and for the future is to be the stewards of the planet. There is no one else who will do it for us, I am afraid, and we are capable of doing it well.

Long ago, our ancestors discovered that to extract the optimum value from the earth they had to cultivate the soil, they had to manage their environment, to establish conditions that would enable sustainable harvest and hunting and gathering. They did not do perfectly, as some would have us believe and sometimes they did it badly indeed, as we have seen with Easter Island, for example. But they tried and often they succeeded, sometimes for tens of thousands of years, as is the case with Australia's aboriginal people. Unfortunately, as a species, we have not yet come to the realization that we need to manage our global environment. Using terminology with which you will be familiar, what we must do is to change our business model.

We are still living on and using the Earth as if we were hunter-gatherers, taking what we need and what we want from the planet, its flora and its fauna, with little heed for the consequences, as if we could move on elsewhere when this particular patch of the universe is worn out. Unlike our hunter-gatherer ancestors, we can't do that, we cannot trade in exhausted pasture for new, untouched land, we cannot trade in an exhausted planet for another. We may be able to do that at some future time, if our technological evolution continues, but, as the Easter Islanders found out a few centuries ago, if we squander the raw materials we have, we will not be able to build new vessels to take us somewhere else in the solar system. We will be stuck where we are, in a great global mess.

> *So now we have to manage the transition, and we have about half a century to complete the job. Most of the changeover has got to come in the next twenty years, and we need to have completely decarbonized our economies by 2050...That won't be easy, but it is the sort of task at which industrial societies excel.*—Gwynne Dyer

This argument holds true regardless of the impact from climate change and regardless of the causes of climate change. However big the Earth may seem to any of us as individuals, our projected global population of eight or nine billion by mid century will destroy the planet's ecology and us along with it by the end of the century, if we do not reduce our use of natural resources—even if only half of those billions live western lifestyles. Climate change, if orthodoxy is followed, would make that day of reckoning come sooner or would it?

My response is grounded in practicality. If the Earth were a business faced with rising costs, shrinking supplies of raw materials, and a deteriorating business environment, what would we do? Would we accept our fate and sit and wait for events to unfold as they please? Would we resort to prayer or devote ourselves to organizing protest marches? Would we expect the government to save us? Or would we do what we can to reduce our costs, find alternative supplies or raw materials or even redesign the business to be something entirely new? Would we take steps to create the future we want or would we let the future tell us what we can have? I say that there is time for us to do what needs to be done and we should get on and do it.

What can we do? What should we do?

Figure 7 illustrates a possible cascade of change resulting from global warming. It is not comprehensive and it does not show the inevitable feedback loops that would guarantee us an unpredictable whirlpool of change, rather than a more predictable cascade. However, despite its limitations, the cascade shows us how far ranging the implications of global warming could be. Of course, a similar cascade (and the accompanying whirlpool) could be constructed for global cooling also. Actually, even without global warming or cooling, we are about to enter a more unstable period in our history anyway, because the era of cheap energy is coming to an end. I am writing this book in the twenty-first century, when we are entering an era of more expensive energy and those who want to profit from that should position themselves accordingly.

If I had been writing this book in the early part of the twentieth century, I might have said that we were heading into an era of cheap and easily accessible energy and that those who wanted to profit from such an era should position themselves to benefit from that. The classic example has to be that of car makers, especially in the USA. For much of the twentieth century, what was good for General Motors (and Ford and Chrysler) was good for the USA, even for the world. Detroit was the epitome of the industrial revolution at its peak, making millions of gas guzzlers to satisfy a seemingly insatiable demand for more power, bigger vehicles and it was all cheap. The cars were cheap, the fuel was even cheaper, cheaper than milk in fact, and most of the oil powering America's cars was American or came from compliant dictatorships in the Middle East. That is not the case now. We have seen that oil will inevitably become more expensive, because of falling supplies and rising global demand.

Figure 7: Change cascade resulting from global warming

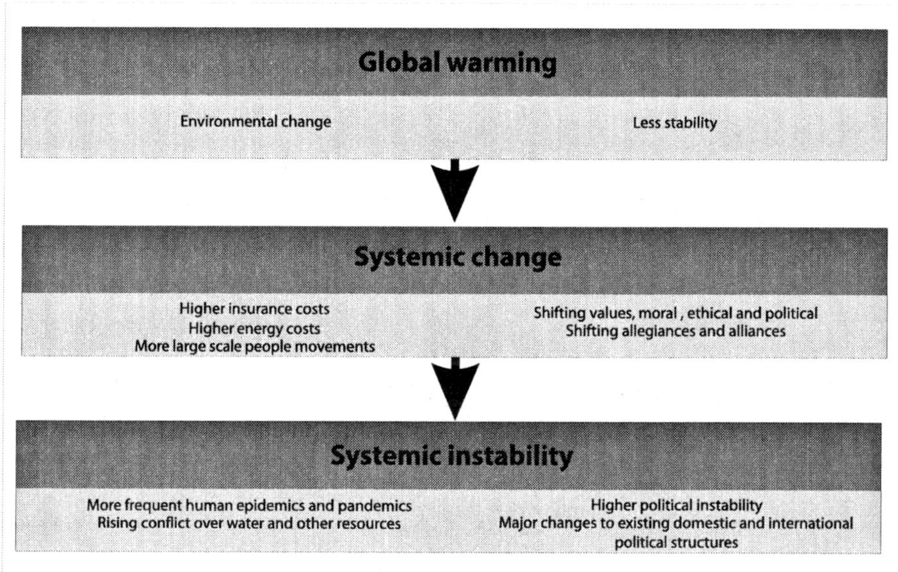

As Thomas Friedman points out, what makes things worse is that much of the oil Americans now buy for their cars comes from what countries that are not America's friends and that are often guilty of supporting, nurturing and funding America's enemies. According to Friedman, "through our energy purchases we are funding both sides of the war on terror…We are financing the US Army, Navy, Air Force, and Marine Corps with our tax dollars, and we are indirectly financing, with our energy purchases, al Qaeda, Hamas, Hezbollah, and Islamic Jihad."[44] Friedman puts a persuasive case, arguing that the USA should lead a green revolution to rid itself of what he calls a dangerous addiction to oil, if nothing else. Gwynne Dyer does the same in his book, with the somewhat scary title of *Climate Wars*. Friedman's approach is more positive, arguing that greening the USA and the US economy would enable the USA to continue

44 At page 80 of *Hot, Flat and Crowded*.

to lead the world, while benefiting the world at the same time. Dyer tries to scare the reader into action, by presenting appalling, but realistic possible futures, including scenarios of global or continental war over water, energy and food.

The advice that follows is tailored to meet the needs of a specific sector of the economy, the financial services sector. Most of what I am about to say is relevant to other sectors, to other people, but not everything. I have broken the advice into three segments, focusing on how to reduce our and our businesses' impact on the environment; on make money from the green wave; and on how to avoid green the green swamp, a place full of unpleasant consequences likely to flow from climate change and from expectations and fears most people have about what climate change will do to our economy and our society in the next few decades. Let's start with the really positive stuff, how to reduce and preferably eliminate what I call our collective resources overdraft.

Eliminating the resources overdraft

You know what an overdraft is. When, with prior permission, you withdraw more money from your bank account than the account actually holds, you have an overdraft. An overdraft is a flexible form of lending most often used in business, especially small or medium size businesses, to even out cash flow. Like any other loans, interest is charged as are penalties if repayments are late or are not made at all. In a business context, an overdraft is a good thing for all parties, provided the overdrawn amount is eventually repaid, in part or entirely, to be drawn down again when needed. How is this relevant to our present concern? Picture the Earth as a resources bank, from which we draw to eat, drink, make rockets and bombs, surf the net and a billion other things. We withdraw from many resources accounts, with water, air, minerals and climate stability being just a few. However, unlike a bank, the Earth cannot replenish the accounts from which we draw. When an account is emptied out by any given generation living on the planet, then future generations miss out entirely.

This is what we have been doing. We have been using up the Earth's resources accounts so quickly and in such quantities that future generations will have little left to spend—and when I say future generations, it could be your grandchildren we are talking about, not the people of centuries to come,. This is why we should start to reduce, if not eliminate our resources overdraft. There are other reasons too. First, what I am about to suggest will reduce your operating costs, if done well. Second, doing the right thing for the environment is likely to increase your attractiveness as an employer, as you will see. Third, sorting out that aspect of your balance sheet—because that is what I am talking about—may well increase the price of your stock or of your business and may help protect your stock valuation from future shocks.

I will start with information and communication technology, which is now an integral part of any business, especially in the financial services industry. This is an area of activity that is energy-intensive, offering great potential for resource overdraft reduction. If you have not noticed, the volume of electronic information received, processed and stored by organizations has been rising dramatically, with consequent increases in costs and energy use. This is because, paradoxically, the cost of computing has been falling, just as dramatically. In 1965, Gordon Moore, co-founder of Intel, suggested that because of the physical nature of computer chip technology, the cost of a given amount of computing power would fall by half every eighteen months, with a consequent doubling of computing power then becoming available at any given price. So far, things have developed much as Moore suggested they would. So, the processing power of desktop computers, laptops, mobile phones and so on has been rising geometrically. Some of this efficiency gain has been used by manufacturers to reduce the price of hardware, though it is more often the case that the price stays the same, but you get more capacity and more features for the same number of dollars. Car makers are doing something similar now, as they try to survive the slump in car sales due to the global economic crisis.

The enormous rise in computing power and the consequent fall in unit costs for storage and processing, has mean that people in organizations have stepped up their use of computing and their desire to have more and more data stored, just in case it might be needed one day. Legislation such as SOX in the USA has made it almost inevitable that businesses would store digitally large numbers of documents, web pages, emails, and audio, video and still images. Recent forecasts (2007) have indicated that enterprises can expect continued increases storage requirements and raw data set sizes "in the range of 30 to 50 percent per year for the next few years".[45] Even in these difficult times, as expenditure on other technology is predicted to fall, expenditure on data storage is predicted to rise, albeit marginally. A recent survey in the USA and the UK shows that the budget allocated to data storage technology is expected to increase by .05% in 2009, whereas expenditure on other hardware is expected to decline by two to three percent.[46] What does all this mean in green terms, both dollars and energy, that is?

According to Gartner (2007), half of the data centers in existence in 2007 would not have enough power and cooling capacity to operate their storage equipment by 2008, while energy costs were likely to emerge as the second highest operating cost in seventy percent of data centers across the world in 2009.[47] As we all now know, energy is going to become more expensive, in years to come, thanks to initiatives to control

45 From Tekrati, at http://computers.tekrati.com/research/8534/, retrieved on 10 March 2009.

46 From Computerworld, 6 March 2009, at http://www.computerworld.com.au/article/279057/survey_data_storage_see_increased_spending_09, retrieved on 10 March 2009.

47 From http://searchstorage.techtarget.com.au/contents/22017-Being-aware-of-energy-consumption-is-critical-to-storage-growth-and-cost-containment, retrieved on 10 March 2009.

climate change, there will be new regulations introduced by governments across the world to reduce energy use, partly for political reasons, of course. And corporate budgets for ICT are not going to be as generous as they have been, as a new era of frugality hits the world of business (and of government). Moreover, companies that do not do their best to reduce their ecological footprint will be increasingly punished by consumers and financial markets alike. As the number of servers continues to grow and demand for storage capacity increases, companies are faced with the challenge of powering and cooling these systems while controlling their energy consumption and complying with environmental regulations. This may be why conserving energy, reducing floor space and managing costs are becoming major priorities for chief information officers in Wall Street, Main Street and Pennsylvania Avenue.

A prominent research company, the Aberdeen Group, has surveyed more than 175 organizations. The evidence from that survey is that the best performing ICT organizations have lower operating costs, improved application and data availability and a better corporate image if they have implementing a green initiative.[48] The results of this survey may not be universally applicable, however. A similar survey in Australia conducted in May 2008 by Macquarie Telecom, found that seventy-three percent of companies" had not presented a business case that incorporated any green IT factors, but 53 percent planned to do so in the next year. Of those businesses with plans to 'green,' the greatest hurdles were: a lack of understanding and an absence of independent data on which IT vendors and technologies have what impact on energy consumption."[49]

Let us cut to the chase. Here are recommended areas for action, chosen because they will benefit the planet, your employees, your customers and your business—and not necessarily in that order. Not all of these will be relevant to you directly, depending on the nature, size and character of your business. For example, you may not own or operate any data centers. However, I am sure I can say that your business will be relying on data center facilities, if not yours, then someone else's. If the former, while I am not a great fan of Microsoft in some areas, I must say that their published approach to data center efficiency is sound. This is how Microsoft describes its approach to designing a data center. They ask us "to look at the building as if it were a big computer that must run 24 hours a day, seven days a week. Computers work best when they are tailored to the specific needs of their users. The same principle applies to data center design; the most resource-efficient designs meet the requirements of the data center's users and specific site conditions. Microsoft continually evaluates many different technologies for power distribution, cooling systems, and server rack/container systems. To optimize the data center environment, Microsoft uses tools like Computational Fluid

48 From http://www.ecommercetimes.com/story/61966.html, retrieved on 10 March 2009.

49 From http://www.macquarietelecom.com/media_room/releases/121008-data_center_greening_case_study.htm, retrieved on 10 March 2009.

Dynamics to test different configurations."[50] So, let us start by focusing on the building (or buildings):

- Review your data center arrangements against best practice standards—you can use standards like BREEAM (BRE Environmental Assessment Method), which is a widely used environmental assessment method for buildings. It sets the standard for best practice in sustainable development and demonstrates a level of achievement. It has become the vocabulary used to describe a building's environmental performance. The BREEAM website is *http://www.breeam.org/*.
- Evaluate energy efficiency—there is quick ROI potential here and there are many ways to do it—and here is an example, provided by 42U, a vendor-independent and technology agnostic company, see *http://www.42u.com/power/data-center-power.htm*. The recommended actions may include the following,
    - redesign the cooling system,
    - reconsider redundancy requirements, focusing on business critical need, rather than business unit wants,
    - deploy scalable and modular systems, a scalable system will let you operate at minimum power requirements and give you the capacity to grow into higher power consumption when you're ready, a bit like some cars nowadays, which can adjust up or down the number of cylinders in use, depending on circumstances.
- Virtualize storage, most servers are grossly underused, perhaps as little as a few percent capacity of any one server is ever required, virtualization will reduce hardware, energy, security and management costs.
- Consider alternative power sources, does your data center have a large roof space that could be used for solar cells or can the heat generated by the center be recycled to run the center...there are many possibilities—I am aware of at least one data center that channels its excess heat into greenhouses, where tomatoes are grown—there is money to be made from the produce and carbon credits are also generated.
- Consider energy use in the office, there are quick returns to be made by cutting down on the number of personal computers, laptops and printers, replacing older equipment with more efficient appliances, and introducing forced power downs at the end of the day and on weekends and other times when the office is closed.
- Consider the potential of cloud computing to reduce the power demands of desktop computing. Companies such as Amazon are already harvesting

50 From http://www.microsoft.com/environment/our_commitment/articles/datacenter_bp.aspx, retrieved on 11 April 2009.

green and financial benefits from cloud computing. In a recent blog, Ken Oestreich asked this question: "How is Amazon Web Services able to charge $0.10/CPU-Hour, (equating to ~$870 per year) when the average IT department or hosting provider has a loaded server cost of somewhere between $2,000-$4,000 per year? What does Amazon know that the rest of the industry doesn't?"[51] Amazon uses a utility computing (or cloud) model. Companies such as Microsoft, Yahoo, Amazon, Google, and IBM have built significant cloud-computing infrastructure and can service large numbers of users. If you have the capabilities in your organization, like Amazon, you can even consider creating your own cloud.

- Change your work practices, for example, consider introducing or expanding teleworking options for your staff.
- Start to measure the more subtle impacts, positive and negative, that your business has on the social and physical environment. This will give you the opportunity to enhance brand value or to remove negative perceptions of your brand—note what has been happening with Google and its alleged hunger for energy—and will also uncover opportunities to cut costs or to create new products and services. The material in appendix 1 will be useful to you here. A note of caution: under promise and over deliver. Expectation management is essential and you may need appendix 2.

Creating green profits

I suggested earlier that sorting out your resources overdraft would be good for your balance sheet. Allow me to explain why and how. If I am right in suggesting that profits come more from the intangible aspects of your balance sheet than from the tangibles, investments in reducing environmental costs must be good for your balance sheet directly and indirectly. Directly because of the impact on costs and indirectly because of higher staff retention rates, higher productivity, greater brand value, better informed investment decisions and greater product and service innovation rates. For example, on that last point, where investments are made in activities that lead to the production of carbon credits, a bank may opt to charge a lower interest rate in return for a share of those credits, either to offset pollution generated by the bank as a business or to use for trading purposes. This approach could be extended to individual account holders with the bank, many of whom will be generating carbon credits through domestic solar power generation or other means. The bank could pool small amounts of credits form individual accounts to create a substantial, marketable quantum of credits, profits from which could then be shared among all contributors.

Engage with your stakeholders, including customers, working together to find

51 From http://fountnhead.blogspot.com/2008/09/inherent-efficiencies-of-cloud.html, retrieved on 11 April 2009.

opportunities to reduce the environmental impact of doing business. Map the whole value chain and identify weak spots. An obvious area for attention is the use of paper, necessitated by the requirement to print account statements and so on. Many banks already offer customers the option to view their statements online and, sometimes, they also offer the option of downloading data to an accounting package on the customer's own personal computer. This is fine, but often customers print those statements anyway, for ease of reference and because people still do not trust their computers, because downloading data can be cumbersome and because not everyone has an accounting package on their personal computer.

This means that the bank has transferred a cost to the customer, but may do little to reduce the overall consumption of paper. Here is an alternative that would achieve that objective. Using the web browser as an entry point, offer your customers a safe place within your ICT environment where they can store, view and analyze their own data, related to accounts they hold with you or to (selected) other accounts. Instead of giving them statements, offer them the opportunity to see their account data within a budget format, tailored for broad home use or for small businesses, with a secondary option to see the same data in a traditional statement format. You could offer a basic service for no charge and a broader range of services, such as word processing or additional data storage, for example, for a modest charge. Allow people to store their photographs on your site, as well as digitized versions of important documents—install a scanner in bank premises to allow people to scan and upload documents.

If your organization does not have the capabilities to do all this, partner with Google or Yahoo, for example, to enable you to do it. The service could be paid for by allowing your partner to run ads on content pages viewed by your customers, ads tailored to the specific circumstances of customers. To maximize take up, offer customers training packages they can run on their personal computer at home and a dedicated helpline. Again, this could be outsourced or you could train some of your customers, retired seniors, for example, on how to provide this service to others. I am offering this as an example. I am sure that by bringing your staff and your customers together many and better ways would be identified to reduce our reliance on paper and ink.

Avoiding the green swamp

As much as the coming decades will provide opportunities, they will also provide us with many challenges. The climate of the Earth we have experienced during our time is not normal, if seen from the perspective of geological time. Our primitive ancestors, before the Holocene, experienced glaciations and inter-glacial periods alike, but no human record has been left to tell us what it was like. Our history is contained entirely within a bubble of relative climate stability, which may be about to end, with or without our contribution. The stage is set for a perfect storm or a great fire and all that is needed is something that will ignite the fire. As with the Great Recession or the Great Depression itself, almost anything would have served as the trigger, once the conditions were right.

Because of the conditions of the climate at present, almost anything could act as the trigger for a slide into instability, and the rise in greenhouse gases due to our obsession with burning fossil fuels might just be it. We live in abnormal times, whether we know it or not, and in abnormal times it is easy to trigger a catastrophe. It took a shot in Sarajevo to start World War 1 and a few tanks rolling into Poland to start World War 2, for example. It did not take much to set off the Great Depression, as we have seen. This is how a novelist, through a letter written by a character in a book set in the midst of the Great Depression, describes what happened to the US banking system in those years.[52]

> *Speaking of the mill in Waterboro, the workers there started a run on the bank in town. There was a story going around that there was a shortage in the bank's funds, and so everyone went to the bank to get their money out. They had to call the police force to keep everyone in line. The newspaper said the bank was $1000 short, but Muriel, who used to work there, says the shortage was much bigger. The newspaper also said there was no danger that the bank would go out of business, but no one believes that either. Truthfully, it all comes down to a matter of belief, doesn't it? If you think the bank is sound, you won't panic, and then the bank will be sound.*

Please read the last two sentences again, because those few words say it all. For the banking system to work, people's belief and trust in the system are essential ingredients. For the system to fail, you need an explosive mixture of fear and ignorance, with the trigger provided by a relatively harmless rumor—even in 1930, $1,000 was not a lot of money, certainly not enough to break a bank. But the bank was broken nonetheless, as people forgot the collective good and scrambled to protect their personal property. The Great Depression was the result of a pandemic of such incidents, as illustrated by Franklin D. Roosevelt's famous contemporary quote, "We have nothing to fear but fear itself".

It may seem strange that fear in the hearts of men and women can bring down an economy, but in abnormal times, complex systems can be disrupted by very small perturbations. This is worth watching, because we humans have a tendency to generalize our fears, which means that having developed a fear about X, we sometimes become fearful of y as well or, in the worst cases, we become fearful of everything. In individuals, this is known as generalized anxiety. Well, societies can also suffer from generalized anxiety. This means that if people become fearful of the impacts of climate change, there is a risk that they may become fearful about their

52 The quote is from page 131 of *Sea Glass*, by Anita Shreve. If you want to know what the Great Depression felt like, this would be a good place to start.

futures and their children's futures and this is not good for the financial system or for the economy.

People who are fearful about the future tend not to invest in the future and become more risk averse. They also tend to be more susceptible to the lures of demagogues, political and financial, who promise certainty and safety in exchange for loyalty and money. If the financial services industry wants to continue to prosper, its interest will be best served by engaging with governments and with the community to combat fear and to stifle any incipient demagoguery. This will have to extend beyond the confines of the industry itself, reaching out into other areas of public concern, such as the environment. Think of it as an anti-fear vaccination campaign, a campaign that will fortify our collective spirit, enabling us to sharpen our appetite for risk, individually and collectively. Rapid innovation and growth can occur only when the appetite for risk among the public is strong. When that appetite wanes, as it did in the 1930s, innovation and growth are stifled. Only a superordinate need, the need to survive, broke that spell and World War 2 gave us that. What would you prefer, a careful investment in building public confidence and public involvement or another global war?

Assuming that you are opting for the former, at the enterprise level it would be advisable to present to the public a corporate image that is founded on solid values, of predictability, reliability, concern for the public good, and engagement with the future, as well as the present, leavened by a component of innovation and creativity. Why do I say this? Modern corporations look and behave like feudal domains, run by a select few to look after the interests of a select few, with CEOs often behaving as if they had a *droit de seigneur* that allows them to pillage company property and company revenues for their benefit. Fairly or unfairly, large transnational corporations are often not seen by people as part of the political and social milieu in which they operate. In many cases, the corporations like it that way, believing themselves to be above and beyond the reach of national interests and national governments and assuming that this will enable them to make faster and greater profits. To make things worse, often the people these corporations use to deal with governments are both arrogant and ignorant of cultural subtleties.

I have represented the Australian Government in its dealings with corporations such as these and I know whereof I speak. Without naming names, I shall mention the case of a north-American company that was most surprised when informed by my staff that the Australian Government would not sign contracts that would require a minister of the Crown to submit to foreign courts in case of any dispute. Their response was, "but no one has complained before". It took a few weeks and a lot of patience on our part, but eventually they understood that in Australia, we prefer to use Australian law. Of course, such arrogance and ignorance as this company displayed vis-à-vis a national government is usually multiplied a hundred-fold when dealing with individuals or with small and medium enterprises. And large domestic companies do it too, when their size and the lack of competition allow them to get away with it.

The impression experiences such as this creates in the collective public mind is one of intentional alienation—these corporations are not part of us, they do now want to be one of us, they are here only to exploit us. Alienation creates fear and loathing, which sometimes manifests itself even in boycotts, vandalism and violence against foreign corporations or their symbols, as we saw at Davos earlier this year, for example, of whenever big business and big governments get together, in G8 or G20 meetings. This is not merely unpleasant for those who get caught up in protests or riots; it is bad for business and, as I have just observed, it may be bad for all of us.

The damage can be undone by extending corporate reporting to cover social and environmental impacts, by democratizing company processes, by adopting a more sophisticated understanding of cultural and social differences across the world, and by engaging openly and freely with the markets and with the community. By the way, the evidence is that long-term survival and profitability are strongly associated with behaviors such as these, which means that altruism is neither essential nor required. The material in appendixes 1 and 2 can help you to implement reporting and stakeholder engagement that will translate into (sustainable) profits and greater product and service innovation. You may also want to consult chapters 4 and 5 of my earlier book, *Compliance and Regulation in the International Financial Services Industry*.

Insurance and the coming green bubble

In *The Ascent of Money*, Niall Ferguson provides a comprehensive analysis of the problem of managing risk through insurance, in chapter 4. He uses the example of New Orleans and the aftermath of Katrina, which left many thousands of householders unable to secure insurance, to make the point that insurance, in whatever form, is becoming too expensive for many. Having discussed hedging, as a new form of risk management that has exploded in size over the last two decades, he says, "The fact…remains that this financial revolution has…divided the world in two: those who are (or can be) hedged, and those who are not (or cannot be). You need money to be hedged…We lesser mortals still have to rely on the blunt and often expensive instrument of insurance policies…or hope for the welfare state to ride to the rescue."[53] The chief inference I draw from this is that the cost of managing (or hedging against) risk is on the way up, as insurance companies act to protect their pool of funds, excluding those who represent a poor risk. In turn, this means that we are likely to see more situations like New Orleans and more calls for governments around the world to "do something". These calls will increase in frequency and stridency, as global weirding creates a less predictable and therefore riskier environment for both insurers and the insured.

53 At page 228.

This is why I suggest you review your insurance requirements and arrangements, to reduce your need for insurance and to optimize value for money. The first question is, what segment(s) of your internal and external environment provide the greatest source of financial risk, remembering that the purpose of insurance is not to transfer risk, but to make good the damage that is likely to occur when a risk becomes reality. The second question is, is greater uncertainty likely to increase or diminish the likelihood of the risk translating into reality and/or of the consequences if that were to occur. Let us assume that you are in the business of financing motor vehicle purchases, for example. What is your risk exposure? The primary concern is default by borrowers. The secondary concern is tied to the size of the market and the consequent scale and profitability of your business.

Which is the greater risk, as we move into the second decade of the twenty-first century? It may surprise you, but I say the latter is. Here is why. I think that the risk of personal default, in the medium term (next ten years) is likely to fall. This is because it seems that the global economy is going to recover reasonably soon; because baby-boomers are the richest generation planet has ever seen, on average; because the Y generation has now learnt that there are rainy days and that saving for them is not such a bad idea; because governments around the world, assisted by financial institutions, are going to foster and encourage thrift; and because purchasers in emerging economies will be people who have had to work hard to get a car and will not want to lose it. Why is the risk greater on the market side of the equation? The rate of growth of motor vehicle sales in the developed economies has probably peaked and when fuel prices start going up again, as they will when the global economy cranks up again and when carbon taxes in various forms start to bite, the sale of traditional vehicles (using carbon-based fuels) in the developed world will fall.

This will be balanced in part by the growth in sales of vehicles using alternative means of propulsion or alternative fuels, but only in part. In the emerging economies, there will be growth in traditional vehicles, but they will be cheaper vehicles, like the *Tata Nano*, offering much smaller margins for profits for both manufacturers and financiers. In any case, even in countries like India and China, by the end of the second decade of this century sales of motor vehicles will be near peak. I say this relying on the experience of countries like Germany, Japan and Italy after World War 2 and noting that the rate of industrialization and economic growth in India and China may even outpace those so-called miracle economies. If I am right, the question for a provider of motor vehicle finance is whether to stay in the business at all or, in the alternative, how to re-structure business models to accommodate a moderate fall in units and a relatively faster fall in profit per unit.

I have run a similar train of thought through the business of real estate insurance and reached similar conclusions, because global weirding, rising sea levels and a possible rise in civil and other disturbances is going to push up the cost of insurance significantly. This is likely to increase the proportion of uninsured property, which reduces revenues and increases costs for those who remain in the insurance pool, creating a vicious cycle that leads to lower and lower take up of insurance. Knowing the world of politics, such a trend would push governments to consider alternative models of insurance, perhaps along the lines of New Zealand's national accident compensation scheme, which effectively nationalized a big chunk of the insurance market. For those who think this is unlikely in countries like the USA, I respond with the very recent examples of de facto bank nationalizations in that country (and elsewhere). When fundamental elements supporting social and economic stability are threatened, governments will do what they must, however reluctantly, to prevent collapse and also to prevent opposition politicians from capitalizing on the situation. Remember that self-interest is always in the race to win.

On the positive side, a thorough search for ways of cutting dependence on insurance can help the bottom line, if that search is done with the right objectives in mind. The right objective is to match the risk with a suitable treatment, thus reducing costs, and not the reverse. Also, those who can think up new ways of protecting people from risk will benefit in a world where risk and perceptions of risk are on the rise, increasing the need and want for insurance, in some form or other. The models of insurance we have now were developed several centuries ago, in the age of mercantilism and they have served us well. Capitalism as we know it would not be possible without insurance, because long distance trade would not have been possible if the intrinsic risks of putting goods on a sail-powered ship crossing an ocean had not been matched by the ability to insure against loss. What we learned then has served us well and sophisticated actuarial practices have enabled us to refine and to improve what, whom and how we insure—and for how much. However, that which has served us well for centuries may not be able to do so for much longer. The combined impact of technology, climate change, and new cultural and social practices is likely to require new ways of insuring against the risk of doing business, in particular. Those who can come up with new models, new products and new services that are in tune with the times will do well.

My suggestion is to develop service offerings that encompass both a compensatory premium, which is what insurance is about nowadays, and services that enable a business or an individual to reduce risk or exposure to risk. By way of illustration, this could be done by providing three types of insurance cover. The first and most expensive would be the traditional model. The insured buys an amount of coverage for damages and/or loss and pays an appropriate amount, determined by actuarial means. The least expensive cover would be provided through a specialized service offering that aims to define the existing risk exposure, to commit the insured to agreed steps, with measurable results, to reduce that exposure and to support a self-insurance fund, by way of a hedge fund of some sort. The cost to the insured would be for the services provided and would be offset, at least in part, by cost reductions resulting from risk reduction and from gains made through the hedge fund. This would be the cheapest option. The middle path would see a mix of the former and latter options, with the self-insurance element replaced by traditional insurance cover, but a lower level than for the first option, with a consequent lower cost. As I said, this is only to illustrate what might be possible. I am not an expert in insurance and I am sure that those who are can do much better than this. But I suggest you get started soon, because this is probably an occasion where first-mover does best.

The next tip is obvious, I think, which is to limit exposure to dirty industries. There are three reasons for this. First, the profits that can be derived from such industries are likely to fall, as governments around the world start to levy a cost for what is now considered to be an economic externality. Dirty industries have done well because they have not had to pay anything like the full cost, if anything, of the damage they do to the environment, to their workers or to the communities that host them. This de facto tax exemption will not last for much longer. When it goes, profits will fall and it will become harder and harder to find both finance and markets. Second, just as it is now unthinkable in developed countries to light a cigarette in the workplace or in a restaurant, within ten-fifteen years it will become unthinkable to use products that pollute. As with smoking, the initial steps towards new behaviors may be small and even seem slow and inadequate to some, but once the wagon starts rolling, it will pick up momentum and what seemed normal only yesterday will soon seem abnormal, unacceptable or even unthinkable. Third, the value pool is shifting from dirty to clean and the change will be quick. When the USA switched from clean to dirty, from electric cars to the internal combustion engine, the change was rapid. I suspect that the reversal from dirty to clean will be equally rapid. Remember the discussion of crowd behavior and of the fundamental human traits that underpin and shape the economy?

Humans are a herd animal, be they consumers, investors, advisers, or financiers or politicians—and what we do in our own small world is usually replicated in the larger world. As with the second point, once the wagon that is taking us from dirty to clean starts rolling, everyone will want to jump on it and start pedaling like mad. There will doubtlessly be a resulting "clean" bubble. Slowly to start with, but unhesitatingly and certainly, attention, power and money will shift to the clean end of the spectrum, whatever the industry, inflating a great big bubble, which might surpass any bubble we have seen so far. My suggestion here, unlike with insurance, is to take it easy and careful. Being first mover may not be a good thing unless you are right at the beginning and know exactly when to get out. And the evidence is that this is hard to do, if not impossible very few, if any, get out at the right time. But there will be opportunities for those who know where to look and there will be opportunities, as always, when the bubble bursts, as it will.

For the moment it looks like the process of globalization is still on track; it looks like the self-interest of the G20 governments (and others) aligned to ensure that the Great Recession did not result in the end of trade liberalization. It may even be the case that the pace of trade liberalization increases, as China and India start to be less dependent on exports to support growth and start to focus on domestic demand. This may seem paradoxical, but when domestic demand becomes the focus of governments, it is because the middle classes are becoming restless. The size of the middle class and its collective purchasing power have grown to the point where economic growth is now dependent on consumer demand and the demand for services starts to grow at a rate outstripping demand for products, with consequent shifts in employment type. At this point, governments become dependent on the middle class vote, rather than the rural vote, as is the case in India, or on the tacit support of industrial workers, as is the case in China. Then, the pressure on governments to allow access to an ever growing range of consumer goods starts to rise and the pressure to protect domestic rural or manufacturing jobs starts to decrease. China and India are likely to reach this point within the next decade, with Brazil and others to follow, which means that, all other things being equal, the general trend towards trade liberalization should accelerate.

Note that I am leaving Russia aside here, because it is a peculiar case. It is peculiar because its economy is still highly dependent on energy production, because its middle class remains weak, for historical reasons tied to seventy years of dictatorship, and because it is neither a democracy like India nor a Confucian state, like China, held together by a compact between the ruler and the ruled that has lasted for millennia, with recurrent interruptions. Russia is held together by naked power, held by a few, and the seemingly infinite capacity of its people to tolerate rule by a few for the benefit of the few. These are traditions that date back to the beginning of the second millennium, when Kiev was the heart of Russia, that continued through the era of the royal czars and the communist czars and which Putin is continuing. Abridging Winston Churchill's famous quote, I would say that Russia remains an enigma, a joker in the pack. My suggestion is, do business somewhere else, because the risk of doing business in Russia is as high as it has ever been; you will get better odds and a fairer turn at the roulette table.

Two more for the road

In chapter 3 I discussed the opportunities and threats arising from changes in how we work and how we relate to each other, driven by the adoption of existing and emerging information and communication technologies. This process of change will occur symbiotically with the changes driven by the growing desire for clean and green. The industrial revolution did not merely transform the nature of work, turning peasants into factory workers. It also changed rural dwellers into citizens and transformed the landscape of entire nations. Before the industrial revolution, England was a land of villages and farms, with few roads and few cities of any consequence. Power was vested in the rural aristocracy and especially in absentee landlords, who perpetuated a form of feudal rule well into the eighteenth century. The power of the political class and of the middle classes was limited. Most people worked on farms and few were employed for pay, which meant that the economy was still fundamentally reliant on barter. Few were educated beyond the basic skills of reading and writing and the church, in its various manifestations, remained a powerful political force. England's empire was primarily made up of its earliest conquests, Scotland, Ireland and Wales.

With the industrial revolution, England, and in parallel Great Britain as a whole, became a country of cities, with a workforce increasingly locked up in poorly ventilated and unsafe factories, and with power moving to the middle classes, which controlled trade and finance, in alliance with a few of the aristocratic families that had managed to transition from a barter economy to an economy that relied on money, trade and profit. More and more of the urban middle classes were educated, the country was united by canals, roads and railroads, and a fledging modern state started to emerge, albeit still defined by the trappings of the past, inherited from the landed aristocracy, such as the monarchy and the House of Lords, and peculiar titles for its political office holders, such as the Chancellor of the Exchequer, for example. Britain's empire, supported by the industrial and bureaucratic machine build to run the domestic empire, now straddled the world. This is why I say that the industrial revolution changed how and where we lived and worked and learned and related to each other and what started in England, soon spread to what we know as the West (and at least to some of its colonies, such as Australia). Technology and our growing desire to be clean and green will have similar impact, but on a global scale. This means that there will be grand opportunities for those who engage with governments, businesses and communities to develop new cities that accommodate new ways of working and interacting.

For example, soon it will be as unusual to see a city without ubiquitous free wireless internet as it is now to see a city without electricity or paved roads. Everyone is talking about optic fiber as the endgame for connectivity, but I think they are wrong. History and my experience tell me that people will want cheap, ubiquitous portable connectivity and that they will trade off a little privacy and security to achieve that.[54] Wireless internet will kill the wired internet, just as cell phones killed fixed phones in the home and wireless radio killed cable radio. Within a decade or a little more, depending on where you are, fiber or cable internet will be relegated to specialized uses, within offices, apartment buildings and where a high level of security is required. My argument is simple. Human intellectual productivity results from four factors.

54 In the recent past, I was responsible for advising the Australian Government on the adoption of new communication technologies, at the then National Office for the Information Economy. My predictive record made me unpopular with some colleagues, but earned me respect in the industry. To sample my thinking, you may want to read "Making Connections", *InformationWeek*, November 2003 (see w**ww.itnews.com.a**u or email me and I will send you a copy).

First, intelligence—the level of grunt, the number of neurons. Second, cycle time—speed of thought, turning thought into action and learning from the reaction. Third, individual spirit—personality, the "animal spirits" that inhabit all of us. And fourth, the environment—how the world reacts to you and what you do (or fail to do).The first three factors compound each other, in a positive sense, while the last can undo the lot. This is also true for a national economy, and in the knowledge era, these are the things that make a nation or an enterprise or a city competitive:

- the quantum (and quality) of thinking infrastructure;
- cycle time, how often do ideas come up? How rapidly are ideas turned into action, dreams into products and services that customers will buy? How quickly does the system learn?
- culture, openness to risk, flexibility, acceptance of diversity, future orientation;
- the environment, how plugged in are we? How accepting is the world of our ideas, of our products and services? Are we players or spectators?
- trust, creating value from social capital.

A fundamental requirement for all these things is connectivity, which, in an online world, increasingly means online connectivity. This is as much the case for government activity as it is for the economy more broadly, and applies both within and between business enterprises that inhabit a shared value chain. An investment in ubiquitous, cheap, fast, reliable and appropriately secure connectivity, with the elements listed above, will lift productivity, innovation and speed to market. My recommendations are to look out for opportunities to exploit connectivity infrastructure provided by others or to collaborate with others to build or to get access to appropriate infrastructure, either for use within your own business or to take service offerings to the market. The unit cost of online connectivity is about to take a big dive and returns from the infrastructure per se will be in line with other utilities. Some say that the profit pool is moving into content, but I think that train has already left the station. The next train to leave the station will be for services that enable people to exploit the virtual worlds that increasingly sophisticated ICT will enable. I don't mean Facebook or Twitter, though there are hints of the future there and getting involved in those spaces may offer you opportunities to see what the future might bring or might need.

Think of the stock market and tell me where the bulk of the action is now; it is in derivatives, in illusions of reality that are given solidity by their usefulness as a sophisticated method to manage risk...if used properly. Within a couple of decades, the same thing will happen to the economy as a whole. It is not possible now to see how that might happen, anymore than IBM or Xerox could have predicted in the 1960s and 1970s that the personal computer would revolutionize the world. They let that one go by them, didn't they, and Steve Jobs and Bill Gates cleaned up as a consequence. Bill

Gates missed the internet bus also to start with, though he managed to scramble on later, and look what Google is doing and is about to do to Microsoft...the same thing Microsoft did to IBM, Xerox and later to Apple. So, my advice is not to try to read the future, but to be prepared for it, to be positioned for it and the way to do it is to invest in connectivity and to free up the productive and creative capacity of your people, together with the value hidden in your stakeholder networks. I have provided the sign posts here and more detail can be found in chapters 3 and 5 and in the appendixes.

Suggested reading

In addition to the references I have already mentioned, here are few more. First, an economist's perspective, as offered by JD Sachs in *Commonwealth. Economics for a Crowded Planet*. For a philosophical take on the same issues, I suggest *A New Earth. Awakening to Your Life's Purpose*, by E Tolle. For a historical perspective, I recommend *Civilizations. Culture, Ambition, and the Transformation of Nature*, by F Fernández-Armesto. To round out the list, two generalist perspectives, starting with *Climate Wars*, by G Dyer, and concluding with *Hot, Flat and Crowded*, by TL Friedman.

CHAPTER 5

Changing of the guard

In this chapter we consider the impact of demographic change over the next twenty years or so, focusing on developed economies such as the USA, the UK, Canada and Australia. Why is this relevant in this book? The odds are, statistically speaking, that if you are reading this book you are a Baby Boomer, like me. The Baby Boomers are the largest generation in history, a result of the post-war boom in births in many of the countries that were leading participants in World War 2. More on the Boomers a little later. We have got used to a world run by and for Baby Boomers and yes, we Baby Boomers like it that way, climate change and Great Recession warts and all. Baby Boomers have had a longer run than most at the steering wheel and we have got a few years left, because—to the chagrin of Generations X and Y—we are not ready to retire just yet.

Certainly not if retirement means driving a *Winnebago* around the country, doing a lot of fishing and sitting around campfires. That is the approach to retirement of our parents' generation, the Veterans, who worked until pension age, with few luxuries and few vacations, unlike their children, who have had the benefit of living in more prosperous times. Baby Boomers are not fond of retirement and even the word itself is rarely used. Using my own situation as an example, I have left behind my public service career, but I am now as busy as I ever was, interspersing work with vacations overseas and at home.

Having said that, even we Baby Boomers will eventually have to acknowledge that death waits for no one and we will gradually fade away, albeit not quietly. As Baby Boomers vacate positions of influence in the economy and in politics, the world as we know it will be handed over to new people to run. This will be a gradual process. Over the next two decades, the influence of the Baby Boomers will wane and generations X and Y will assume more and more influential roles in the workplace and in the marketplace, reshaping both, often into shapes we Baby Boomers may not like. So, if you are a Baby Boomer, get ready for change that you may or may not like. If you are not a Baby Boomer, welcome, and get ready to party.

Before I get much further here, I should say that the notion of the Baby Boomer generation is most apt in the USA, Canada, Australia and New Zealand, and less so elsewhere, because these are the only countries that experienced a true baby boom after the end of World War 2. In the USA, the baby boom generation encompasses births from 1946 to 1964, 1947 to 1966 in Canada and 1946-1961 in Australia. To give you an idea of the size of the baby boom, in the USA The birth rate per 1000 population was 25.3 in 1957, falling to14.8 in 1973, with Generation X, and rising slightly to 16.7 in 1990, with Generation Y, before shrinking again to14 today. In the USA, approximately 79 million babies were born during the Baby Boom.[1] It is obvious that a demographic bulge this big is going to cause change wherever and whenever it appears. The world we know today is a Baby Boomer world, shaped by and around the needs, wants and expectations of that generation. Very little of the world our parents knew is left as it was, after the Baby Boomer tsunami. As with any great wave of change, its passing will also have a significant effect. What that will be will be for other generations to determine.

People of the world

According to the International Monetary Fund, the world's population will reach 9.1 billion by 2050, with almost all the growth occurring in developing countries (see figure 8). World Bank data show that population in less developed countries is increasing as a proportion of world population, growing from seventy percent in 1960 to eighty-one percent in 2001, while infant mortality rates are decreasing.[2] The annual rate of growth of the world's urban population should be 1.8 percent a year between 2000 and 2030, almost twice as fast as global population growth. By 2007, most of the world's people will live in urban areas, with more and more mega-cities—three billion urban dwellers in 2005 will grow to five billion in 2030. The number of people aged 60 or over in less developed countries is expected to exceed the number of 12- to 24-year-olds by 2045, matching what happened in developed countries in the late 1990s.[3] This means that at that point they would resemble Italy, where total fertility rate now is 1.3 children per woman or Japan, where it is 1.2. In those countries, unless substantial immigration programs are put in place to attract younger people to work there, by 2050, people sixty and older will make up thirty-nine percent of Italy's population and forty-four percent of Japan's.[4]

1 Matt Rosenberg, "Baby Boom. The Population Baby Boom of 1946-1964 in the United States", by About.com, retrieved on 8 January 2009 from http://geography.about.com/od/populationgeography/a/babyboom.htm.

2 Brief review of world socio-demographic trends, retrieved on 9 January 2009, from http://gsociology.icaap.org/report/demsum.html.

3 From "Picture This", *Finance and Development*, September 2006, Volume 43, Number 3.

4 From Foreign Policy, retrieved on 8 January 2009 from http://www.foreignpolicy.com/story/cms.php?story_id=3981.

Figure 8: Population growth rates[5]

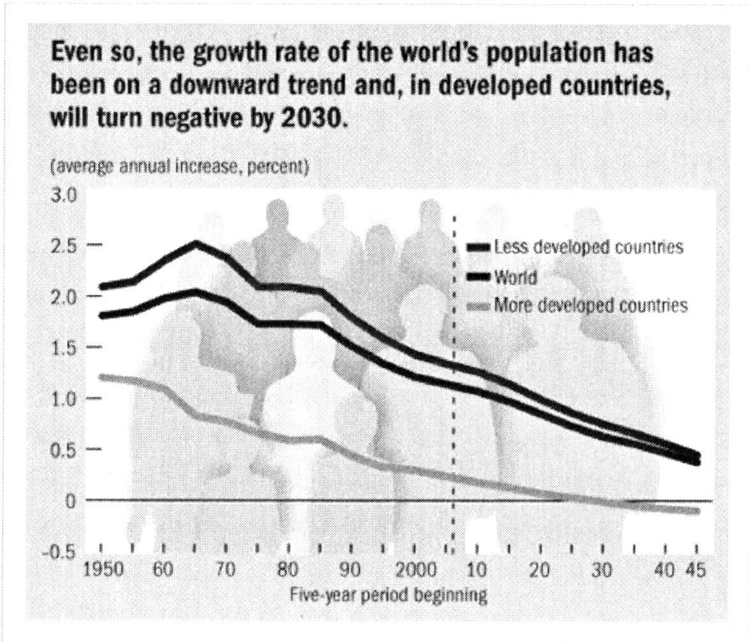

Figure 9: World population growth[6]

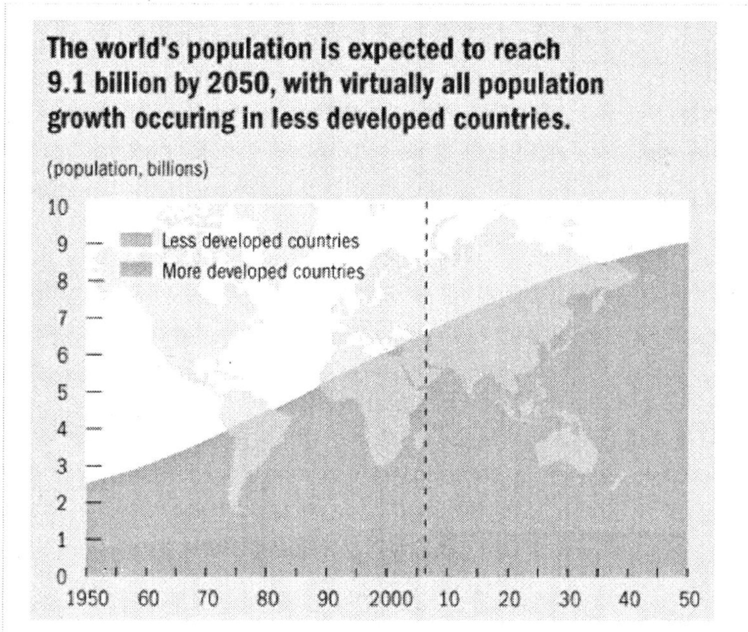

5 Idem.
6 Idem.

As if this degree of change were not enough, there are social trends developing that accompany and compound demographic change. Each year, more and more people get the opportunity to go to school, to college and to university. Each year, even in developing countries, the proportion of women receiving an education continues to grow, despite the best efforts of reactionary groups ranging from the Exclusive Brethren to the Taliban.[7] The World Bank has noted that in the year 2000 in developing countries the illiteracy rate was about half what it was in 1970.[8] Each year, the proportion of women earning an income grows and, increasingly, women are the backbone of small business, as the service sector dominates national economies and international trade. The experience of peer to peer lending organizations like Kiva is that women are much more entrepreneurial than men in developing economies and there is a strong correlation between the engagement of women in the economy and social and economic well being in those countries.[9]

New culture, new society, new economy

What will all this mean for work and workplaces in general and for the financial services industry in particular? Think back to the 1950s and 1960s and compare those days with the present. Then, women were in the workforce only until they got married, were in junior or supporting positions or in the so-called caring industries, such as teaching and nursing. The incidence of university education was low and most men entered the workforce in their mid to late teens, starting with poorly-paid unskilled work in an office or as a laborer or factory hand, because the bulk of employment was still in manufacturing. Those in the workforce could expect to stay with the same employer or, at worst, to remain in the same industry for their entire working lives. Change, skipping from job to job or career hopping, was frowned upon and loyalty was rewarded by employers and by the system. Most children grew up in a nuclear family, with mother at home and siblings to play with. Television was still a relative luxury and vacations abroad were for the rich and famous.

Families would have one car and one telephone for all to share and homes tended to be small by today's standards, with little privacy for teenagers, which meant that, as soon as they could afford it, Baby Boomer children left the parental home and struck off on their own, often also marrying young, in their late teens and early twenties. In the workplace, controls were strict, with people clocking on and off and limited

7 The Exclusive Brethren belong to an Evangelical Protestant Christian church that adheres to fundamentalist notions of Christianity and in being separate from the world; children of the Brethren are not allowed to go to university. The Exclusive Brethren do not discriminate between women and men in this regard, both are treated equally badly; this is not the case with the Taliban, who believe that only religious education is permissible — and even that is only for boys and men, not women. In either case, the result is the same: ignorance wins.

8 Brief review of world socio-demographic trends, retrieved on 9 January 2009, from http://gsociology.icaap.org/report/socsum.html.

9 See www.kiva.org.

opportunities for breaks. The workplace was just like school, with older people giving orders and younger people doing as they were told. In many countries, employers were still obliged by law to reserve job opportunities for war veterans, who were seen by the younger employees as a road block, an impediment to both change and promotion opportunities, echoing the present complaints by generations X and Y. Most workers, outside the USA perhaps, would plan for their old age on the assumption that a state pension would be provided and did little to build up private investments, except for what was spent to purchase the family home. This was then.

Now, because of much greater personal wealth, families in the suburbs live in large homes, with plenty of private space for children and teenagers, cars, telephones and televisions for all, frequent short and longer vacations, often abroad. Mother and father both work and many households have only one child, which means that the process of socialization of children is quite different from what it was. Most jobs are in the services sector and there are few opportunities to start at the bottom. Would-be employees are expected to have both university degrees and work experience, which is often acquired through vacation or part-time employment. Without university students, restaurants in most cities would find it difficult to secure enough staff it seems nowadays. Unlike their parents, the children of Baby Boomers tend to stay at home for as long as their parents will support them. Hey, can you blame them? Free bed, free board, free 'phone, free everything and you get your washing done as well, plus, your boy/girl friend can stay over and share your bed and ensuite bathroom, thanks to what we think of as more enlightened parental attitudes. Workers now have to change or else. If you are not prepared to change jobs, change careers, change industries and change towns, you may find yourself out of a job or left behind on the career fast track.

As for state pensions, don't count on it, because even where they exist, it is becoming harder and harder to get one and the amount you get is not likely to support a Baby Boomer style retirement. Now everyone has investment plans and investment advisers, brokers, accountants and assorted hangers-on and the topic of interest at parties is more often the stock market than the job market or the football game at the weekend. In the workplace, we have a confused and confusing set of expectations at work, which is driving everyone to work longer and longer hours, despite the growing appetite and capacity to support leisure time and activities. The topic of work life balance is on everyone's lips, though few workers and few workplaces actually ever get it right. Enough said, I think. The point is that life in the first decade of the twenty-first century is vastly different, in some ways better and in some ways worse, than it was forty years ago. And forty years from now or even twenty?

My expectation is that present conditions will hold for about ten years more, when most Baby Boomers will have left positions of influence in the economy—note, I did not say retired. This means that workplaces, in general, will remain a confused and confusing place to be. Most new work opportunities will continue to be generated in the services industry, though there will be niche growth in highly specialized manufacturing segments, using new materials, and in mining, in countries like Australia and Canada, at least. The rate of mobility of the workforce will continue to increase, as new economies take their place at the forefront of the global marketplace, including, among others, Brazil, China, India, Indonesia and Vietnam. The world's brightest young people, as always, will flock to the bright lights, whether they shine in London, Rio de Janeiro, Hanoi or Shanghai, to name but a few examples. Increasingly, in addition to university qualifications, employers will start to expect their people to have a practical edge, acquired through experience or through technical education or through a combination of these. They will need to, because everyone has an MBA these days, so how do you choose? New types of qualifications will be developed to meet expectations and needs of employers and prospective employees, combining academic learning and competence-based training. Members of Generation Y, in particular, value the acquisition of learning and the transmittal of knowledge and wisdom through mentoring, which could develop into a twenty-first century form of apprenticeship.

All this is very general stuff and that is all one can sensibly do, realizing that the future is a different place and that, to paraphrase a common saying, you can't see there from here. This is because the future will be shaped by those who follow us, not by us and, just like our parents could not have predicted from their vantage point what our lives would be like, I doubt we can predict what the lives of our children and grand-children will be like. However, while we cannot see the future, we can with some confidence assess which elements of the present are likely to continue and how they might be altered as time goes by; we can discern trends. I think I can discern what will be the best way to manage people in years to come, as generations X, Y and so on, take over the workplace and the marketplace. What follows is practical guidance on how to manage and lead to get the best sustainable return from the future workforce.

Generations at work

In most organizations in countries like the USA, Australia, Canada and the UK, there are four generations at work right now, Veterans, Baby Boomers, and generations X and Y. Each generation has its own values, which shape how people see and interpret their environment, including how they view family, work and life balance, career, training and development, loyalty, expectations of leaders, expectations of themselves, and the work environment. As you read these brief characterizations, please remember that, like newspaper horoscopes, they cover a lot of people and that they are generalizations. Not all the folks in the each generation will be as described, as I can attest from personal experience. Also, remember that there will be cultural differences overlaying generational differences. For example, an Australian Boomer may exhibit quite different values and behaviors than might an American or Canadian from the same generation. However, the tone of the character and behavior of each generation is pretty close to what you are about to read. Let us start with our parents, the Veterans, who, having struggled through the Great Depression and a world war, plus one or two minor wars subsequently, gave up the reins of power to the Baby Boomers in the 1980s and 1990s.

The Veterans were born before 1946, grew up during wartime, tend to be disciplined and to respect law and order. Generally, they like consistency and are not comfortable with change, preferring a directive, command and control management style. They are also likely to have fixed views on gender roles, at home and at work. This is the generation whose character was forged in hard times. They had to work hard for what they had, they made do if they could not afford to buy, they hated having to borrow money, and they were used to doing what they were told, with no complaint. Not many had a university education, unless they came from a wealthy background, and their social values were closer to the Victorian era than to the age of Rock and Roll. They would have thought of themselves as having old-fashioned values, while their children would have said that their views on social and cultural issues were rigid and unforgiving. Now they are almost all in retirement, though a few are still hanging on in both business and politics, and especially in the latter field, which means that the influence of this generation has not yet waned entirely.

Their children are the Baby Boomers. The Baby Boomers, of whom I am one as I said, were born between 1946 and 1964 (some would say 1960) and are the largest generation in history. Even in countries that did not have a significant post-war baby boom, Baby Boomer values are dominant, thanks to their dominance in the realm of culture and especially popular culture. Baby Boomers were or at least saw themselves as open minded and rebellious in their youth, in the 1960s, but tend towards more conservative views later in their lives, as they acquired families and work responsibilities. If asked, they may deny this, but do not believe them. Baby Boomers were brought up in an age characterized by rising wealth and by greater social and cultural freedom, but they lived during the Cold War and under the shadow of nuclear war. This has caused them to be more than a little self-centered, not to say egotistical. Baby Boomers are not afraid to take what they want, re-shaping society to suit them and their needs and expectations. Education became more freely available during their time, as did, for the first time in history, control over personal fertility, chiefly in the form of the contraception pill.

Freed from most of the traditional gender restrictions and by the ever-present demands of their fertility cycles, Baby Boomer women joined the workforce in record numbers. In most developed economies, women now have half the jobs, though they do not always have parity of income or equal access to senior roles. While they tend to be ignorant or dismissive of this fact, the lifestyle that women in generations X and Y now take for granted was won for them by their mothers, who joined the workforce, attacked the glass ceiling with gusto, and, in collaboration with a better educated and more open-minded generation of men, re-shaped the home and the workplace. Baby Boomers tend to be optimistic, ambitious, loyal, believing employment is for life—one person, one career—which makes job status and symbols important to them. They may talk about inclusive leadership, as a reaction to the Veterans' preference for command and control, may not have the required skills to practice it. Deep down, Baby Boomers hanker for the certainties of their parents' generation and do not believe in their hearts what they say about leadership, often resorting to command and control methods even when they know that they are not effective. To some extent, that of the Baby Boomers is a conflicted generation, as is Generation X, though for different reasons.

Generation X includes those born between 1965 and 1979. Generation X children often had both parents working and many were latchkey kids, because their mothers were not at home, unlike their mothers before them. Most Baby Boomers were brought up in traditional households, with mother at home and father working, while most members of Generation X were not. Perhaps because of this, Xrs tend to be insecure and it is not unusual to hear from members of this generation that they feel squeezed between the Baby Boomers and Generation Y. Their cry is that their parents had it easy, with full employment and cheap everything, while Generation Y has it easy, because of full employment and access to lifestyle choices they feel they did not have. Of course, their Baby Boomer parents think that Xrs are spoilt and the Generation Y kids think they are a mob of whiners. There is some truth in all these perceptions and there is truth in the observation that Generation X has been caught between a rock and a hard place, though this by no means a universal experience. In any case, because they see themselves as such, I would call this generation the *In-betweeners*. On the positive side, members of Generation X tend to be resourceful, individualistic, self reliant and skeptical of authority, focusing on workplace relationships, outcomes, their rights and their own skills. Often they are not interested in long-term careers, corporate loyalty or status symbols, which means that they are easy to recruit, but hard to retain and are likely to have many careers and many employers, with at least one stint of self employment.

Now let us turn too Generation Y, which covers those born after 1980 (up to 1996?). They are also known as the Millennium or Net Generation, for self-explanatory reasons. Paradoxically, members of Generation Y tend to have similar values to the Veterans—optimistic, confident, sociable, strong morals and with a sense of civic duty. Their motivations are different though. The Veterans complied because they had to, while the Millennials comply because they want to. Unlike the Veterans, they are comfortable with people of differing ethnicity and gender and both women and men expect greater workplace flexibility, something that may change, to some extent, as a result of the Great Recession. In the workplace they are different from the rest of the workforce—they are likely to have more careers than even Generation X and will gravitate towards self-employment, interspersed with stints as an employee and long breaks from the workforce, to study or to travel. Generation Y is apparently comfortable with managerial models and organizational structures that align best with emerging economic reality and, for this reason, they may leapfrog over Generation X members, capturing top jobs and leading political roles in numbers disproportionate to the size of the respective cohorts.

So, now you have seen them all, Veterans, Baby Boomers and Generations X and Y. For now, all these generations are still represented in the workforce and in politics, though the influence of the Veterans in top management roles has waned almost entirely. Veterans still remain strong in politics, where age is not always a disadvantage and where merit is not always a determining criterion. By 2030, Baby Boomers will be in the position now occupied by the Veterans and the alphabet generations will be writing books about the changes new generations are expected to usher in. The world in 2030 will be a different place indeed, but the change will not be sudden or immediate, it will be gradual. Whichever generation calls you its own, you have time to adapt. Having said all that, individuals are just that, individual. Being part of a particular generation does not mean that a person will be the same as all the others in that generation. It would be dangerous to assume that how people in the workplace are managed should be determined solely by demography.

Keeping an eye on the research

For example, people have different ways of taking in, processing and storing information. Some people absorb information well only if they can read it at their leisure; others like to have the opportunity to hear information and then to discuss it with others; many need to experience what the information means, what it feels like, before they can absorb it and understand it. This means that providing written instructions, for example, and expecting people to follow them is courting disaster. Some will not understand what they mean, some will not even notice, a few may even resent that their communication preferences are once again being ignored. This would destroy trust and would put at risk the ability of the organization to act as expected. This is where technology can help. The family of technologies known as the social media, wikis, blogs and so on, can help us to build trust to achieve better communication, bridging generational gaps and learning preferences.

Available research suggests that, if used wisely, these technologies can be useful elements of an organization's trust-building strategy. A global survey conducted in 2007 indicated that social media could be used to improve employee engagement, internal collaboration, the development of internal communities, and dialogue with senior executives. It also found that by 2008, almost sixty percent of business organizations would have some sort of social media in place.[10] Following on from the study, Melcrum, an international research and information company, suggested that organizations

10 *How to Use Social Media to Engage Employees*, Melcrum Publishing 2007.

consider using social media, noting at the same time that most organizations would lack the skills to do so. Melcrum advised that organizations should:

1. Assess their cultural readiness
2. Focus on the people, not on the technology
3. Think about the business purpose of the tools
4. Understand the difference between traditional and social media
5. Prepare to relinquish control and share the process
6. Be experimental and involve employees
7. Clarify what employees can and can't do
8. Take a hands off approach to marketing the tools
9. Work with they have and integrate new tools
10. Don't obsess about the numbers (measurement)

These are sensible guidelines. Using them we could experiment, to develop principles on which new management practices could be develop, with the aim to foster trust and thereby increase productivity and creativity within our organizations.[11] It is never too late and it is never impossible. A case study on how SAP has made use of social media indicates that even conservative organizations can re-make themselves and their image to the benefit of the business, as illustrated by the following quote:

> *SAP was formerly viewed as rigid, monolithic, and overly process-oriented. Our SDN and BPX communities have dramatically shifted that view, to the surprise and delight of many….if you look at the blog posts or the media coverage, it's been very good…. We are now viewed as open and collaborative.*[12]

It is worth noting that among Generation Y, social networking ranks first as an option among a broad series of activities. When asked what they would do if they had fifteen minutes of time, seventeen percent of people between fourteen and twenty-nine indicated in a recent survey that they would check out social networking sites, matching talking on the telephone and beating watching TV, surfing the web, playing video games, instant messaging, listening to an MP3 player or listening to the radio.[13] This suggests that an organization offering social networking options to younger employees might succeed in capturing the time and attention of those employees, diverting them from competing interests. Adult social networking sites like www.linkedin.com point the way. LinkedIn is an online network of more than seventeen million professionals from around the world, representing one hundred and fifty industries. Its purposes for members are:

11 An example of such a strategy can be found at http://www.ddmcd.com/managing-technology/how-to-develop-a-business-aligned-social-media-social-networ.html.

12 From http://www.socialmediatoday.com/ClientFiles/2b461d74-0b05-4149-a6fd-33257181a2c7/sapnetworks.pdf.

13 "Never Ending Friending. A Journey into Social Networking", Fox Interactive Media 2007.

- Find potential clients, service providers, subject experts, and partners who come recommended
- Be found for business opportunities
- Search for great jobs
- Discover inside connections that can help you land jobs and close deals
- Post and distribute job listings
- Find high-quality passive candidates
- Get introduced to other professionals through the people you know

It is possible to see in this list at least the potential for business use within an organization like a bank, which will increasingly be relying on Generation Y to fill essential roles and to boost its customer base, remembering that its customer base will increasingly be made up of members of Generation Y. This is what I suggest you do.

Creating business value through trust

> *Big brands disappear all the time… Cingular Wireless was on most Top 100 brands lists. Once AT&T (T) took over BellSouth, it dropped Cingular completely. Compaq was one of the most visible PC brands in the world. It began to fade away after it was bought by Hewlett-Packard. The IBM PC brand…no longer exists since it was acquired by Lenovo…several years ago.* — Douglas A. McIntyre

We live in interesting times, an era during which change and turbulence dominate the business environment. Coping successfully with a turbulent environment requires new solutions. Haeckel has put forward a promising model. Haeckel's solution—the sense and respond model—is a combination of "adaptive system design" and "a governance system that provides 'context and coordination' for empowered teams".[14] An adaptive system design is a framework that ranks strategic options and sets boundaries for behavior, expressed as set of processes, rather than a plan. Context and coordination are the replacement for the command and control model typically used by "industrial age firms". Citing examples of success, such as Motorola, Haeckel argues that

> *Sense-and-respond firms will require a modular, fluid, organic organization to respond effectively to dynamic non-linear change ... this means networks of skills, assets, cross-functional processes, information and knowledge that are linked to capabilities, which are in turn linked into processes for creating product and service responses to customer needs.*[15]

14 S H Haeckel, "Adaptive Enterprise Design: The Sense and Respond Model", *Planning Review*, May/June 1995.
15 At page 9.

This he calls a "synergy strategy", a method for integrating sub-systems within the organization while allowing management of the content of those sub-systems to remain with the people who work within them. My contribution is to extend this sense and respond model beyond the boundaries of the organization, to encompass customers, clients, suppliers and the community, as well as government and the regulating environment. I do this because these days no organization is self-sufficient and because to succeed an organization must extend its influence throughout its value chain, upstream and downstream. This means that to succeed, we have to engage people or organizations that have an interest in what our organization does. This is what stakeholder management is all about.

The objective is to develop a circle of trust within which the organization can go about its business with minimum interference. The means to achieve that objective are many, but the essence of successful stakeholder management is effective communication, where effective communication is *the reciprocal transmission of meaning without unintended confusion or ambiguity*. To put it plainly, effective communication is getting and receiving the intended message. The test of effective communication is that each party acts as the other party expected. This builds trust among the parties, as we will see. We will shortly see why trust is important, but first let's consider the subject of efficiency and effectiveness.

Defining efficiency and effectiveness

I would say that effectiveness is "the degree to which predetermined goals are achieved", whereas efficiency refers to the economical manner in which goal-oriented operations are carried out—something of an input/output ratio".[16] Time is a qualifier of effectiveness. While survival is the ultimate measure of organizational effectiveness, in the everyday world managers need short term and intermediate term measures or indicators. Suggested short-term measures are production, efficiency and effectiveness, while suggested intermediate measures are adaptation to environmental changes and the internal development of the organization, including the level of trust and collaboration.

I am pointing this out to illustrate the point that issues such as trust and concern for an organization's general climate and morale are not do-gooders' issues. There is a definite and definable connection between how well an organization treats the people it deals with and its long-term success, as explained in appendix 1. One of the fundamental reasons for Google's success is how it treats its people...and sacking people may cost your business more than you think.[17] How do you treat your people well, while keeping an eye on the bottom line and on competitors? You do it by building trust.

16 JH Jackson et al, *Organization Theory: A Macro-perspective for Management*, Prentice-Hall, 1986.

17 "Layoffs cost more than you think", *Fortune Magazine*, March 17, 2009, retrieved from http://money.cnn.com/2009/03/16/magazines/fortune/colvin_layoffs.fortune/index.htm.

The ability to build trust is a key competency for leaders today. Great leaders don't dictate, they influence. And influence comes from a leader's ability to engender credibility and inspire people to both believe them and believe in them.—Stephen R Covey

How to build trust

If I trust the competence of other drivers, of the road designers and builders and the car manufacturers, it is likely that I will be able and willing to drive faster than if I do not. What is true on a road is also true of any other network, including within organizations or stakeholder networks. If I trust the various components that make up the network, the other users of the network and the operators of the network, I will be prepared to have fewer checks and balances operating in and on the network. In turn, this will free up the movement of data on the network, lifting the speed of traffic on the network. This makes the network more efficient and effective in moving information and in enabling sharing of knowhow.

Most of us work in service industries. The value produced by service industries is made up of several factors, but the dominant factors are knowhow (or knowledge) and information. The quality of food in a restaurant or of service in a bank or the success of government policy, all depend on the knowhow of the workers involved in the process and on the quality of information flows. Both knowhow and information are essential. For example, a competent waiter who does not understand the language of a customer is more likely to give poor service. On the other hand, an incompetent waiter who is fluent in the language of his or her customers is also more likely to give poor service.

Knowhow is also a factor in farming and manufacturing, of course, as is information, but they are not dominant factors, often playing second fiddle to capital and capital goods, such as machinery and raw materials, or are dependent on the quality of the land and the vagaries of climate. Because of the twin requirements of knowhow and information, service industries are the natural home of knowledge workers. According to Peter Drucker, "The terms "knowledge industries", "knowledge work" and "knowledge worker" are only forty years old. They were coined around 1960, simultaneously but independently; the first by a Princeton economist, Fritz Machlup, the second and third by this writer."[18] Knowledge workers make their living primarily by thinking, rather than doing, which means that not all who work in an office are knowledge workers and not all knowledge workers are to be found in office buildings. Knowledge workers work best when they are trusted and feel trusted.

18 *The Economist*, "The Next Workforce. Knowledge workers are the new capitalists", by Peter F. Drucker, November 1, 2001, from http://www.druckerinstitute.com/whydrucker/why_articles_nextworkforce.html, retrieved on 14 March 2009.

I have developed a model to show how trust and communication are linked, at figure 10. The assumption underpinning this model is that we cannot have trust without effective communication and we cannot have effective communication without trust. I define trust as *reliance, certainty based on experience*. In other words, what you have experienced in relating with someone gives you a reasonable degree of predictability about the future behavior of the other. Within this broad definition, I see three types of trust:

- Self-disclosure trust—which emerges with mutual self-disclosure and sharing
- Contract trust—which emerges from making and keeping agreements
- Safety trust—which evolves from reading another person's intentions and being confident that the other person means no harm

Figure 10: Model linking trust and communication

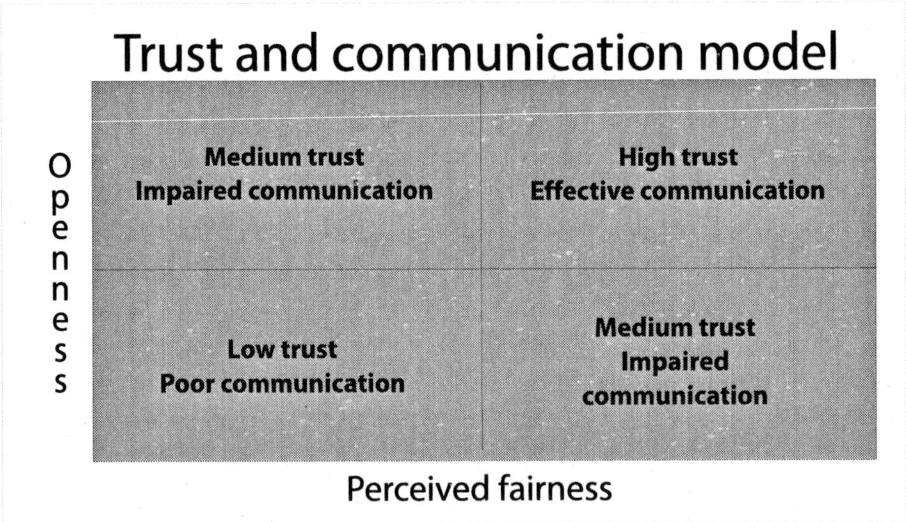

How do we achieve trust? We build up **self-disclosure trust** by sharing information freely and not holding on to knowledge as it were property; by encouraging and receiving feedback—and being seen to treat that feedback with appropriate respect; by disclosing a portion of who we really are to others, sharing some information about our private lives—this does not mean disclosing secrets or details about others; and by being prepared to admit ignorance, to say "I don't know". Building **contract trust** requires following through on promises and commitments, on doing what we say. It also means that if we can't keep a promise, we face up to the consequences. We explain why we can't and we take steps to make good any direct or collateral damage. On the other hand, it means giving others a bit of latitude that perhaps we would not allow for ourselves, being forgiving of small or infrequent lapses by others.

Safety trust is achieved by making sure that we at least do no harm in our relationships with others. It does not mean refraining from giving someone bad news or from making decisions that are not palatable to others. It means doing what we do professionally, with no malice and no deceit, and being always ready to explain why something has to be done. Safety trust requires self-disclosure and contract trust as conditions precedent. If there is low contract and self-disclosure trust, it is not possible to achieve safety trust. Without safety trust, morale in organizations will be low and productivity will be lower than it can be, at both the firm level and affecting whole economies.[19]

There are common elements in these three types of trust. My hypothesis is that trust in an organization—or in any relationship, really—requires sustained openness and perceived fairness, where openness is an *attitude of ready accessibility without concealment, not secretive,* and fairness is evidenced by *judgments that are free from negative discrimination or dishonesty*. Attitudes and judgments are somewhat nebulous concepts. To make it easier for you I have come up with a list of behaviors that are likely to build trust, which are in table 4. In that table you will also find a list of behaviors that are likely to destroy trust. These behaviors are relevant in relationships between individuals, between organizations, and between organizations and individuals. They are as relevant in dealing with employees, bosses, suppliers, partners and spouses.

As you build trust, it is vital that you also stop doing anything that destroys trust. It is vital because any perceived inconsistency in behavior will in and by itself destroy any results you might hope to achieve by doing the right things. Also, remember that the more senior you are in an organization, the more power your actions have. If you are perceived to behave even slightly inconsistently, that venial sin will become a mortal sin overnight in the eyes of those below you in the hierarchy. On a brighter note, this phenomenon applies to the positive behaviors as well, which means that, provided you act consistently, if you stick to the left hand side of the table you will achieve much more than you might think.

I should add that the behaviors I have suggested are not a menu, from which you can pick and choose to suit a particular situation. Ideally, all these behaviors should be part of your everyday repertoire, in all circumstances. Of course, from time to time you will lapse—we all do. However, you will find that if you have built up a reservoir of trust, the odd lapse will be easily and quickly forgiven. Without a reservoir of trust, the well of forgiveness will remain dry. These principles apply more strongly the higher you are in the pecking order. The more senior the manager, the more scrutiny s/he will have to endure by others in the organization. The more senior the manager, the more likely that a venial sin will be considered to be a mortal offence by others in the

19 GW Fairholm, *Leadership and the culture of trust*, Greenwood Publishing Group (1994); A Lyman, "Building trust in the workplace", *Strategic HR Review*, Volume 3 Issue 1 November/December 2003; R Putnam, *Making Democracy Work Civic Traditions in Modern Italy*, Princeton University Press (1993).

organization. This may not seem fair, but that is how it is. This is one of the reasons why senior management need to especially adept in the art of building trust. Sadly, most are not and the company bottom line suffers as a consequence.[20]

Table 4: Actions that build or destroy trust

ACTIONS THAT BUILD TRUST	ACTIONS THAT DESTROY TRUST
Behave consistently	Behave inconsistently
Accept ideas	Dismiss ideas put forward by others
Tolerate faults	Embarrass people
Criticize the idea, not the person	Blame others for one's own mistakes
Clarify, understand before seeking to be understood	Avoid eye contact
Be inclusive	Ignore people
Ask for feedback	Withhold feedback
Work together	Interrupt when others are talking
Play together	Withhold credit that is due
Protect confidences—when you have said that you will	Fail to keep a confidence
Follow through on your promises	Break a promise
Provide accurate information	Withhold information that is important to making a decision
Observe the niceties, say thank you, please, good morning and so on	Be rude, discourteous

If you do all this right and you do it consistently, you will keep all the generations happy, because you will be addressing all of the generational value sets, concurrently. Veterans will appreciate the clarity and certainty of your approach, as well as the good manners, while Baby Boomers will appreciate the open and flexible character of the organization, and the younger folk will love the free access to information, knowledge and wisdom, as well as the evident honesty. If you keep all your generations happy and engaged, you will profit from higher morale, greater commitment and much better productivity. There is ample research and frontline evidence for that. Next are a few more strategies I recommend you adopt to keep your people working diligently for the benefit of the business and for their own benefit also.

20 HS Harung and T Dahl, "Increased productivity and quality through management by values: a case study of Manpower Scandinavia", *The TQM Magazine*, 1995, Vol. 7(2), pages 13—22.

Harnessing people to serve the corporate good, as volunteers

Many organizations have understood the value of giving employees a share in the company's fortunes, through performance pay, share and option schemes and so on. This is a good practice, in theory. The problem is that by picking a few winners, you are making many losers. To put it another way, tools such as performance pay focus individuals on how they can benefit from the company, placing each member of staff in competition with every other—for personal benefit, not to the benefit of the corporation.

As Stephen Covey explains, reward systems must reflect the values of the corporate mission statement. If the mission statement is predicated on collaboration and information sharing, as it should be, then the reward system must be aligned to those values.[21] At table 5, you will find a generic value model, which is what I suggest you use as the benchmark to align work and workers to what the organization values. I suspect that all of the components will be relevant to most organizations, but they will have different weightings depending on the type of business and the specific circumstances in which the business operates. Of course, the weightings can be adjusted from time to time, to reflect changes in priorities or in the business environment. This model ties individual rewards very firmly to corporate performance, while allowing scope for individual brilliance—but not at the expense of the whole.

Table 5: Generic value model

	Value components	Indicators
1.	Cycle time	Fewer processes, simpler processes, no rework, on-time
2.	Cost	Fewer inputs, lower TCO, less waste, no rework, on budget
3.	Sustainability	More customers, new markets, new products, higher margins, longer product life
4.	Return generated	Higher ROI, higher sales volume, rate of innovation, productivity per hour, quicker revenue gathering
5.	People	360° feedback, appropriate staff turnover rates, greater diversity, staff satisfaction index

The best design for a corporate reward program is achieved by balancing the value of personal initiative with the value of collaboration. There should be two levels of performance assessment: corporate and individual. The program should apply equally

21 Covey (1999).

at all levels of the organization. This would not produce equal rewards, because base salaries would be different, but the model for allocation of rewards would be fair to all and would be seen to be fair by all. Corporate performance should be determined by the weighted sum of value components 1-5 in your organization's value model, along the lines of table 5. Individual performance should be composed of 75% for 1-4 and 25% for 5, again reflecting weightings that are relevant to your organization. There should be no separate performance assessment at business unit or other intermediate levels, to avoid fragmenting commitment to corporate goals. Speaking of corporate goals, the problem of dealing with non-performance is ever with us and the new generations are especially concerned that non-performers be dealt with firmly, but fairly, putting them closer to the Veterans than to the Baby Boomers in this regard. And the problem may be about to get worse, rather than better, because life at work is getting more and more complicated.

Change is a constant. We live in a globalised economy, characterized by the growing importance of information as the raw material for value creation, and by the diminishing importance of distance as a barrier to market. The speed of change is increasing and the rules governing value creation and competitiveness are under challenge. Everything is speeding up: remaining viable and being competitive in the decades to come will require business to deal with much faster economic cycles. While it took the telephone a century to become a universally available tool, it has taken only a decade or two for the internet to do the same.[22] Creative destruction, a term introduced by Schumpeter early in the twentieth century, is a ubiquitous phenomenon. Creative destruction occurs when something new, an innovation, destroys an existing product, or company or even a whole industry.[23]

If you don't watch out, your organization may well be the next entry on the list of extinct corporate species. Yes, change is a constant and organizations cannot afford to keep people who are not comfortable with change. This does not mean that anyone who opposes any change should be dismissed instantly. Opposition to any particular change is not a problem; rather, the problem is with those individuals who have an ingrained, unthinking resistance to change generally.

The culture of the company should be such as to discourage such individuals from even considering joining or, if they have joined and are not prepared to change themselves, it should be such as to encourage them to make an early departure, with your assistance to find a more suitable place of employment. This may seem harsh, but it is not, if the focus is on helping people to embrace change, to benefit from change, while dealing humanely and sensibly with those who will not do so. The alternative is to allow a negative influence to fester within your organization, damaging all who have a stake in it. This is unfair to the vast majority of stakeholders, including employees.

22 Gleick (1999).
23 Schumpeter (1975).

Executives owe it to the organization and to their fellow workers not to tolerate nonperforming individuals in important jobs.

PF Drucker

Recommended action

Review your recruitment and promotion processes, to ensure that the ability to change and to help others to manage change are identified and rewarded. Train managers and supervisors to identify resistance to change and to deal with the problem when they find it, rewarding those who do so in the best interests of all concerned. If an employee proves to be consistently resistant to necessary change, take steps to help that employee to resolve the problem. If that does not produce the desired result, then assist that employee to find suitable, alternative employment. Make these expectations clear to all who work with you or who would like to join your organization and make the connection to your value model explicit, so that the reasons for these policies are understood. This can be done by adopting the approach to people issues incorporated in table 5, using component 5. Make sure you apply these policies fairly and consistently, regardless of the rank or position of the person concerned, remembering that, as the saying goes, the fish goes rotten from the head.[24] If you want more detail on how to deploy these strategies, I suggest you get hold of a copy of my earlier book, *Compliance and Regulation in the International Financial Services Industry.*

Impact on planetary ecology and recommended reading

The new generations with new ambitions, expectations and desires will change the world, re-shaping cultures, societies and the global economy. This is as it should be and as it has always been. Those who follow us will also literally re-shape the world, as we have see in chapter 4, taking one of two directions. Like us, the Baby Boomers, they could continue to muddle on, dealing with ecological crises as they come dealing with them as if they were a war. This is an attitude we baby Boomers have inherited from the Veterans and that we have kept, unfortunately. I guess it suits the modern desire for constant stimulation and excitement. Making war on carbon pollution is a somewhat more exciting call to action than reducing our environmental overdraft. I suggested in chapter 4 that we need to ditch the metaphor of war, because it is leads us towards courses of action that will not deal with the substance of the problem, any more than

24 For interesting reflections on corporate governance and rotting fish, see the speech by Mr. John Phillips, Chairman, The Australian Gas Light Company; Chairman, Foreign Investment Review Board; Chancellor, University of Western Sydney, at http://www.ausncp.gov.au/content/docs/144_145_20021001_phillips.pdf.

the television show *Big Brother* deals with the problems of real life. My suggestion is to opt for a managerial or, better still, a stewardship metaphor and that is another course open to those who follow us, if we have not grasped the nettle ourselves. I think I need say nothing more than that here and I ask you instead to go on to chapter 6, where we discuss what can be done, what should be done and what must be done to meet the challenges presented by waves of change that are coming our way.

Suggested reading

As for further reading, I suggest *Generation Blend. Managing Across the Technology Age Group*, by Rob Salkowitz, which offers useful guidance on how to make the best of the engagement between the coming generations and the never ending ICT revolution. Bernard Salt, an Australian, writes with humor and perspicacity on what he sees as the main social issues of this century, in *Man Drought and Other Issues of the New Century*. Another useful (and entertaining) book is *Wikinomics: How Mass Collaboration Changes Everything*, by Don Tapscott and Anthony D. Williams, though I believe that the authors have exaggerated a little the potential of the Wiki model to affect how we live our lives and earn our living. *Coming of Age in a Globalized World: The Next Generation*, by J. Michael Adams and Angelo Carfagna is worth reading, because it seeks to transcend national and cultural boundaries. There are thousands of blogs that cover generational issues and I have picked out just one, to get you started. It is an Australian site, www.openforum.com.au, which describes itself as "Open Forum is an independent collaborative think-tank built around an interactive discussion website hosted and moderated by Global Access Partners (GAP). It provides a platform for focused dialogue on social, political, economic, ecological and cultural issues and challenges." I will declare right now that I blog here, following my policy of declaring biases and prejudices.

CHAPTER 6

What is to be done

... we must not regard our knowledge as ready-made and unalterable, but must determine how knowledge emerges from ignorance, how incomplete, inexact knowledge becomes more complete and more exact. — Lenin

One of the oldest puzzles of politics is who is to regulate the regulators. — John Kenneth Galbraith

If we are to solve the problems that face us and new problems that will arise, we must start by acknowledging our collective ignorance, by accepting the limitations of our knowledge and then seeking to learn more. We must also accept that utopia is just that, it is nowhere. A perfect system of regulation, a system incapable of error, is not within our grasp, at least not for the foreseeable future, anymore than we can hope to make the global financial system proof from shock. If we can accept these limitations, then we can start to do what is needed, fixing what can be fixed and allowing ourselves scope to learn from our future mistakes, as well as from the mistakes of the past.

In earlier chapters, I flagged that we should consider financial markets as providing a utility service, like energy providers or suppliers of potable water or manufacturers of food. We regulate utilities through standards, requiring each element of the supply chain to comply with requirements based in science that also satisfy the public and downstream users that the integrity of the chain is being preserved. I pointed out that we require manufacturers of food to behave according to standards, with compliance backed up by legal sanctions and by open scrutiny of the manufacturing and distribution processes. I also pointed out that we place more strictures on casino operators than we do on hedge fund managers, which is strange, because customers of casinos assume risk voluntarily, whereas all of us, whether we know it or not, bear a share of the risk generated by large financial institutions.

I also explained—and we will return to this theme shortly—that because financial markets are essential to preserve a society's economic health, we should learn from the discipline of epidemiology, which concerns itself with preserving and enhancing public health. What follows in this chapter builds on these arguments and on the notion that a complex system can be regulated effectively through a few simple rules, a concept borrowed from Darwin and Lamarck. If a few rules can keep planetary evolution going, I am sure we can do the same for the financial services industry.

Why am I arguing for a few rules only? First, to keep overheads low, for government, for industry and for customers. Red tape costs money and time and also acts as a wet blanket, stifling opportunities and the fire of innovation. Second, research shows that we humans can keep only so many concepts in our heads at any one time and that we are more likely to remember and to comply with rules if they are few and simple. Third, a thicket of rules actually helps those who prefer to avoid scrutiny and supervision. This is because complex rules are more likely to generate inconsistencies, obscurities, loopholes and gaps, creating nooks and crannies where the dishonest and the crooked can hide and creating excuses for weak or incompetent regulators, when prosecutions fail or never even start. Fourth, research establishes that complex systems can be designed and run with only a few rules and, as an aficionado of Ockham's razor, I fail to see why more would be better, if this is the case.

> *"We can't solve problems by using the same kind of thinking we used when we created them."* – attributed to Albert Einstein

A regulatory framework based on a few simple rules can be designed and deployed effectively if we understand how complex systems operate and evolve, if we accept that the stock market, for example, is in a sense alive. As such, it functions just like us, through a complex mixture of reason and emotion, of science and superstition, of fear and greed. We also need to remember that humans tend to behave irrationally, despite the contrary claims of orthodox economics, and that our individual irrationality is accentuated dramatically when we form a mob, when we become prey to the famed animal spirits that, their peak, can overcome any rational safeguard. We also need to be cognizant of the trap that awaits us if we assume that someone else is going to mind the commons, if we act as if somehow, things will turn out all right. Lastly, we need to be aware that bad or excessive regulation will choke the goose that gives us our golden eggs.

All these elements inform the proposal for change that I make in this chapter. My proposal is to regulate financial markets through a global, federated network of trust. In formulating this proposal, I have taken into account that the next decade or two may be especially challenging, as the world struggles to come to terms with the realization that we cannot continue to exploit our planet at the present rate and as new generations take over the levers of power. The confluence of these forces for change will present governments, business enterprises and individuals with difficult choices. The first big choices are: how do we reduce our environmental overdraft without destroying our way of life; how do we re-shape the workplace and society to accommodate new ways of working and new ways of living; how do we collaborate within industries, within societies and globally to deal with problems that are increasingly intractable within the boundaries of their creation; and how do we learn lessons from the past that we can apply wisely to design a better future? This chapter is about that last question, focusing on the need to redesign global financial markets, without throwing the bay out with the bathwater.

My proposal is predicated on the use of market forces to ensure that the market has the right balance of regulation and freedom to fail or succeed, without necessarily guaranteeing success to anyone or any business in the market. The specific forces to which I will make reference are competition (or contestability) and pricing (price signal). The former creates a self-sustaining drive towards innovation and continuous improvement, while the latter pushes the market in the direction of greater efficiency, both in terms of production and allocation. For once, I will make use of the favorite tools of economists, formulae and equations, but for a different purpose. My purpose, as the proponent of change, is to provide the means by which my proposals can be tested, to see if they take us in the right direction and to check on progress made. These are the reasons why I am putting forward an equation of (economic) value.

From equation of exchange to equation of value: speed matters

Why focus on speed? Have you noticed that everything is getting faster and that time to get things done is getting shorter? This is not a mere impression. For example, the design and marketing cycle is shrinking, quickly. The article in *The Futurist* I quoted at the beginning of the book tells us that "As late as the 1940s, the product cycle stretched to 30 or 40 years. Today, it seldom lasts 30 or 40 weeks." That same article also tells us that "All the technical knowledge we work with today will represent only 1% of the knowledge that will be available in 2050. Industries will face much tighter competition based on new technologies. Those who adopt state-of-the-art methods first are likely to prosper. Those who ignore them eventually will fail.

Brand names associated with quality are becoming even more important in this highly competitive environment. Lifelong learning is a necessity for anyone who works in a technical field--and for growing numbers who do not." While the authors of this study may have erred in predicting where the financial cycle was going next, I think these predictions, if you pardon a small pun, are right on the money. On this basis, I am proposing we assume that value or wealth creation will depend increasingly on reducing cycle times and on speeding up the rate of innovation (you may wish to revisit the material in the introduction, in chapter 1 and in appendix 1).

A fundamental premise of this book is that business and government should focus on creating value, but economics says little about measuring value and not much about identifying drivers of value, especially at the macroeconomic level. However, in economics there is the concept of the equation of exchange (or **M** x **V** = **P** x **Q)**, where

- **M** is the amount of money in circulation in an economy at any one time
- **V** is the velocity of money or how often each unit of money is spent
- **P** is the average price level for the economy
- **Q** is the number of items purchased during the month

The equation of exchange is used to study the notion of inflation, a phenomenon that occurs when too much money is chasing too few goods. I will borrow some of the elements of this equation to formulate an "equation" of economic value. My starting point, as discussed earlier, is that in the twenty-first century, economic success and economic stability will continue to depend on competitiveness, which, in turn will rest on new perspective on the velocity of money (or **V**)—how quickly value (or $\mathbf{M^+}$) is turned over, whatever form value takes, tangible and intangible, with these enablers:

- the speed of the flow of information across the economy and across economies (or $\mathbf{S^i}$);
- effective and efficient knowledge management, where knowledge is the sum of information and consequent action; the capacity for innovation, which I define as ideas translated into sustainable products and services is a lead indicator of the capacity of the economy to manage knowledge well (or **PS**); and
- effective and efficient governance of the state, of the economy, and of the financial sector in particular (or **G**).

This equation differs from the orthodox approach because it includes externalities, thus, in my opinion, getting closer to giving us an accurate estimation of the potential of an economy to create value. That potential would be determined by the result of the equation ($\mathbf{M^+}$ x **V)**, where **V** is equivalent to $\mathbf{S^i}$ x **PS** x **G**. Unlike the equation of exchange, this is not a mathematical equation. It is a combination of quantitative and qualitative indicators. However, each of the qualitative indicators has reliable and measurement methods available for use. Velocity of money is something we already measure and

I am comforted by the fact that there is evidence that how quickly money cycles through the economy has a positive effect on GDP.[1] For **G**, we can use the Financial Development Report, a comprehensive analysis of financial systems and capital markets in fifty-two countries conducted by the World Economic Forum (WEF)[2] or the Global Governance Index complied annually by the World Bank, which covers over two hundred economies.[3] We could complement these with ratings assigned to sovereign governments by ratings agencies. The speed of the flow of information (or $\mathbf{S}^i$) could be measured by reference to the Networked Readiness Index, compiled by the WEF, in collaboration with INSEAD.[4] The capacity to manage knowledge (**PS**) could be assessed by reference to the quality of education systems. The United Nations, through UNESCO, conducts regular analyses of comparative indicators across its global membership.[5]

My proposed model for managing the economy and, in particular, the financial sector, rests on the proposition embedded in this equation. Just as the value of a telecommunications network is proportional to the square of the number of users of the system (n^2)—remember Metcalfe's law—the value of an economy in the twenty-first century will be proportional to the volume of use of information by the financial system (or more accurately its participants). The challenge for regulators is to allow the maximum use possible, while preventing abuse of the system or of participants in the system. The opportunity for participants is to use knowledge management to push to use of the system to the limit, without pushing it over the edge. How do we avoid going over the edge, how do we generate more and more value without creating a bubble and the inevitable bubble burst that will follow? I will explain how by reference to epidemiology and the study of epidemics and pandemics, but the gist of it that just as we control speed on our highways, we must learn how to control speed on the financial super-highway and we must build better vehicles and train better operators.

Swine, pandemics and the stock market

How does a pandemic start? I will use the so-called swine 'flu', which is more accurately called Novel Influenza A (H1N1), as an example. While it is not known for certain, it is suspected that it first emerged in Mexico, soon followed by an outbreak in the USA. In the former country it caused quite a few deaths, while in the latter it has not. The virus became a global issue within a few months of the first cases diagnosed in Mexico. According to the Centers for Disease Control and Prevention (CDC) in the USA, Novel

1 See Sun Shuibo, "Does Transaction Velocity of Money Work on GDP? An Empirical Study.", retrieved from http://papers.ssrn.com/sol3/papers.cfm?abstract_id=340281 on 24 June 2009.

2 See http://www.weforum.org/en/initiatives/gcp/FinancialDevelopmentReport/index.htm, retrieved on 24 June 2009.

3 See http://info.worldbank.org/governance/wgi/index.asp, retrieved on 30 June 2009.

4 See http://www.insead.edu/v1/gitr/wef/main/fullreport/index.html, retrieved on 24 June 2009.

5 See http://www.uis.unesco.org/ev.php?ID=6292_201&ID2=DO_TOPIC, retrieved on 24 June 2009.

influenza A (H1N1) is a virus of swine origin first detected in April 2009. The virus is infecting people and is spreading from person-to-person, through the coughs and sneezes of people who are sick with the virus.[6] As at 5 June 2009, the World Health Organization reported that sixty-nine countries have reported 21,940 cases of A (H1N1) infection, with 125 deaths attributed to the virus. About eighty percent of reported deaths have been in Mexico.[7] This last piece of information is especially interesting, as we will see shortly.

So, now we know where this new virus started to infect people and we know how many people have been infected and how many have died so far. However, we know nothing of the origins of the virus and how it became capable of infecting humans and we have a puzzling disconnect between the extent of the pandemic and where the bulk of the deaths occurred. We actually do not even know that it originated among swine; it may be that it did not. Swine influenza is common among pigs, with many strains of virus reported, and from time to time people working with pigs have contracted a strain of swine flu. On the back of this history, some commentators and researchers hypothesized that the sudden emergence of a new swine virus that infected humans was due to intensive pig farming practices in the USA, where pigs and poultry are raised in cramped conditions, in large populations, and tended to by the same staff.[8]

It made for a good story. However, until 2009 there were no reported cases of infection from human to human involving swine flu, until the new virus, H1N1 emerged, allegedly from the world's pig population As it happens, H1N1 was a bird flu virus, which jumped the fence and started affecting humans, killing tens of millions of people during the so-called Spanish flu pandemic that followed World War 1. We humans then gave it to pigs and it has remained as a swine virus for nine decades. However, the latest information on the new virus that is affecting humans now is that while it contains elements found in swine flu viruses, it has not been isolated in pigs. In fact, according to the American Veterinary Medical Association, while there is "a H1N1 virus that is a common cause of seasonal human influenza infection…it is not the same virus as the swine H1N1". We will see how this plays out in future months, as more evidence is gathered and analyzed.

For our purposes, let us assume that the intensive pig farming hypothesis is correct. If so, the argument would run this way. In the pursuit of greater profits, larger and larger piggeries were established in the USA, which enabled pig farming to become a much more efficient enterprise, thanks to the benefits of scale. With increased scale of pig farming, greater and greater risks started to accumulate, because, for the first time, large populations of pigs were housed together, in close proximity and in conditions that did not match up to an environment in which the animals could maintain optimum health.

6 See http://www.cdc.gov/H1N1FLU/, retrieved on 5 June 2009.
7 See http://www.who.int/csr/don/2009_06_05/en/index.html.
8 For example, see "Swine flu: is intensive pig farming to blame?", 28 April 2009, from the www.guardian.co.uk.

Also, more and more people were placed in contact with the animals and with the large quantities of animal waste that accumulate in large, intensive farming establishments. These conditions provided an ideal environment for viruses to thrive, for viruses to mutate and for those mutations to survive and become viable. Eventually, one of those mutations affected humans and, within those humans, mutated to become capable of infecting other humans directly, without the need for a pig to be the host. Then we had a global human pandemic. In more vulnerable environments, with less robust health care arrangements, such as Mexico, the new virus was quite powerful and deadly, whereas in other, less vulnerable environments, with more robust health care arrangements, the virus was much less deadly.

If you study any pandemic, you will find a similar pattern. For example, the great waves of plague that devastated Europe over several centuries developed this way. The disease was first recorded in Europe just after the fall of the Roman Empire, in the sixth century, but it did not become a great killer until the fourteenth century and it remained a great killer, in wave after pandemic wave, until the modern era. The disease, in both its bubonic and pulmonary forms, is caused by a bacterium that uses a flea as the host, with the flea, in turn, using a species of rat as host. Why did it follow this pattern? From the fall of the Roman Empire until the Middle Ages, Europe was a land of villages and peasant farmers. This meant that there was not a suitable environment for rats to breed in large numbers and to then come into close contact with humans. In turn, this meant that the flea that carries the plague bacterium could not find enough suitable hosts to reproduce, which also means that the bacterium itself had a hard time reproducing, let alone thriving. When towns started to grow in number and size across Europe, with generally poor sanitation, all this changed.

Suddenly, rats had food aplenty, many places to live and breed and many opportunities to come into contact with humans, directly or through their feces. As the rats did well, so did the fleas and the plague bacteria and the deadly pandemics followed, for several centuries. This occurred in China, which was also highly urbanized, for similar reasons. The end of the plague was not due to any great medical discovery. It was due to better sanitation in cities, due to the introduction of reliable clean water supply and the availability of safe sewerage disposal, together with generally higher standards of personal and public hygiene. These changes in behavior again created an environment that made it difficult for rats, fleas and bacteria to live and multiply and to come into contact with humans. Unfortunately, in the past humans have not understood this and have tried to deal with plagues and disease in other ways, generally with poor or even disastrous effects. And we are still at this stage of development when we have to confront investment crises, though we do better in other fields.

Computer plagues

The world of computers is as vulnerable to viruses and other vectors of disease as we are and how we defend ourselves from "disease" in the ICT world is very similar to what we do in the real world. We rely on building robust systems, vaccinating regularly, and by responding quickly and effectively to crises, thanks to a federated global network, with national control, that enables sharing of knowledge and prompt diffusion of remedies, curative and preventive. That model is known as CERT, which is short for Computer Emergency Response Team Coordination Center (CERT/CC). There are CERTs in government agencies and in corporations. Each CERT operates independently, a creature of its owners, but they coordinate their activities across the world, voluntarily, recognizing that this is the only way to deal with a global threat to a complex global system originating from many sources. I will refer to this as the CERT model. The CERT model focuses both on responses to specific incidents, which is where it has its origins, and on identifying and addressing existing and potential threats, notifying system administrators and other technical personnel of these threats, and coordinating with vendors and incident response teams globally to address the threats. And it all seems to work, because the model focuses sharing, managing and exploiting knowledge acquired or developed by many for the collective good of all.

This approach makes the CERT model capable of learning as it deals with each problem or incident and once it has learned something useful, the model easily socializes that learning across the globe, quickly reaching those who need to know. CERT also supports activities intended to harden the system against known or probable threats, for example by assisting critical infrastructure owners and operators to assist them to identify vulnerabilities in computer systems and related networks, and to test their ability to resist exploitation and attack. In Australia, the Government CERT provides financial assistance to do this and access to a panel of vetted and trusted consultants. This seems to be a more sustainable approach than forcing financial institutions to undergo expensive stress-testing, which is conducted too rarely to be of any real value in strengthening the system.

But in the world of finance we obstinately stick to the logic people used in the Middle Ages. We think each time we face a crisis we are dealing with something new; we retreat behind national or corporate moats; we blame individuals for causing or spreading the plague; and we fiddle at the edges, ignoring the real causes of the problem. As we have seen, bubbles are part and parcel of the market system and, like the poor, they will always be with us. Individuals do not cause a bubble to burst, though they may seem to be doing just that; once a bubble has inflated, anything will serve to puncture it, if the conditions are right. Like vinegar flies, crooks and charlatans will always be attracted by a market gone sour and will seek to profit from it, but they are not the cause of the problem. It is not individual greed that causes a bubble, but our collective greed. Focusing on overpaid executives is scapegoating, channeling the anger of the crowd onto a few individuals so that we can avoid accepting our own share of the collective guilt, just as Jews and others were scapegoated in medieval Europe whenever a pandemic of plague broke out, because our ancestors did not understand that their poor hygiene and a liking for crowding into towns were to blame for the disease and death that had befallen them.

Enough of death and disease, for now, let us return to our core interest, the well being of the global financial system. What does all this stuff about disease and computers tell us about the stock market, financial markets and investment bubbles in general? It tells us quite a lot, actually. It tells us that the risk of the market going septic will rise significantly and rapidly if the pursuit of profit is not accompanied by adequate treatment of concomitant and inevitable risks. It also tells us that greater scale provides a great breeding environment for unsafe practices and for those who want to take advantage of prevailing circumstances for their own benefit, at the cost of others. Then it tells us that even when the market goes sour, some will be affected more than others and that this is due to differences in how robust and responsive the system is when presented with a crisis. Next to last it tells us that a crisis will come in its own good time, because the point at which the latent risks become manifest is very hard to identify, let alone predict. Lastly and most importantly it tells us that there are steps we can take to make the system more robust, less prone to crisis and, should a crisis strike, better able to respond quickly and effectively—it also tells us of the converse, that some responses are not effective and may even be counterproductive, as we will see shortly.

What happens if the wrong methods are used?

Continuing with the metaphor of the pandemic and responses to pandemics, derived from the discipline of epidemiology, it is possible to formulate a catalog of responses to both pandemic and financial crisis that are unlikely to succeed and may even be counter-productive. Let's consider what history tells us about responses to pandemics:

- emotional reactions, such as searching for those who are thought to have spread the disease or even to have caused it, such as witches or *untori* (or anointers), people who are believed to spread the disease by anointing doors with substances taken from the sick—what happens then is greater and consequent disruption to rational efforts to deal with the problem;[9]
- segregation (or quarantine), locking in the sick and locking out the world, is another option, at the household, neighborhood, city, regional or even national level—this can work if the quarantine is absolute, which is difficult

9 As happened in Milan, Italy, in 1630, when rumors about anointers caused panic such that people who acted suspiciously were beaten by mobs or turned over to the authorities, who often had them put to death (see Untori, by Alexandra Queen, at http://www.pikerpress.com/article.cfm?form.id=1415, retrieved on 24 January 2009.

on a large scale and for a any length of time, but bad for the system, because everything comes to a halt, no trade or social intercourse is possible;

- flight, running away—this does not solve the problem—and the plague might follow those who escape (because they had not developed symptoms, but were nevertheless infected) or travel with them, in their clothes or their possessions or animals; and
- treating the symptoms—alleviates the problem, does not solve it, and may create an illusion of safety, which weakens the organism and the system further.

Translating these observations on pandemics and plagues to financial crises is not difficult. First, there are the emotional reactions, with people blaming overpaid executives, of alleged fraudsters or the government or foreigners—does this resonate with your experience? *Post-hoc*, seemingly dispassionate analysis can also be as unreliable as contemporary, emotional characterizations. As Galbraith observes on the causes of the Great Crash of 1929, the conventional view that the increase in liquidity in 1927 prompted by actions of the Federal Reserve is attractive but misguided.

> *It is simple, and it exonerates both the American people and their economic system from any substantial blame. The danger of being guided by foreigners is well known… The explanation is a tribute only to a recurrent preference, in economic matters, for formidable nonsense.*[10]

Alternatively—or as well as—governments are exhorted or volunteer themselves to do the opposite of whatever is supposed to have caused the problem. So, if lax regulation is thought to be at fault, the response is a lot more regulation, if too much regulation is thought to be at fault, the response is to let the market do what it will. Second, some economies might seek to sequester themselves from the rest of the world, as Malaysia sought to do during the Asian financial crisis in the 1990s. Third, people move their capital, to another type of investment, to cash, to another country where banks have guaranteed deposits, to a supposed safe haven, like Switzerland. Fourth and last, governments will want to act and to be seen to be acting to deal with the crisis, which usually means an endless series of announcements that is rarely founded on strategy or evidence.

When a complex system is at risk of death, resources are withdrawn from the periphery (this is what happens when we get frostbite, for example) and are used to protect the core. Thus, in any financial crisis, entities at the periphery will always suffer more, for longer. This applies to the poor in any given economy, to industries that are not crucial to economic survival—e.g. tourism and leisure—and to whole economies that are distant from the global financial epicenters. The experience of Australia in the

10 1997, page 11.

Great Depression in the 1930s is a good example of this, as we will see shortly, but the experience of the last couple of years is also pertinent. After the global financial crisis started to engulf the world, the Australian dollar, which had reached parity with the US dollar for the first time in several decades, tanked badly, against almost all major currencies. I found this puzzling, because Australia has been the least affected of all major economies, has a very strong financial sector and is stable and safe. One might have thought that, because of its safety, strength and stability, Australia's currency would have attracted lots of buyers. Yet, our dollar plunged even against the Indian Rupee! Why was this so? It was so because the global financial system was bringing its lifeblood back home, to the USA and Europe in particular, thus starving the Aussie dollar of attention and shrinking it rapidly in value. Whatever the intrinsic value of the Australian economy might be, the Australian dollar's value rises and falls as the global tide of money sloshes in and out of the core economies. Its value goes up in the good times, when people are prepared to let money trickle south and goes down in bad times, when the world puts its money under its metaphorical mattress.

The Great Depression was a time of extreme hardship around the world, but it was especially bad for Australians. At the time, Australia was a small, isolated semi-independent nation, with a strong agricultural base that depended on exports and a developing industrial base that depended on domestic consumption and government support, in the form of tariffs. The domestic financial markets were tiny and almost entirely dependent on British investors, who withdrew their funds to protect their home base. The British Government also insisted that the Australian Government repay relatively large loans, despite the economic circumstances, further reducing liquidity in the economy and depriving the Australian Government of the capacity to spend to keep the economic wheels turning.

As the global economy crashed, demand for Australian agricultural exports fell away and unemployment rose dramatically from an already high level—before the stock market crash on Wall Street, unemployment in Australia was already at ten percent. After the crash unemployment in Australia more than doubled to twenty-one percent in mid-1930; it peaked at thirty-two percent in mid-1932. As the ranks of the unemployed swelled, domestic consumption dried up, contributing to a vicious cycle of shrinking investment, liquidity and expenditure in the economy. Arguably, only the advent of the Second World War pulled Australia out of a lingering two-decade long depression. Across the world to the Western Hemisphere, Canada suffered in a similar fashion, for similar reasons. Like Australia, Canada's economy was commodity driven, financially strapped and over-dependent on another economy, the USA. Like Australia, Canada was caught by a simultaneous dip in exports and consumption, just like Australia. In Canada, between 1929 and 1933 the gross national product dropped forty percent and unemployment reached thirty percent in 1933. In the same year, Gross National Expenditure was forty-two percent lower than the 1929 level.

Drawing lessons

What lessons can and should we draw from all when a bubble bursts. First, if markets are driven by a blend of rational and non-rational forces, it is essential that we respond with a mix of solutions that can deal with this mix. So, we should resist emotional responses that would push us to regulate more or to deregulate everything, depending on where we are in the cycle and, whatever we do, we should not do it in the heat of the moment. When a fire burns, the first step is to put it out and to save what we can. The time for inquiring into the causes of the fire comes later, when the ashes are cold and the mind free from immediate concerns. Similarly, when an investment bubble bursts, we should deal with the problems at hand, rather than conducting hasty witch hunts or selectively highlighting personal greed as the cause of our problems, because the cause is our collective greed and not what any one individual or firm may or may not have done. Take action to preserve jobs and to keep the economy alive and pay no heed to the bleating about excessive executive salaries. The herd has caused the damage and culling the odd bull or steer is not going to do us any good. In fact, it can cause damage, by distracting us from focusing on the real problem and by further damaging confidence in the financial system. By all means acknowledge the problem, but make sure people understand that it will be dealt with later, when normality or something like it is restored.

Second, do not segregate your firm or your industry or your economy from the broader economy. While the temptation to pull up the drawbridge may be strong and while doing so may protect you in the short term, it will damage you and the whole economy in the medium to long term. When the banks stopped lending to each other after the subprime crisis, whole economies came to a sudden stop and a huge stockpile of consumer and business confidence was burnt up in very short while. The overriding imperative when a bubble bursts is to keep the system working, to keep credit flowing and to take steps to reduce any negative impact on vulnerable elements of the economy, which requires leadership by government. Doing so will help limit any tendency to panic and will stem any tendency to flight or retreat, fostering a virtuous cycle and preventing a vicious cycle from taking form. When the crisis is dying down and passions have cooled, then take time to identify and treat the causes of the crisis and, if possible, to develop a "vaccine", a way of immunizing the economy against that particular financial fever. Allow me to illustrate these points by reference to a real epidemic.

AIDS and the subprime crisis

When AIDS hit Australia, in the mid-1980s, the response by the authorities was two-pronged: to create awareness among the public of the risk of contagion, through a hard hitting media advertising campaign, and to engage the at risk communities, gays and drug users, in a broad-ranging prevention campaign, which focused on promoting safe sex and safe injecting practices. Later, as drugs became available to treat or to retard the progression of the disease, the Government subsidized these drugs, to ensure wide use. This approach worked. About 16,692 people were living with HIV in Australia at the end of 2007. From the start of the epidemic until the end of 2007, there have been 27,331 diagnoses of HIV and 10,303 diagnoses of AIDS and the country has recorded 6,767 AIDS deaths.

The incidence of AIDS in Australia (0.9 per 100,000 people) is similar to that in the UK and Canada (1.4 and 0.8 respectively) and much lower than in the United States (12.8). Compare this situation with countries where authorities have not cooperated with groups at risk or have pretended that the problem did not or does not exist or adopted an ideological approach, decrying the use of condoms for example. Take Zimbabwe, where one in seven adults has HIV1 and an estimated 565 adults and children become infected with the virus every day; by comparison, in 2007 Australia experienced fewer than 1200 HIV infections during the whole year.

Perhaps you might say that this is not a fair comparison, between a first world country and a country that is a disaster zone...fair point. But what about the USA, where stated earlier, the incidence of AIDS is almost thirteen times Australia's? As it says on the website from which I have taken this information, in the USA "Stigma and discrimination towards HIV positive people still persist and thousands of uninsured Americans struggle to access good HIV care and antiretroviral therapy."[11] There you have the difference between a successful approach and one that has not worked. In Australia the authorities developed a rational approach to tackle the real causes and put substantial effort into making it work. In the USA, the authorities embarked on or allowed by default a non-rational blame the victim approach and did not take the steps needed to deal with the problem. In Australia, health outcomes were pursued and secured through a network based on trust; in the USA, mistrust poisoned any attempt to get to the root causes of the problem, instead focusing attention on red herrings.

Steps towards a federated network of trust

Turning back to the world of finances, what would be the steps required to develop a federated network of trust? I suggest the following steps, to take us towards a new and better way to manage the global financial system:

- Develop a risk engine and apply an appropriate risk mitigation strategy—a little later in this chapter I will suggest how this should be done

11 Retrieved from http://www.avert.org/, on 11 April 2009.

- Develop scenarios based around desired futures and undesirable, but possible future, with at least one bad future that is an outlier (quite unlikely)
- Develop integrated monitoring, using scenarios and keep feeding data into the risk engine
- Develop a global capability to respond to crises, using the CERT experience as a model, leaving intact national and corporate sovereignty—the financial equivalent of CERT could be called FERN or the Financial Emergency Response Network
- Use FERN to develop global, national and corporate capability to assist vulnerable entities/sub-systems (rationalize various international banking structures or, at least, create a common operating model, a system of systems)
- Use the risk engine/scenarios and FERN to develop "vaccines", embedding in the system and in all its elements greater resilience–these vaccines would take the form of standards, as I will explain later
- Use the value equation I proposed earlier to test the impact of any proposed solutions, remembering most importantly, that the first obligation is to do no harm

Because I do not believe that we need an all powerful transnational regulator, while I also do not believe, unlike Prime Minister Gordon Brown, that each state knows best, I think we need to agree on principles that are to be used to reform national regulatory systems. Adoption of these principles would safeguard national sovereignty, while mitigating the risk to the global commons. Here are my suggested principles, which should be used to design national regulatory systems.

A model national regulatory system

My proposal for change includes the development of a model national regulatory system. I will explain later how this would work, but remember that the fundamental objective is to ensure that all components of the financial system can operate within a trusted network. Trust is obtained when we have mutual self-disclosure and sharing (self-disclosure trust); when people make and keep agreements (contract trust); and when people can read another person's intentions and be confident that the other person means no harm (safety trust). We build up self-disclosure trust by sharing information freely and not holding on to knowledge as it were property; by encouraging and receiving feedback—and being seen to treat that feedback with appropriate respect; by disclosing a portion of who we really are to others, sharing some information about our private lives—this does not mean disclosing secrets or details about others; and by being prepared to admit ignorance, to say "I don't know". This is true of organizations as much as it for individuals.

Building contract trust requires following through on promises and commitments, on doing what we say. It also means that if we can't keep a promise, we face up to the consequences. We explain why we can't and we take steps to make good any direct or collateral damage. On the other hand, it means giving others a bit of latitude that perhaps we would not allow for ourselves, being forgiving of small or infrequent lapses by others. Safety trust is achieved by making sure that we at least do no harm in our relationships with others. It means doing what we do professionally, with no malice and no deceit, and being always ready to explain why something has to be done. Safety trust requires self-disclosure and contract trust as conditions precedent. If there is low contract and self-disclosure trust, it is not possible to achieve safety trust. Without safety trust, morale in organisations will be low and productivity will be lower than it can be, at both the firm level and affecting whole economies.[12]

As I observed earlier, my proposition for change is predicated on using market forces to ensure that the market has the right balance of regulation and freedom to fail or succeed. Those forces are competition (or contestability), to create a self-sustaining drive towards innovation and continuous improvement, and a price signal, to push the market in the right direction. Contestability would be created by using standards to make explicit to the public, not just to the cognoscenti, the level of competence of fundamental elements of the market. Armed with that information, investors would be better placed to make informed choices and regulators would be better equipped to identify and to deal with systemic risk. The level of competence within a specific economy would be correlated with the capacity of the system to sustain risk, providing a price signal to the economy that would steer it towards higher levels of competence and, consequently, towards higher levels of productivity and profitability.

The model is predicated on my belief that a standards based approach, as explained in *Compliance and Regulation*, is most likely to deliver the level of flexibility, reliability and sustainability required by the twenty-first century economy.[13] Standards are ubiquitous and increasingly pervasive in our society; they are embedded in our lives, from computers, to telephones, to cars, and in other things too, like food or services. The effect of using standards is that the behavior of those using those standards is being controlled or, at least, influenced by external forces that are not necessarily visible or obvious. I think about it this way: a train is a powerful, fast device, capable of transporting huge weights, but it is easily controlled by the implied design of railway transport. A train can go only where the tracks go. Standards and standardized procedures work the same way.

12 GW Fairholm, *Leadership and the culture of trust*, Greenwood Publishing Group (1994); A Lyman, "Building trust in the workplace", *Strategic HR Review*, Volume 3 Issue 1 November/December 2003; R Putnam, *Making Democracy Work Civic Traditions in Modern Italy*, Princeton University Press (1993).

13 Some elements of this model are drawn from the regulatory structures assigned to the Food Standards Australia New Zealand, see http://www.foodstandards.gov.au/aboutfsanz/.

Lessons from history

Because I am a student of history, when discussing standardization it occurs to me that we have been here before and that it may be useful to understand our previous experience in this domain, to avoid repeating the same mistakes. We need to go back a few centuries, to the fourteenth and fifteenth centuries, the golden age of the guilds in Europe. Note here that I am not claiming that the guild is a European invention, since the Indians were here first, by several millennia. The focus on the European guilds is due to the closer cultural similarity between their circumstances and ours. Aside from the direct cultural connection, western European society in the fourteenth and fifteenth centuries being re-shaped by globalization and the internationalization of trade, just as we are now, and new rules had to be created to accommodate new realities. Among those realities was the discovery of a whole continent that had yet to be colonized by capitalism, North America, just as capitalism is now colonizing Asia, and China and India in particular. Lastly, then as now, a lone superpower, Spain then and the USA now, dominated the economy of the western world, but incipient new superpowers were beginning to manifest themselves, England, the Netherlands and Portugal then, India, China, Brazil and Russia now.

In Europe, The guilds were at the center of manufacturing from the thirteenth to the sixteenth century. The guilds enjoyed rights granted by state that gave them a privileged position in the burgeoning town economies, often amounting to a monopoly. For example, in Florence, my native city, there were seven major guilds, the judges and notaries, bankers and international traders in cloth (the *Calimala*), the money changers, the silk merchants, the doctors and apothecaries, the wool merchants, and the dealers in furs. There were also five lesser guilds, the butchers, the shoemakers, the smiths, the stonemasons, and the secondhand dealers. Collectively, the guilds elected the six priors who ruled Florence as supreme magistrates, much as Republican Rome was ruled by two consuls and the USA by a President and Vice-President.[14]

The guilds, which provided the foundations of the Florentine state and also were its commercial lifeblood, carved up among themselves the right to carry out certain trades and regulated who could perform which trade and how the requisite skills could be acquired, by apprenticeship. These oligopolies were created and secured their commercial ends through regulation. This was a universal characteristic of guilds throughout Europe. Regulation was also used to ensure that no guild member could usurp to himself too large a share of the pie.[15] For example, in London in the thirteenth century no cordwainer could employ more than eight journeymen. In

14 Actually, the similarity with the situation in the USA is even greater, because the President and Vice-President are elected by an Electoral College that is intended to represent the interests of the electorate, much as the guilds represented the interests of their members.

15 I say himself because the guilds were an almost exclusive male bastion, while women in the Middle Ages were involved in trade, it was rare for a woman to be allowed to join a guild.

Venice in the fifteenth century no silk weaver could have more than six looms. Some of you may remember that Savings and Loans banks in the USA were once restricted to operating within a tight geographic area or the strict differentiations that once generally applied to what savings and merchant banks could do.

European guilds imposed long, standardized periods of apprenticeship, much as the medical profession does today. The guilds, aided and abetted by the state that harbored them, also made it difficult to gain access to materials or knowledge needed to set up a new business in a regulated trade or craft, and controlled who could sell what and where, again much as medical practitioners or lawyers, for example, do today. Essentially, a business could not be established or operated without the continuing consent of the relevant guild—once in, standards had to be maintained, without fail, and corners could not be cut. If anyone did not play by the rules, they were dealt with, swiftly and effectively, because this was in the interest of the members of the guild—and in the interests of the state's economy as a whole. The success of any member of a guild depended on the success of the guild as a whole and the success of the guild depended on its collective reputation as a reliable supplier of quality products or services, in a virtuous cycle of quality improvement. If you wanted quality wool or a reliable merchant bank, you would turn to the Florentine guilds. If you wanted lace, you would go to Bruges, and so on, giving international trade a relatively stable and reliable platform on which to build ever-growing prosperity.

Like any strength, the strength of the guild system had its dark side, which was eventually to contribute to its destruction. The dark side of stability and reliability is blind conservatism, the reluctance to embrace innovation, which eventually limits the capacity of business to meet the changing expectations of its customers. However, the guilds could perhaps have remedied this flaw, in time, if the world had not changed radically, making their survival impossible. The guilds thrived while the city-state was the fundamental unit of governance. The guilds needed the close-knit world embraced by the city walls to survive. Once city-states started giving way to nation-states, the guilds could not survive—the eco-system that had spawned and nurtured them was no more. As modern capitalism took shape and took hold, the closed world of the guild was doomed to be replaced by a new entity, the corporation, the child of capitalism, and new rules would have to be created to regulate this often unruly child, the rules which, broadly speaking, are now reaching their use by date.

What can we learn from this that would be of use today? First, we know that a well-structured regulatory regime developed cooperatively by the state and industry can facilitate the development of a business environment that is friendly to private enterprise. Second, it seems that standards can provide the backbone of a successful regulatory environment. Third, compliance need not be predicated on enforcement, but can rest on foundations provided by standards and a strong attachment to quality.

All these characteristics could be replicated in our time, though not in the same way as the way of the guilds, and we will return to this theme later in the book.

How we develop standards

If my proposal were adopted, to do business, financial services providers would have comply with standards in the Code and regulators would comply with relevant elements of the Code. Standards established by the Code would be legal requirements and non-compliance would attract penalties. Sustained compliance of a high standard would be acknowledged through incentives that reward the provider and benefit the system. Inadequate performance by the regulator(s) would also attract appropriate sanctions, tied to the performance of the system, measured against the criteria I set out earlier and by using the value equation I have proposed.

The Code would comprise:

- national and international standards;
- codified practice manuals;
- specifications;
- handbooks; and
- guidelines, including the management of FERN.

Wherever possible and desirable, the Code would rely on international standards, supplemented by specific national standards, specifications and so on. The standard adoption and development process would involve an evaluation of the risk to the system and to the economy as a whole of any proposed change to the Code and the impact of the regulation on the financial services industry and any international obligations. The Code would provide standards for:

1. Regulators and regulation.
2. Corporate governance.
3. Professional conduct (for executives, managers, accountants, lawyers, advisers and so on).
4. Development of products and services.
5. Deployment of products and services.
6. Training and qualifications of industry participants.
7. Sanctions, penalties and rewards.
8. Independent supervision of the Code.

The purpose

The purpose of the Code is to enable the financial system (the System) to meet the requirements of the economy as whole and of its constituent elements, including meeting any international obligations. The desired state is a sustainable, stable and reliable system, and well-informed consumers. The operating principles are openness, transparency, predictability, accountability and responsiveness to changing circumstances and expectations. To ensure public confidence in regulatory decisions, the approach should be collaborative, including national and international regulatory partners, financial services providers, broader industry, consumer organizations, government bodies and other stakeholder groups. The method of operation should rest on a standards-based approach, where a standard is a set of specifications and procedures designed to ensure products, services and systems are safe, reliable and perform as intended.[16] What I am proposing is that a *Financial Services Standards Code* (the Code) be developed, to govern the global financial system. The Code would complement the work of FERN, by providing a context within which FERN would operate. The performance of the Code—and of FERN itself—would be continuously assessed against these criteria, which are derived from the discussion in earlier chapters.[17]

1. The System creates minimum overheads

By working within the Code, individuals, businesses and governments can do what they need or want to do, safely, with little red tape and without fear of breaking the rules.

2. The System is sustainable and reliable

The Code gives everyone confidence that the financial products and services they are developing or using are safe, reliable and will perform as intended. Standards help consumers make informed choices between one product or service and another. Standards also enable the regulators to stay ahead of the risk curve, facilitating prevention and minimizing the need for cures.

3. Innovation is ubiquitous and sustainable

Standards provide a platform on which to turn ideas into innovation, into new value, however defined.[18] As the world changes, standards change to reflect new technologies, shifting perceptions and community expectations.

16 This is a modified version of the definition used by Standards Australia, see http://www.standards.org.au/cat.asp?catid=2.

17 Again, these success criteria owe much to the work of Standards Australia.

18 Drucker, in the *The Discipline of Innovation*, says this about innovation, "It means having a clear mission. It means defining what you mean by results. It means the ability and willingness to abandon where you don't get results. And then–when you find the real opportunity, the unique opportunity where you can make the greatest difference, zone in on it, and reassess and reassess and reassess. This is a discipline. This is not being brilliant, it's being conscientious."

4. Production and productivity grow faster than international benchmarks

Standards save time and money and enable the development of new capabilities. They drive economies of scale, enable the reduction of energy consumption and support useful new technologies.

5. Businesses and the economy are more competitive

Financial services providers that comply with the Code have a competitive edge over those that do not, because their product and service offerings are both reliable—they do the job—and trusted.

6. International trade is easier

Businesses that comply with the Code are automatically accepted as trusted and reliable providers around the world, removing entry barriers to international markets.

7. Markets work better

The Code helps governments to protect the community and the economy and provide a defense against crime, malfeasance and terrorism, by ensuring the System is open, transparent and accountable.

How it would work

When a wildfire or a hurricane approaches, people are told of the strength and dimensions of the event and of the likely level of risk they face. Armed with that information, people can make their own choices, to flee or to stay, to stay in the house or to seek shelter somewhere else, and so on. When it comes to fires, the level of sophistication in estimating the likelihood and probable consequences of a fire is very high. In Australia we have a Forest Fire Danger Index (FFDI), which is a composite measure of humidity levels, wind speed, temperature, and combustibility of fuel. The FFDI has proven itself to be highly reliable. I am proposing that we develop a measure similar to the FFDI for financial markets, with two levels of measurement, for the market as a whole and for significant segments. This measure could be called the Financial Markets Risk Index (FMRI).

The FMRI, which would be produced by the FERN, would be a composite of the level of competence of the regulator(s); the level of sophistication of the market's soft and hard infrastructure; the level of deviation of the market from established measures, such as price to earnings ratios, for example; the stability of the host economy; the level of competence of ratings agencies; the medium-term trajectory of the host economy; and the level of sophistication of the host civil society. The FMRI would be compiled and published by the FERN, as I said, and would be produced at the national level, under government supervision, and as a global index, under the supervision of the body that governs FERN at the global level.

The level of competence of the regulator(s) would be determined by reference to standards adopted globally, let us say against a scale of 1 to 100, where the latter point represents perfection or total compliance. Each year (and perhaps more frequently during times of turmoil), national regulators would be audited by an independent international panel and rated against these standards. When I say competence, I mean the capacity to perform effectively a given function or functions or role—one either can or can't do it; there is no in-between rating. Let me illustrate my point. Would you use a brain surgeon who is almost capable of performing surgery or trust an airplane pilot who can almost fly an aircraft? I think not. You would not trust your own life or the lives of several hundred to such people. So, why is it that do we not apply the same logic in the case of people or organizations that control the future of millions or even billions? Why is it that we put our future and our children and grandchildren's future in the hands of people whose competence has never been tested objectively? After all, these are the same people who allowed Bernard Madoff to get away with fraud on a grand scale for decades. These are the same people who have run banks and other financial institutions that have been found sorely wanting.

I say we should stop trusting those who have proven they do not deserve our trust. Those appointed to be a regulator should be competent to do the job and should be tested regularly, to keep them on their toes. This is why, by the way, I do not support the proposition that we should have some sort of global or trans-national regulatory agency. We would end up with the same sort of people who have fallen well short of the mark every time they have been put to the test, because the same sort of people who have failed in the USA exist elsewhere, for the same reasons. It is a club of those in the know who then pretend to police their fellow members. Allow me to illustrate this, by recounting a story told by Robert Manne, an Australian political commentator, in an essay titled "Neo-Liberal Meltdown".[19]

> *James Lieber in the* Village Voice *tells a fascinating story. One of the engine rooms of the derivatives market was the London-based financial-products arm of the (later bailed-out) American insurance giant AIG. In 2000, the chief legal officer of AIG asked the head of insurance regulation in New York whether he would like to audit their business. The New York regulator politely declined.*

In the same essay, Manne turns to the erstwhile darling of the markets, Alan Greenspan, observing that Greenspan, the chief regulator of the US financial markets and indirectly of the whole US economy, was such a blind believer in the ideology of the market that he could see no need to regulate derivatives, including, of course, the type of instrument that triggered the subprime crisis. A competent regulator should not be

19 *The Monthly*, March 2009.

driven by ideology or fear or self-interest, noting that the class of people who most benefit from investment bubbles is the same class from which regulatory positions, high and low, are filled. In the absence of international standards, I will substitute my own judgment here and, because of the intrinsic flaws in the US regulatory regime and because of the track record of regulators, I conclude that it is likely that the American regulator(s) would fail against many of the requisite elements of competence. To be charitable, I might give a rating of 20 from 100 possible points, rather than fail them altogether. This is not the rating the World bank assigns to the USA; the Bank gives a higher score, but I beg to differ, noting that the USA, even according to the World Bank, rates behind suitable comparators.[20]

Next is the level of sophistication of the market's soft and hard infrastructure. US markets are highly developed and sophisticated, if one considers the very broad range of products traded there and the plethora of companies and advisers that populate that market. However, the profession of financial adviser in the US seems to have come a cropper in recent years, behaving like a flock of sheep, rather than like leaders should. Again, in the absence of accepted standards, I will substitute my own judgment, assigning good marks for the hard infrastructure and poor marks for the soft, adding up to 60 in the total, made up of 40 from 50 for the former and 20 from 50 for the latter. I should say that this is not what the World Economic Forum has concluded in developing its first Financial Development Report in 2008, which ranked the USA first and the UK second. Given the events of the last few years, perhaps the WEF needs to re-think the components of its index. I will stick to assessing results, if they are available, rather than mere potential.

The level of deviation of the market from established measures, such as price to earnings ratios, for example, would have registered off the scale in the lead up to the subprime crisis, as shown by Professor Shiller (see figure 11), but was falling sharply by 2006, reaching a level of twelve or thereabouts. A study by Professor Jeremy Siegel, of Wharton, has concluded that US stocks are fairly priced at an average price earnings ratio of about fifteen times earnings.[21] If we were to assume a level of twelve, we would score the market as being on the positive side of risk, perhaps producing a rating of 60 out of 100, noting that in previous periods twelve was a point struck on the way down to even lower levels. Please note that I am not proposing here that the FMRI would rely on price to earning s ratios only; we will need something more sophisticated than this, preferably relying on research that identified solid, reliable, indicators. I am doing what I am doing here to illustrate my point, not to produce a working index.

20 See http://info.worldbank.org/governance/wgi/sc_chart.asp, retrieved 30 June 2009.

21 "Equity Risk Premium Forum, November 8, 2001", *Historical Results I*, Jeremy J. Siegel, Wharton School of Business, Philadelphia, Summary by Peter Williamson, Amos Tuck School of Business Administration, Dartmouth College.

Figure 11: Historical price to earnings ratios for the US S&P 500

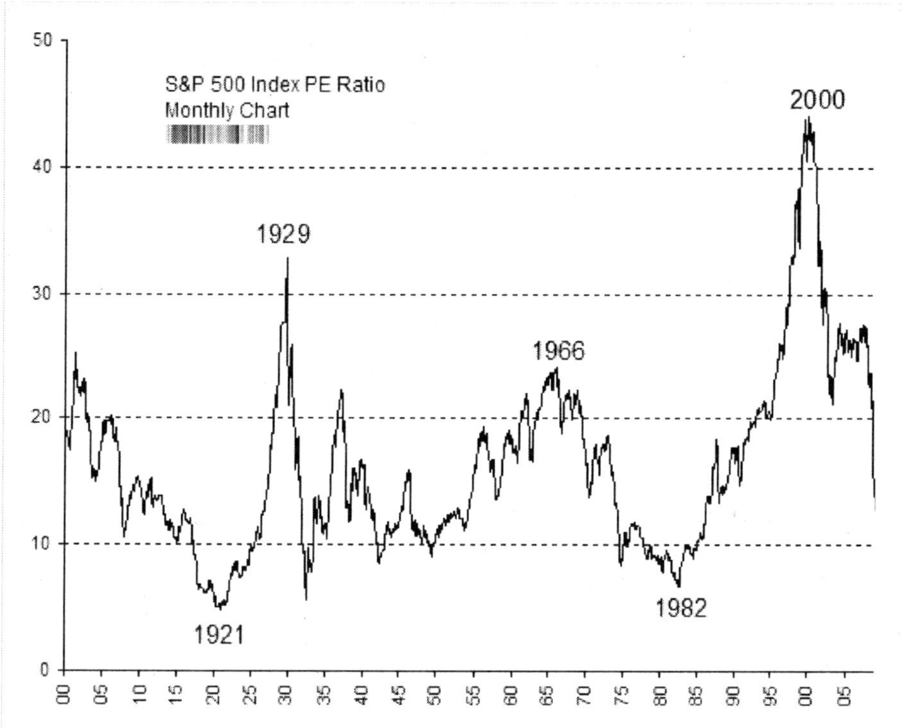

The stability of the host economy also would need to be gauged by reference to a composite basket of indicators. However, it is likely that the USA would score well here, with the major flaw being the high level of debt, especially to China. Perhaps we could be a bit generous here and assign a score of 70 from 100. Next, we judge the level of competence of ratings agencies, again in the absence of established standards. The consensus reached by commentators is that ratings agencies have performed abysmally, so let's say 20 from 100 points for this item. Then we look at the medium-term trajectory of the host economy. To keep things simple, here I will use trends in productivity, assuming that if productivity is not rising, the economy is likely to slow at some subsequent point. The signs have been around since 2006 and 2007 that US productivity was slowing.[22] Let's give the US a score of 50 from 100 here. Lastly, we are assessing the level of sophistication of the host civil society. Here the US does especially well, thanks to its strong media, its commitment to freedom of speech, of assembly and so on. My suggestion is that we use the Freedom Index here, published by Freedom House annually. In 2008 the USA was rated as free (with many other countries) and the consequence is a score of 100 from 100.[23] Again, please note that I am using this index

22 "US Productivity Growth", Willem Buiter, 10 August 2007, from FT.com, retrieved on 25 March 2009.
23 Retrieved on 25 March 2009 from http://www.freedomhouse.org/template.cfm?page=410&year=2008.

to illustrate a point. If I were to look at freedom of the press alone, for example, the USA ranked only 36th in the world in 2008, according to Reporters Without Borders.[24]

What does all this add up to? It adds up to 380 from 700, which is equivalent to about 54.3 from 100. Without a normative framework, this is not very meaningful. To provide a comparison, let's rate Australia also. Again, the level of competence of the regulator(s) would be determined by reference to standards adopted globally, against a scale of 1 to 100, where the latter point represents perfection or total compliance. Australia has one of the best regulatory regimes in the world, judging by its comparative performance against similar economies. However, even Australia falls short of the optimum, because it does not deal adequately with systemic risk. On balance, a rating of 80 points would seem fair.

Next is the level of sophistication of the market's soft and hard infrastructure. Australian markets are highly developed and sophisticated, if one considers the very broad range of products traded there and the plethora of companies and advisers that populate that market. However, Australia suffers a little by comparison with the USA, for example, for reasons of scale. Again, in the absence of accepted standards, I will substitute my own judgment, assigning good marks for the hard infrastructure and average marks for the soft, adding up to 75 in the total, made up of 40 from 50 for the former and 35 from 50 for the latter.

As in the USA, a price earnings ratio of about fifteen times earnings is considered to be fair value and I would assign Australia a similar rating on this criterion, of 60 out of 100. Next we consider the stability of the host economy, where given the performance of the economy over the last twenty years and given Australia's strong record as a stable democracy, we should rate Australia highly, perhaps assigning 80 points from 100. Then we judge the level of competence of ratings agencies, again in the absence of established standards. The consensus reached by commentators is that ratings agencies in Australia have performed better than in the USA, though the ratings game needs improvement there also, so let's say 60 from 100 points.

Turning to the medium-term trajectory of the host economy, Australia traditionally lags comparable economies in terms of multifactor productivity.[25] In particular, as shown by research by the Australian Government Treasury," Despite a series of broad and deep macroeconomic and microeconomic reforms boosting Australia's productivity growth, the level of Australia's GDP per capita remains well below that of the United States."[26] However, until 2009, Australia has had almost two decades of continuous growth. Australia's prospects remain good, given its growing trade links with China, based on mineral exports. Let's give Australia a score of 70 from 100 here. Lastly, we are

24 Retrieved on 25 March 2009, from http://www.rsf.org/article.php3?id_article=29031.

25 Australian Productivity Commission research, at http://www.pc.gov.au/research/productivity/estimates-trends/trends, retrieved on 6 April 2009.

26 Comparing Australian and United States productivity, Jyoti Rahman, Australian Government Treasury, Canberra 2005, see http://www.treasury.gov.au/documents/987/PDF/04_comparing_productivity.pdf.

assessing the level of sophistication of the host civil society, which is strong in Australia, as evidenced, for example, by voluntarism.[27] My suggestion is that we use the Freedom Index here, published by Freedom House annually. In 2008 Australia was rated as free (with many other countries) and the consequence is a score of 100 from 100.[28] Australia ranked 28th in the world in 2008 for press freedom, according to Reporters Without Borders.[29]

What does all this add up to? It adds up to 525 from 700, which is equivalent to about 380 points from 700, which is equivalent to about 75 from 100, compared with the rating for the USA of 54.3 from 100. I must repeat here that this is not a real rating exercise, it is merely an illustration of how a rating system might work, though the hypothesis that Australia would rate better than the USA, at least for now, is likely to be valid. By way of corroboration, Australia's four major banks all continue to have strong ratings, despite the global and local financial turmoil and the Australian Government retains a strong AAA rating.[30]

Using the Financial Markets Risk Index (FMRI)

How would the index be used and what would happen if it were used? These are good questions. Let me see if I can provide equally good answers. As I said earlier, the ratings would be compiled by an independent national authority, the FERN. Such bodies would have to be compliant with international governing standards, perhaps overseen by the (almost) new Financial Stability Board (FSB), the revamped Financial Stability Forum or, alternatively, by the global FERN federation. As indicated in official media releases following the April G20 meeting in London, the FSB is supposed to be "a mechanism for national authorities, standard setting bodies (SSBs) and international financial institutions to address vulnerabilities and to develop and implement strong regulatory, supervisory and other policies in the interest of financial stability."[31] The ratings could be published by the FSB and would have to form part of any documentation made available to the public by all financial services providers, by force of domestic law and by application of international standards. So, when Mr and Mrs Public apply for a loan or Ms Gen Y receives advice from a broker, they would be advised, among other things, of the rating of the relevant economy at that time and would also be given trend information.

27 Australian Government, Social Policy Research Paper Number 28, published by the former Department of Families, Community Services and Indigenous Affairs, retrieved from http://www.facs.gov.au/research/prp28/exec.htm on 6 April 2009, which shows Australia performing better than most, though not as well as Canada, Finland, France and the United Kingdom.

28 Retrieved on 25 March 2009 from http://www.freedomhouse.org/template.cfm?page=410&year=2008.

29 Retrieved on 25 March 2009, from http://www.rsf.org/article.php3?id_article=29031.

30 See http://www.businessday.com.au/business/moodys-to-review-bank-ratings-20090219-8c4g.html, retrieved on 6 April 2009.

31 See http://www.fsforum.org/press/pr_090402b.pdf, retrieved on 6 April 2009.

The advice, based on a substantial statistical base that would have to be developed, might read like this for someone who is considering buying listed stocks: the rating for the USA at present is 53.4, which means that the risk rating for investment in the stock market is high. The trend for the next twelve months is steady, with a tendency to improve, with a likely rating of medium-high by the second quarter of 2010. A rating of high means that there is a substantial risk (more likely than not) in the short to medium term (one to three years) that the value of the investment will decrease by more than thirty percent and may decrease by as much as fifty percent. A rating of medium-high suggests that there is a substantial risk of a short to medium term decrease in value of fifteen percent, with a possible decrease of as much as thirty percent. The risk ratings for other economies would also be provided.

What would the recipients of this advice do as a consequence of receiving it? They may decide not to invest in the stock market, for the time being, perhaps waiting to see if the projected fall in risk eventuates. Their money might be left in the bank or they might consider alternative forms of investment, such as real estate or bonds, where the risk rating might produce different projections of likely outcomes. They might also consider investing the money in another economy, which has a better risk rating. These alternatives illustrate how the FMRI would assist the global financial system to move resources to where they are most likely to be used optimally. Mr and Mrs Public might also decide to proceed with their purchase of stocks, because their investment perspective is long term, not short term, or because they are comfortable with the level of risk they are incurring. Their money, their call. The intent of the FMRI is not to stifle or to limit individual choice; its role is to help inform consumers trying to make sense of a complex market.

This is a micro level example. What could happen at a macro level? The FMRI would work in a way similar to an electrified fence on a cattle ranch. The current is not actually strong enough to stop a beast that is intent on running through the fence, but it is strong enough to cause a pause for reflection and, generally, a wired fence will keep the herd corralled where the rancher wants it to be. My expectation is that the FMRI would operate on our own animal spirits in a similar manner. It would not stop an investor who is determined to graze on the other side of the fence, where the bulls are, but it would give that investor—and the market as a whole–pause for thought. The FMRI would cool down any undue exuberance in the market. But it would do more, over time. It would act as a stabilizer, by funneling risk towards those elements of the global system that are best placed to handle it at that time.

If the FMRI does its job properly, its impact at the macro level in a high risk environment would be to divert money from hot spots to cooler spots, to stop firewood being piled onto a highly flammable pyre. If implemented properly, within a new regulatory regime that professionalizes the entire market, keeps regulators on their toes, and provides actors with maximum information, the FMRI would slow down the inflation of bubbles and act as a homeostatic device within the economy. Homeostasis is the property of a system that regulates its internal environment, maintaining a stable, constant condition. It is how the human body works, keeping the heart beating, the lungs breathing, and our body temperature constant, without our conscious intervention. Homeostasis is perhaps what Adam Smith imagined when he wrote about the invisible hand. The problem is that the economy needs an invisible brain, not an invisible hand.

As Wikipedia explains, "homeostatic control mechanisms have at least three interdependent components for the variable being regulated: The receptor is the sensing component that monitors and responds to changes in the environment. When the receptor senses a stimulus, it sends information to a control center, the component that sets the range at which a variable is maintained. The control center determines an appropriate response to the stimulus. In most homeostatic mechanisms the control center is the brain. The control center then sends signals to an effector, which can be muscles, organs or other structures that receive signals from the control center. After receiving the signal, a change occurs to correct the deviation by either enhancing it with positive feedback or depressing it with negative feedback."

The receptor is the global system of collection, analysis and publication that would support the FMRI. The control center, the brain, is the web of international standards I have proposed, mediated by appropriate domestic and international institutions. The FMRI is the signal sent by the brain to all those who have a stake in the operation of the financial services industry, not just those who are in the know, the members of the club, the insiders. The collective response by stakeholders to the signal will be either positive feedback, "designed to push levels out of normal ranges", or negative feedback, driving the system towards "a set and narrow range". [32]

> *"Successful investing is anticipating the anticipations of others."*–John Maynard Keynes

Summing up

In summary, the FMRI, together with FERN and my proposed Code would act as stabilizers for the financial system, keeping it within more manageable parameters, reducing potential swings up and potential falls, without tying everything up in red tape or making us all hostage to the lowest common denominator. The FMRI and the FERN would limit the speed of the System to a manageable level, while constantly improving

32 From http://en.wikipedia.org/wiki/Homeostasis, retrieved on 6 April 2009.

the capacity of the System to handle higher and higher speeds. I am confident that it would work and I have put forward the means for testing my confidence. Yes, what I am proposing seems like a radical departure from the status quo, but is that not what we need now? The status quo has served us well, more or less, for six decades, but it has now reached its use by date. If you do not agree, tell me again what you will do when the next bubble bursts? I thought so, you are not sure. Well, just in case my proposals are not accepted, allow me to suggest a few things you could do, as well as some books you may want to read, in chapter 7.

CHAPTER 7 Hints and tips

Here we get down to the practicalities of turning all this knowledge and understanding into wisdom, into something useful in running a business or working in one. First, we will focus on how to avoid getting caught up in a bubble or in a dodgy Madoff-like scheme. Then I will provide indicators of an inflating bubble and to strategies that you can use to benefit through this process—without pumping more air into the bubble. Lastly, we will consider strategies to use when a bubble has burst. In putting forward suggestions, I will refer to the thinking and wisdom of others, of course. I have chosen four books as sufficient to provide a broad view of diagnosis, prognosis and cure.

There are many more now in the marketplace, but most of these are sensationalist or shallow in their approach and do not tell us much of value. The books I have chosen are from a hands on investor who fancies himself as a philosopher, George Soros; by JK Galbraith, a stalwart of Keynesian thinking and a very lucid and sharp writer and thinker; by Paul Krugman, winner of the Nobel Prize in economics and someone who is prepared to challenge the status quo; and by Niall Ferguson, a historian with a deep understanding of economic theory and practice. I will extract from these books any guidance I think might help us here and then draw from it lessons that may help us to avoid repeating past mistakes.

Learning from the past

Let us start with George Soros. In *The New Paradigm For Financial Markets. The Credit Crisis Of 2008 And What It Means*, Soros puts forward what he calls policy recommendations.[1] His rationale is not dissimilar from mine, as he observes that regulators are human and are also bureaucrats and that "...going overboard with regulations could severely impede economic activity." His conclusion, like mine, is that "systemic risks need to be managed by the regulatory authorities" and cannot be left to market participants and that access to regulation is essential for effective market regulation. Soros suggests that regulation should encompass credit creation, as well money supply, which poses an interesting question. Since credit creation is an important generator of money supply, how is it that regulating the latter does not include regulating the former? Soros then

1 In chapter 8, which begins at page 142.

goes on to say that the recent housing bubble in the USA and what he calls the "super-bubble" are the result of the "excessive use of leverage" and that leverage should be "controlled". That is about it for his proposals to deal with systemic risk; the rest of the chapter concerns itself with dealing with the specifics of the US housing bubble.

I have already discussed Galbraith's book on the 1929 crash, as I sought to gain from the past a better understanding of how to read the present, but let me focus here on his proposed remedies, rather than on the diagnosis. In chapter ix, Galbraith identifies five weaknesses, which he believed to have had "an especially intimate bearing on the ensuing disaster" of the Great Depression. [2] The first weakness is the "bad distribution of income". Galbraith argues that the economy at the time was unwisely dependent on "a high level of investment or a high level of luxury consumer spending or both". The stock market crash wiped out a large portion of the capacity of the rich to spend and invest, thus weakening the underlying economy. The second weakness is "bad corporate structure", which had resulted, in Galbraith's words, from the "fact that American enterprise in the twenties had opened its hospitable arms to an exceptional number of promoters, grafters, swindlers, impostors, and frauds". Tied to this wave of what he calls "corporate larceny" was "the vast new structure of holding companies and investment trusts". This posed a risk to the economy because dividends from utility, railroad and entertainment businesses paid the interest on the bonds of holding companies. When the dividend flow dried up, the river of bond debt could not be contained and holding company after holding company went broke. As more and more of the remaining income was put to the task of repaying debt, "borrowing for new investment became impossible", creating a self-sustaining deflationary spiral.

Next, Galbraith focused on the bad banking structure, which was highly fragmented, creating the potential for a domino effect, which was soon realized, as "When one bank failed, the assets of others were frozen while depositors elsewhere had a pregnant warning to go and ask for money." Using terms which readers of this book will understand easily, Galbraith describes how "when income, employment, and values fell as the result of a depression bank failures could quickly become epidemic". What made things worse is that even where deposits were not lost, a pervasive fear of loss swept the whole economy, destroying confidence and swiftly killing off any green shoots of recovery. The next weakness is the "dubious state of the foreign balance", meaning the position of the USA as a creditor in global markets. How was this a problem? It was a problem because many of the debtors were not in a position to re-pay the debt or even the interest owing and to get around this problem, US banks made a string of new loans available, to countries such as Peru, for example. As Galbraith explains, while the amount of debt grew, debtor nations "had either to increase their exports to the United States or reduce their imports or default on their past loans." The first option was eliminated, because the US Government increased tariffs significantly, and this, in turn,

2 This chapter begins at page 168.

reduced even further whatever capacity there was for debts to be repaid to the US. Large scale debt default followed, with an accompanying fall in US exports.

The last weakness was what Galbraith called the "poor state of economic intelligence", as shown by the preceding discussion on the handling of foreign debt. In Galbraith's view, "the economists and those who offered economic counsel in the late twenties and early thirties were almost uniquely perverse", meaning that their advice was generally to the exact opposite of what ought to be done. In particular, this was to balance the budget, preventing any increase in government outlays and removing any capacity to reduce tax. This was a position driven by belief and ideology, not science or reason. Essentially, it was believed that because thrift was good and extravagance was bad, then the solution to the day's economic woes could be found only in being good, in being thrifty. Another piece of ideological irrationality was the continuing attachment to the gold standard, which, it was argued, protected against inflation. Of course, in a time of severe deflation a little push toward inflation would not have been a bad thing, but, in any case, the rationale for keeping the gold standard was fundamentally flawed. As Galbraith points out, "Until 1932 the United States added formidably to its gold reserves, and instead of inflation the country was experiencing the most violent deflation in the nation's history." The sum of these attachments to traditional values was rightly characterized by Galbraith as "...a triumph of dogma over thought."

This is a good point at which to move on to consider Paul Krugman's book, titled *The Return of Depression Economics And The Crisis Of 2008*. Like Galbraith's book, this is an updated version of an earlier book, first released in 1999. Krugman picks up where Galbraith leaves off, it seems at first glance, observing that "Most economists...regard the Great Depression of the 1930s as a gratuitous, unnecessary tragedy" and that since then economists and policymakers have learnt their lesson.[3] In other words, Krugman suggests, modern policy, guided by contemporary economics would avoid repeating the mistakes so well identified by Galbraith and discussed above. However, Krugman thinks this might not be so and he uses the Asian crisis of the 1990s and the 2008 crisis to argue that those lessons have not been learnt or at least that they are not being applied as smartly as they should be, adjusting for changed circumstances. He quotes himself from the 1999 version of the book as saying, "...it was as if bacteria that used to cause deadly plagues, but had long been considered conquered by modern medicine, had reemerged in a form resistant to all the standard antibiotics...Well, we were foolish. And now the plague is upon us."[4] Later in the book, Krugman quotes Robert Lucas, another Nobel Prize winner in economics, claiming in a speech in 2003 that the "central problem of depression prevention...has been solved, for all practical purposes."[5] Much of the book is then taken up by Krugman's arguments as to why Lucas was wrong.

3 At page 3.
4 At page 5.
5 At page 9.

Arguably, though we are not yet out of the woods entirely, it may that Lucas was indeed right, though perhaps for the wrong reasons. In mid 2009, it seems that policies have been put into place that seem to have prevented a second great depression. This is most evident in my homeland, Australia, where a strong system of financial regulation, a government prepared to spend and invest and a banking sector that has not suffered a single default, seem to be carrying the country's economy through the crisis with relatively little damage. This could be read to imply that Krugman was wrong, if indeed Lucas was right. However, as I have already said, Lucas was right for the wrong reasons. Lucas thought that a new depression was not possible, Krugman argues, because he thought that the business cycle had been "tamed", and, indeed, that little would be gained by doing more. The events of the last two years establish that Lucas was wrong; the business cycle has not been tamed, it is as wild and unpredictable as ever, as we have seen in earlier chapters, and that it will remain so. However, this time around we have reacted better, on the whole, and more swiftly, with positive results, so far at least. This seeming contradiction, which has both Lucas and Krugman in the right and in the wrong at the same time, makes it worthwhile to read Krugman's book. In particular, the last few pages are worth special attention, starting from page 162, when he discusses depression economics.

Here Krugman puts the boot into supply-side economics, labeling it a "...crank doctrine that would have had little influence if it did not appeal to the prejudices of editors and wealthy men", and pushes strongly his theory that the focus should be on the demand side of the economy instead. For this is where Krugman sees "depression economics", because the "...failures on the demand side of the economy—insufficient private spending to make use of the available productive capacity—have become the clear and present limitation on prosperity for a large part of the world." Krugman puts forward a two phase solution. First, he argues, the world needs a "rescue operation", to "get credit flowing again and prop up spending." Then, when the crisis has past, we need "financial reform". The source of the problem in Krugman's view is that international financial flows have been increasing vastly and without adequate controls; that the growth of "the shadow banking system" has "set the stage for latter-day bank runs on a massive scale (through) mouse clicks rather than frantic mobs outside locked bank doors...". And his solution is to extend the kind of regulation that has covered the mainstream banking world. Krugman proposes that "Now that we've seen a wide range of non-bank institutions create what amounts to a banking crisis, comparable regulation has to be extended to a much larger part of the system."[6] Am I alone in finding this a bit of a letdown in a book with such a grand title? I will come back to Paul Krugman later, but first let us see what Professor Ferguson, the historian, has to offer.

His book is titled *The Ascent of Money. A Financial History of the World*, a publication that has met with such acclaim that it has been turned into a well-received television

6 At page 190.

series with the same name.[7] As you may have observed, I tend to value the perspectives historians bring to the understanding and resolution of complex contemporary problems, including financial problems. The book provides a great deal of historical material that, in my view, underpins the analysis and the proposals for change I have put forward in this book, including my warning about the risk that China's economy and its interrelationship with the US economy pose to the global economy. In a chapter with the fascinating title of "From Empire to Chimerica", Ferguson explains how the growing US dependence on Chinese credit creates the potential for the US economy as a whole to be labeled and treated as a "sub-prime economy". Ferguson compares this co-dependence with the relationship between Imperial Britain and the new nation of Germany in the19th Century, an imbalanced relationship that eventually led to two global wars and terminated the nineteenth century version of globalization. At some point, whether because of fear of the future or because of conflict, perhaps over Taiwan or North Korea, the IOU to China from the people of the USA may be called in. It may also happen as the people of China grow wealthier and want to repatriate their money so that they can put it to work in their own country or so that they can spend it, creating their own investment bubbles. Or it may be that none of these things will happen and that Chinese thrift will continue to support the American way of life. Only time will tell. What is certain, however, is that the wealth imbalance between China and the USA creates a reservoir of risk that has to be studied, understood and managed. And if the US does not want this done, the rest of us may have to persuade them otherwise, because as a slightly reworded version of a famous saying goes, when the elephants dance, the mice should be afraid, very afraid.

Ferguson concludes his book by observing that "...financial markets are like the mirror of mankind, revealing every hour of every working day the way we value ourselves and the resources of the world around us. It is not the fault of the mirror if it reflects our blemishes as clearly as our beauty."[8] I wish I had thought of it first! In any case, this is a good point at which to turn from description to analysis.

What should we learn from history?

For me, Galbraith's analysis remains the most useful, if we shift the focus from the US to the global scene. This is why. Galbraith identified five weaknesses: the "bad distribution of income"; "bad corporate structure"; bad banking structure; the "dubious state of the foreign balance"; and the "poor state of economic intelligence", with dogma triumphing over thought. If we look at the global economy and at the global financial system, we can soon see that all these weaknesses are present, though in different guises, perhaps. Income distribution across the world is grossly imbalanced. Global income inequality

7 You can buy the DVD of the series as well as the book from any major book retailer.
8 At page 358.

is perhaps greater than it has ever been, with the richest one percent of people in the world receiving as much as the bottom fifty-seven percent.[9] If, as Krugman argues, the economy is dependent on demand to support prosperity, this kind of imbalance presents a problem, as it did in the USA at the time of the Great Depression. If, for some reason, the rich stop spending or are unable to spend, perhaps because of a credit crunch originating in the USA following the repatriation of Chinese funds lent to Americans, the global economy could enter a period of deflation that would make the Great Depression feel like a picnic.

I have discussed elsewhere in this book, as well as in my earlier book (*Compliance and Regulation in the International Financial Services Industry*) the problems afflicting global and national banking and I have proposed solutions. The very least we should do is what Krugman suggests in his book, which is to extend the present regulatory regime to encompass non-banking financial institutions. However, we should note that this would be a bandaid at best, because the creativity of humans is without end. However far we push the regulatory boundary, someone somewhere will find ways around it. The only permanent solution is to re-think why and how we regulate and to do it in such a way that the system becomes self-adjusting, self-repairing. Both Professor Ferguson and I have spoken of the problem of the foreign balance, especially as it relates to China and the USA. But this is not the only problematic area. At the moment, the world economy runs on Chinese demand for commodities and on Chinese capital. Historically, the Chinese have been great savers and they may continue to be as they get wealthier and have increasing freedom to spend their wealth as they wish. But we cannot take this for granted. What if the propensity to save is associated negatively with growth in disposable income? If that were so, as the latter goes up, the former would come down. This, of course, would contradict Denison's law, which holds that the overall rate of savings in a given economy is inelastic, meaning that it changes little if at all over decades and it seems that household savings are particularly steady.[10] I guess we shall have to wait and see, but I suggest you keep an eye on Chinese savings trends.

Then we have the twin evils of poor economic intelligence and the ever present threat of dogma as a way of making policy. For many years in Australia we had a conservative government that prided itself on being a good economic manager. One of its claims to fame was that it for most of its almost twelve years in power produced a budget surplus. One of its mantras was that budget surpluses are good and budget deficits are bad, whatever the circumstances. As it happens, they lost government in 2007 and have been in opposition through the present crisis. Throughout the crisis they have continued to assert that government budgets should not go into deficit and have attacked the (Labour) Government for its vigorous efforts to support demand and to keep credit flowing, because this has required the Government to borrow.

9 See http://ucatlas.ucsc.edu/income.php, retrieved on 28 June 2009.
10 See http://bear.cba.ufl.edu/bomberger/papers/dtext.pdf, retrieved on 28 June 2009.

It seems reasonable to assume that if the conservatives had not lost power in 2007, they would have stuck to their dogma and would not have supported flagging demand and infrastructure building, if that had required them to go into debt. Similar cries have been heard in the USA also, where President Obama has been declared a spendthrift and labeled a communist because of his spending and interventionist policies. The cries have come from economists as well as politicians and commentators. It seems that poor economic intelligence and dogma are alive and well and always ready to make their contribution. Whatever your politics, I urge you always to consider the evidence, rather than the rhetoric, and I have provided material in this book that can be used to distinguish between evidence and rhetoric.

Dodging the bubble and its effects

I will assume that my proposals in chapter 6 have not been accepted. I am not an expert in charting, so I am not going to offer any wisdom related to that craft. However, I think that charting has something to offer, if the example I provided earlier in the book is anything to go by. My focus is more on behavioral and other hints that the market itself and the players in it are likely to display as a bubble inflates. I will also assume that we are concerning ourselves with what goes on in a mature economy, with well developed financial markets, free media and a strong civil society. Also, let me say here and now that I am not trying to scare anyone from being in the stock market. In the long-term, the stock market will give you a better return than most other forms of investment. Also, as they say, it is time in the market that matters and not timing the market, which is not actually possible with a sufficient degree of accuracy and reliability. Go forth and invest, but be aware of the risk, is what I am saying. The question is, in the absence of an accepted, visible and public risk indicator, as proposed in chapter 6, how do we know that a bubble is forming? How do we assess the risk?

First, keep an eye on trends in long-term aggregate indicator of market performance. If the long-term trend for price to earnings is fifteen and the market is starting to diverge from that significantly, for example, that is an indicator of trouble to come. But one indicator is not sufficient to make a decision one way or the other. However, the stock market is not a random machine, a lotto numbers generator that is free of the restraints that apply to all complex systems, restraints that are best understood by reference to statistics and, in particular, trend analyses, of which charting is a specialized manifestation.[11] Also, remember Drucker's view that a speculative bubble has a life of about eighteen months. If the market, when you do your due diligence, has been outside long-term trends for several months, without crashing, you can assume that the time the bubble has left before it is punctured is running short.

11 See "Price-Earnings Ratios as Forecasters of Returns: The Stock Market Outlook in 1996", by Robert J. Shiller, retrieved from http://www.econ.yale.edu/~shiller/data/peratio.htmlhttp://www.econ.yale.edu/~shiller/data/peratio.html, on 10 April 2009.

Second, be alert to the intensity of news reports concerning what is going on in the market, especially stories written by observers, commentators and experts that describe the future state of the market by reference to an extrapolation of the recent past and of the present. You know what I mean, stories that say something like this: because the market was x last year and is twice x now, it will be four times x next year. I recall many such claims being reported in the media in 2006. I am surprised that Google has not come up with a stock market fever indicator yet! You can build your own rough fever indicator using Google news or any similar online tool.[12] Set up an account and choose key words that will harvest stories for you that give an indication of the level of heat in the market. Then, keep tabs on the volume of stories and any hot spots that appear within the overall picture, either sector related or pointers to specific economies. The keywords you may want to consider would include the leading economies, up and coming economies, and words that would bring up commodity prices, known names of speculative stocks, stories on bond yields and so on. You can have many keywords, which will harvest many, many news stories, because I am not suggesting you actually read the stories—though you may want to read a small selection.

The purpose of this exercise is merely to focus on numbers of stories on particular topics, assessing whether the number of stories on speculative stocks is going up and up, for example, while the number of stories on gold is going down. That kind of pattern would suggest that the attention of the media—and of the audience—is shifting to the riskier end of the spectrum. It may also be worth tracking the number of stories on luxury goods, houses, cars, holidays and so on. My hunch is that as the appetite for risk grows, so does the appetite for luxuries. None of these things will prove anything in and by itself, but a few such indicators may paint a vivid picture of the economy going red in the face through over-exertion! If you see such signs, it may be time for you to assume that a bubble burst is on the way. Of course, this approach can be used in reverse also, to see if and when an economy might be coming out of bad spot. As things get better, the media will start to focus more and more on positives, rather than negatives.

Another way of taking the pulse is this. If everyone you meet is talking about how much they have made in the market, from the bank manager, to the checkout operator, to the taxi driver, to the person who makes your hamburger, then you are seeing indicators of market fever, of which you should take note. If everyone is making money in the market, regardless of knowledge, understanding or skill, be afraid, be very afraid. Just as in a casino, when the gaming house closes for the evening, the only guaranteed winner is the house and the rest of us must split into winners and losers. Not everyone can be a winner. If it looks like everyone is a winner, then the economy and the market are drawing down on funds that are not there or that will soon be exhausted. At the same time, you are also likely to see a proliferation of offerings of things (derivatives) to buy in the market, because the salesmen among us will scent an opportunity to dip

12 See http://news.google.com/.

into the river of money that is flowing past their door. Also, money will be easy to find. Lenders will be calling you to see if you want to borrow more, if you want your credit limit on your Amex card increased, or to tell you that since you now have some equity in your home, you could use that money to invest in the market or in some special opportunity the bank itself has devised.

Of course, by now, when all these signs are evident, the bubble may well be well on its way to bursting. If you have missed the early signs, the best you can do, if you are already in the market, is to take steps to hedge your bets. First, you could start selling stock that has produced a good capital gain, but is paying low dividends. This combination is an indicator that the particular stock may not have the stamina to survive a bear market and you may be better off without it. Take the cash from the sale and invest it somewhere else, preferably somewhere contrary, countercyclical, if you have the appetite for that sort of risk, or if you do not, try government or strong corporate bonds. They should be relatively cheap at that time and, when the bubble bursts and interest rates and dividends drop, you will look and feel like a genius. When interest rates rise again, as the economy recovers, you will get a good capital return from the investment in bonds.

You may also want to pick up any stock that pays a solid dividend that is above the prime lending rate; the caution here is that a solid dividend may become shaky as the slow down takes hold. If you want something even simpler and less risky, in the medium to long term, pay off your home mortgage. You will instantly save money, because in times of bubbles interest rates will be high, and you will save money in the long-term, by reducing your contingent liability. Also, when the bubble bursts, the banks might consider you a good enough credit risk to lend you money against the equity in your home. You will then have money to get a few bargains in now falling stock market.

None of what I have suggested here is a solution in and by itself, because, as discussed in chapter 6, the problem is systemic and can be fixed or I should say managed, because wicked problems cannot be fixed, only at that level. This is why my chief recommendation is that, using the material in appendix 2, you do whatever you can to build a coalition for change. My secondary recommendation is that while systemic change is designed and implemented, you take the approach embedded in appendix 1 to transform how your business understands, creates, manages and harvests value. That is because by doing so you will be helping to make your business more resilient to the temptations that will come your way as the next bubble inflates and you will also be vaccinating your business against the worst consequences of the next bubble toburst.

APPENDIX A

Australian Guiding Principles on Extended Performance Management

A Guide to Better Managing, Measuring and Reporting Knowledge Intensive Organizational Resources

Final Draft, November 3-4, 2005
GAP Congress on Knowledge Capital, Parliament House, Melbourne,

SOCIETY FOR KNOWLEDGE ECONOMICS

PRODUCTIVITY AND PERFORMANCE THROUGH KNOWLEDGE AND INNOVATION

These draft *Guiding Principles* have been prepared by Christina Boedker, on behalf of the *Society for Knowledge Economics*.

Acknowledgements

All errors and omissions are the responsibility of the author. Please do not quote without the permission of the *Society for Knowledge Economics*. These draft *Guiding Principles* could not have been made possible without the valuable contributions of the following people, to whom the author is grateful. The author is especially thankful to Steve Vamos and Mark Bezzina for making possible this project; to Professor James Guthrie for his mentorship and support; and to Julie King, Warwick Watkins and Bruce Hills for their valuable support with the mini-case studies.

- Cameron Barnsley, University of New South Wales
- Mark Bezzina, StanCert
- Dr. Suresh Cuganesan, Macquarie Graduate School of Management
- John Dumay, University of Sydney
- Richard Fabricius, Hewitt Associates
- David Fox, CPA Australia
- Professor James Guthrie, University of Sydney
- Bruce Hills, Westpac Banking Corporation
- Nicholas Kearns, University of New South Wales
- Julie King, New South Wales Department of Lands
- Kevin Lewis, CPA Australia
- Chris Liell-Cock, KnowledgeAbility
- Beatrice Maestri, Bocconi University
- Professor Jan Mouritsen, Copenhagen Business School
- Tamara Plakalo, Fairfax Business Media
- Dr. Federica Ricceri, University of Padova
- Nick Ridehalgh, PricewaterhouseCoopers
- Professor Goran Roos, Intellectual Capital Services
- Steve Vamos, Microsoft Australia
- Warwick Watkins, New South Wales Department of Lands

Contact Information

Mark Bezzina	**Christina Boedker**	**Tamara Plakalo**	**Chris Liell-Cock**
Executive Director Tel. 0413 101 096 bezzina@stancert.com.au	Research and Guiding Principles Tel: 0422 928 103 c@boedker.net	Communications and International Development Tel. 0403 011 391 tplakalo@yahoo.com.au	Industry Projects and Liaison chrislc@bigpond.net.au

Committee of Management

Steve Vamos, President; Alex Malley, Vice-President and Director; Mark Bezzina, Executive Director; Andrew Gale, Director; Patrick Callioni, Director; Tamara Plakalo, Director.

Contents

Foreword

The global economy is increasingly connected and evolving towards service-based industries that thrive and survive only to the extent that they can learn, innovate and evolve with the needs of their customers and business partners. Organizations, regardless of sector, have obligations to better manage their knowledge intensive resources, - to innovate and be more sensitive to their stakeholders.

Ten years ago, businesses like eBay, MSN Hotmail, Google and Amazon were embryonic and beyond the comprehension of most people. However, today, these organizations have achieved scale and prominence that is phenomenal by any measure. More than ever before, people, organizations and the economies they shape are connected and services based. Resources such as knowledge, relationships and the capability to innovate are significant drivers of success.

The reality however is that many of the management and measurement tools we depend on to drive organization performance are inadequate in this new environment. Managing a business, government agency or an economy requires new disciplines and measurement systems in this connected economy.

The role of the *Society for Knowledge Economics* is to provide best practices tools and guidelines, that address this need and by doing so make Australia a leader in driving productivity and performance through knowledge and innovation.

Steve Vamos
President, Society for Knowledge Economics

The arrival of the "Knowledge Economy" has been much heralded but what does this actually mean for organizations, government and the public at large?

Any attempt to improve the management and measurement practices of knowledge intensive organizations must first and foremost involve a deeper understanding of the characteristics of knowledge intensive resources.

The *Society for Knowledge Economics* has been founded to help advance the management, measurement and reporting of such resources. As an initial step, the Society is working on these *Australian Guiding Principles on Extended Performance Management*–a set of industry guidelines intended to inspire Australian organizations to better manage their knowledge intensive resources. We invite you to join us in testing and developing these draft *Guiding Principles.*

I would like to thank the Department of Finance and Administration (AGIMO) for supporting and endorsing the creation of the Society. I would also like to thank the Society's Committee of Management, our founding members, the Institute or Actuaries of Australia, CPA Australia and AGCCKC, as well as the many stakeholders who have helped us develop this early draft of the Guiding Principles.

One final and important point is that I would like to recognize and convey my appreciation to Christina Boedker for her outstanding work in preparing these draft Guiding Principles.

Mark Bezzina,

Executive Director, Society for Knowledge Economics

Background – Society for Knowledge Economics

This publication has been commissioned by the *Society for Knowledge Economics* (SKE). The *Society* was established in June 2005 following a mandate from the Australian Government Consultative Committee on Knowledge Capital (AGCCKC) and the Australian Government Information Management Office (AGIMO). At present, the Society's founding members include CPA Australia, the Institute of Actuaries of Australia, AGCCKC and Microsoft, Australia.

The objective of the *Society for Knowledge Economics* is to help improve organizational productivity and performance through the better management of knowledge and innovation.

The motivation to focus on the management of knowledge and innovation is driven by two macro-level drivers of change. One is the transition from the industrial economy (making tangible goods) to the service economy (delivering knowledge solutions), with a growing proportion of Australian GDP attributable to the effective management of knowledge intensive resources. The other is to address the well documented concerns regarding changing workforce demographics, with a large proportion of Australian knowledge workers scheduled for retirement over the forthcoming decades. Thus, increasing the productivity of a smaller work force is a critical national priority.

We believe these socio-economic transformations call for new business models, management skills and organizational practices, - practices, which maximize the productivity and performance of organizations' knowledge intensive resources, be they *relational, structural* or *human*.

The *Society for Knowledge Economics* aims to take a leadership role in advancing the development and uptake of best practices management principles in this growing field of practice. Among others, we aim to:

1. **Guiding Principles:** develop and test a series of guiding principles to enhance the management of knowledge and innovation within public, private and third sector organizations;
2. **Community of Practice:** establish and promote a community of practice to provide thought leadership consistent with the best practice guiding principles;
3. **Research:** prove through research the value, challenges and benefits associated with managing knowledge intensive resources;
4. **Professional Certification:** develop professional certification and high quality learning opportunities to improve the skills and competencies of the Australian workforce in the management of knowledge and innovation; and
5. **Partnerships:** partner with governments, professional associations, universities and public and private sector organizations to articulate and promote the value and benefits of **the** management of knowledge and innovation.

This publication is one in a series of planned publications intended to guide Australian organizations in the management of knowledge intensive resources. The publication is intended for the benefit of Australian organizations, the individuals that work for Australian organizations, the communities they affect and the national economy they seek to advance.

Mark Bezzina,
Executive Director, *Society for Knowledge Economics*

Executive Summary

Over the past century, organizations have witnessed major transformations in the economy within which they operate. The speed of doing business is faster than ever, technological progress is unprecedented and global economic growth has reached record highs.

Modern economists attribute such exceptional achievements to a fundamental transformation in the factors of economic production. It is the emergence of a "new economy", in which conventional economic theory is challenged. Knowledge, with its increasing, not diminishing, returns to scale is changing business fundamentals and providing new opportunities for economic growth.

The Australian economy, which traditionally has sustained its wealth from natural resources and manufacturing, is no exception, with over 73 percent of its workforce employed in knowledge intensive services, contributing more than 52 percent to national GDP in 2003. Successful organizations operating in today's knowledge economy increasingly derive their wealth from their knowledge intensive resources, be they *relational*, *structural* or *human*.

In the midst of this dynamic, fast moving environment remains one comforting pillar of stability. That is the 500-year-old accrual accounting system, which continues to be the foundation for measuring organizational success (and failure) in the 21st century. Traditional financial accounts provide a source of predictability and certainty; an assurance of life to continue "as is".

However, during recent years, critics have started to question the adequacy of traditional financial accounts in a changed economy. They criticize financial accounts for their historical focus, failure to record important intangible resources, and bias towards bottom line results, resulting in short-termism and opportunistic behavior.

Critics are particularly concerned about the lack of recognition of the "new" factors of production on the balance sheet, - these invisible, so called intangible, knowledge intensive resources, which drive growth and competitive advantage to a larger extent than physical assets, remain largely unaccounted for. The International Financial Reporting Standard (IFRS) has done little to improve the situation, with the top 100 Australian organizations writing off $7.5bn in intangible assets in 2005.

There is also a concern about the failure of the profit and loss statement to shed light on how organizations utilize and develop their knowledge intensive resources. Stakeholders, in particular investors, want information about the drivers of business value and how such drivers are managed, not merely the bottom line results of past performance.

To make up for the limitations of traditional financial accounts, modern practitioners and theorists have started to propose new ways in which to account for organizational performance. They talk about:

- Intellectual Capital Statements
- Corporate Social Responsibility Reports
- Balanced Scorecards
- Triple Bottom Lines

These "new accounts of performance", which we call extended performance accounts, are encouraging signs for those concerned with sustaining organizational performance in a fast changing, global economy. They "make visible" the often overlooked, taken-for-granted knowledge intensive organizational resources, thus creating new opportunities for management intervention and financial valuation. They provide a broader, more balanced, perspective on organizational wealth and shed light on the capacity an organization has to create value in the future. Some even argue that these new performance accounts are paving the way for a fundamental rethink of the way in which organizational performance is thought of, and accounted for.

A central, yet unanswered, question in the debate on extending traditional management and financial accounting practices, however, relates to the gains and benefits that accrue to organizations from doing so.

Skeptics are quick to point out the weaknesses of extended performance accounts, highlighting the competitive disadvantage resulting from greater transparency; the lack of validity, accuracy and objectivity of extended performance information; the incomparability of such information across organizations, industries and time; and the resource requirements and complexity associated with tracing the value that accrues from investing in knowledge intensive resources.

There is no single uniform answer with which to counter these concerns, and evidence thus far is inconclusive. However, trends are starting to emerge substantiating the benefits that flow to organizations that measure and report the value of their knowledge intensive resources.

A recent study by KPMG, which investigated the management practices of 1600 of the largest companies around the world, found that organizations produce extended performance accounts to reduce risk exposure, improve employee motivation and enhance workplace innovation.

These objectives were confirmed, to varying degrees, by the 150 Danish organizations, who participated in the preparation of intellectual capital statements over a five-year-period. Many of these organizations reported heightened levels of employee motivation, a larger pool of candidates to recruit from, a greater capacity for customer retention, and improved employee awareness of organizational activity, strategy and objectives.

In the US, statistical analysis of extended performance information supports these findings and shows a correlation between employee attitudes, customer satisfaction and financial performance, thus confirming, as one would expect, that investments into knowledge intensive resources increase financial returns.

In the capital market arena, research shows that extended performance accounts can positively affect share price. Markets reward, and increasingly expect, organizations to increase transparency. Transparency, in turn, reduces uncertainty, thus resulting in lower risk premiums and more accurate company valuations.

At the heart of this search for business evidence substantiating investment decisions however lies a number of critical questions. These pertain, among others, to reflecting on what constitutes good corporate performance management, measurement and reporting in the 21st century. Is the pursuit of quantifiable representations of business performance and reliance on financial data the best means of organizational performance (e)valuation? If not, what type of performance indicators do we assign to measure the success (and failure) of knowledge intensive organizations in the 21st century? How do we best identify and value knowledge intensive resources given their subjective, invisible and often value-laden character? And within which structure and with what means (narratives, images or numbers) do we best report on their performance?

These *Australian Guiding Principles on Extended Performance Management* (EPM) attempt to answer some of these questions. We provide insights into the structure and content of contemporary EPM frameworks, highlighting how they differ from traditional financial accounts. We also propose a framework and a series of management steps intended to help organizations produce extended performance accounts and, as a result, develop new understandings of the value that accrues from their knowledge intensive resources.

Besides professional bodies and public, private and third sector organizations, we appeal to Australian government officials and public policy makers interested in staying in tune with national and international trends and developments in this field. We provide insights into international trends such as the Danish and Japanese guidelines on intellectual capital and intellectual property measurement and reporting; the UK Operating and Financial Review (OFR), which now requires organizations to publicly disclose information about their knowledge intensive resources; Austrian legislation, which requires certain public sector organizations to produce intellectual capital reports; and the United Nation's Global Reporting Initiative (GRI), which sets a benchmark for international standards in social, economic and environmental reporting. We raise questions as to what is the role and contribution of Australia to these developments and how can we best position and promote Australia as a leading knowledge economy within the international community?

We invite readers to work with us in advancing the position of Australia as a knowledge economy. And we are particularly interested in extending an invitation to public and private sector organizations to participate in testing the *Guiding Principles on Extended Performance Management*.

1. Scope and General

1.1. Motivation and Scope

Traditional accounts of organizational performance have often been criticized for their failure to illustrate the value of intangible, knowledge intensive organizational resources. These *Australian Guiding Principles* respond to this criticism and introduce the concepts "extended performance management" and "extended performance accounts".

Extended performance accounts differ from traditional financial accounts by "making visible" an organization's knowledge intensive resources not recorded and accounted for in traditional financial statements. In doing so, they provide managers and others with new insights into organizational performance and open up new opportunities for management intervention and financial valuation.

An extended performance account complements the three existing financial accounts. Some even refer to it as the "fourth" account of organizational performance.

In brief, extended performance accounts are:

- **strategic in nature**, placing knowledge intensive resources within the strategic business context in which they rightfully belong;
- **forward looking,** providing insights into how an organization is positioned to create value across different time horizons; and
- **often simple in structure,** providing a one-page snapshot of the organization's knowledge intensive resources and activities.

Extended performance accounts can be used for different purposes, depending on an organization's specific needs, requirements and circumstances. Some organizations use the account for **internal management purposes**, as a tool to provide managers and others with new insights into the value and performance of the organization's knowledge intensive resources. Extended performance accounts have also been used as brainstorming and planning tools to improve the effectiveness of resource allocation and strategy formulation; as change management tools to transform workplace culture; and as motivational devices to improve employee productivity and stakeholder awareness of organizational identity, activity and intent.

Some organizations also choose to use their extended performance account for **external reporting purposes.** The objective here is to aid the decision making processes of stakeholders, such as potential employees, investors customers and others, by disclosing information about the organization's knowledge intensive resources, not accounted for in traditional financial accounts.

We provide illustrations of such usages in our two mini case studies with the NSW Department of Lands and Westpac Banking Corporation.

We learn from these "early innovators" that extended performance accounts must be embedded into management thinking and reflect managerial activities and courses of action. An extended performance account is not a disengaged corporate report, driven by regulatory requirements. It is neither a marketing collateral striving to gain public acceptance. It is instead a dynamic account, which helps organizations reflect on their "identity", their "DNA", and start a journey in which Purpose (i.e. "where they we going?") and Means ("how do we intent to get there)" are centered around the strategic management of knowledge intensive organizational resources.

We propose a framework and series of management steps to guide organizations interested in preparing an extended performance account. We use the label *extended performance management* (EPM) to signify the management processes organizations are likely to go through as they prepare the account.

In brief, we find that EPM can help organizations:

- take a broader perspective on the drivers of organizational performance and focus on the often invisible and taken-for-granted knowledge intensive organizational resources, be they *relational, structural* or *human;*
- engage in a process of reflection and innovation in which managers gain new ideas, inspirations and perspectives on business management;
- create an infrastructure, which allows for, and encourages, reciprocal communication flows between the organization and its key stakeholder groups; and
- reflect on their efforts in creating a sustainable organization taking into consideration the external impacts and contributions of organizational activity, be they social, environmental or ethical;

Our pilot projects tell us that by placing at the center of attention the often taken-for-granted knowledge intensive resources, EPM opens up new opportunities for organizational value creation. Possible the main benefit is an improved capacity among managers and leaders to reflect on how they manage, utilize and develop knowledge and innovation. It is the acknowledgement that knowledge and innovation, despite their intangible character, needs to be explicitly managed, and developed within a strategic context. The value thus lies in an enhanced capacity among managers to conceptualize the role, functioning and effects of managing knowledge and innovation. We refer to this as "making visible the invisible".

Other benefits that may flow to organizations who engage in EPM include, but are not limited to:

- improved financial performance and sustainable organizational health;
- improved stakeholder relations and increased awareness of stakeholder needs and perspectives;
- a stronger reputation and corporate image;
- a greater capacity for customer acquisition and retention;
- better information to inform resource allocation and strategy formulation;
- reduced risk exposure due to improved employee awareness of organizational activities, objectives and strategy;
- a greater capacity for innovation, learning and development;
- heightened levels of employee motivation and trust; and
- a lower cost of capital and improved share price valuation.

However, a number of challenges may also await organizations that embark on the journey of producing an extended performance account. These may include, but are not necessarily limited, to:

- attracting resources;
- developing and sustaining interest and commitment from executives, employees and others;
- attracting (visionary) teams leaders;
- determining levels of responsibility and accountability;
- project planning;
- overcoming employee resistance and challenging the status quo; and
- identifying and tracking the value and performance of knowledge intensive resources.

1.2. Objectives

The objectives of these *Australian Guiding Principles* are four-fold:

1. to raise public awareness of how to strategically manage knowledge intensive organizational resources and activities;
2. to propose and initiate the testing of a framework and series of management steps to assist Australian organizations to better understand the value and performance of their knowledge intensive resources;
3. to help place Australia on the map as a leader in the management and development of workplace knowledge and innovation; and advance the testing, and uptake of best practice in this emerging field of management; and
4. to increase awareness among users of organizational performance information, be they employees, customers, shareholders or others.

1.3. Readers and Target Audience

These *Australian Guiding Principles* are intended for, but not limited to, the following audiences:

- Australian public, private and third sector organizations seeking to engage in the preparation of extended performance accounts;
- government officials wishing to become familiar with the latest trends and developments in extended performance management, internationally and in Australia; and
- investors, professional bodies and other community groups seeking to increase their understanding of the structure, content and effects of extended performance accounts.

1.4. Structure and Content

These *Australian Guiding Principles* are structured accordingly.

Section 2 defines the terminologies used in the *Guiding Principles*.

Section 3 contextualizes extended performance management and provides an overview of the macro-level drivers of change, outlining the transformations in the national economy and the factors of economic production.

Section 4 provides a comparative analysis of existing frameworks for managing, measuring and reporting knowledge intensive resource and activities. We compare extended performance accounts with traditional financial accounts, highlighting the differences in reporting categories between the two types of organizational performance accounts. We conclude with a brief review of some of the work place and financial effects documented thus far, illustrating the benefits that may flow to organizations that measure and report the value of their knowledge intensive resources.

Section 5 proposes a framework for developing an extended performance account. The framework is simple in structure, strategic in nature and future oriented. We also provide practical examples of extended performance accounts produced by Australian organizations during early stage pilot projects.

Section 6 proposes a series of management steps intended to help Australian organizations create an extended performance account and in doing so, facilitate a strategic approach to the management of knowledge and innovation.

Section 7 concludes the *Guiding Principles* with a review of national and international trends and developments in legislation, guidelines, codes of conducts and standards. We also review some of the challenges facing organizations and information users in advancing extended performance management, and point towards a series of action points to help pave the way forward.

2. Definitions of Terms

Practitioners, public policy makers and researchers alike are faced with a plethora of definitions and terminologies to make sense of when discussing the resources and characteristics of the knowledge economy. We hear talk of intangible assets, intellectual resources, knowledge based assets, knowledge capital, intellectual capital and intangible resources.

The purpose of this section of the *Guiding Principles* is to reduce the level of ambiguity surrounding this plethora of terminologies. We aspire to influence the development of a common language and propose a series of definitions to inform our discussions.

1. **Accountability**
   Accountability refers to the adoption of sustainable business management, measurement and reporting practices, which seek to reduce the negative

impacts and enhance the positive impacts of organizational activity, be they societal, environmental, ethical or economic.

2. **Accounting**
   Accounting refers to the systematic identification, analysis, recording and reporting of information about organizational resources, activities, performance and impacts.
3. **Accounting Information**
   Accounting information comprises financial and non-financial performance information. The purpose of accounting information is to enable internal and external stakeholder to make informed decisions about the organizational performance.
4. **Accounting System**
   An accounting system records information about an organization's activities, resources, impacts and performance. It compromises systematic processes and repositories, which allow for the collection, storage and dissemination of organizational performance information.
5. **Asset**
   An asset is a resource that is controlled by the enterprise as a result of past events (for example, purchase or self-creation) and from which future economic benefits (inflows of cash or other assets) are expected (International Financial Reporting Standard (IFRS)).
6. **Extended Performance Accounts**
   Extended performance accounts differ from traditional financial accounts of organizational performance by placing knowledge intensive resources and activities at the center of attention. They "make visible" the often overlooked, taken-for-granted intangible resources, be they *relational, structural* or *human*. Extended performance accounts are:
   - **strategic in nature**, placing knowledge intensive resources within the strategic business context in which they rightfully belong;
   - **forward looking,** providing insights into how an organization is positioned to create value across different time horizons; and
   - **often simple in structure,** providing a one-page snapshot of the organization's knowledge intensive resources and activities.
7. **Extended Performance Management (EMP)**
   The objective of EPM is to help organizations prosper by providing them with the tools, ideas and philosophies for better managing their knowledge intensive resources, be they *relational, structural* or *human*. EMP entails:
   - adopting a more strategic and complete approach to managing intangible, knowledge intensive resources and activities;
   - establishing reciprocal communication flows between the organization and the groups of individuals it seeks to create value for, thus taking

into account the value perspectives and needs of key organizational stakeholder groups; and

- taking into account the external impacts of organizational activity, be they social, environmental or ethical, thus creating better conditions for sustained organizational and community performance.

Operationalizing EPM may be informed by the proposed management steps outlined in section 6 of these *Guiding Principles.* One outcome of EPM is an extended performance account, as exemplified in the mini case studies of the NSW Department of Lands and Westpac Banking Corporation in section 5.2.

8. Extended Performance Management Frameworks

Extended performance management frameworks are used to manage knowledge intensive organizational resources in a balanced and strategic manner. They help visualise and measure the value and performance of knowledge intensive organizational resources and activities. Examples include, but are not limited to, the Balanced Scorecard, the Scandia Navigator, the Intangible Asset Monitor, the ValueReporting™ framework, the Intellectual Capital Statement model and the framework proposed by the United Nation's Global Reporting Initiative.

9. Extended Performance Measures

Extended performance measures are organizational performance measures, which are not derived from the three financial statements: the balance sheet, the profit and loss statement and the cash flow statement. Extended performance measures complement financial measures to provide a broader, more balanced perspective on organizational health and future prospects. They:

- help identify, measure and illustrate the value that accrues from knowledge intensive organizational resources and activities. Examples include, but are not limited to, employee morale, community relations, employees' innovative capacity etc;
- include lagging and leading indicators, of which the latter provide insights into how an organization is positioned to create value now and in the future; and
- illustrate the managerial activities and efforts which go into the value creation process, not solely the financial outcomes of organizational activity.

10. Financial Resources

Financial resources refer to an organization's financial capital and profile. They include, but are not limited to, an organization's liquidity, borrowing capacity, credit rating, working capital, depreciation policy, risk profile, revenues, expenses, profit margin, tax rate, cash flows from operating, investing and financing activities, weighted average cost of capital, $-value of assets (cash reserves, receivable balance, provisions, inventory balance), $-value of liabilities (loans, accounts payable, unearned revenue), and shareholder equity.

11. Intangible Asset

The terminology "intangible asset" is derived from accrual accounting. According to the IFRS, an intangible asset is defined as an identifiable non-monetary asset without physical substance. To be recognized on the balance sheet, an intangible asset must be identifiable, controllable, reliably measurable and provide future economic benefits (such as revenues or reduced future costs).

An intangible asset is identifiable when it:

- is separable (capable of being separated and sold, transferred, licensed, rented, or exchanged, either individually or as part of a package); or
- arises from contractual or other legal rights, regardless of whether those rights are transferable or separable from the entity or from other rights and obligations.

The IFRS requires that:

- research, start up, internally generated goodwill, training, relocation and advertising costs are expensed;
- internally generated intangible assets (e.g. mast heads, brand names etc that arise other than by way of acquisition) are not recognized as assets and must also be expensed;
- intangible assets are subject to amortization and impairment testing; and
- intangibles are only re-valued if there is an active market for the asset.

Intangible assets may be categorized as:

- marketing related: trademarks, brands, trade names, trade dress, internet domain names, newspaper mastheads, non-competing agreements;
- customer related: customer lists, order or production backlog, customer contracts;
- artistic related: plays, operas, ballets, books, magazines, newspapers, musical works, pictures, photographs, videos, films, television programs;
- contract based: licensing, royalty and standstill agreements, contracts for advertising, construction, management, service or supply, lease agreements, construction permits, franchise agreements, operating and broadcasting rights, use rights such as drilling, water, air, mineral, timber cutting and route authorities, servicing contracts, employment contracts; and
- technology based: patented technology, computer software, unpatented technology, databases, and trade secrets.

12. Information Management

Information management describes the means by which an organization efficiently plans, collects, organizes, uses, controls, disseminates and disposes of its information, and through which it ensures that the value of that information is identified and exploited.

13. Intellectual Capital

Intellectual capital is the organizational perspective (or worldview) that is adopted to identify and address the management of an organization's knowledge intensive resources. It pertains to making visible the often taken-for-granted knowledge intensive organizational resources, not recorded and accounted for in the traditional financial statements.

14. Knowledge

Knowledge is two dimensional, being either explicit or tacit.

- **Explicit knowledge** *can be documented and codified in the form of manuals and operating procedures.*
- **Tacit knowledge** *is personal and context-specific. It exists in people's heads and is described as being accumulated, experiential and represented in a person's skills and competence. It is hard to formalize and communicate.*

15. Knowledge Intensive Resource

A knowledge intensive resource exists in two forms:

- **An explicit knowledge intensive resource** *comprises a tangible element (such as a computer) and a knowledge element (such as the know-how of how to start the computer). The two co-exist. The tangible resource is made operational when knowledge is applied to it, and vice versa. Examples include software, information technology, customer relations, distribution channels etc.*
- **A tacit knowledge intensive resource** *has no substance. It exists on its own without the intervention of tangible resources. It is enacted through action, conversation, and human interaction. Examples include culture, norms, behavior, rituals, routines, problem solving skills and others.*

Knowledge intensive resources are classified into a tripartite scheme as follows:

- **Structural (Internal) Capital** includes, but is not limited to, corporate culture, management philosophy, organizational structure, management processes, information systems and networks, intellectual property, contracts, research and development and new product development.
- **Relational (External) Capital** includes, but is not limited to, corporate name and brands, alliances and partnerships, licensing and franchising agreements, supplier and distribution channels and relations, community relations, government relations, industrial relations, customer relations, and financial relations.
- **Human Capital** includes, but is not limited to, employee demographics, employees' innovative capacity, employee diversity, learning and development abilities, educational and work-related qualifications, leadership and top management quality.

Knowledge intensive resources are likely to possess the following characteristics. They are:

- not easily identifiable or readily visible and therefore often taken-for-granted and overlooked;
- not easily controllable or separable from the owner or object, and thus more risky to invest in than tangible assets;
- often a source of organizational competitive advantage and core competency;
- often unique and company specific, and therefore difficult to compare across organizations; and often subjective, qualitative and value-laden and thus more complex to quantify and value in $-terms.

Contrary to physical assets, which decrease in value when used, knowledge is cumulative. The more knowledge is used and shared, the more new knowledge is generated. Knowledge intensive resources thus provide increasing returns to scale.[1]

An example includes the knowledge developed by a management consulting team as they solve a client problem. In the process of solving the task, the team leverages their existing knowledge. They however also build new knowledge, which they subsequently share with the client organization and subsequent clients to whom they consult. The more the team utilizes and shares their knowledge, the more the team learns, and the more the client(s) learns.

Another example includes joint product development whereby organizations include suppliers, customers and other key stakeholders in the product development process. In the process of jointly designing the product, the parties share knowledge and learn from each other. In the process, they each develop new knowledge.

Thus, the more we utilize and share knowledge, the more we learn and the more new knowledge we develop. Knowledge is therefore cumulative, and provides increasing returns to scale.

16. Knowledge Management

Knowledge management refers to the management of the organization's knowledge intensive resources, be they *relational, structural* or *human.*

Knowledge management is not to be mistaken for information management. Information is codifiable knowledge and thus information management concerns the management of codifiable knowledge. Examples may include an organization's standard operating procedure, user manuals and customer lists.

Knowledge, in contrast, exists in the form of tacit knowledge (see definition above). An example of tacit knowledge includes the innovative capacity of a member of staff. Here, tacit knowledge is seen to exist in people's heads and has proven difficult to codify. Case studies of attempts to codify tacit knowledge

1 See endogenous growth theory (e.g. Romer, 1986, Romer, 1990 and Gylfason, 1999)2

often show that the value of tacit knowledge is lost as managers try to capture, codify and control it (i.e. you cannot capture an employee's innovative capacity; at best you can ensure it prospers and is allowed to flourish).

17. Management

Management comprises six reiterative, un-sequential processes:

1. Identification
2. Analysis
3. Action planning and strategy formulation
4. Implementation
5. Measurement
6. Reporting

18. Market Analysis

Market analysis comprises an analysis of the macro-environmental and industry specific factors which impact the organization and its value creation activities and abilities. These are classified into seven categories:

1. Competitors
2. Political Factors
3. Economic Factors
4. Societal Factors
5. Technological Factors
6. Environmental Factors
7. Legal Factors

19. Organizational Resources

Organizational resources are classified into three broad categories:

- *Financial resources*
- *Physical resources*
- *Knowledge intensive resources.*

20. Physical Resources

Physical resources refer to tangible resources such as plant, property, equipment and inventory.

21. Reporting

Reporting refers to the documentation of information. Reporting may be used for internal management purposes or for external disclosure purposes. External reporting may be voluntary or driven by legislative reporting requirements.

22. Resource Analysis

Resource analysis refers to the identification and analysis of an organization's resources. For the purpose of these Guiding Principles, we focus on the analysis of knowledge intensive organizational resources. The objective of resource analysis is to provide an inventory of the knowledge intensive resources the organization has at its disposal. Examples include, but are not limited to: number of employees; number of customers; type of customer; number of strategic alliances and partnerships.

Resource Management Analysis

Resource management analysis comprises an analysis of the activities undertaken to manage the organization's knowledge intensive resources relative to its strategic objectives. Resource management activities are classified into five broad categories:

1. Acquisition of knowledge intensive
2. Development of knowledge intensive
3. Utilization of knowledge intensive
4. Maintenance of knowledge intensive
5. Disposal of knowledge intensive

23. Stakeholders

Stakeholders include all persons, or groups of people, external or internal to the organization, who affect, or are affected by, the organization's operating activities. External stakeholders include, but are not limited to:

- Capital Market Actors
- Community
- Customers
- Distributors
- Suppliers
- Government
- Education Providers
- Non-government Organizations.
- Internal stakeholders include, but are not limited to:
- Board Members
- Consultants
- Contractors
- Employees such as Senior Executives, Managers and Staff.

24. Stakeholder Analysis

Stakeholder analysis refers to the identification and analysis of the expectations, perspectives and needs of internal and external organizational stakeholders. It helps managers better understand their organizations by facilitating reciprocal, as opposed to one way, communication flows between organizations and the people they serve and affect. Stakeholder analysis may be facilitated through interviews, surveys, focus groups or other means of stakeholder engagement and feedback.

25. Sustainability

Sustainability refers to the adoption of business practices, which prioritize long-term survival and value creation. It comes from the verb to sustain, which means to hold up; to support; to maintain; to keep going; to prolong;

to support the life of. By paying attention to sustainability, organizations can confront and adjust over time those activities that may provide both short term financial returns and ensure long term business health. The 1987 Brundtland report noted that sustainable development is "to meet the needs of the present without compromising the ability of future generations to meet their own needs".

3. Drivers of Change–Economic Transformations

Traditional financial performance accounts have for long been criticized for not recognizing critical intangible, knowledge intensive resources. In this introductory section of the *Australian Guiding Principles*, we seek to contextualize this critique and provide an overview of the macro-level drivers of change. We introduce the notion of the knowledge economy, highlighting the changes in the structure of the Australian economy over the past centuries and the transformations in the factors of production (Table 1).

Table 1: Economic Transformations

	ECONOMIC ACTIVITY	FACTORS OF PRODUCTION
Agricultural Economy Pre-1800	Harvesting	Land Landowners and workers
Industrial Economy 18th to 20th century	Manufacturing	Labour Machinery Raw material
Knowledge Economy 20th century and onwards	Mediation of Knowledge and Services	Relational capital Structural capital Human capital

3.1. The Rise of the Knowledge Economy

The past century has witnessed major transformations in the structure of the Western economy. These transformations have been driven by the growth in service-based industries in which knowledge intensive resources constitute the main part of the value creation process. Today, service-based industries comprise over 68 percent of world GDP, up from 61 percent in 1990. Goods producing industries contribute 28 percent, down from 34 percent in 1990; and agriculture contributes 4 percent, down from 5 percent in 1990.

The contribution of service-based industries to Australian GDP is slightly lower than global averages, given the continued reliance on natural resources and manufacturing in Australia. The 2005 Yearbook *100 years of Change in Australian Industry* by the Australian Bureau of Statistics shows that:

- services contributed almost half (48.4 percent) to GDP in 2000-01, up from 31 percent in 1900-01;
- government administration increased its contribution to 4.1 percent in 2000-01, slightly higher than in 1900-01 and 1950-51;
- manufacturing, the next largest industry, contributed 11.9 percent, slightly less than its 12.2 percent contribution in 1900-01, but half of its contribution of 22.4 percent in 1950-51, reflecting the increase in development of manufacturing during World War II;
- dwelling rent contributed 9.8 percent to GDP, only slightly less than its contribution in 1900-01, but almost four times as much as its contribution 1951;
- both the mining and construction industries contributed 5.6 percent in 2000-01. Mining's share had more than doubled since 1950-51, but was still only around half its share of GDP in 1900-01; and
- agriculture, the largest individual industry in 1900-01, contributing 19.4 percent to GDP, was only 3.7 percent in 2000-01.

The growth in service based industries is also reflected in the changes in employment data with over 73 percent of the Australian workforce employed in services in 2000 (Table 2). The four main employment sectors at the turn of the century included: Retail Trade; Property and Business Services; Health and Community Services; and Education.

The greatest increase from 1995 to 2000 occurred in Property and Business Services (31.9 percent), followed by Construction (17.9 percent), and Personal and Other Services (16 percent). The greatest decrease occurred in Electricity, Gas and Water (24.4 percent).

Table 2: Australian Employment Trends

	1994-95(A) '000 PERSONS	1999-2000(A) '000 PERSONS	INCREASE
Goods Producing Industries -			
- Agriculture	403.3	437.5	8.5
- Mining	86.1	78.2	-9.2
- Manufacturing	1,115.3	1,113.1	-0.2
- Electricity, Gas and Water	86.8	64.5	-25.6
- Construction	589.8	695.4	17.9
- Total	2,281.3	2,388.7	4.7
Service industries -			
- Wholesale Trade	493.6	494.9	0.3
- Retail Trade	1,187.0	1,324.6	11.6

	1994-95(A) '000 PERSONS	1999-2000(A) '000 PERSONS	INCREASE
- Accommodation, Cafes and Restaurants	377.2	432.8	14.7
- Transport and Storage	381.4	407.3	6.8
- Communication Services	148.4	169.3	14.1
- Finance and Insurance	312.9	327.5	4.7
- Property and Business Services	749.8	988.7	31.9
- Government Administration and Defense	357.3	345.8	-3.2
- Education	555.6	609.3	9.7
- Health and Community Services	720.2	828.1	15.0
- Cultural and Recreational Services	189.2	217.1	14.7
- Personal and Other Services	303.7	352.3	16.0
- Total	5,776.2	6,497.8	12.5
Total All Industries	8,057.4	8,886.5	10.3
Service Industries as a Percentage of All Industries	71.7	73.1	

3.2. Knowledge Intensive Resources Are the "New" Factors of Production

The emergence of a knowledge intensive economy has implications for the factors of economic production. Many organizations and national economies today derive their competitive advantage from their intangible, knowledge intensive resources, be they *relational, structural* or *human*. Managing relationships, business structures and processes, and human capital is critical to organizational wealth and health in the knowledge era.

A core driver of change is the emergence of new technologies and the creation of "virtual" relationships and instant "knowledge exchanges". In 1994, Australia had one million mobile phones and almost no homes connected to the internet. Today, there are twenty million mobile devices in the market and millions of homes connected to the internet. Such new technologies enable knowledge to be exchanged, shared and traded across national and organizational boundaries, in ways thought impossible two decades ago.

The proliferation of "virtuality" and "interconnectivity" has implications for the nature and structure of contemporary business models. We see the traditional value chain, in which tangible resources dominated, being replaced by value shops and value networks, in which problem solving (i.e. consulting firms) and mediation of exchanges (i.e. eBay) comprise the new factors of production. The notion of a connected, knowledge intensive and innovation based economy is developing rapidly before our eyes.

A 2003 survey conducted by Accenture with senior executives from twenty-seven countries and nineteen industries supports the notion of a globally connected knowledge economy in which intangible knowledge intensive resources dominate wealth creation. The survey finds that 49 percent of executives believe intangible resource are the most important sources of shareholder wealth creation; 26 percent find tangible and intangible resources to be of roughly equal importance; and only 25 percent of executives find that they rely primarily on tangible assets for shareholder wealth creation.

A recent survey by McKinsey (2005) supports the above findings and illustrates the changing information needs of senior executives. It shows that company directors are looking for more information about organizations' intangible, knowledge intensive resources. In order of importance, the 1016 company directors surveyed wanted to know more about the following areas: 1) Market Health (customer profitability/satisfaction, competitors' market share and products, suppliers, brands); 2) Organizational Health (employee retention/satisfaction, capabilities and skills, organizational structure, culture, values); 3) Network Health (regulatory changes, government policies, public opinion, community views); 4) Financial Performance (cash, costs, EBITDA, margins, return on capital); and Operational Health (buildings, inventories, patents, product pipeline, production rates). The survey concludes that directors sometimes lack the information needed to make sound decision making. This compromises their ability to fully understand the objectives and risks of their companies.

However, despite this consensus of the growing importance of intangible, knowledge intensive resources, there is limited agreement among practitioners, professionals, policy makers and researchers as to how to define, measure and report these "invisible" resources. Professional accounting standards have taken a conservative stance and restricted the recognition of intangible resources to those which are identifiable, reliably measurable, controllable, and acquired from external parties, thereby excluding a wide range of important knowledge intensive resources. The result today is a continued focus on tangible resources, bottom line results and prioritisation of short term financial performance setting aside the qualitative, intangible aspects of organizational health and wealth.

These *Guiding Principles* aspire to broaden existing perspectives on corporate performance management, measurement and reporting, and increase awareness of the issues surrounding intangible, knowledge intensive resources.

The first step we take towards realizing this objective is to provide a broader classification of intangible, knowledge intensive resources (Figure 1), thus encouraging recognition which extends beyond traditional financial accounting standards. Our classification scheme comprises **structural capital** (the structures and processes employees develop and deploy in order to be productive, effective and innovative); **relational capital** (the organization's relationships with external stakeholders be they suppliers, customers or others); and **human capital** (the skills, attitudes, abilities, competencies and qualities of the organization's employees).

We acknowledge the inherent difficulties associated with identifying, controlling and reliably measuring these 'invisible' resources. We also acknowledge that these resources have very different characteristics to the traditional tangible resources. Thus, we emphasize that for business managers to better manage and derive value from knowledge intensive resources they need to first develop an appreciation of the characteristics of such resources and how they differ to the conventional, tangible factors of economic production.

In brief, intangible, knowledge intensive resources are:

- not easily identifiable or readily visible, and therefore often taken-for-granted and overlooked;
- not easily controllable or separable from the owner or object, and thus more risky to invest in than tangible assets;
- often subjective, qualitative and value-laden and thus more complex to quantify and value in $-terms;
- often a source of organizational competitive advantage and core competency; and
- often unique and company specific, and therefore difficult to compare across organizations.

The second step towards raising awareness of the issues surrounding the management, measurement and reporting of knowledge intensive resources is to review existing frameworks for "visualising" such resources. We label these extended performance management frameworks (see section 4).

Figure 1: Knowledge Intensive Resources

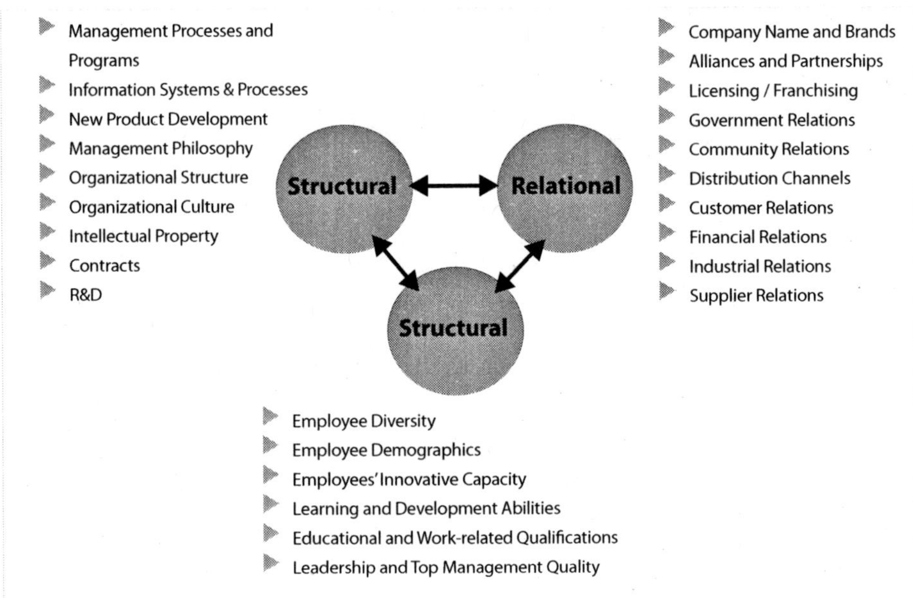

4. Overview of Extended Performance Management

The previous section introduced a classification scheme for conceptualizing and categorizing knowledge intensive resources (Figure 1). It also alluded to the limitations of professional accounting standards in recognizing the value of such resources. In this section of the *Guiding Principles*, we examine contemporary responses to this critique and introduce the concepts of extended performance management (EPM) and extended performance accounts.

We start by providing a comparative summary of existing frameworks, which extend the traditional approach to measuring and accounting for organizational performance. We then compare the reporting categories of traditional financial accounts with those of extended performance accounts. This is followed by an examination of the type of performance measures commonly reported in extended performance accounts. We conclude with a brief review of empirical evidence developed by researchers thus far to illustrate the benefits that may flow to organizations who embrace the agenda of EPM.

4.1. Extended Performance Management Frameworks

The conservative stance of professional accounting bodies in the intangible discourse has given rise to a growing criticism of traditional financial accounts and performance measures. Critics claim that the stocks of tangible resources recorded on the balance sheet and the $-outcome measures shown on the profit and loss statement, however useful, no longer fulfill the information needs of organizational stakeholders, be they managers, investors, employees, governments, customers, suppliers or others. Financial performance measures inform only one part of the overall "picture" required to evaluate organizational performance.

Critics are particularly concerned about the lack of recognition of the "new" factors of production on the balance sheet, with many intangibles being expensed, not capitalized, thus acting as a potential disincentive to investing into *relational, structural* and *human capital*. The new International Financial Reporting Standard has done little to rectify the situation, with the top 100 Australian organizations writing off $7.5bn in intangible assets in 2005.

Critics are also concerned about the failure of the profit and loss statement to shed light on *how* organizations utilize and develop their intangible, knowledge intensive resources. Simple question such as "to what extent do organizations realize the full potential of their *relational, structural* or *human capital*?" and "what actions to they take to maximize the utilization and development of such resources?" currently goes unanswered.

Stakeholders, in particular investors, want information about the drivers of business value, not merely bottom line results. They are looking for future oriented performance information which show how an organization is positioned to create value across different time horizons. Thus, there is a growing demand for dependable performance information, which goes beyond the traditional financial performance accounts.

The criticism and limitations of traditional financial accounts have led to the emergence of a series of "new" frameworks, intended to broaden the traditional approach to measuring and accounting for organizational performance. We label these frameworks extended performance management frameworks.

EPM frameworks can broadly be grouped into two categories (Figure 2):

1. Corporate social responsibility and sustainability frameworks, which trace stakeholder perspectives and external impacts of organizational activity, be they environmental, social, or economic.
2. Scorecard and intellectual capital frameworks, which focus on internal management activities and impacts and place the management, measurement and reporting of organizational knowledge intensive resources within a strategic context.

Figure 2: Extended Performance Management Frameworks[2]

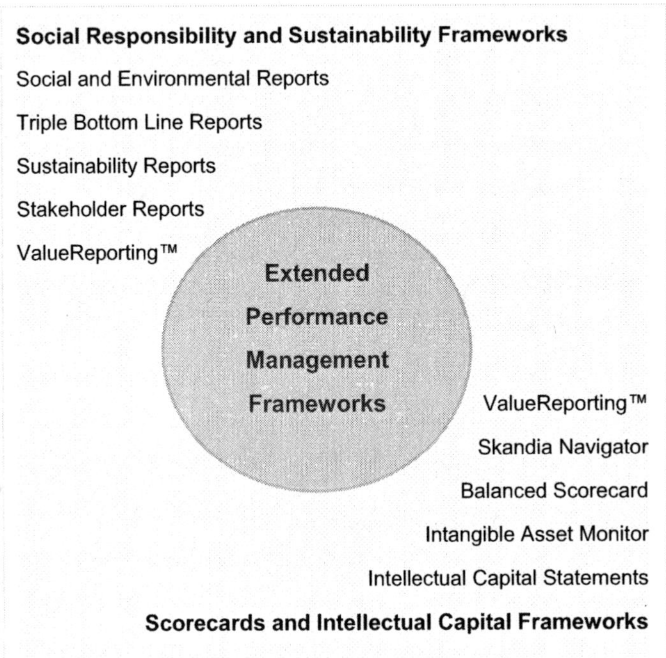

Contemporary literature and research on EPM illustrate how such frameworks are useful to organizations. Among others, they:

- enable managers and others to visualize the value and performance of the organization's knowledge intensive resources, not recorded and accounted for in traditional financial accounts;
- provide systematic processes and structures for measuring and reporting the value and performance of knowledge intensive resources;

2 The ValueReporting™ framework addresses both external impacts of organizational activity and internal management activities, hence the double listing of this framework.

- facilitate a more balanced perspective on resource performance, and provide a broader scope for strategy formulation and resource allocation;
- shed light on the drivers of business value, and how these value drivers are currently managed, thus extended the traditional $-based approach to performance evaluation;
- provide opportunities for stakeholder identification, engagement and dialogue, resulting in reciprocal communication flows, strategic feedback and organizational learning;
- reduce information asymmetry between internal and external stakeholders, thus opening up new opportunities for financial valuation;
- increase awareness of organizations' social, economic and environmental impacts and contributions; and
- provide new opportunities for organizational learning, development and innovation.

To better understand the structure and characteristics of EPM frameworks, we have identified seven leading frameworks and examined their differences and similarities in accordance with seven predetermined criteria. The seven criteria raise the following questions:

1. Does the EPM framework identify the level and type of activities undertaken by management to manage the organization's knowledge intensive resources? Examples of such activities may include customer relationship management, human resources management, information management, technology management etc.
2. Does the EPM framework link the knowledge management activities to the organization's strategic objectives? An example may include aligning a management activity, such as a new learning and development programme, to a strategic objective, such as service excellence.
3. Does the EPM framework facilitate the reporting of extended performance measures? Examples of such measures may include customer satisfaction, employee turnover and new product development (see section 4.3 for more examples).
4. Does the EPM framework report performance against established targets? An example may include a target indicator for customer retention of 67 percent versus actual achievement of only 64 percent.
5. Does the EPM framework facilitate stakeholder consultation and feedback? Examples may include opinion polls and surveys, which investigate and surface the value perspectives and needs of key stakeholder groups.
6. Does the EPM framework consider the external impacts of organizational activity? Examples may include contributions to national GDP, assessment of environmental impacts, community donations, etc.
7. Is the EPM framework used for internal and external reporting purposes?

Table 3 summarizes the outcome of the comparative analysis, illustrating the differences and similarities of the seven EPM frameworks.

Table 3: Comparative Summary of Extended Performance Management Frameworks

	1. Identifies Knowledge Management Activities	2. Links Knowledge Management Activities to Strategy	3. Reports Non-financial Performance Measures	4. Reports Performance Against Target	5. Facilitates Stakeholder Consultation and Feedback	6. Considers External Impacts (Social, Economic and Environmental)	7. Used for Both Internal and External Reporting Purposes
Balanced Scorecard1	Y	Y	Y	Y	Y	N	N
GRI–Sustainability Reports2	Y	Y	Y	Y	Y	Y	Y
Intangible Asset Monitor3	N	N	Y	Y	Y	N	Y
Intellectual Capital Statements4	Y	Y	Y	N	Y	N	Y
Skandia Navigator5	Y	Y	Y	N	Y	N	Y
Triple Bottom Line Reports6	Y	N	Y	Y	Y	Y	Y
ValueReporting™7	Y	Y	Y	Y	Y	Y	Y

The following general observations can be made in regards to Table 3:

- All frameworks consider the activities associated with the management of knowledge intensive resources (column 1). The frameworks provide insights into the way in which the knowledge intensive resources are managed, thus helping to answer the "how" question that traditional financial reports do not answer.
- All frameworks prioritize stakeholder consultation and engagement (column 5). This reflects the growing emphasis on reciprocal information flows between organization and the people the organization seeks to create value for.
- The Balanced Scorecard, the Intellectual Capital Statement model, the Skandia Navigator, and the Intangible Asset Monitor do not explicitly consider the external impacts of organizational performance, such as community impacts, contributions to GDP or environmental impacts (column 6). These frameworks focus to a larger extent on internal management activities and impacts. All frameworks, with the exception of the Balanced Scorecard, are used for both internal and external reporting purposes (column 7). The Balanced Scorecard is predominantly used for internal reporting purposes[3].

The above analysis has provided a brief introduction to the content of some of the most commonly used EPM frameworks. In the following sub-section, we extend the analysis of EPM frameworks to provide illustrations of the reporting categories of such frameworks, and how they differ from the reporting categories of traditional financial accounts.

3 It should be noted that some public sector organizations have published their Balanced Scorecards to external stakeholders.

4.2. Extended Performance accounts

The EPM frameworks, discussed in section 4.1, help facilitate the preparation of what we call "extended performance accounts". In this section, we examine the most common reporting categories of such extended performance accounts, and contrast these with the reporting categories of traditional financial accounts. The objective is to gain an insight into the differences in reporting content of the traditional versus the "new" accounts of organizational performance.

Table 4 summarizes in table format the differences in reporting categories between the two types of performance accounts. It illustrates the vast amount of information not recorded on the balance sheet (non-shaded areas). This is contrasted by the limited amount of intangible resources accounted for in the traditional balance sheet (shaded area in upper left hand corner).

The key point to note in Table 4 is that extended performance accounts recognize and record an organization's knowledge intensive resources, be they *relational, structural* or *human*. They help "make visible" these strategically important resources, thus providing new perspectives on organizational performance and creating new opportunities for management intervention and financial valuation.

Table 4: Differences in Reporting Categories[4]

	Traditional Financial Accounts			Extended Performance Accounts		
	Monetary	Physical	Intangible	Structural	Relational	Human
Tangible Resources	Cash Receivables Payables Securities	Property Plant Equipment Inventory	Intellectual Property Customer Lists Brands Contractual Agreements	Documented Operating Policies Documented Company Programs (i.e. TQM, JIT, Six Sigma, SPC etc).	Contractual Agreements with Alliance Partners and Joint Ventures	Employment Contracts Training Manuals In-house Learning and Development Programs
Intangible, Knowledge Intensive Resources	Credit Rating Borrowing Capacity Strength of Balance Sheet	Plant Flexibility Tradability of Assets Quality of Inventory	Infrastructure Working Capital Managemen	New Product Development Management Processes and Programs Information Systems and Processes Software Programs Organizational Structure and Culture Management Philosophy	Government Relations Community Relations Distribution and Supply Channels and Relations Customer Relations Financial Relations Industrial Relations Company Name and Brands	Employee Demographics Employees' Innovative Capacity Employee Diversity Learning and Development Abilities Educational and Work-related Qualifications Leadership and Top Mngt Quality

4 It should be noted that according to the IFRS, the intangible resources featured in the shaded area of the table can only be recorded when purchased externally. The definitions section of the Guiding Principles provides a complete list of intangibles recognizable on the balance sheet according to the IFRS. The table is adapted from Ballow, Burgman, Roos and Molnar (2004, exhibit 4, p. 7).

4.3. Extended Performance Measures

In this section we elaborate on the differences between the traditional and the "new" accounts of organizational performance and take a closer look at the performance measures reported in extended performance accounts. We label these extended performance measures.

Table 5 provides a summary of some of the most commonly used extended performance measures. The summary is inspired by the GRI Reporting Guideline, the Australian Bureau of Statistics' publication on Measuring a Knowledge Based Economy, the UK Operating and Financial Review, the Danish Guideline on Intellectual Capital Reporting, the German Guideline on Intellectual Capital, and a general review of published extended performance accounts, such as Corporate Social Responsibility reports, Intellectual Capital statements, ValueReporting™ reports and Triple Bottom Line reports.

Table 5 groups the various performance measures into three categories, as follows:

- **Stock:** Column one lists the stocks of the organization's knowledge intensive resources. Similar to the balance sheet, it records the level and types of the knowledge intensive resources and shows the position of the resources at a given point in time. Some of these resources may be classified as a liability (i.e. a high level of workplace accidents) or an asset (i.e. an increase in the number of strategic customers).
- **Investments:** Column two lists the investments made into the knowledge intensive resources. The term investment is used in a broader sense to signify not only capital investment, but also other types of resource investments such as time, energy, expert knowledge etc.
- **Effects:** Column three lists the possible effects of the investments made into the knowledge intensive resources. Similar to the profit and loss statement, this column shows the outcomes of performance for a given period of time. The result of a given investment may, for example, be an increase in work place productivity or an increase in community perception of corporate conduct.

One of the main points to note in Table 5 is the focus on organizational effects (column 3). Thus far, demonstrating the value that accrues from investing in knowledge intensive resources has been a challenge to researchers and practitioners alike, possibly serving as a barrier to increasing the uptake of EPM. There are a number of reasons for this.

One reason is the difficulty of excluding intervening variables and determining in isolation the effect of a given action. For example, an increase in customer satisfaction may be due to a number of simultaneous management activities and investments, such as new product development, staff training or an extension of distribution channels. Determining in isolating the cause of the change in performance outcome is thus a key challenge to understanding the value that accrues form investing into knowledge intensive resources.

A second reason is the challenges associated with isolating the time period for determining the effect. For example, a new automobile advertising campaign launched at the beginning of the year may trigger a customer to purchase the product at year end, or the following year. The challenge thus lies in determining the timing of the inflow (capital or other) that accrues from the given investment.

A third reason pertains to the issue of *circularity* and the fact that most performance measures are both input and output measures. For example, a measure of customer satisfaction is commonly seen as an output of past strategy. It tells the effectiveness of past business performance. It is however also commonly seen to be an input into (the formulation of) future business strategy. For example, in a scenario where customer satisfaction proves to be lower than expected, strategy is likely to be amended to alleviate points of dissatisfaction. Thus, the challenge lies in determining the role and meaning of extended performance measures. What is the cause and what is the effect?

Understanding the issues impacting the use, effects and meaning of extended performance measures remains a challenge to researchers and practitioners alike. It is, however, a prerequisite for justifying investments into knowledge intensive resources, and thus, more testing and empirics are required to establish their value.

We welcome readers of this publication to participate in pilot projects facilitated by the *Society for Knowledge Economics* to increase empirical evidence substantiating the effects and benefits that flow to organizations who measure and report the value and performance of their knowledge intensive resources.

The extended performance measures summarised in Table 5, differ to traditional financial performance measures in a number of ways (Table 6).

Table 6: Traditional versus Extended Performance Measures

Traditional Performance Measures	Extended Performance Measures
• Lagging indicators (i.e. historical performance) • Stocks of tangible resources • $-based outcome measures • Unit inputs and output • Production optimization	• Lagging and leading (i.e. future oriented) • Stocks and flows of intangible resources • Insights into resource use and development • Cause-effect relations • Strategic significance

Table 5: Examples of Extended Performance Measures[1]

	1.Stocks of Knowledge Intensive Resources and Activities	2. Investments (Time, Capital, Resources etc) in Knowledge Intensive Resources	3. Effects
Structural	Number and types of innovation projects / teams Number of patents, licenses and trademarks Number of six sigma projects completed Number of cross-functional teams Number and type of operating and policy procedures	Expenditure on innovation as a proportion of total expenditure Investment made into process reengineering Expenditure on ICT infrastructure Investment made in culture change program Investment made into corporate governance program	Financial: • Share price/ EPS • ROE • ROA • Leverage • Working capital ratios Customers: • Satisfaction, • Retention/ churn • Acquisition • Segments proliferation • Share of market according to customer segment or geographic location • Change in stock indicators
Relational	Number of strategic customers Three largest customers as percent of turnover or profit Number and/or types of strategic alliances and partnerships Number and/or types of research projects with universities or scientists Number of analyst briefings held Number of employees represented by trade unions Number of products/services sold through online media	Marketing expenditure as a proportion of sales or profit Investment in customer surveying and analysis Investment made into environmental management programs Donations to community as proportion of profit Investment made into non-core business infrastructure, i.e. schools in local communities Investment into supplier chain management activities Investment into developing or improving distribution channels	Employees: • Satisfaction • Morale • Retention and turnover • Change in stock indictors Business Processes: • Productivity • Efficiency • Effectiveness levels Environmental: • Levels and/or type of omission gasses • Waste levels • Water consumption • Energy use by energy source
Human	Workforce demographics (age, gender) Workforce competency profile, i.e. number of researchers, accountants Number of staff enrolled in training / education courses Number of staff having completed designated training / certification / leadership courses. Number and type of workplace accidents	Investment made in leadership development program Expenditure on education or training per employee as a proportion of sales or expenses Average number of training / education hours per employee according to employee category Investments made into staff surveying Investments made into OH&S Investments made into diversity and equal opportunity programs	Social: • Public perception of corporate conduct • Impact of operations on community • Bribery and corruption Economic: • Contribution to GDP • Tax payments • Cost of goods, services and products purchased according to region or country • Total payroll by region or country

1 These measures are not exhaustive but intended as sample measures only. It should also be noted that the measures in the three columns are displayed as independent measures, and have, in the current display, no relationship with each other.

Extended performance measures:

- **are forward looking (leading well as lagging indicators)**, and provide insights into how an organization is positioned to create value in the future. Customer retention is an example of a leading indicator of future financial performance. It is based on the assumption that higher retention rates positively affect future financial performance. However, as previously mentioned, customer retention is also a lagging indicator, telling a story of the past success of the organization's business strategy. Thus, it is both a leading and a lagging indicator;
- **provide insights into the flow of resources**, not merely the stocks of tangible resources. Extended performance measures show how an organization's knowledge intensive resources are used and developed over time, thus extending the traditional short-termist focus on bottom line results. An example may include the recoding of the number of innovation projects or investments made into a leadership development program; **track the cause-effect relations of management activities** across functional structures, work groups and value networks, not merely unit inputs and outputs. Tracking the cause-effect relations is commonly done through statistical analysis whereby a change in investment or expenditure is correlated with changes in performance outcomes,
- be they operational, customer related, financial, community related or other; and **emphasize the strategic significance of management activities, thus ext**ending the traditional short-termist focus on production optimization. For example, extended performance measures can be used to track investments made into culture change programs, research activity and community development activities. Such investments have a longer time horizon for benefits realization when compared to operational measures o**f unit inputs and outputs. They are of strategic significance and help** build organizational sustainability and competency.

We conclude this section by proposing a mind map for thinking about the different types of extended performance measures available to organizations who engage in the creation of an extended performance account. The purpose is to emphasize that performance measures must be set within a broader, strategic context of market trends, organizational strategy and operations, stakeholder value and environmental impacts and contributions. Figure 3 provides a graphic illustration of the mind map, grouping the measures into four broad categories:

- **Market Trends and Business Strategy**: These measures show how an organization is positioned in the market place and outline the macro and industry forces that are affecting its performance.
- **Products, Services and Business Processes**: These measures show how an organization is managing and developing its products, services and internal business processes to maximize value **creation.**

- **Stakeholder Value Perspectives and Needs**: These measures show how an organization's stakeholders perceive of its ability to create value.
- **External Impacts and Contributions**: These measures show how an organization affects its external environment, including its social, environmental and economic contributions and impacts. **We revert to the concept of extend**ed performance measures and how such measures can be used within a strategic business context in sections 5 and 6, where we detail the proposed framework and management processes for preparing an extended performance account.

Figure 3: Mind Map: Contextualizing Extended Performance Measures [5]

4.4. Effects and Benefits of EPM

The previous section outlined the many challenges associated with demonstrating the value that accrues from investing in knowledge intensive resources. In this sub-section, we provide a brief review of some of the empirical evidence provided thus far, illustrating the benefits to organizations who embrace the agenda of EPM.

Needless to say, determining the effects and benefits of EPM is critical to justifying investments into knowledge intensive resources. Executives and business managers need evidence illustrating the financial gains and broader workplace benefits that accrue to organizations from investing in EPM.

5 The overview of measures illustrated in this figure has been inspired by Exhibit 3 in McKinsey's (2005) survey "The View from the Boardroom", and a general review of the literature on extended performance measures (see the list of Referenced Documents in section 8).

Table 7: Effects and Benefits of EPM

Financial Effects		Work Place Effects	
Share price	US and European research has shown that an increase in disclosure of extended performance information improves transparency, thus reducing information asymmetry and uncertainty. This leads to a tighter range of share price estimates and a reduction in beta, resulting in more accurate share price valuation and a reduction in the cost of capital. An example includes an experiment conducted by PwC in which one group of analysts was provided with standard financial data whilst another group was provided with both financial data and an intellectual capital statement. The experiment showed that those analysts given both sets of performance data had a lower spread of earnings and assigned a higher share price valuation to the given company.	**Cultural**	Extended performance accounts have proven to have positive effects on organisational culture and work place practices. Danish studies illustrate that working with intellectual capital statements can help facilitate organisational change and aid the development of a knowledge-based organisational identity (Kjaergaard, 2003). They can help transform employees' work attitudes and lead to heightened levels of trust and motivation, resulting in a greater capacity for innovation, learning and development.
IPO valuation	US studies on Initial Public Offerings (IPOs) likewise find that extended performance information, such as information about product development, R&D and the competitive environment, reduces information asymmetry and assist IPO pricing (Guo, Lev and Shou, 2005).	**Reputation**	Extended performance accounts have also been proven to increase transparency, provide a vehicle for stakeholder feedback and improve stakeholder communication. Better stakeholder relations positively impact brand values and image, resulting in a larger pool of candidates to recruit from and a greater capacity for customer acquisition and retention.
Profitability	Statistical analyses of organisational performance data have found cause-effect relations between employee attitudes, customer satisfaction and financial performance, thus confirming, as one would expect, that investing in knowledge intensive resources improves financial performance (Ricci et al, 1999).	**Managing Knowledge and Risk**	Extended performance accounts have also shown to help managers and others better visualise an organisation's knowledge intensive resources, resulting in improved utilisation, management and development of these invisible resources. Knowledge is made manageable and accessible for intervention as performance information is recorded in an extended performance account (Mouritsen and Thorsgaard Larsen, 2005). EPM has also proven to increase employee awareness of organisational activity, strategy and objectives, which in turn helps reduce organisational risk exposure.

Table 7 (previous page) provides a summary of emerging trends in the business and academic literature illustrating the effects and benefits of EPM. The effects are categorized into financial (quantitative) and work place (qualitative).

It should be noted that contemporary studies often emphasize that EPM is a subjective exercise with no so to speak 'magical' recipe for success. The value of EPM may not lie in the framework chosen or be realizable in the form of short term financial results. Rather, the value often lies in the processes of implementation and the impact EPM has on employee behavior, attitude and morale. So whilst we acknowledge the role and importance of the financial effects, we also emphasize the importance of the behavioral and often subjective and qualitative effects that accrue to organizations who engage in EPM.

5. Proposed Framework and Practical Example

In this section of the *Australian Guiding Principles*, we extend our learnings from the previous sections and propose a simple framework to assist organizations in the development of an extended performance account. We illustrate the use and relevance of the proposed framework by providing practical examples of extended performance accounts prepared by Australian organizations during current pilot projects.

5.1. Framework

Figure 4 outlines the proposed framework for structuring the extended performance account. We propose a one-page account, which provides a summary of the value and performance of the organization's knowledge intensive resources and activities relative to its strategic objectives. The account may possibly be thought of as he "fourth" performance account, complementing the three existing financial accounts: the balance sheet; the profit and loss statement; and the cash flow statement. The proposed extended performance account framework is valuable in that it is:

- **strategic in nature**, placing knowledge intensive resources within the strategic business context in which they rightfully belong;
- **forward looking,** providing insights into how an organization is positioned to create value across different time horizons; and
- **simple in structure,** providing a one-page snapshot of the organization's knowledge intensive resources and activities.

The proposed framework also meets the seven assessment criteria deployed in section 4. It furthermore extends existing frameworks by providing a simple structure, which, similar to the traditional financial accounts, provides a one-page snapshot of organizational performance. In this case, the focus is on the invisible, knowledge intensive resources not recorded in traditional financial accounts.

Time scarce business managers and other organizational stakeholders others often only

Figure 4: Proposed Framework for Structuring an Extended Performance Account

	Strategic Objectives	Managerial Efforts		Indicators (External and Internal)		
		Current Activities	Planned Actions	Indicators	Past / Current	Target
Relational Capital						
Structural Capital						
Human Capital						

require a one-page snapshot of organizational performance. The qualitative performance information seen in, for example, corporate social responsibility reports, however valuable, is time consuming to digest and often subjective of nature.

The proposed framework also differs to existing frameworks in that it: 1) combines a broad classification of knowledge intensive resources (y-axis), with a review of the organization's efforts in managing its knowledge intensive resources relative to its strategic orientation (x-axis); and 2) extends beyond internal management activities of knowledge intensive resources to encourage an analysis of external impacts of organizational activity, be the social, environmental or economic (see section 6 for more details).

Importantly, extended performance accounts can be used for different organizational purposes, depending on the organization's specific needs, requirements and circumstances. Some organizations use the account for **internal management purposes**, as a tool to help managers and others gain new insights into organizational performance. The accounts have also been used as brainstorming and planning tools to improve the effectiveness of resource allocation and strategy formulation; as change management tools to transform workplace culture; and as motivational devices to improve employee productivity and awareness of organizational identity, activity and intent.

Some organizations also use their extended performance account for **external reporting purposes.** The purpose is to provide stakeholders external to the organization with a broader perspective on the organization's value creating activities and abilities. The account help achieve this objective by showing the value and performance of the organization's knowledge intensive resources not accounted for in traditional financial accounts.

In regards to the structure of the extended performance account, the y-axis categorizes the knowledge intensive resources into *relational, structural* and *human,* as previously illustrated in section 3.

The x-axis of the framework comprises three columns:

- **Column one, labeled Objectives**, lists the Business Objective for each of the resource areas: *relational; structural;* and *human*. An example of a strategic objective for say relational capital may be to "develop and sustain profitable customer relations".
- **Column two, labeled Managerial Efforts**, is divided into Current Activities and Planned Actions. The Current Activities lists the current management activities. An example may be a marketing campaign conducted during the year. The Planned Actions lists the initiatives management plans to take in the future. An example may be the planned implementation of a culture change program. The Planned Actions are set relative to the Business Objectives, listed in column one.
- **Column three, labeled Indicators, is divided** into three areas: 1) Name of Indicators; 2) Performance of the Indicators (past and current); and 3) Target Performance for the Indicators. The column labeled Indicators lists the name of the performance indicators. This may be customer satisfaction, employee turnover or any other extended performance measure. The column labeled Current / Past Indicators shows the outcome of past performance. The column labeled Target Indicators shows the set target for the performance indicators. The Target Indicators are set relative to the Planned Actions listed in column two and the Business Objectives listed in column one.

The management activities and processes, which inform the creation of the extended performance account, are discussed in more detail in section 6. We wish to emphasize that the proposed framework outlined in this section of the *Guiding Principles* is provided in draft format. Our medium to long term objective is to test the framework with a larger group of Australian organizations. Processes of trial and error, modifications and learnings await us as we embark on this process. We invite you to embark on this journey with us.

5.2. Practical Examples

A number of Australian public and private sector organizations have embarked on the journey of preparing extended performance accounts. In this section we introduce two of these organizations. We discuss their learnings and provide examples of their draft extended performance accounts.

The two case study organizations are the New South Wales Department of Lands (NSW) (hereafter Lands) and Westpac Banking Corporation (hereafter Westpac).

To both pilot organizations, the overarching objective of preparing the extended performance accounts has been to better understand the value and performance of their intangibles, knowledge intensive resources.

The extended performance accounts prepared by the two pilot organizations however serve different purposes to the organizations. Lands has a dual objective and is using the extended performance account for both internal management and external reporting purposes.

Westpac, in contrast, is intending to use the extended performance account for internal performance management only.

We learn from these "early innovators" that extended performance accounts must be embedded into management thinking and reflect managerial activities and courses of action. An extended performance account is not a disengaged corporate report, driven by regulatory requirements. It is neither a marketing collateral striving to gain public acceptance. It is instead a dynamic account, which helps organizations reflect on their "identity", their "DNA", and start a journey in which Purpose (i.e. "where they we going?") and Means ("how do we intent to get there)" are centered around the strategic management of knowledge intensive organizational resources.

MINI CASE STUDY 1

NSW Department of Lands

The NSW Department of Lands developed its first extended performance account for the accounting year 2004/2005. The project was initiated by Warwick Watkins, the Director General in 2003, and facilitated through relations with members of the Australian Government Consultative Committee on Knowledge Capital.

Lands was created in April, 2003, integrating three separate operating divisions: Land and Property Information (LPI), the provider of land and property information for NSW; Crown Lands, the administrator of all crown lands comprising over half of all land in NSW (which includes around 29mn hectares of land valued at over $8.3bn); and Soil Services, a specialist conservation earthmoving and soil consultancy business.

Lands had three main reasons for starting the project

1. **The first reason is the need to better understand the value and performance of the organization's knowledge intensive resources.** When interviewed, the Director General commented:

   "The greatest value of organizations in today's business environment is in intangible assets. However, in most organizations, senior executives pay little attention to the greatest asset in their organizations; that is the knowledge or intellectual capital. Decision-making is skewed towards short-term materialistic gains, which undervalues the real value and influences whether an organization is sustainable or not. At the moment, organizations are undervaluing their true wealth. We need to develop a greater sense and appreciation and awareness of the true value of what the intangibles are, and in doing so, be able to better allocate financial and other related resources.

We need to be able to, in a structured sense, have an objective discussion about where we should be cutting or increasing our resource allocation. Our objective is to get a better understanding of what constitutes the organization, the value of the organization, and how we can use that knowledge generally, augmented with other tools, to bring about better decision making."

2. **The second reason is Lands' ageing workforce**, with up to 44 percent of staff scheduled for retirement over the next three to five years. Critical questions have been raised as to how to capture and transfer the knowledge held by the retiring staff to sustain the existence of Lands. A representative from Finance explained:

   "Knowledge loss is expensive. If we relinquish expert knowledge, we are letting go of a host of things that we need to retain for the health of the business. If a key person with the background, experience and knowledge leaves without having passed on the knowledge, you might need two people in order to undertake that same task, so there are cost and financial implications involved."

3. **The third reason pertains to the use of performance information by external stakeholders.** Executives raised questions as to how governments and others can adequately judge, value, assess and make forecasts about organizational performance without having access to critical information about the knowledge intensive resources and activities that underpin the organization's value creation activities and abilities. The executives at Lands seek to address the limitations of traditional financial reports by creating an extended performance account illustrating the value, utilization and performance of the organization's knowledge intensive resources.

Project Aims

Measuring: Clarify the need to identify, agree and assign metrics to assess the efficient use of organizational knowledge intensive resources.

Reporting: Develop a framework to communicate, in a balanced way the value created through the knowledge intensive resources.

Managing: Identify and prioritize management challenges in creating sustainable value.

Approach and Methodology

- Involved establishing existing management, measurement and reporting practices within the Department, and recommending a possible extended performance account and action plan for the agency.

- Involved the creation of an Organizational Capabilities Project Team responsible for consulting and driving forward the project across the operating divisions and support functions.
- Involved visionary leadership and engagement of managers and staff through participation and consultation.
- Involved primary research through semi-structured interviews and secondary research by means of content analysis and review of internal documents.

Actions

1. Agreement on what knowledge intensive resources are and why they are important.
2. Agreement on an extended performance management framework.
3. Development of divisional projects and project teams.
4. Implementation of data gathering systems.
5. Agreement on the content of the extended performance account.

Outcomes & Deliverables

1. Identified key management challenges and initiatives from a knowledge perspective.
2. Identified the gap between "perceived importance" and "actual management" of the organization's knowledge intensive resources.
3. Created an extended performance account.
4. Raised awareness of issues surrounding the management of knowledge within the Department.

Lessons Learned

1. The project raised awareness of knowledge intensive resources within the three divisions and the importance of viewing the money spent on the development of knowledge intensive resources as an investment in the future and not a current cost.
2. The project facilitated the initiation of "strategic conversations" which involved discussions about organizational identity, strategic priorities and management challenges. It helped management reflect on the way in which the organization addresses its strategic issues and how these issues are viewed through the lens of knowledge. The Chief Information and Technology Officer pointed out:

   "The project is giving us the ability to see ourselves and what we are made of, our DNA. It helps us initiate a process of self-reflection, and to better clarify and describe who we are and what we are doing. It helps us to start to see ourselves differently. It is also a way of envisioning the future and assessing where we can go, how we can change and how we can better organize ourselves to move forward. It is helping us create a healthier organization".

3. The project was at times hampered by difficulties with breaking down organizational barriers that prevented the communication of important information and impeded progress. Clear objectives, strong leadership and the communication of practicable outcomes, both in regards to engaging staff and measuring results, are pre-requisites for project success.
4. "The process is iterative; as we learn more about knowledge and how it creates value, our assumptions concerning appropriate measurement and reporting are challenged." (Senior Policy Officer at Lands)

Recommendations·

- Further research on appropriate measures particularly in relation to knowledge and relationships is required.
- Keep the language simple and further develop consensus on clear definitions. Ambiguous terminologies and unclear definitions can negatively impact the engagement of management and staff, causing confusion and (unproductive) debate.
- Develop a community of interest to facilitate sharing of experiences and learning in relation to the management, measurement and reporting of knowledge intensive resources.
- Extend the process to other government agencies.

Figure 5: Draft Extended Performance Account (NSW Department of Lands)

	Objectives (Business Orientation)	Managerial Efforts		Indicators (External or Internal)					
		Current Activities	Planned Actions	Indicator	02/03	03/04	04/05	Trend	Target[14]
Relational Capital	Better Management of External Stakeholder Relationships	Collaborative Research with Universities Liaison and Collaboration with Professional Associations Interagency Committees	Stakeholder Consultations Customer Survey	Number of Significant Commit-tees with Statutory Bodies	40	32	36	↗	
				Research Partner-ships	2	2	6	↗	
Structural Capital	Improve Service Delivery	Development of Marketing Tools Analysis of Client Profiles Quality Management Methodology IT	Assessment of Distribution Methods (face-to-face versus web based) Ongoing Transition to Web Based Technologies	Average Number of (monthly) Internet Feedback Requests	-	-	285		
				Average Number of Hits on Website (monthly)	-	-	1.8mn		
Human Capital	Better Management of Employee Demographics	Learning and Development Training Apprenticeships External Studies Internal Seminars IT	Identification of Tacit Knowledge in the Workforce Mentoring Programme Employee Satisfaction Survey	Number of Full Time Staff	1458	1441	1427	↘	
				Average Age of Employee	-	-	45		
				Number of Staff Attending External Courses	-	246	-		
				Number of Staff Attending Internal Courses	-	462	-		
				Number of Staff as Being NEBS	15.3	15.7	15.3	↗	
				Women as a Percent of Total Staff	34.8	35	36.4	↗	

MINI CASE STUDY II

Westpac Banking Corporation

Westpac Banking Corporation is currently in the early stages of developing its first extended performance account. The project was initiated by Bruce Hills, Head of Risk, and facilitated through the Australian Government Consultative Committee on Knowledge Capital.

The pilot project is conducted by the Business Technology Solutions and Services (BTSS) group. BTSS is a shared services unit that delivers back-office functions for all of Westpac's products. The group defines the overall information technology architecture; supports and enhances software systems; and manages and implements major projects. BTSS also provides infrastructure support for cash management, fraud, physical security, business services and records management. Overall, BTSS can be considered the backbone of the organization and the enabler of the interfaces that satisfy the day-to-day banking requirements of Westpac's diverse customer base.

Westpac's motivation for embarking on the EPM project

The main reason for embarking on the extended performance management project is to demonstrate the intangible value delivered by BTSS to: 1) its partner business units; and 2) the end user of Westpac's products and services.

The value that BTSS creates for its partner business units and end customers is invisible. Indeed, the internal accounting system charges Westpac business units for their use of BTSS resources. The result is that BTSS is considered a cost rather than a source of value. Overall, BTSS faces the challenge of articulating how spending on its knowledge intensive resources are investments in long-term capability and value to the end customer, rather than costs and detriments to the 'bottom line'.

The anticipated benefits of the EPM project relate to:

- improved resource allocation due to availability of better information for business decision making;
- improved service delivery to partner business units and end customers, resulting in heightened levels of customer satisfaction;
- enhanced business performance across the partner business units due to BTSS' better understanding of their service requirements and needs;
- heightened levels of employee engagement and commitment due to enhanced understanding of business objectives, service delivery and strategy;

- improved understanding and management of knowledge flows between BTSS and the partner business units; and
- heightened levels of work place and employee innovation.

Project Aims

Measuring: Examine existing measurement and reporting systems and processes and the extent to which they: (a) capture attributes of strategically important knowledge intensive resources; (b) communicate and measures the value that BTSS provides to its partner business units and end customer.

Reporting: Investigate the impact of extended performance accounts on managerial decision making and performance evaluation.

Managing: Assess the knowledge flows and transfers from BTSS to its partner business units and end customer.

Approach and Methodology

The project at BTSS tests the proposed management steps for developing extended performance accounts recommended by the Guiding Principles on Extended Performance Management. This involves six process steps, grouped with three management phases, as follows:

- **Business Orientation**, in which the strategic orientation of BTSS is established, highlighting issues of use value and service delivery.
- **Business Analysis**, in which BTSS' business environment, stakeholder needs, resource composition and resource management activities are analyzed.
- **Performance Evaluation**, in which the current performance of BTSS relative to its stakeholder needs is understood and assessed.

Section 6 of the *Guiding Principles* provides more details about the management steps.

The following methods are applied to facilitate the project at BTSS:

- Analyses of internal and external business documentation to determine the strategic orientation and intent of BTSS, relative to the organization's broader strategy, and relative to the measurement and reporting systems and processes currently applied to evaluate the performance of BTSS.
- Interviews with key stakeholders to understand the services provided by BTSS; the extent to which value delivery is successful; and the ways in which the performance of BTSS is currently understood and assessed by key stakeholder groups.

Planned Actions

1. Scoping and project planning, including agreement on the purpose, content and intended use of the extended performance account.
2. Awareness raising exercises in the form of presentations and brainstorming sessions.
3. Identification of key stakeholder groups and development of project team(s).
4. Recommendations on the preparation of an extended performance account.
5. Interviews and workshops.
6. Data analysis.

Outcomes & Deliverables

The overarching objective of the pilot project is to develop a draft extended performance account for BTSS to use in demonstrating the value it provides to its partner business units and the end user of Westpac's products and services.

Lessons Learned and Recommendations

The project is at the early stages and thus lessons learned and recommendations are not yet available.

6. Operationalizing Extended Performance Management

In this section of the *Australian Guiding Principles*, we provide guidance to help organizations operationalize EPM. We introduce six process steps, categorized within three management phases, intended to help organizations prepare an extended performance account. Our intent is to broaden the traditional approach to measuring and accounting for organizational performance and facilitate a strategic approach to the management of knowledge intensive resources.

We wish to emphasize that the primary objective of these *Guiding Principles* is to encourage better management and development of knowledge and innovation within organizations and across the Australian economy. Any perceived emphasis in this document on reporting, whether for internal or external use, is not done so for the sake of reporting itself. We believe the role of reporting is to support management efforts to produce better organizational performance.

We also wish to emphasize that the management phases and process steps outlined in this section are in draft format. Our medium to long term objective is to test the principles with a larger group of Australian organizations. This will help establish the empirical validity required to influence the creation of guiding principles for national Australia. We acknowledge that processes of trial and error, modifications and learnings await us as we embark on this process. We invite you to join us on this journey.

6.1. Management Phases

Extended performance management must be set within a strategic context, comprising Business Orientation, Business Analysis, and Performance Assessment (Figure 7):

Figure 7: Management Phases

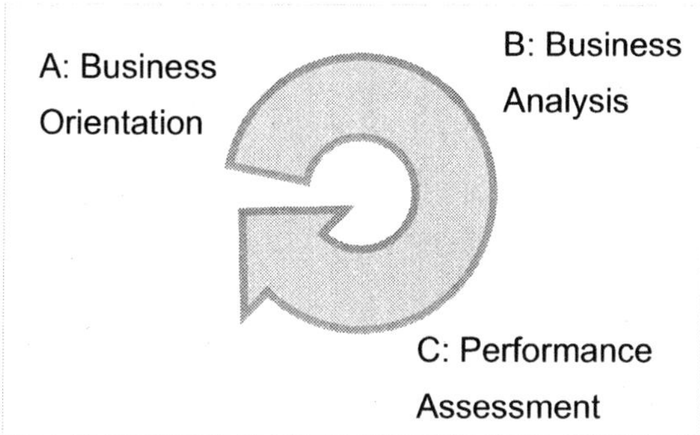

6.2. Process Steps

The three management phases, Business Orientation; Business Analysis; and Performance Assessment, comprise six process steps. These are discussed within the respective management phase in the following.

A: Business Orientation

Business orientation is the first management phase and comprises one process step (Figure 7, and Figure 9). In this phase, managers are faced with a number of key questions:

- **Organizational Identity:** What is our identity as a group of people, and how do we communicate this identity to organizational stakeholders?
- **Vision for Creating Use Value:** Where do we intend to go, and how do we envision to get there? What "use value" do we envision to create for our stakeholders and how do we intend to create and deliver this value?
- **Knowledge Gaps:** What knowledge do we need in order to succeed in delivering and creating use value to our stakeholders? E.g. what do we know we know? what don't we know? and what do we need to know to succeed in creating and delivering use value?

The outcome of the business orientation phase is an identification of the organization's strategic business objectives, relative to its identity, vision for creating use value and knowledge gaps.

B: Business Analysis

Business analysis is the second management phase and comprises four process steps (Figure 7 and Figure 9), as follows:

Market analysis

Market analysis includes an analysis of the macro-environmental and industry specific factors that affect the organization. The objective of market analysis is to identify changes in the external environmental and illuminate how external factors, trends and developments may impact on the organization and its ability to create value for the stakeholders it serves and affects. Market analysis can help close knowledge gaps and ensure that the organization is aware of risks and opportunities arising from changes in the external environment.

The following factors and actors are considered in the market analysis:

- Competitors
- Political Factors
- Economic Factors
- Societal Factors
- Technological Factors
- Environmental Factors
- Legal Factors

The outcome of market analysis is a summary of the threats and opportunities the organization faces as a result of changes in the external environment.

Figure 7: Process Steps

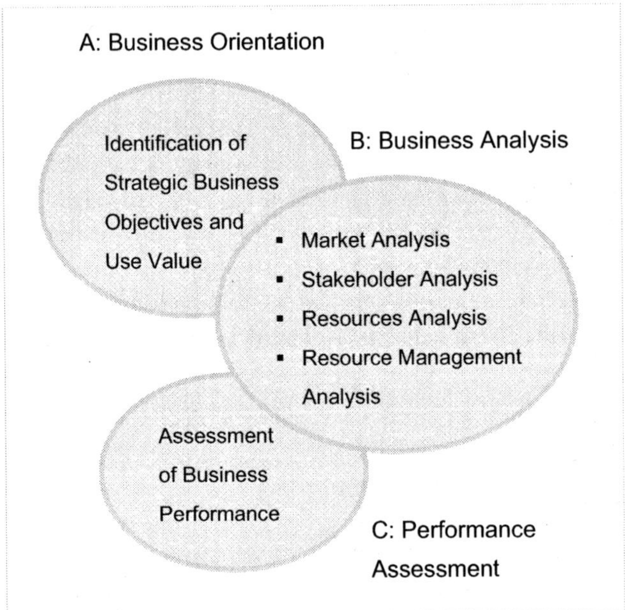

Stakeholder Analysis

Stakeholder analysis pertains to the identification and analysis of the expectations, perspectives and needs of internal and external organizational stakeholders. Stakeholder analysis facilitates reciprocal, as opposed to one way, communication flows between organizations and the people they serve and affect. It provides organizations with new knowledge about the needs and perspectives of key stakeholder groups, thus creating opportunities for reflecting on existing management activities and devising new avenues for organizational development.

Stakeholders include those people external or internal to the organization, who affect, or are affected by, the organization's operating activities. External stakeholders include, but are not limited to:

- Capital Market Actors
- Community
- Customers
- Distributors
- Suppliers
- Government
- Education Providers
- Non-government Organizations

Internal stakeholders include, but are not limited to:

- Board Members
- Consultants
- Contractors
- Employees such as Senior Executives, Managers and Staff

Stakeholder analysis may be facilitated through interviews, surveys, focus groups or other means of stakeholder contact and feedback.

Examples of possible questions to be raised during the stakeholder analysis phase include:

- Customers: What do customers think about the organization, its products and services, community practices and ethical conduct?
- Employees: What do employees think about the organization? Is the work environment motivating and stimulating? Are they given opportunities for feedback, career advancement? Do they participate in decision-making? Are they given opportunities for ownership and personal growth?
- Environment: What do environmental groups think about the behavior and conduct of the organization? What are the organization's environmental impacts and contributions?

The stakeholder feedback may be represented in the form of a scorecard quantifying and/ or qualifying the value perspectives and needs of stakeholders according to stakeholder category.

The main outcome of stakeholder analysis is the creation of new insights into the value perspectives and needs of the people, or groups of people, the organization serves and affects. It induces management with new knowledge on which to base decision making and strategy formulation.

Resource Analysis

Resource analysis pertains to the identification and analysis of the organization's resources (Figure 7 and Figure 9). Organizational resources may be categorized into:

- Knowledge intensive resources:
  - Relational resources
  - Structural resources
  - Human resources
- Monetary resources
- Physical resources

For the purpose of these *Guiding Principles*, the objective of resource analysis is to provide an inventory of the knowledge intensive resources the organization has at its disposal in its pursuit of value creation. If appropriate, the analysis may be extended to include the physical and monetary resources reported in the balance sheet.

Resource analysis includes recording the composition of the organization's knowledge intensive resources. Examples include, but are not limited to:

- Structural: Number and type of software licenses; number and type of new product developments; number of cross functional teams.
- Relational: Number and type of strategic alliances and partnerships; number and type of customers (i.e. strategic versus casual).
- Human: Number of employees; age profile of employees; employees skills and vocations.

The outcome of resource analysis is an inventory of the composition (or stock) of the organization's knowledge intensive resources. It complements the balance sheet by recording the intangible resources not recognized by existing accounting standards.

Resource Management Analysis

Resource management analysis comprises an analysis of the activities undertaken by management to manage the organization's knowledge intensive resources relative to its strategic objectives.

Resource management activities are classified into five broad categories:

1. Acquisition of knowledge intensive resources
2. Development of knowledge intensive resources
3. Utilization of knowledge intensive resources
4. Maintenance of knowledge intensive
5. Disposal of knowledge intensive resources

Examples of such managerial activities include, but are not limited to:

- Structural: Process reengineering; organizational restructuring; leadership development programme.
- Relational: Creation of advertising campaign; community development activities; formation of strategic alliance.
- Human: Sourcing of employees; implementation of learning and development programme; workplace innovation project; retrenchment of staff.

The outcome of the managerial activity analysis is an identification and analysis of the efforts taken by the organization to manage its knowledge intensive resources relative to its strategic objectives.

C: Performance Assessment

Performance Assessment is the last of the six process steps. It comprises an assessment of the progress made by the organization at managing its knowledge intensive resources relative to its strategic objectives.

Performance assessment is informed by the market analysis, stakeholder analysis, resource analysis, and resource management analysis (Figure 8).

Figure 8: Performance Assessment

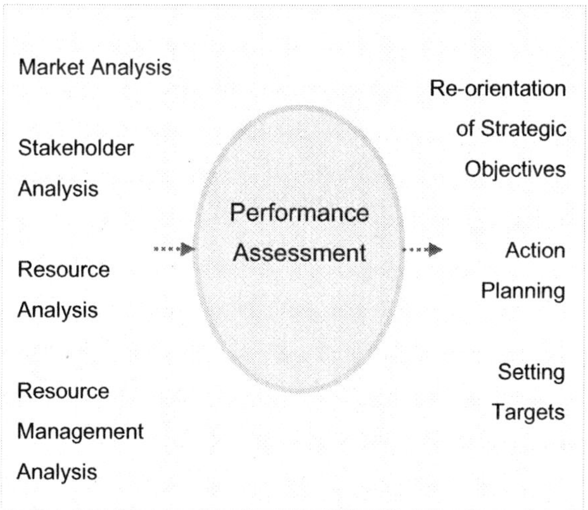

Performance assessment is a continuous process of matching organizational performance against stated targets. It enables managers to reflect on past performance and facilitates the identification of future management action. Information about past performance provides input into action planning and the setting of new strategic business objectives.

Such new strategic business objectives may be informed by extended performance measures, in line with those illustrated in Table 5 in section 4.3. One activity possibly undertaken is an analysis of the effects of a given investment activity. This may incorporate statistical analysis to establish the cause effect relations between investments, stakeholder perspectives and behavior and / or financial outcomes.

Figure 9 provides a detailed graphical illustration summarizing the three management phases and the six process steps.

We also wish to point out that organizations that embark on the journey of producing an extended performance account are likely to face a number of important decisions and possible challenges. These may include, but are not necessarily limited, to:

- attracting resources;
- developing and sustaining interest and commitment from executives, employees and others;
- attracting (visionary) teams leaders;
- determining levels of responsibility and accountability;
- project planning;
- overcoming employee resistance and challenging the status quo; and
- identifying and tracking the value and performance of knowledge intensive resources.

The *Society for Knowledge Economics* aims to establish knowledge forums for organizations to come together and share their challenges, learnings and experiences on the preparation of extended performance accounts.

7. How Does the Future Look?

In this last section of the *Australian Guiding Principles,* we review recent trends and developments in national and international legislation, guidelines and codes of conduct. We also comment on the challenges facing practitioners and public policy makers in advancing the uptake of EPM, and point towards a series of action points to help pave the way forward.

7.1. International Trends and Developments–Legislation and Guidelines

In this first section, we provide a brief overview of the trends in legislation, codes of conduct or national guidelines on EPM.

The key findings of our analysis are summarized in Table 8, which shows an increase in international standards and guiding principles on how to manage, measure and report knowledge intensive organizational resources.

Figure 8: Process Steps Undertaken in Extended Performance Management

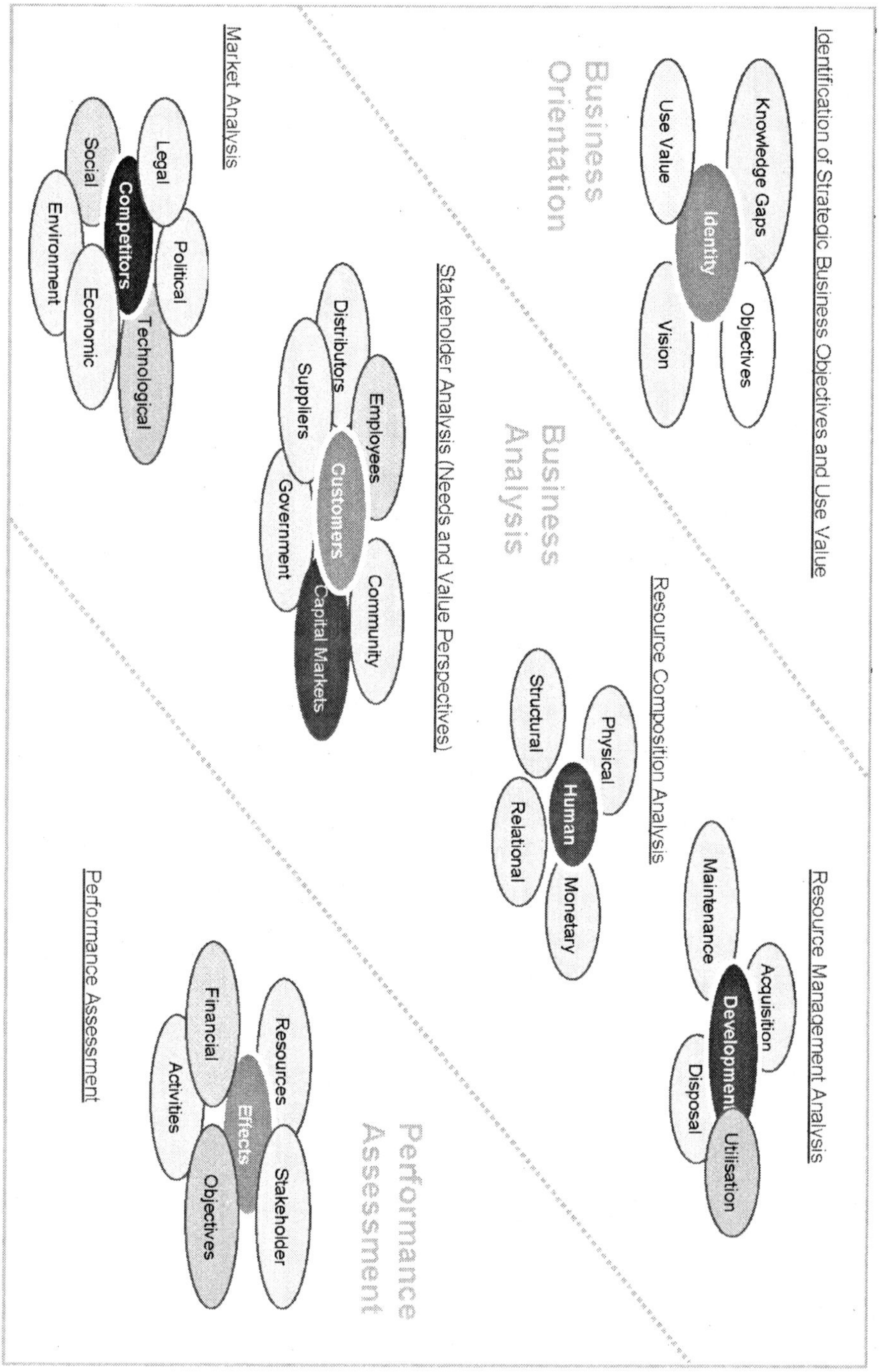

Key trends include:

- **The UK Operating and Financial Review**, which now mandates UK public listed organizations to report on environmental, competitive and regulatory factors, risks and uncertainties, business objectives, and strategies for achieving the business objectives. To the extent necessary, the OFR also requires organizations to report on stakeholder relations, social and community issues, environmental matters, employees, customers, and key performance indicators. The OFR came into effect on April 1, 2005 (see Appendix A for more details on the OFR).
- **The 15th Corporate White Paper on Corporate Social Responsibility,** issued by the Japanese Association of Corporate Executives, the Keizai Doyukai, proposes a draft CSR standard called *Practical Tools for Evaluating the Current Situation and Setting Goals to Enhance Comprehensive Corporate Value*. The aim is to assist organizations in performance evaluation, goal setting, discovery of best practices and risk management. It outlines 110 CSR indicators, which are grouped into five categories: Market, People, Environment, Society and Corporate Governance (see Appendix B for details).
- **The Intellectual Capital Reporting Guideline,** issued by the Danish Ministry of Science, Technology and Innovation in 2003, consists of two parts. The first part informs organizations on how to prepare intellectual capital statements. The second part informs users on how to read and analyse the statements. An intellectual capital statement reports on an organization's management challenges, knowledge resources, knowledge management activities and performance measures. The reporting categories are set within a strategic context and consider customer use value and the organization's knowledge narrative. The reporting model has been piloted by over 150 Danish organizations over a five-year period (see Appendix C for more detail about the structure and content of intellectual capital statements).
- **The Austrian Universities Organizations and Studies Act**, which came into effect on 1 January 2004, requires Austrian Universities to produce intellectual capital reports. The reports must be structured into *relational, structural* and *human capital* and include an obligatory set of performance measures for each category (see Appendix D for more details).
- **The Australian Stock Exchange Principles on Good Corporate Governance**. The ASX reporting principles provide a guide to listed entities on best practices in corporate governance and disclosure, emphasizing the need for corporate accountability and transparency. It outlines ten Corporate Governance Principles, which among others comment on: Board Structure; Enhanced Performance; Recognizing and Managing Risk; Recognizing the Interests of Stakeholders; Ethical and Responsible Decision Making; and Timely and Balanced Disclosures (see Appendix E for more details).

Notably, Table 8 shows an increase in guidelines on the management and reporting of knowledge intensive organizational resources in the international sphere.

Australia, despite initiatives to increase triple bottom line reporting and the recent ASX principles on corporate governance, appears to lag behind its international counterparts. Existing practices in Australia show a strong focus on environmental reporting, yet there is limited evidence of practices which consider the management and measurement of knowledge intensive organizational resources.

Several factors may help explain the lagging position of Australia in the uptake of EPM. One possible explanation is the lack of a peak body leading the way forward. A second possible explanation is the continued perception of Australia as a mineral and raw material producing, manufacturing economy, resulting in a lack of acknowledgement of the role and importance of knowledge, innovation and technology in sustaining and improving national and organizational productivity and performance. A third explanation may be the lack of prioritization of strategic initiatives in the area of knowledge and innovation by professional associations, government officials and education providers.

The lagging position of Australia within the international community poses questions as to which initiatives are required to better position and promote Australia as a leading knowledge economy. It also raises questions as to who will lead the way for the implementation and uptake of such initiatives.

The vision of the *Society for Knowledge Economics* is to take on this responsibility and to lead the way in establishing best practice examples on the management and development of knowledge and innovation in the Australian economy. We believe there is ample space for Australia to take a leadership position in this important and growing field of practice and study.

Our objective is first and foremost to increase awareness of the role of knowledge and innovation in national and organizational productivity and performance. We also aspire to help provide Australian organizations with the ideas, tools and philosophies to better manage, measure and report on their knowledge intensive resources. Such initiatives, we believe, will help advance the productivity and prosperity of Australian organizations, the individuals that work for Australian organizations, the communities they affect and the national economy they seek to advance.

Table 8: Trends in Legislation and Guidelines[6]

Legislation		Guidelines, Codes of Conduct and Standards	
Australian Corporations Act/CLERP 9	Requires public listed companies to report on their operations and financial position, business strategies and prospects and performance in relation to environmental regulations	**AA1000 AccountAbility Guideline**	The Guideline provides guidance on how to establish a systematic stakeholder engagement process. This is used to identify indicators, targets and reporting systems to enhance overall performance.
Australian Financial Services Reform Act	Requires fund managers and financial product provides to disclose the extent to which labour standards or environmental, social and ethical considerations are taken into account in the selection, retention or realisation of the investment.	**Australian Greenhouse Challenge Programme**	Members commit to preparing emissions inventories and forecasts, identify and undertake abatement plans and reporting progress against the action plan.
Austrian Universities Organisations and Studies Act	Mandates Austrian Universities to produce intellectual capital reports. The reports must be structured into human, structural and relationship capital. For each category, an obligatory set of ratios are required to be reported.	**Australian Guideline for Triple Bottom Line Reporting**	Consistent with the GRI principles, the guideline provides guiding principles for reporting environmental performance.
Belgium Bilan Social	Requires organisations to report data on the evolution of employment (i.e. training)	**Australian Minerals Industry**	The industry has issued a framework for Sustainable Development "Enduring Value". Members commit to publish sustainability reports on an annual basis. Metrics are informed by the GRI. Independent verification of reports is required.
Canadian Securities Commission	Requires public companies to report the operating and financial effects of environmental protection requirements, be they future or current.	**Australian Securities Institute's Disclosure Guidelines**	Guideline for product issuers to disclosure about labour standards or environmental, ethical, and social considerations in Product Disclosure Statements.
Canadian Bank Act	Requires financial institutions with equity of USD 1mn or more to report their contributions to the national economy.	**ASX Principles on Good Corporate Governance**	Provides a comprehensive guide to listed entities on best practices in corporate governance and disclosure. Emphasises the need for corporate accountability and transparency. The guideline includes ten Corporate Governance Principles.
Danish Financial Statement Act	Requires intellectual capital resources and environmental aspects to be reported if it is material to providing a fair view of the organisation's financial position.	**Danish Guideline on Intellectual Capital Reporting**	Provide a structured framework for organisations to manage, measure and report their knowledge resources and knowledge management activities within a strategic context.
Finnish Accounting Act	Requires certain public companies to report material non-financial issues in their annual report.	**Danish Social And Ethical Accounts**	Provides guidance on how to report social and ethical initiatives and activities.

6 This table has been adapted from KPMG's International Survey of Corporate Responsibility Reporting 2005.

EU Integrated Pollution Prevention and Control Directive	Member states are required to register emission data from large companies.	**Dow Jones Sustainability Index**	The Dow Jones Sustainability Index was the first index to try to assess the ability of businesses to create long-term shareholder value. It focuses on identifying future value potential and uses a defined set of criteria to assess the opportunities and risks deriving from economic, environmental and social developments. A major source of information is the SAM questionnaire, which is completed by companies participating in the annual review.
French Law no2001-420	Requires public listed companies to report their environmental and social impacts	**EMAS**	The EUR Eco-Management and Audit Scheme enables organisations to evaluate, report and improve their environmental performance.
Germany Bilanzrechts-reformgesetz	Requires German organisations to report non financial performance indicators such as environmental and employee issues.	**German Guideline on Intellectual Capital Statements**	Issued by the Federal Ministry of Economics and Labour in 2004, the guideline provides guidance on how to prepare an intellectual capital statement. It traces the experiences of a sample of organisations who participated in the pilot projects.
Japanese Law	The Law of Promotion of Environmentally Conscious Business Activities requires certain entities to publish an annual environmental report.	**Global Reporting Initiative**	Describes itself as a global multi-stakeholder process and independent institution that disseminates and develops globally applicable sustainability reporting guidelines. Encourages organisations to report on the environmental, social and economic dimensions of their services products and activities.
Japan's Pollutant Release and Transfer Register Law	Requires organisations to report releases to the environment of certain chemical substances.	**Italy's CSR-SC project**	Encourages organisations to produce social statements according to predefined guidelines and criteria.
Norwegian Accounting Act	Requires inclusion of social, environmental and health and safety issues and the implementation of measures to prevent or reduce negative impacts and trends.	**International Standards Organisation**	Has developed a wide range of standards, including corporate responsibility in the areas of quality and the environment (ISO 9000 and 1400 series).
Spain's Resolucion de 25 de marzo de 2002	Requires reporting of environmental assets, provisions, investments and expenses in financial statements.	**MERITUM Guideline**	Initiated by the European Commission in 1998; MERITUM stands for Measuring Intangibles to Understand and Improve Innovation Management. Six European countries (Finland, France, Denmark, Norway, Spain and Sweden) participated in the project. The objective was to produce guidelines to measure and disclose intangibles to improve decision-making for managers and stakeholders.
Sweden's Annual Accounts Act	Requires certain companies to include a brief disclosure of environmental and social information in the annual report.	**Japanese Guidelines for Environmental Reporting**	The Ministry of the Environment has issued two guidelines. One on Environmental Reporting and one on Environmental Performance Indicators.
The Netherlands'	Requires the largest polluters to report on their environmental impacts.	**Japanese Keizai Doyukai**	The Japanese association of corporate executives has issued its 15th Corporate White Paper on Corporate Social Responsibility. It

Environmental Protection Act			proposes a draft CSR standard called "Practical Tools for Evaluating the Current Situation and Setting Goals to Enhance Comprehensive Corporate Value".
UK Operating and Financial Review	The OFR requires public listed UK organisations to report on environmental, competitive and regulatory factors, risks and uncertainties, business objectives, and strategies for achieving the objective. To the extent necessary, organisations must also report on stakeholder relations, social and community issues, environmental matters, employees, customers, and key performance indicators.	**Japanese Guideline on Intellectual Property**	This guideline has been issued by the Ministry of Economy, Trade and Industry. It focuses on strategic IP related issues and provides guiding principles for disclosing information about IP, technology, business strategy and R&D.
US Sarbanes Oxley	Imposed new reporting requirements for public listed companies to increase corporate transparency and governance.	**OECD Multinational Enterprise**	Provides voluntary principles for responsible business conduct in areas such as human rights, disclosure of information, anti-corruption, taxation, labour relations, environment, and consumer protection. Governments of the countries adhering to the Guidelines agree to promote their implementation by enterprises operating in or from their territory. Used by MNEs from the OECD group of 30 countries plus Argentina, Brazil, Chile, Estonia, Israel, Lithuania and Slovenia
US Securities and Exchange Commission	Requires appropriate disclosure of environmental impacts and expenditure on control facilities and legal proceedings on environmental matters	**Sweden's Accounting Standards Board**	Provides guidelines on environmental reporting in the Directors' section of the annual report.
US Toxic Release Inventory	Requires companies with more than ten employees to submit data on specific toxic chemicals to the Environmental Protection Agency.	**UK Public Environmental Reporting Initiative**	Provides tools for organisations to produce a balanced perspective on their environmental policies, practices and performance.
		United Nations Global Compact	Encourages companies to adhere to ten guiding principles in the areas of labour, human rights, environment and anti-corruption.
		US Enhanced Business Reporting Consortium	Encourages increased transparency in business reporting, e.g. "Better Information Leads to Better Management . . . Better Governance . . . Better Markets". Proposes the EBR framework which in intended to put structure around external reporting of information not currently covered under GAAP (i.e. management strategy and plans, risks and opportunities faced by a company, industry-specific, process-oriented value drivers and financial and non-financial key performance indicators).

7.2. Challenges

Despite the increase in national and international codes of conduct and the trends towards standard setting, discussed in the previous section, there are still significant challenges to advancing the uptake of EPM. These challenges may be perceived from the perspective of users external to organizations, be they capital market investors, customers, future employees or others, and stakeholders internal at the organization, be they board members, company directors, managers or others. Certain challenges are generic across both stakeholder categories. Figure 9 is illustrative.

Figure 9: Challenges to EPM

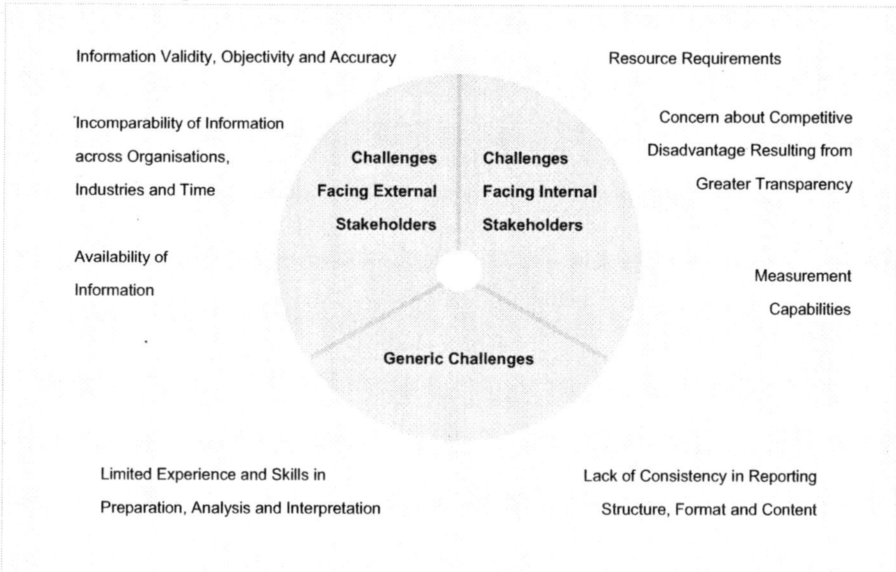

7.2.1 Challenges Facing External Stakeholders

External stakeholders, be they customers, investors, suppliers, public sector agents or others, face three main challenges to advancing the uptake of EPM.

Validity, Objectivity and Accuracy of Extended Performance Information Possibly the greatest barrier is the lack of assurance of the validity, objectivity and accuracy of extended performance information. Contrary to financial accounts, extended performance information is reported on a voluntary basis. This poses questions as to whether external stakeholders can be assured that the information reported in extended performance accounts is accurate and complete. The lack of assurance has created some skepticism among public users, who maintain there is a tendency towards "cheery picking", whereby organizations turn performance information into a glamorous marketing collateral focusing solely on the success stories, leaving out the negative stories.

In an effort to counter this, the past three years have witnessed the introduction of two new global assurance standards intended to help improve the validity, accuracy and reliability of extended performance information. The two standards, which guide the work of assurance providers, include:

- the International Standard on Assurance Engagement issued by the International Auditing and Accounting Standards Board in December 2003. The standard strives to ensure that assurance is carried out with independence and professionally; and
- the AA1000 Assurance Standard issued by AccountAbility in March 2003. This standard requires assurance providers to report their findings against the three principles of materiality, completeness and responsiveness.

However, despite the advancement of global assurance standards, the uptake of assurance still remains low in relative terms, both internationally and in Australia. A survey commissioned by CPA Australia (2005), which investigated the level of sustainability reporting among Australian private (top 500) and public sector (Commonwealth and state government business enterprises and local governments) organizations, found that only thirteen (54 percent) of separately disclosed reports had been subjected to any form of audit or verification. A global survey by KPMG (2005) of the top 250 Global Fortune companies shows a more positive number and finds that reports with formal assurance reached 30 percent in 2005, up from 29 percent in 2002.

Incomparability of Information across Organizations, Industries and Time

A second challenge facing external stakeholders is the incomparability of extended performance information across organizations, industries and time. This is influenced by the fragmentation of existing measurement and reporting systems and the lack of standard reporting criteria and frameworks to guide the disclosure of extended performance information. The Global Reporting Initiative (GRI) by the United Nations is increasingly seen to pave the way at an international level for advancing consistency in reporting criteria, with 40 percent of companies in the Global Fortune 250 using the GRI to decide on reporting content (KPMG, 2005).

Availability of Information

The third challenge is the lack of consistency in the availability of extended performance information. Since most disclosure is done on a voluntary basis, the type and level of disclosure is discretionary and information availability is subject to the willingness of individual organizations to publicly report extended performance data. The lack of consistency in availability makes identification and comparison across companies difficult.

In regards to the level of disclosure, recent surveys show a positive trend towards an increase in external reporting. KPMG's (2005) survey of international reporting practices found that 52 percent of the top 250 Global Fortune companies published separate corporate responsibility reports in 2005. This was a positive increase, up from 45 percent in

2002. The survey also shows that there is a change in the type of disclosure with an increase in sustainability information (social, economics and environmental) over earlier years where environmental, health and safety dominated.

In regards to levels of national reporting, the KPMG (2005) survey found that 80 percent of Japan's and 71 percent of the UK's top 100 companies published a separate corporate responsibility report. These two countries were far ahead of the next best, Canada (41 percent). Australia ranked 11th, with only 23 percent of companies issuing a stand alone corporate responsibility report.

Besides the KPMG survey, limited data is available on the reporting practices of Australian organizations. The most advanced is the 2005 survey commissioned by CPA Australia, which investigates the level of sustainability reporting in Australia. The survey finds that twenty-four private corporations published separate sustainability reports in 2003, seventeen of those were in the Materials industry, three in Capital Goods, two in Energy, one in Telecommunication and one in Banking. The report also outlines reporting levels in the public sector and finds limited uptake in separate reporting documentation with only one Commonwealth government business enterprise (GBE) and 3 state GBEs disclosing a separate sustainability report.

It should be noted that the aforementioned surveys focus solely on corporate responsibility reports. Neither of the surveys investigated the use of intellectual capital statements, balanced scorecards, ValueReporting™ statements and other extended performance accounts.

7.2.2. Challenges Facing Internal Stakeholders

Internal stakeholders likewise face a number of challenges to advancing the use and adoption of EPM.

Resource Requirements

An important challenge facing internal stakeholders wishing to engage in EPM is the time, commitment and resources required to successfully identify, analyze, measure and report their knowledge intensive resources and activities. The previous sections of the *Guiding Principles* outlined the proposed management phases and process steps to produce extended performance accounts. Depending on an organization's capability levels, embarking on this process may be a challenging and time consuming affair, requiring vision, leadership, commitment and resources.

Competitive Disadvantage Resulting from Greater Transparency

Possibly the greatest challenge facing organizations in advancing external reporting is the fear of disclosing competitively sensitive information to external stakeholders. Managers are particularly concerned about competitors gaining insights into strategic information, which may disadvantage them in the market. Competitive intelligence experts reject this concern. They claim that 98 percent of information is available through public channels and extended performance accounts provide limited information which is not already publicly available.

Measurement

The third challenge facing organizations relates to the complexity associated with tracing the value that accrues from investing in knowledge intensive organizational resources and activities, as discussed in section 4.3. Only during recent years have researchers begun to establish empirical support of cause-effect relations between investing into knowledge intensive resource and financial outcomes[7]. Measurement techniques and practices are, however, still in the infancy stage and require more empirical testing through research and practice.

7.2.3. Generic Challenges

Internal and external stakeholders share two generic challenges to advancing the uptake of EPM.

Limited Experience and Skills in Preparation, Analysis and Interpretation

The first is the general lack of awareness of extended performance management processes and techniques. Accountants, investors and business managers are brought up with years of training in financial accounting techniques, focusing on quantitative interpretations and analyses of accrual accounting and cash flow information. Yet, less attention is attributed to the qualitative drivers of business performance including understanding the value of knowledge intensive organizational resources. The challenge lies in increasing visibility and awareness of how to identify, analyze, measure and report the value of knowledge intensive organizational resources.

The Lack of Consistency in Reporting Structure, Format and Content

The second generic challenge is the lack of consistency in reporting structure, format and content, possibly influenced by the aforementioned fragmentation of existing measurement and reporting practices and the lack of consistency in reporting criteria. The 2005 survey (p. 19) commissioned by the CPA finds that "there is significant diversity in the format and scope of the sustainability disclosure practices of sample companies notwithstanding that over 70 percent of them operate in the same industry". The reports concludes that the "diversity of reporting scope and format impedes comparison of environmental and social performance between entities".

Contrary to financial statements, extended performance accounts, be they intellectual capital statements, balanced scorecards or corporate responsibility reports, are experimental

7 See Roos and Pike (2004, p. 248 onwards) for an overview of trends in measurement theory and a summary of existing measurement methodologies.

of nature and therefore dissimilar in structure, format and content. Such inconsistency may be attributable to the "early stage" of extended performance accounts in the product life cycle. The accrual accounting system has over 500 years of heritage. Extended performance accounts have barely a couple of decades on the back.

Furthermore, whereas traditional financial accounts require reporting of quantitative data and have specific content requirements and clear, unambiguous reporting structures, extended performance accounts comprise qualitative, often subjective information. Thus, a challenge is how to create consistency in reporting and measurement practices, given the subjective, often value-laded and qualitative nature of intangible, knowledge intensive resources.

7.3. Action Points

The discussions and analyses undertaken throughout this concluding section of the *Australian Guiding Principles* point towards a series of action points in order to advance the notion and uptake of EPM among Australian organizations, policy makers and professional agencies.

The aforementioned report commissioned by the CPA supports this observation and highlights the importance of the establishment and development of new methods and techniques for managing and accounting for organizational performance. The report (2005, p. 19) states that "the inability or reluctance of organizations to modify or develop tools, processes and frameworks through which they can report their direct and indirect economic, social and environmental impacts to stakeholders provides a challenge for the accounting profession and policy makers. In particular there is a need to develop more accessible approaches and guidelines to enable entities to discharge a broader accountability than is currently reflected in reporting practices in the public and private sectors in Australia". We extend this focus on social, economic and environmental impacts to also include the effective management of knowledge intensive resources internal at organizations.

We propose a number of key action points to help address these issues and advance the awareness, uptake and proliferation of extended performance accounts among Australian organizations. These action points pertain to:

1. Influencing the development of national and possibly international guiding principles to ensure consistency in reporting structure, format and content and advance the comparability of extended performance measures[8] across organizations, industries and time[9];

   Advancing the development of assurance standards to improve information validity, objectivity and accuracy;

8 This may involve the establishment of benchmarking studies and criteria to influence the development of standards on extended performance measures.

9 An example includes the GRI guideline on sustainability reporting, which identifies eleven principles intended to help ensure comparability and reliability. These include: Transparency; Inclusiveness; Completeness; Relevance; Sustainability Context; Accuracy; Neutrality; Comparability; Clarity; Timeliness; and Auditability.

2. Facilitating research into EPM to examine the:
   a Type, and levels of use, of EPM frameworks in Australia, whether for internal management or external reporting purposes;
   Challenges and benefits that accrue to organizations that measure and report the value and performance knowledge intensive organizational resources.
3. Increasing awareness among practitioners, investors and others of how to interpret and analyze extended performance accounts, possibly facilitated by education, conferences, workshops and professional certification;
4. Aiding and influencing public policy makers in setting the agenda for extended performance management.

The *Society for Knowledge Economics* aspires to be the peak body paving the way for the realization of these action points.

We invite government officials, public and private sector organizations, industry bodies and professionals to work with us in advancing the position of Australia as a leading knowledge economy within the international community. We are particularly interested in extending an invitation to public and private sector organizations to participate in testing these draft *Guiding Principles on Extended Performance Management*.

8. Referenced Documents

Accenture (2004), 'A New Paradigm for Managing Shareholder Value', Accenture Institute for High Business Performance, July 2004.

Accenture (2003), 'Intangible Assets and Future Value', An Accenture Survey, conducted by the Economist Intelligence Unit, 2003.

AccountAbility (2005), 'Beyond Reporting: Creating Business Value and Accountability', AccountAbility, June 2005.

AccountAbility (2004), 'Strategic Challenges for Business in the Use of Corporate Responsibility Codes, Standards and Frameworks', AccountAbility, October 2004.

Ambler, T., Barwise, P. and Higson, C. (2001), 'Market Metrics: What Should We Tell the Shareholders?', retrieved from *http://www.icaew.co.uk/*

Arbouw, J. (2005), 'Looking Beyond the Bottom Line', *Company Director*, July 2005, cover story.

Australian Bureau of Statistics (2002), 'Measuring a Knowledge Based Economy and Society: An Australian Framework', Discussion Paper, ABS, 2002.

Australian Yearbook (2005), 'Industry Structure and Performance Article – 100 Years of Change in Australian Industry', *http://www.abs.gov.au/Ausstats/abs@.nsf/0/06359B2064A5C169CA256F7200832F6A?Open*

Ballow, J., Burgman, R, Roos, G and Molnar, M. (2004), 'A New Paradigm for Managing Shareholder Value', Accenture Institute for High Business Performance, July 2004.

Boedker, C., Guthrie, J. and Cuganesan, S. (2005, forthcoming), 'An Integrated Framework for Visualising Intellectual Capital', *Journal of Intellectual Capital*, Special Edition: 'Management

Consulting Practices on Intellectual Capital', Vol. 6, No 4, 2005.

Buffini, F. (2005), 'Earnings Hit as Rules Erase $17bn', *Australian Financial Review*, September 27, 2005, cover story and p. 52.

Bukh, P. N. and Johanson, U. (2003), 'Research and Knowledge Interaction: Guidelines for IC Reporting', *Journal of Intellectual Capital*, Vol. 4, No. 4, 2003.

Bukh, P. N., Rimmel, G., Koga, C., Nielsen, C., Tandanori, Y. and Sakakibara, S. (2005, working paper), 'Intellectual Capital in Japanese and Danish IPO Prospectuses: A Comparative Analysis', working paper.

CPA Australia (2005), 'Measuring Intellectual Capital: Something to Think About', *Australian Accounting Review* Issue 36, Vol. 15, No. 2, July 2005.

CPA Australia (2005), 'Sustainability Reporting: Practices, Performance and Potential', CPA Australia, July 2005.

Davenport, T. H. and Prusak, L. (1998), '*Working Knowledge: How Organizations Manage What They Know*', Harvard Business School Press, Ch. 4 'Knowledge Codification and Coordination'.

Department of Industry, Science and Resources (2001), 'Invisible Value: The Case for Measuring and Reporting Intellectual Capital', DISR, Canberra, Ch. 1 'Introduction', Ch. 2 'The Economics of Intellectual Capital', Ch. 3 'IC: Concept and Why It Is Important', pp. 19–25, Ch. 4 'Conventional Accounting of Intangible Assets', pp. 25–29.

Enhanced Business Reporting Consortium (2004), 'Business Plan', retrieved on Oct. 17, 2005 from *http://www.ebrconsortium.org/download/EBRC_Business_Plan.pdf*

Federal Ministry of Economics and Labour (2004), 'Intellectual Capital Statement–Made in Germany', Federal Ministry of Economics and Labour, *www.bmwa.bund.de*

Financial Review (2004), 'Special Report–Knowledge Management', pp. 10–16.

Fincham, R. and Roslender, R. (2003), 'The Management of Intellectual Capital and Its Implications for Business Reporting', Research Report for the Research Committee of The Institute of Chartered Accountants of Scotland, Edinburgh, Scotland.

Global Reporting Initiative, *www.globalreporting.org/guidelines/2002.asp*, accessed in August, 2005.

Guo R., Lev B. and Zhou N. (2005), "The Valuation of Biotech IPOs", working paper, New York University, accessed on October 17 2005, *http://pages.stern.nyu.edu/~blev/docs/ExplainingIPO%20Anomalies%20by%20RD-JBFAConference-May%*,

Guthrie, J. and Ricceri, F. (2002), 'Quantify Intellectual Capital: Measuring and Reporting to Demonstrate Value of KM to Stakeholders', Knowledge Management Australia: Building and Improving on Knowledge Management Initiative for Commercial Proficiency Conference, Merchant Court Hotel, Sydney, 4 December 2002.

Gylfason T. (1999), 'Principles on Economic Growth", Oxford University Press.

Hansen, T., Nohria, N. and Tierney, T. (1999), 'What is Your Strategy for Managing Knowledge?', *Harvard Business Review*, March–April 1999.

Holland, J. (2003), 'Intellectual Capital and The Capital Market–Organization and Competence', *Accounting, Auditing and Accountability Journal*, Vol. 16, No. 1, 2003, pp. 39–48.

Institute of Chartered Accountants in England and Wales (2003), 'Information for Better Markets:

New Reporting Models for Business', ICAEW, 2003.

Johanson, U. (2003), 'Why Are Capital Markets Ambivalent to Certain Information about Certain Indicators on Intellectual Capital', *Accounting, Auditing and Accountability Journal*, Vol. 16, No. 1, 2003, pp. 31–38.

Kaplan R. and Norton D. (2005), *www.Balancedscorecard.org*, accessed in August, 2005.

Kaplan, R. and Norton, D. (1992), 'The Balanced Scorecard: Measures that Drive Performance', *Harvard Business Review*, January–February 1992.

Kjaergaard, I. (2003), 'Constructing a Knowledge Based Identity: Experiences from Working with Intellectual Capital Statements', *Corporate Reputation Index*, Vol. 6, No. 3, 2003, pp. 266–275.

KPMG (2005), 'KPMG International Survey of Corporate Responsibility Reporting 2005', KPMG International.

KPMG (2004), 'Transitioning to International Financial Reporting Standards: Key Issues for Australian Industrial Companies', retrieved from *www.kpmg.com.au* in December 2004.

Kreiner, K. (2002), 'Tacit Knowledge Management: The Role of Artefacts', *Journal of Knowledge Management*, Vol. 6, No 2, 2002, pp. 112–123.

Marr, B., Gray, D. and Neely, A., (2003), 'Why Do Firms Measure Their Intellectual Capital?', *Journal of Intellectual Capital*, Vol. 4, No. 4, 2003, pp. 441–464.

Marr, B., Schiuma, G. and Neely, A. (2004), 'The Dynamics of Value Creation: Mapping Your Intellectual Performance Drivers', *Journal of Intellectual Capital*, Vol. 5, No. 2, 2004, pp. 312–325.

Massingham, P. (2004), 'Linking Business Level Strategy with Activities and Knowledge Resources', *Journal of Knowledge Management*, Vol. 8, No. 5, 2004, pp. 50–62.

McDermott, R. and Dell, C. O. (2001), 'Overcoming Cultural Barriers to Sharing Knowledge', *Journal of Knowledge Management*, Vol. 5, No. 1, 2001, pp. 76–85.

McKinsey (2005), 'Views from the Boardroom', *McKinsey Quarterly*, January 2005.

MERITUM (2001), 'Guidelines for Managing and Reporting on Intangibles (Intellectual Capital Report)', EU.

Mouritsen, J. and Thorsgaard Larsen, H. (2005), 'The 2nd Wave of Knowledge Management: The Management Control of Knowledge Resources through Intellectual Capital Information', *Management Accounting Research*, Vol.16, 2005, pp. 371–394.

Mouritsen, J., Thorsgaard Larsen, H. and Bukh, P.N. (2005), Dealing with the Knowledge Economy: Intellectual Capital versus Balanced Scorecard', *Journal of Intellectual Capital*, Vol. 6, No. 1, pp. 8–27.

Mouritsen, J., Bukh, P. N. and Marr, B. (2004), 'Reporting on Intellectual Capital: Why, What and How', *Measuring Business Excellence*, Vol. 8, No. 1, pp. 45–54.

Mouritsen, J., Bukh, P.N., Flagstad, K., Thorbjørnsen, S., Rosenkrands Johansen, M., Kotnis, S., Thorsgaard Larsen, H., Nielsen, C., Kjærgaard Jensen, I., Krag, L., Jeppesen, G., Haisler, J. and Stakemann, B. (2003), 'Intellectual Capital Statements – The New Guideline', published by the Danish Ministry of Science, Technology and Innovation (DMSTI), *http://www.videnskabsministeriet.dk/cgi-bin/theme-list.cgi?theme_id=100650&_lang=uk*, retrieved in April 2004.

Mouritsen, J., Bukh, P.N., Rosenkrands Johansen, M., Thorsgaard Larsen, H., Nielsen, C., Haisler, J. and Stakemann, B. (2003), 'Analysing Intellectual Capital Statements', published by the

Danish Ministry of Science, Technology and Innovation (DMSTI) retrieved from *http://www.videnskabsministeriet.dk/cgi-bin/theme-list.cgi?theme_id=100650&_lang=uk*, in April 2004.

Mouritsen, J., Bukh, P.D., Larsen, H.T., Johansen, M.R. (2002), 'Developing and Managing Knowledge through Intellectual Capital Statements', *Journal of Intellectual Capital*, Vol. 3, No. 1, pp. 10–29.

Nielsen, C. (2005), 'Business Reporting: How Transparency Becomes a Justification Mechanism', working paper, Aarhus School of Business.

Nonaka, I. and Takeuchi, H. (1995), *The Knowledge-creating Company*, Oxford University Press, Oxford.

Offsey, S. (1997), 'Knowledge Management: Linking People to Knowledge for Bottom Line Results', *Journal of Knowledge Management*, Vol. 1, No. 2, December 1997, pp. 113–122.

Petty, R. and Guthrie, J. (2000), 'Intellectual Capital Literature Review: Measurement, Reporting and Management', *Journal of Intellectual Capital*, Vol. 1, No. 2, 2000, pp. 155–176.

Picker, R. and Hicks, K. (2003), 'Countdown 2005: Derecognition Looms for Corporate Intangibles', *Australian CPA*, June 2003, pp. 78–80.

Plakalo, T. (2005), 'Accounting for the Unaccountable', *Managing Information Strategies*, cover story, retrieved on 9 February 2005 from *http://www.misweb.com/magarticle.asp?doc_id=24257&rgid=2&listed_months=0*

PricewaterhouseCoopers (2005), *www.pwc.com*, accessed in August 2005.

PricewaterhouseCoopers (1998), 'ValueReporting™ in Australia–Improving Competitiveness in Capital Markets', retrieved on 10 December 2004 from *http://store.barometersurveys.com/db_pages/sub.php?id=8*

Romer, RM. (1986), 'Increasing returns and long-run growth', Journal of Political Economy, 94(5): 1002-1037

Romer, P.M. (1990), 'Endogenous technological change', Journal of Political Economy, 98(5 pt. 2): 71-102.

Roos, G., Pike, S. (2004), 'Mathematics and Modern Business Management', Journal of Intellectual Capital, vol. 5, no. 2, 2004, pp. 243-256

Roos, G., Pike, S. and L. Fernström (2004), 'Valuation and Reporting of Intangibles - State of the Art in 2004', International Journal of Learning and Intellectual Capital, Vol. 1, No. 3, 2004.

Rucci, A., Kirn, S. P. and Quinn, R. T. (1998), 'The Employee-Customer Profit Chain at Sears', *Harvard Business Review*, January– February 1998, pp. 83–97.

Schaffhauser-Linzatti, M. (2004), 'Intellectual Capital Reporting for Austrian Universities–A Thrilling Work in Progress', forthcoming.

Skandia's website, *www.skandia.com*, accessed in August 2005.

Storey, J. and Barnett, E. (2000), 'Knowledge Management Initiatives: Learning from Failure', *Journal of Knowledge Management*, Vol. 4, No. 2, 2000, pp. 145–156.

Sveiby's Intangible Asset Monitor (2005), *www.sveiby.com*, accessed in August 2005.

Sveiby (2004) '28 Models of IC', *www.sveiby.com*, accessed on 30 July 2004.

Sveiby, K.E. (1997), 'The New Organizational Wealth', Berrett-Koehler Publishers, Inc., (?) San Francisco, Ch. 1.

SustainAbility (2004), 'Risk and Opportunity: Best Practices in Non-Financial Reporting',

SustainAbility, London.

SustainAbility (2002), 'Trust Us: The Global Reporters 2002 Survey of Corporate Sustainability Reporting', SustainAbility, London.

Systematic's Intellectual Capital Statement (2004) retrieved on 10 December 2004 from h*ttp:// www.systematic.dk/UK/About+Us/Intellectual+Capital+Reports.htm*

The New Zealand Ministry for the Environment (2002), 'Triple Bottom Line Reporting in the Public Sector Summary of Pilot Group Findings', retrieved on 22 August 2005.

The World Bank (2005), 'World Development Indicators', data retrieved on 19 August 2005, h*ttp:// www.worldbank.org/data/wdi2005/wditext/Section4.ht*m

Tissen, R., et al. (1998), 'What Ever Happened to the Industrial Age?', *Value Based Management*, Ch. 3, pp. 47–57, Longman, Netherlands.

UK Accounting Standards Board (2005), 'Reporting Standard 1: Operating and Financial Review', Accounting Standards Board, May 2005.

Zack, M. (1999), 'Developing a Knowledge Strategy', *California Management Review*, Vol. 41, Issue 3, 1999, pp. 125–145.

Appendix A: The UK Operating and Financial Review

The UK Department of Trade and Industry has issued a mandatory statutory requirement which requires public listed UK companies to prepare and disclose an 'operating and financial review' (OFR) as part of their annual reports. The mandate came into effect in April 2005. The UK Accounting Standards Board is responsible for the statutory requirements of the OFR.

The OFR has been designed to help shareholders get a more complete picture of a company's business by enabling them to assess a company's strategies and the potential of them to succeed.

The OFR is intended to strengthen corporate Britain. The idea is that investors equipped with higher-quality information are able to make better informed decisions.

The OFR mandates UK organizations to report on:

- The nature of the market including environmental, competitive and regulatory factors and developments;
- Risks and uncertainties that may affect the entity's long term value;
- Business objectives, and strategies for achieving the objectives;
- Stakeholder relations which are likely to influence the performance of the business (to the extent necessary);
- Social and community issues (to the extent necessary);
- Environmental matters (to the extent necessary);
- Employees (to the extent necessary);
- 'The KPIs (key performance indicators), both financial and, where appropriate, non-financial, used by the Directors to assess progress against their stated objectives' (to the extent necessary) (ASB, 2005, p. 14, paragraph 40). Examples of KPIs are provided in the report and include, among others, customer churn, social risk in the supply chain, employee morale, products in the development pipeline, waste, environmental issues and market share (see p. 50 onwards); and
- Other performance indicators (to the extent necessary).

The mandate states (pp. 7–18):

- The OFR shall have a forward-looking orientation, identifying those trends and factors relevant to the members' assessment of the current and future performance of the business and the progress towards the achievement of long-term business objectives.

- The OFR shall complement as well as supplement the financial statements, in order to enhance the overall corporate disclosure.
- The OFR shall be comparable over time.
- The OFR shall provide information to assist members to assess the strategies adopted by the entity and the potential for those strategies to succeed. The key elements of the disclosure framework necessary to achieve this are:
  - The nature of the business, including a description of the market, competitive and regulatory environment in which the entity operates, and the entity's objectives and strategies;
  - The development and performance of the business, both in the financial year under review and in the future; and
  - The resources, principal risks and uncertainties and relationships that may affect the entity's long-term value.
- To the extent necessary to meet the requirements set out in paragraph 28 above, the OFR shall include information about:
  - Environmental matters (including the impact of the business of the entity on the environment);
  - The entity's employees;
  - Social and community issues;
  - Persons with whom the entity has contractual or other arrangements which are essential to the business of the entity;
  - Receipts from, and returns to, members of the entity in respect of shares held by them; and
  - All other matters the directors consider to be relevant.
- The OFR shall include a description of the business and the external environment in which it operates as context for the directors' discussion and analysis of performance and financial position. The OFR shall discuss the objectives of the business to generate or preserve value over the longer-term. The OFR shall set out the directors' strategies for achieving the objectives of the business;
- To the extent necessary to meet the requirements set out in paragraph 28 above, the OFR shall include the key performance indicators, both financial and, where appropriate, non-financial, used by the directors to assess progress against their stated objectives.
- Directors shall also consider the extent to which other performance indicators and evidence shall be included in the OFR.
- The OFR shall analyze the main trends and factors that directors consider likely to impact future prospects.

- The OFR shall include a description of the resources available to the entity and how they are managed.
- The OFR shall include a description of the principal risks and uncertainties facing the entity, together with a commentary on the directors' approach to them.
- To the extent necessary to meet the requirements set out in paragraph 28 above, the OFR shall include information about significant relationships with stakeholders other than members, which are likely, directly or indirectly, to influence the performance of the business and its value.

Appendix B: Keizai Doyukai's White Paper on Corporate Social Responsibility

Prepared by: Nicholas Kearns, University of New South Wales

'Keizai Doyukai' (Japanese association of corporate executives) has issued its 15th Corporate White Paper on Corporate Social Responsibility (CSR) management. Japanese companies started to engage with CSR management and reporting in 2003, following the spate of corporate misfeasance and collapses, such as Yamaichi Securities and Hokkaido Takushoku Bank. Simultaneously, Socially Responsible Investment (SRI) funds, which evaluate companies on their environmental performance, social contributions, employment and consumer relations, have started to emerge in the capital market sector.

Keizai Doyukai highlights that there are three approaches to CSR in Japan:

- Corporate Ethics Approach–places corporate ethics at the center of CSR.
- Stakeholder Approach–central issues are accountability to stakeholders, transparency and fairness.
- Sustainability Approach–meet the needs of today without sacrificing the ability of future generations to satisfy their own needs.

Keizai Doyukai's White Paper proposes a draft CSR standard called 'Practical Tools for Evaluating the Current Situation and Setting Goals to Enhance Comprehensive Corporate Value'. The aim of the standard is to assist in performance evaluation, goal setting, discovery of best practices and risk management (p. 22). The standard is not exclusively intended for external reporting, but focuses on management principles to enhance sustainability.

The standard outlines 110 CSR indicators, which are grouped into five categories: Market, People, Environment, Society and Corporate Governance, as shown in the figure below. The following table illustrates in more detail the processes and performance indicators deployed to analyse, manage and report organizational practices in the five aforementioned categories.

Components of the CSR Standard

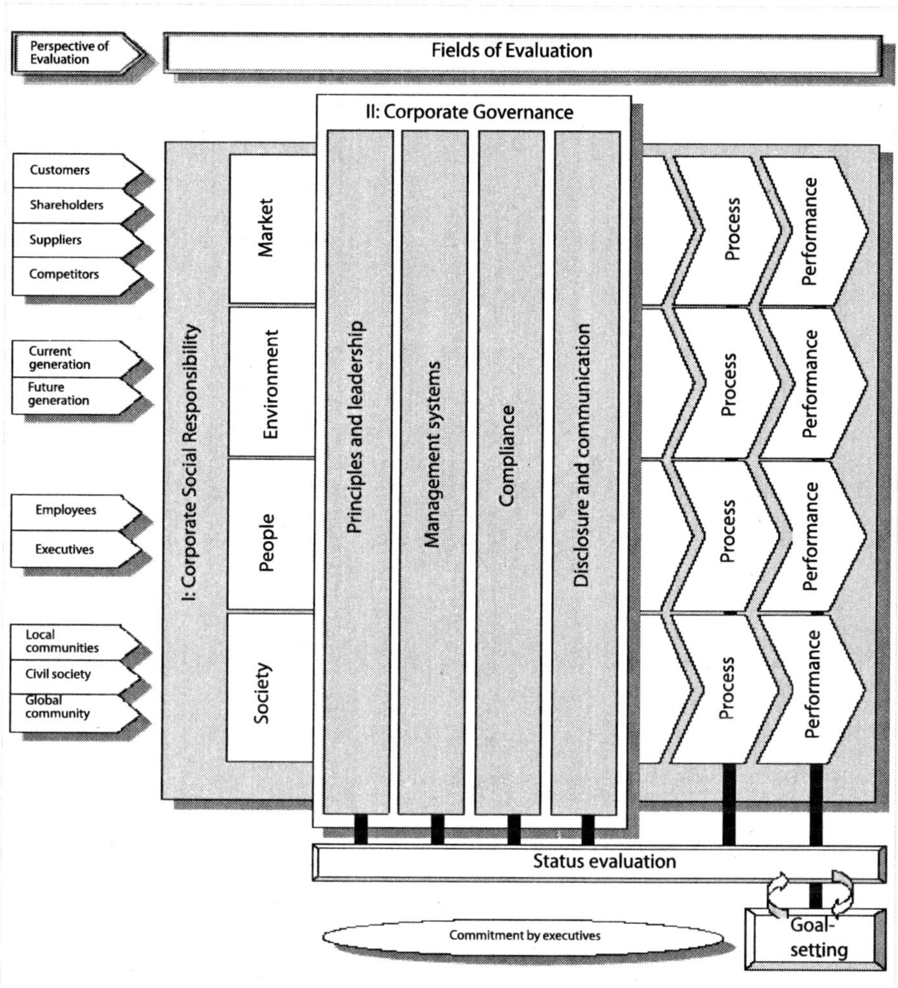

Source: Keizai Doyukai website: http://www.doyukai.or.jp/en/policyproposals/

Overview of Processes and Performance Indicators in CSR Standard

Source: Keizai Doyukai website: http://www.doyukai.or.jp/en/policyproposals/

I: Corporate Social Responsibility (CSR)	
1. Market	
(Process)	(Performance)
Initiatives for sustained value-creation and creation of new markets 1) core competence management 2) marketing 3) collaboration in knowledge 4) intellectual property strategies 5) brand management **Providing value to customers** 6) customer satisfaction survey 7) complaint management 8) risk & crisis management 9) privacy policy **Providing value to shareholders** 10) IR division 11) IR feedback 12) general meeting of shareholders **Free, fair and transparent transactions and competition** 13) fair trade policy 14) CSR procurement standards 15) rigorous compliance with fair trade and fair competition)	**Initiatives for sustained value-creation** 1) profitability 2) productivity 3) number of patents registered **Providing value to customers** 4) customer satisfaction level **Providing value to shareholders** 5) earnings per share 6) total market value of shares 7) performance forecasts and percentage gap to actual performance **Building trust** 8) number of violations of laws and ordinances concerning consumers 9) number of violations of laws and ordinances concerning fair trade and fair competition
2. Environment	
(Process)	(Performance)
Establishment of environmental management system 1) policies 2) employee education 3) acquisition of external certifications 4) environmental accounting **Initiatives for reducing environmental burden** 5) resource saving 6) recycling 7) energy saving 8) assessment of products and services 9) green purchases and procurement **Disclosure and communications** 10) environmental reports 11) third-party environmental review 12) social contribution activities	**Establishment of environmental management system** 1) acquisition of external certifications **Initiatives for reducing environmental burden** 2) total materials use 3) total energy use 4) total water use 5) greenhouse gas emissions 6) total amount of waste 7) ratio of recycled and re-used resources 8) green purchases and procurement ratio 9) production and sales ratio of eco-friendly goods and services **Building trust** 10) Number of violations of environmental laws and ordinances)

3. People	
(Process)	(Performance)
Employing and utilizing highly skilled and competent personnel 1) equal opportunity 2) internal recruitment and FA systems 3) capacity and performance assessment **Improving employability** 4) education and training 5) leadership programs **Creating a family-friendly work environment** 6) consideration of family responsibilities 7) support for child care and long-term nursing care **Creating a pleasant work environment** 8) employee satisfaction survey 9) flexible working hours and styles of employment, consideration of safety, sanitation and human rights)	**Employing and utilizing highly skilled and competent personnel** 1) ratio of female directors 2) ratios of female managers 3) ratio of foreign managers in domestic offices 4) ratio of foreign directors in overseas offices 5) ratio of employees with disabilities **Improving employability** 6) amounts spent for employee education and training) **Creating a family-friendly work environment** 7) annual paid holidays used 8) monthly hours of overtime 9) number of employees using leave of absence for child-rearing 10) number of employees using leave of absence to provide long- term nursing care) **Creating a pleasant work environment** 11) level of employee satisfaction)

4. Society	
(Process)	(Performance)
Promoting activities for contribution to society 1) basic policy 2) utilizing management resources and special strengths 3) supporting the volunteer activities of employees **Disclosure and partnership** 4) sustainability reports 5) dialogue and collaboration with NGOs and NPOs) **Establishing proper relations with politics and government** 6) Relations with politics and civil servants **Cooperation with global community** 7) observing international rules and norms observing local laws, culture and practices 8) contributing to solution of global problems	**Promoting activities for contribution to society** 1) amount expended 2) number of student interns accepted 3) number of employees taking advantage of system of holidays and leave of absence of volunteer work 4) number of collaborations with NGOs and NPOs **Building trust** 5) number of violations of laws in connection with domestic politicians and civil servants 6) number of violations of laws in connections with foreign politicians and civil servants

II: Corporate Governance (CG)	
1. Principles and Leadership	2. Management Systems
Clear and transparent management principles 1) efforts for clarification and transparency 2) level of clarification of stakeholders 3) transparency of stakeholders **Exercise of leadership** 4) direct participation by CEO 5) communication with employees 6) communication from employees	**Functional powers of board of directors and board of auditors (or auditors)** 1) participation in real discussion 2) integration of external perspectives 3) opinions of auditors/board of auditors 4) support given to auditors **Appointment and assessment of CEO** 5) appointment 6) assessment and removal 7) decisions on remuneration **Establishment of CSR-related management systems** 8) creation of CSR office 9) SRI of pension funds
3. Compliance	4. Disclosure and Communication
Formulation and education of corporate code of conduct 1) formulation and publication 2) education 3) application or recommendation to group companies **Establishment of compliance system** 4) creation of compliance office 5) consultation and advisory desk 6) internal complaints desk 7) checking of compliance status 8) inclusion in performance assessment	**Establishment of management systems for promoting disclosure and communication** 1) basic policy 2) scope and contents of disclosure 3) feed-back 4) dialogue with stakeholders

The Keizai Doyukai gives the following reasons as to why Japanese companies need to re-examine their social responsibilities: Growing mutual influence of business and society.

- Society's changing (more critical) view of the corporation.
- Rectifying the excesses of 'shareholder capitalism'.
- Changing individual values.

Appendix C: Danish Guideline on Intellectual Capital Reporting

The Danish Ministry of Science, Technology and Innovation published two guidelines on intellectual capital (IC) reporting in 2003. The first guideline informs organizations on how to prepare IC reports. The second guideline informs users on how to read and analyze IC reports. The guidelines were piloted by more than 150 Danish organizations over a five-year period.

The first guideline consists of five parts, as follows:

Part 1 outlines the elements of the IC statement and provides examples of how an IC statement looks and is structured. It introduces the IC statement model which consists of four categories as illustrated in Figure 5 below.

Figure 5: Mouritsen et al.'s (2003) IC Statement Model

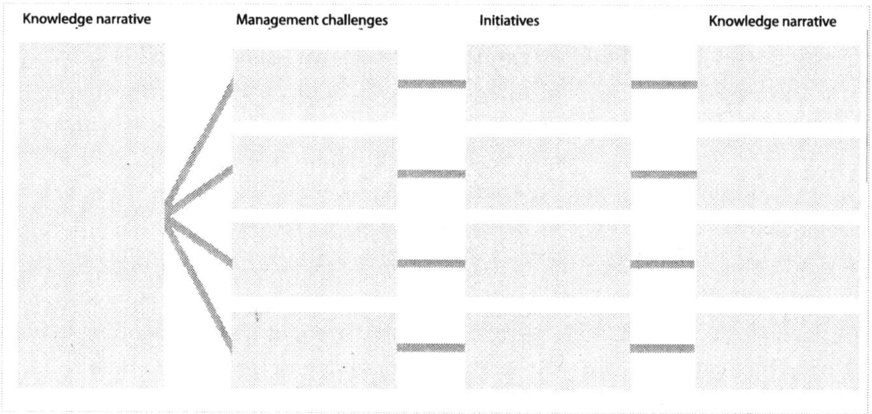

Source: Mouritsen et al. (2003) in conjunction with the Danish Ministry of Science, Technology and Innovation 'Intellectual Capital Statements – the New Guideline'

The **Knowledge Narrative** explains:
- What product or service does the company provide?
- What makes a difference for the consumer?
- What knowledge resources are necessary to be able to supply the product or service?
- What is the relationship between value and knowledge resources?

The **Management Challenges** detail:
- What challenges is the organization experiencing?
- Which existing knowledge resources should be strengthened?
- What new knowledge resources are needed?

The **Initiatives** detail the actions taken by management to overcome the management challenges:
- What initiatives can be launched?
- What initiatives should be prioritized?

The **Indicators** measure the effectiveness of the knowledge management initiatives:
- Which indicators can each initiative have? Indicators can measure:
  - Effects;
  - Activities; and
  - Resource mix.

Part 2 describes in more detail how to prepare an IC statement. It outlines how to populate the four elements in the reporting model and how to identify, build, develop and anchor a company's knowledge resources.

Part 3 provides directions on how to communicate and write IC statements to external stakeholders. It raises questions such as:
- Who is the target audience?
- What is the principle message?
- Which media to use? Should the IC statement be part of the annual report or separate?
- What are the legal requirements?
- What are the resource allocations (time and cost / man hours, etc.)?

Part 4 outlines the work process involved in preparing an IC statement and provides suggestions for how to organize the IC project and project team.

It raises questions such as:
- Who is part of the project team?
- What is the role of senior management?
- What is the time schedule and deadline?
- How to ensure management commitment?
- How can data collection be automated?
- Is there a need for an auditor's verification?

- How is the IC statement used as a management tool in practice?
- How can the company ensure the IC statement will become embedded in the organization?
- Is there an opportunity to participate in Experience Groups where companies come together to brainstorm, share ideas and knowledge on how to prepare an IC statement?

Appendix D: Austrian University Act

On 1 January2004, the University Organization and Studies Act came into effect for all state universities in Austria. The act mandates Austrian universities to produce intellectual capital reports (see Figure 1 below). The act is part of a government initiative taken to restructure the educational and legal framework of universities.

Figure 1: Reports According to the Austrian University Organization and Studies Act

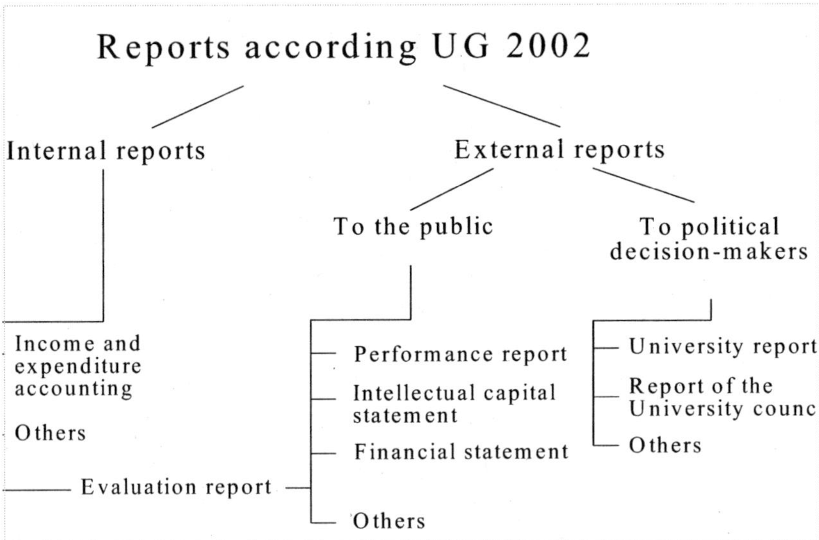

Source: Schaffhauser-Linzatti (2004)

The purpose of the IC statement (Schaffhauser-Linzatti, 2004, pp. 2–6) is as follows:

- The IC statement is designed as an inventory of the existing intellectual capital within the university.
- Knowledge, or similar intellectual capital, is the most relevant production factor for universities and hence should be made visible.
- The new reporting system enforces transparency inside and outside universities.
- Externally, the IC statement shall represent a possibility to publicly account for the use of tax money and to publish the university's performance.
- Internally, it shall deliver information for management and control.

- The statement serves as an important basis for the university's budgetary reimbursement; the IC information will inform performance-oriented budget allocation from the Federal Ministry and from private institutions.

The IC statement is (envisioned) to contribute to:

- Reallocation and a more effective and efficient use of resources;
- improvement in management decision making and forecasting; and
- enforcing competition on public and private resources, resulting in an increase in the performance of Austrian universities.

Content and Structure (pp. 13–14):

- The IC statement is structured into human, structural and relationship capital.
- Human capital is defined as the knowledge of the academic and non-academic staff that is relevant to perform all university tasks; structural capital as non-personal equipment; and relationship capital as networks of social relations that support universities' performances and help acquire knowledge from outside the university (article 12 (11) RV).
- For each category, an obligatory set of ratios is enlarged by specific sets for defined fields of studies and research (i.e. medicine or arts). Further ratios may be added voluntarily. A verbal interpretation allows for evaluating the ratios and for embedding them into the university's strategy.
- Examples include:
- Human capital: number of academic staff.
- Structural capital: available m^2.
- Relationship capital: partnerships with other universities.

Appendix E: ASX Principles of Good Corporate Governance and Best Practice Recommendations

Prepared by: Cameron Barnsley, University of New South Wales

In March 2003, the recently formed ASX Corporate Governance Council released a report entitled 'Principles of Good Corporate Governance and Best Practice Recommendations', with the primary aim of providing a comprehensive guide to listed entities and their external stakeholders as to best practices in corporate governance and disclosure. The report emphasizes the need for corporate accountability and transparency by promoting the disclosure of corporate governance practices, but does not dictate 'black letter' disclosure–instead, the report provides guidance to listed entities as to what disclosures should be made. These guidelines are supported by ASX Listing Rule 4.10.3, which requires that listed companies must provide '[a] statement disclosing the extent to which the entity has followed the best practice recommendations set by the ASX Corporate Governance Council during the reporting period'. If the entity has failed to follow one or more of the recommendations, a disclosure must be made outlining the reasons why the company has failed to comply.

There are ten Corporate Governance Principles which are dealt with by the report. The following is a brief description of the principles, making specific reference to any issues surrounding the disclosure of non-financial information. Emphasis is placed on any non-financial disclosures which form part of the principles.

- Solid Foundations for Management and Oversight: In terms of disclosure, this principle focuses on the division of responsibility and contributions of the board and senior management of a particular entity. Such disclosures, it is argued, will help promote greater understanding by financial report users of the accountabilities and contributions of individual parties within the board and the management structure. The recommendation also suggests that a 'statement of matters reserved for the board or a summary of the board charter or the statement of delegated authority to management' should be disclosed by the entity.

- Structuring the Board to Add Value: This principle focuses on the independence of directors and structuring the board to ensure that it adequately discharges its duties to shareholders. Disclosure of the independence of directors is recommended to be made in the Annual Report, in addition to the tenure (or the period of office) of each director. In addition, the recommendations suggest an independent Chairperson and a separation of the roles of the Chairperson and the Chief Executive Officer, as well as the establishment of a Nomination Committee. Relevant disclosures which form part of the recommendation include the following:
- The relevant skills, experience and expertise of directors.
- The independence of directors, including the company's materiality thresholds with reference to independence.
- Whether there exists a procedure by which directors can seek professional advice at the expense of the company.
- The term of office of each director.
- The members and attendance records of the Nomination Committee.
- A description of the procedure for the appointment of new directors.
- The charter of the Nomination Committee (summarizing the role, rights and responsibilities of members).
- The Nomination Committee's policy for appointment of its members.
- Promoting Ethical and Responsible Decision Making: This recommendation emphasizes the need for the board of a publicly listed company to establish a code of professional conduct, and a policy in relation to the trading activity of employees and directors. Disclosure of these two policies should be made in the Annual Report of the entity.
- Safeguarding the Integrity of Financial Reporting: The fourth principle focuses on mechanisms and review structures to ensure the truthful and factual reporting of an entity's financial position and performance. In addition to a requirement for the CEO and CFO to report to the board regarding the truthfulness and fairness of a company's financial reports (which has now been legislated under the *Corporations Act 2001* (Commonwealth) as part of the CLERP 9 reform package), the recommendation focuses on the establishment of an Audit Committee which should report to the Board of Directors. In terms of disclosure, the recommendation suggests detailed disclosure about the membership and functions of the Audit Committee, the attendance records, as well as information about the committee's charter and appointment mechanisms.

- Timely and Balanced Disclosures: This recommendation emphasizes compliance with ASX Listing Rules by introducing mechanisms which ensure equal and timely access by investors to market disclosures. In terms of non-financial disclosure, this recommendation requires a summary of the policies and procedures which the company has in place to ensure compliance with the disclosure requirements of the *ASX Listing Rules.*
- *R*especting the Rights of Shareholders: It is argued that a company has the obligation to empower its shareholders through open and effective communication, balanced and understandable information about the organization and future proposals, ensuring that shareholders are able to participate effectively at General Meetings. In terms of disclosure, this recommendation suggests that a*n entity should des*cribe the arrangements it has in place to promote communication with shareholders within the corporate governance section of its Annual Report.
- Recognizing and Managing Risk: The seventh recommendation includes a requirement for listed entities to put in place systems which identify, assess and monitor organizational risk, and inform the public about changes in the entity's risk profile. A description of such systems and procedures is required within the corporate governance section of an entity's Annual Report.
- *Encouraging Enha*nced Performance: This recommendation involves the encouragement of enhanced board and management effectiveness, and the review of individual and collective performance. As with the previous recommendation, in terms of non-financial disclosure, all that is required is a description of the process for performance evaluation of board members and senior management.
- Fair and Respo*n*sible Remuneration: In order to achieve corporate governance best practice, this recommendation mandates disclosure in relation to remuneration policies and reporting the link between corporate performance and executive and director remuneration. The key disclosures which are to be made under this recommendation include:
- The company's remuneration policies;
- details of the company's Remuneration Committee;
- the existence and terms of any schemes for retirement benefits (other that statutory superannuation) for non-executive directors; and
- the charter of the Remuneration Committee, including the rights, responsibilities and roles of members.
- Recognizing the Legitimate Interests of Stakeholders: This final recommendation identifies that companies have wider responsibilities beyond shareholders which extend to employees, customers and the wider community. The report states that organizations should establish, and disclose the existence of, a code of conduct in relation to its legal and other obligations to stakeholders.

The report provides guidelines for such a code, and such guidelines must be disclosed in the corporate governance section of an entity's Annual Report.

In addition, in line with the CLERP 9 regulatory changes, ASX Listing Rule 12.7 now requires that companies included in the S&P All Ordinaries Index must have an Audit Committee attached to their Board of Directors. This committee must follow the Corporate Governance Best Practice Recommendations if the relevant entity is amongst the top 300 listed entities at the beginning of its financial year.

Appendix B: Stakeholder Management

How a company makes its goods or performs its primary services will not be its number one priority in the future, but rather, how it manages its stakeholder relationships that determine its brand equity. - T Duncan and S Moriarty

The purpose of this manual is to help individuals and organisations to design, implement and review strategies to work effectively with their stakeholders. When I mention stakeholders, I mean, "those groups without whose support the organisation would cease to exist".[1] The model works equally well for individuals, for teams, for organisations and for coalitions of organisations or individuals. The material in the manual is intended for a sophisticated audience, an audience that understands the value of money, of time, of personal effort. My value proposition is simple: the advice and the tools in this manual will make it easier for you or for your business to achieve your objectives.

1 Stanford Research Institute, 1963, as quoted by Murray Rees in a paper titled "Stakeholder Reporting Process – A Link to Balance the Balanced Scorecard".

Many others make this promise, but few if any will add this to their proposition: all the strategies I proposed can be implemented without using external consultants. Amy medium or large enterprise will have within its walls the skills needed to use the tools to achieve what you want to achieve.

I am confident that I can make this promise because the advice and tools in this guide are the product of many years of experience, they have been tested in the workplace and I know that any competent manager or executive can use them as well or better than I can. Where I have borrowed from others, I have made sure that the same test has been applied, that there is evidence that the tool will work, if used properly. I have provided just enough theoretical context to ensure proper use, with additional reading suggested for those who want to delve more deeply into that context. I look forward to feedback from readers on whether I have got the balance right between theory and practice.

The context

We live in interesting times, an era during which change and turbulence dominate the business environment. Coping successfully with a turbulent environment requires new solutions. Haeckel has put forward a promising model. Haeckel's solution - the sense and respond model - is a combination of "adaptive system design" and "a governance system that provides 'context and coordination' for empowered teams".[2]

An adaptive system design is a framework that ranks strategic options and sets boundaries for behaviour, expressed as set of processes, rather than a plan. Context and coordination are the replacement for the command and control model typically used by "industrial age firms".

Citing examples of success, such as Motorola, Haeckel argues that

> *Sense-and-respond firms will require a modular, fluid, organic organisation to respond effectively to dynamic non-linear change ... this means networks of skills, assets, cross-functional processes, information and knowledge that are linked to capabilities, which are in turn linked into processes for creating product and service responses to customer needs.*[3]

This he calls a "synergy strategy", a method for integrating sub-systems within the organisation while allowing management of the content of those sub-systems to remain with the people who work within them. My contribution is to extend this sense and respond model beyond the boundaries of the organisation, to encompass customers, clients, suppliers and the community, as well as government and the

2 S H Haeckel, "Adaptive Enterprise Design: The Sense and Respond Model", Planning Review, May/June 1995.
3 At page 9.

regulating environment. I do this because these days no organisation is self-sufficient and because to succeed an organisation must extend its influence throughout its value chain, upstream and downstream. This means that to succeed, we have to engage people or organisations that have an interest in what our organisation does. This is what stakeholder management is all about.

The objective is to develop a circle of trust within which the organisation can go about its business with minimum interference. The means to achieve that objective are many, but the essence of successful stakeholder management is effective communication, where effective communication is *the reciprocal transmission of meaning without unintended confusion or ambiguity*. To put it plainly, effective communication is getting and receiving the intended message. The test of effective communication is that each party acts as the other party expected. This builds trust among the parties, as we will see. We will shortly see why trust is important, but first let's consider the subject of efficiency and effectiveness.

Defining efficiency and effectiveness

I would say that effectiveness is "the degree to which predetermined goals are achieved", whereas efficiency refers to the economical manner in which goal-oriented operations are carried out - something of an input/output ratio".[4] Time is a qualifier of effectiveness. While survival is the ultimate measure of organisational effectiveness, in the everyday world managers need short term and intermediate term measures or indicators. Suggested short-term measures are production, efficiency and effectiveness, while suggested intermediate measures are adaptation to environmental changes and the internal development of the organisation, including the level of trust and collaboration.

I am pointing this out to illustrate the point that issues such as trust and concern for an organisation's general climate and morale are not do-gooders' issues. There is a definite and definable connection between how well an organisation treats the people it deals with and its long-term success. One of the fundamental reasons for Google's success is how it treats its people...and sacking people may cost your business more than you think.[5]

Wicked problems and the organization

Something else we need to understand is that organizations are complex systems. A complex system is a system that behaves in ways that cannot be explained by studying its component parts. The actions of a complex system are inherently unpredictable,

4 JH Jackson et al, Organization Theory: A Macro-perspective for Management, Prentice-Hall, 1986.

5 "Layoffs cost more than you think", Fortune Magazine, March 17, 2009, retrieved from *http://money.cnn.com/2009/03/16/magazines/fortune/colvin_layoffs.fortune/index.htm*.

beyond a very limited period of time, and almost impossible to replicate exactly. Allow me to illustrate. A combustion engine can be taken apart, analyzed, understood and put together again–and, if all the parts are re-assembled correctly, it will work. A combustion engine is a complicated system, having many parts, but it is not complex. Any competent mechanic or engineer could deduce the function of such an engine and how it works by reference to a few components only. Also, what a combustion engine does is both predictable and amenable to precise replication.

On the other hand, one cannot take a human being apart and then re-construct the body and bring it back to life. We cannot even do it with a mouse or a worm, because these are complex systems, though, a worm, for example, is not that complicated. A complex system has meaning beyond the mere sum of its parts and understanding any complex system is a wicked problem indeed. Mapping the human genome is not the same as taking an engine apart. Having the map of an organism's DNA does not enable us to replicate it. Nor does it enable us to predict precisely what it would do if we were able to. Remember Dr Frankenstein and his monster? Or what about Dolly, the first cloned sheep? Scientists were stunned when it died so young, as if its ageing process had been greatly accelerated. Whether the cloning process caused Dolly to die earlier than average or not is in doubt, but the fact is that those who cloned her did not expect it.

It is hard enough to map and understand the DNA of a single organism. Try working out what thousands, millions or billions of organisms might or might not want to do. This is what economics is supposed to be about, but it is not, because economists have generally assumed that people are rational organisms and consistently make rational choices. If you assume this, then you will conclude that the economy can be reduced to and understood through a series of complicated mathematical equations. This is what economics has been turned into, numbers and formulae, whereas it is about people and organizations.

The economy is a complex entity, not amenable to disassembly and re-assembly–and hard to predict or replicate. This is why economics is not a science; it is a craft, practiced by people who pretend they are physicists, making extensive use of mathematical incantations to cover up their lack of understanding of what is actually going on and why. This is because economists assume that the economy is governed by something called "economic laws". Wrong. The economy is a specialized application of the same rules that govern the rest of human society and their laws, insofar as there are any such things, derive from sociology, psychology, biology and physics.

There is nothing fundamental in economics that cannot be explained by reference to one or more of those disciplines. I should say at this point that I am not comfortable using the term "law", because a law is a set of rules made and enforced by institutions–law is normative. In science, a law is at best descriptive–it is never normative. The laws of physics, for example, are generalisations based on empirical observations–they are reliable hypotheses of how the universe is thought to work. In economics not even this level of reliability is possible, which is why economists have resorted to using the term "natural laws". By using the adjective natural, they are implying that their so-called laws are like gravity, an intrinsic characteristic of the physical world. Again, wrong! The natural laws of economics are unproven and usually improvable assumptions about how the world works; they are an act of faith, not a product of science.

Let us consider two of these laws, to illustrate my point, two laws that are fundamental to the whole edifice of economics: the law of economizing and the law of economic rationality.[6] Taken together, these state that people tend to economise, maximising gains for a given cost, and minimising costs for a given gain, and that human action is economically rational if one's preferences are consistent and if one economizes. In simpler terms, this means that people are rational beings, who always make the optimum economic choice. Do you know anyone who is like that? I don't and I think there are none. The reason for that is that people are not rational beings and that is not an assertion, it is a generalization based on empirical observations, it is science.

To their credit, some economists recognize this fallacy at the core of their discipline. Paul Ormerod, for example, has stated in plain terms that the idea that economics is based on Rational (Wo)man or *Homo Economicus* is not based in reality and has observed that most of the Nobel prizes for economics in the twenty-first century have gone to economists working beyond rationality.[7] The seminal thinker on this issue in economics is Herbert Simon, who developed a behavioral theory based on "bounded rationality".

The theory is simple. People face uncertainty about the future and costs in acquiring information in the present (I would add that information is also imperfect and often not available). This limits the extent to which people can make rational decisions. What we do, according to Simon, is to exercise "bounded rationality", setting an aspiration level which, if achieved, will be enough to "satisfice" us, which will be probably short of the theoretical optimum towards which *Homo economicus* is supposed to strive. Of course, a first year student in psychology could tell you that, as could any parent or manager or, indeed, anyone at all out there in the real world.[8] If we understand this, we have embarked on the path towards building trust, a platform on which everything else rests.

6 I am relying on a list published at *http://www.progress.org/2004/fold379.htm*, retrieved on 27 March 2009.

7 See the bibliography for suggested reading.

8 See the excellent article on Homo Economicus on Wikipedia, at *http://en.wikipedia.org/wiki/Homo_economicus*, which I consulted on 27 March 2009.

How to build trust

If I trust the competence of other drivers, of the road designers and builders and the car manufacturers, it is likely that I will be able and willing to drive faster than if I do not. What is true on a road is also true of any other network, including within organisations or stakeholder networks. If I trust the various components that make up the network, the other users of the network and the operators of the network, I will be prepared to have fewer checks and balances operating in and on the network. In turn, this will free up the movement of data on the network, lifting the speed of traffic on the network. This makes the network more efficient and effective in moving information and in enabling sharing of knowhow.

> *The ability to build trust is a key competency for leaders today. Great leaders don't dictate, they influence. And influence comes from a leader's ability to engender credibility and inspire people to both believe them and believe in them.* – Stephen R Covey

Most of us work in service industries. The value produced by service industries is made up of several factors, but the dominant factors are knowhow (or knowledge) and information. The quality of food in a restaurant or of service in a bank or the success of government policy, all depend on the knowhow of the workers involved in the process and on the quality of information flows.

Both knowhow and information are essential. For example, a competent waiter who does not understand the language of a customer is more likely to give poor service. On the other hand, an incompetent waiter who is fluent in the language of his or her customers is also more likely to give poor service.

Knowhow is also a factor in farming and manufacturing, of course, as is information, but they are not dominant factors, often playing second fiddle to capital and capital goods, such as machinery and raw materials, or are dependent on the quality of the land and the vagaries of climate. Because of the twin requirements of knowhow and information, service industries are the natural home of knowledge workers.

According to Peter Drucker, "The terms "knowledge industries", "knowledge work" and "knowledge worker" are only 40 years old. They were coined around 1960, simultaneously but independently; the first by a Princeton economist, Fritz Machlup, the second and third by this writer."[9] Knowledge workers make their living primarily

9 *The Economist*, "The Next Workforce. Knowledge workers are the new capitalists", by Peter F. Drucker, November 1, 2001, from *http://www.druckerinstitute.com/whydrucker/why_articles_nextworkforce.html*, retrieved on 14 March 2009.

by thinking, rather than doing, which means that not all who work in an office are knowledge workers and not all knowledge workers are to be found in office buildings. Knowledge workers work best when they are trusted and feel trusted.

I have developed a model to show how trust and communication are linked, at Figure 1. My assumption is that we cannot have trust without effective communication and we cannot have effective communication without trust. I define trust as *reliance, certainty based on experience*. In other words, what you have experienced in relating with someone gives you a reasonable degree of predictability about the future behaviour of the other. Within this broad definition, I see three types of trust:

- Self-disclosure trust – which emerges with mutual self-disclosure and sharing
- Contract trust – which emerges from making and keeping agreements
- Safety trust – which evolves from reading another person's intentions and being confident that the other person means no harm

How do we achieve trust? We build up **self-disclosure trust** by sharing information freely and not holding on to knowledge as it were property; by encouraging and receiving feedback – and being seen to treat that feedback with appropriate respect; by disclosing a portion of who we really are to others, sharing some information about our private lives – this does not mean disclosing secrets or details about others; and by being prepared to admit ignorance, to say "I don't know".

Building **contract trust** requires following through on promises and commitments, on doing what we say. It also means that if we can't keep a promise, we face up to the consequences. We explain why we can't and we take steps to make good any direct or collateral damage. On the other hand, it means giving others a bit of latitude that perhaps we would not allow for ourselves, being forgiving of small or infrequent lapses by others.

Safety trust is achieved by making sure that we at least do no harm in our relationships with others. It does not mean refraining from **giving** someone bad news or from making decisions that are not palatable to others. It means doing what we do professionally, with no malice and no deceit, and being always ready to explain why something has to be done. Safety trust requires self-disclosure and contract trust as conditions precedent. If there is low contract and self-disclosure trust, it is not possible to achieve safety trust. Without safety trust, morale in organisations will be low and productivity will be lower than it can be, at both the firm level and affecting whole economies.[10]

10 GW Fairholm, *Leadership and the culture of trust*, Greenwood Publishing Group (1994); A Lyman,

There are common elements in these three types of trust. My hypothesis is that trust in an organisation – or in any relationship, really – requires sustained openness and perceived fairness, where openness is an *attitude of ready accessibility without concealment, not secretive*, and fairness is evidenced by *judgments that are free from negative discrimination or dishonesty.* Attitudes and judgments are somewhat nebulous concepts. To make it easier for you I have come up with a list of behaviours that are likely to build trust, which are in Table 1. In that table you will also find a list of behaviours that are likely to destroy trust. These behaviours are relevant in relationships between individuals, between organisations, and between organisations and individuals. They are relevant in dealing with employees, bosses, suppliers, partners and spouses.

As you act to build trust, it is vital that you also stop doing anything that destroys trust. It is vital because any perceived inconsistency in behaviour will in and by itself destroy any results you might hope to achieve by doing the right things. Also, remember that the more senior you are in an organisation, the more power your actions have. If you are perceived to behave even slightly inconsistently, that venial sin will become a mortal sin overnight in the eyes of those below you in the hierarchy. On a brighter note, this phenomenon applies to the positive behaviours as well, which means that, provided you act consistently, if you stick to the left hand side of the table you will achieve much more than you might think.

Figure 1: Trust and communication model

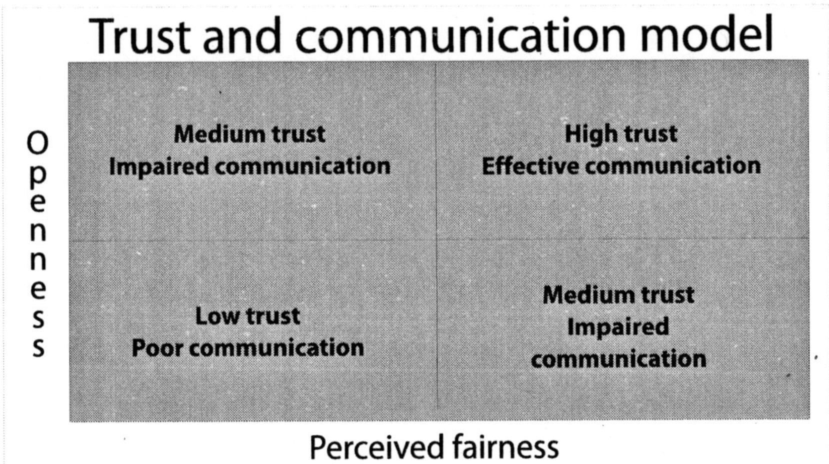

"Building trust in the workplace", Strategic HR Review, Volume 3 Issue 1 November/December 2003; R Putnam, Making Democracy Work Civic Traditions in Modern Italy, Princeton University Press (1993).

I should add that the behaviours I have suggested are not actually a menu, from which you can pick and choose to suit a particular situation. Ideally, all these behaviours should be part of your everyday repertoire, in all circumstances. Of course, from time to time you will lapse, we all do. However, you will find that if you have built up a reservoir of trust, the odd lapse will be easily and quickly forgiven. Without a reservoir of trust, the well of forgiveness will remain dry.

These principles apply more strongly the higher you are in the pecking order. The more senior the manager, the more scrutiny s/he will have to endure by others in the organisation. The more senior the manager, the more likely that a venial sin will be considered to be a mortal offence by others in the organisation. This may not seem fair, but that is how it is. This is one of the reasons why senior management need to especially adept in the art of building trust. Sadly, most are not and the company bottom line suffers as a consequence.[11]

Table 2: Actions that build or destroy trust

ACTIONS THAT BUILD TRUST	ACTIONS THAT DESTROY TRUST
Behave consistently	Behave inconsistently
Accept ideas	Dismiss ideas put forward by others
Tolerate faults	Embarrass people
Criticise the idea, not the person	Blame others for one's own mistakes
Clarify, understand before seeking to be understood	Avoid eye contact
Be inclusive	Ignore people
Ask for feedback	Withhold feedback
Work together	Interrupt when others are talking
Play together	Withhold credit that is due
Protect confidences – when you have said that you will	Fail to keep a confidence
Follow through on your promises	Break a promise
Provide accurate information	Withhold information that is important to making a decision
Observe the niceties, say thank you, please, good morning and so on	Be rude, discourteous

It is now time to get to the substance of what this manual is about, how to manage stakeholders.

11 HS Harung and T Dahl, "Increased productivity and quality through management by values: a case study of Manpower Scandinavia", *The TQM Magazine*, 1995, Vol. 7(2), pages 13 – 22.

Understanding the environment

Mark Moore, from Harvard, has developed a model, which he calls the strategic triangle, to explain how managers in the public sector can apply Michael Porter's five forces (see figure 2) to shape the strategy of their organization. Moore's model has three elements, as we can see in figure 3: the authorising environment, where politicians provide direction and legitimacy, the operating environment, where bureaucrats shape action to give effect to the will of elected representatives, for the purpose of creating public value, which is the third element or third apex of the "strategic triangle".

Figure 2: Porter's Generic Strategies

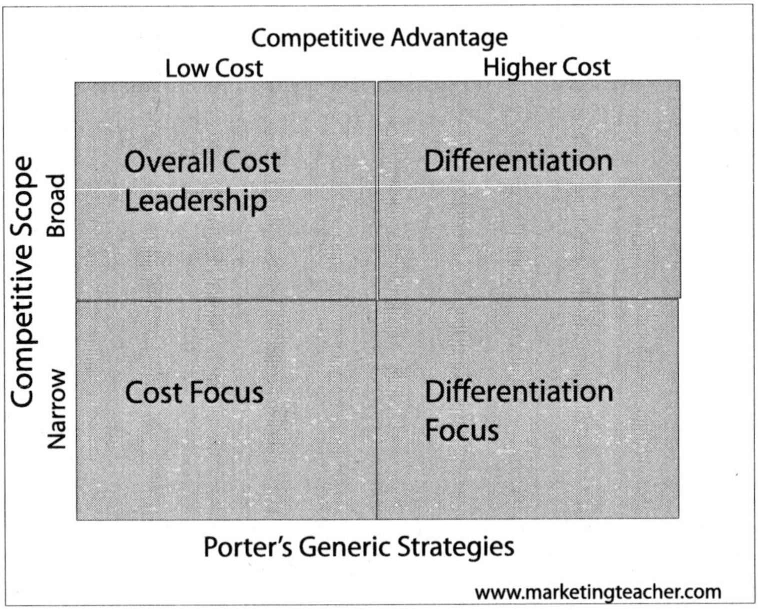

According to Moore, the purpose of the strategic triangle is to help public sector managers position their organisation ("enterprise") in "complex, dynamic environments", to "distribute managerial attention across their task environment and their authorizing environment, and to "help them envision a sustainable public value proposition to be pursued". I think the concepts underpinning the strategic triangle can be used in the private sector, as well, and I have adapted Moore's model to reflect that, as seen in figure 4, which is my influencing model.

Figure 3: Moore's strategic triangle

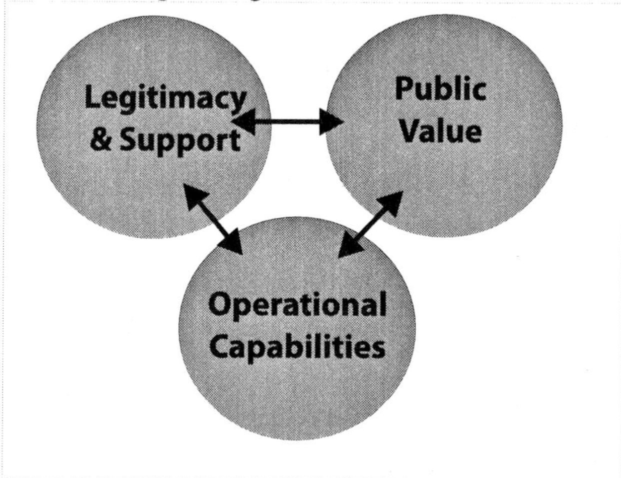

My version of the model is shown as a set of interlocking gears. The complex of gears can be put in motion by operating on or influencing any one of the separate gears. For example, by operating at the governance level (where strategy is set and significant or systemic decisions are made), it is possible to effect changes in the organisation's (or the network's) capability platform (what the system is capable of doing), which, in turn, will have an effect on the type and or quantum of value produced. Alternatively, by identifying new or better ways to generate value, it is possible to re-shape the capability platform, which, in turn, will affect the decision-making at the corporate level. Then again, by changing the capability platform, it is possible to influence what goes on at the governance level and to re-shape the organisation's value proposition, simultaneously.

Figure 4: Internal influencing model

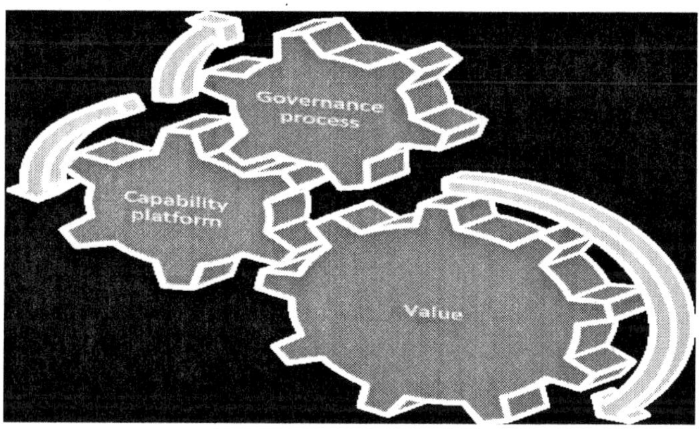

What figure 4, which has an internal focus, does not show is that the influencing model is actually a nested model (see figure 5). In the nested influencing model you will see that you can influence the internal environment of the organisation by operating on its external environment and, of course, vice-versa. You will also see that you can exert influence by operating at the macro or societal level (e.g. through regulation).The operational logic shown in figure 5 is the same as that for figure 4. If you change the regulatory environment, you will affect the environment within which the organisation operates and, in turn, you will have an impact on the internal environment, and so on.

Figure 5: Complete influencing model

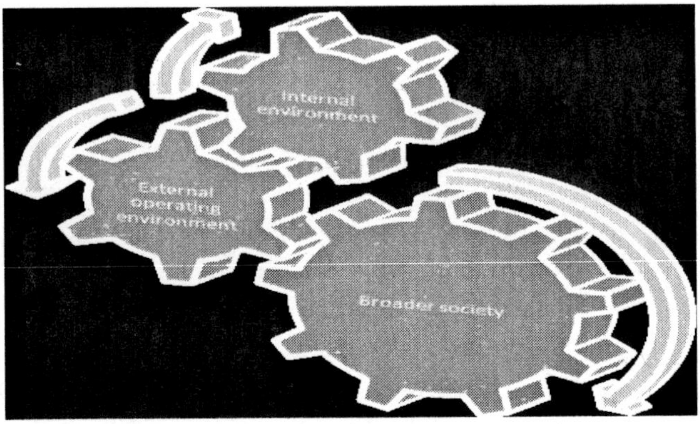

You can choose any element of the influencing model(s) as your starting point. So, if you are an engineer and your strengths are in building organisational capability, it may be best for you to develop an influencing strategy that builds on your strengths. On the other hand, if you are a middle manager, you may find it opportune to exploit any connections you may have with the governing processes in the organisation. If you are outside the organisation, a supplier for example, you may want to influence what happens within the supply chain or even at a broader regulatory level. A classic example of this last scenario is the strategy adopted by suppliers to dominant players in the supermarket arena. Because of the asymmetric relationship in this case, where all the power was with the supermarkets, the best option for farmers and other suppliers was to approach the regulators – and the politicians who hold the regulator's political and purse strings.

It is at this point that I explain to you that while this is called a stakeholder management manual, what actually e on is something quite different. In my opinion, stakeholders cannot be managed, they can only be influenced, which is why from now on we will speak of how to lead stakeholders. By leadership, I mean creating the circumstances within which people will do voluntarily what needs to be done, through influence, rather than coercion.

How to lead stakeholders

Stakeholder leadership facilitates these activities, if done well:

- obtain information/intelligence needed to achieve business objectives
- obtain stakeholder commitment and support
- avoid or manage risks
- minimise any adverse impacts on stakeholders
- enable the realisation of business objectives
- calibrate/improve effectiveness and efficiency of KPIs and measurement against KPIs

Because building trust requires consistency of behaviour, stakeholder leadership should be understood and practised as a process, not an activity. It is or should be an integral part of business operations and should not be seen as an add-on or something that is done to facilitate change or to ease the implementation of a significant project or initiative.

Figure 17: typical constellation of stakeholders

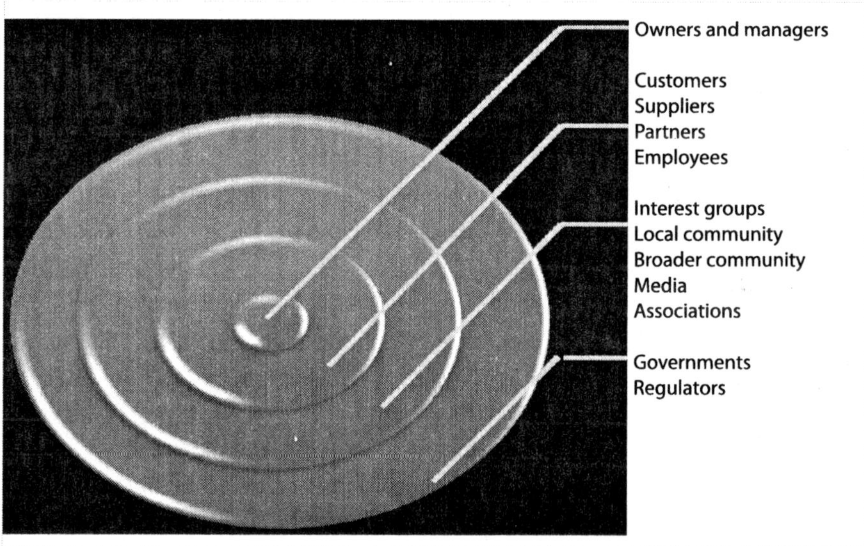

The process of stakeholder management has these elements, which iterate:

1. Identify stakeholders (see figure 6 for a typical constellation of stakeholders)
2. Analyse stakeholders' needs, wants and expectations
3. Develop consultation plan
4. Consult with stakeholders
5. Complete stakeholder matrix

6. Implement appropriate actions
7. Return to 1 and continue cyclically.

The cycle should be aligned with your strategic and operational plans, so as to inform those plans and, in turn, so as to be informed by the consequences of implementing those plans.

An essential contextual element is the type of organisation in which you operate – and how the various interested parties perceive that. It may be that most stakeholders perceive themselves as operating within a cultural context, for example – they see the organisation as a place where they can socialise…and do a bit of work. If that is so, regardless of how **you** might see the world, that is the context within which you should structure your intervention. Otherwise, it will be as if the Tower of Babel curse had struck again!

If your stakeholders expect a dialogue structured around meaning and relationships and you offer them a determinist, machine-like approach, I can almost guarantee that you will not get what you want and that they will not get what they need. So, cast your reasoning, your arguments, your presentations, and your pitch, to suit your stakeholders (or at least the more influential among them).

Table 2: Stakeholder management matrix

STAKEHOLDERS	ORGANISATION IS ACCOUNTABLE FOR ...	MEASURED HOW?	BY WHOM?	WHY? (PRIMARY REASON)
Customer/ client				
Shareholder				
Regulator(s)				
Interest groups				
Community				
Partner				
Suppliers				
The Board				
Senior Management				

How to use this matrix

The first question is: at what level are you operating? At the whole of organisation level (the enterprise, for example)? Or at a business unit or departmental level"? Or from the perspective of a team - or even from an individual perspective? Each of these points of reference is valid and the template can cater from any or a combination of these. If the analysis extends to two or more perspectives (for example, from both an enterprise and business unit level), complete a template for each and then note the *points of difference*, for later use.

The data to complete the matrix can be obtained from your existing stakeholder management plan, if you have one. Otherwise, use your understanding of the circumstances. If we are looking at the world from the point of view of an enterprise the list in column one of the templates is likely to be close to the mark, but a generic list will not do the job – you, perhaps working with colleagues, must identify the groups that are relevant to you.

Having completed the list of interested parties – and I suggest, if you are working on your own, that you validate your list with a couple of trusted sources – move on to determine what your stakeholders value, because our purpose is value creation (return less cost).

The concept of value is relative, but the generic value model in Table 2 can be used to formulate a model of value that is relevant specifically to your organization and its stakeholders. There are other ways of doing this, discussed below. In considering what is of value to your organisation, you may wish to note a recent survey by McKinsey showing that company directors are looking for more information about organizations' intangible, knowledge intensive resources.[12] The survey concludes that directors sometimes lack the information needed to make sound decisions. This compromises their ability to understand fully the objectives and risks of their companies. Total Cost of Ownership (or TCO) is a model that brings together costs associated with a capital purchase during the lifetime of the asset. The main elements of TCO are acquisition, installation, financing, commissioning, energy, repair and maintenance. However, TCO also factors in implicit costs, such as productivity, risk and disposal. There are many commercially available tools for TCO analysis.

If it is worth something, measure it

Private and public sector managers use resources to produce value for their stakeholders. They may differ in value systems, environments, resources and productive capabilities. We need to go deeper, to consider issues more essential to the efficiency, effectiveness and value of an organization operating in the changing and unstable environment

12 *McKinsey (2005).*

in which we find ourselves. In the public sector, as in the private sector, the function of an organization is to create wealth (or value) by using the factors of production to best advantage. There is no need to enter the public choice debate, noting that public enterprise, like private enterprise, is motivated by a range of factors related to the peculiar perspective of each actor.

The material difference is that the private sector is concerned with creating private value, while the public sector is concerned with creating public value. The objectives of private sector organisations ("the firm") and of non-commercial public sector organisations ("the agency") are indistinguishable in their nature, though they may differ in form and in presentation. It is possible to start from the assumption that both private and public sector organisations are about creating value for buyers, an approach reflected in the purchaser/provider model.

Apart from government business enterprises (GBEs), the value created in the public sector is not always measurable by reference to a monetary yardstick or by a measure such as return on investment ("ROI"). The wealth created by a government agency is defined by reference to the meaning and importance attributed by a significant observer to a particular activity, set of activities, outcome(s), process(es) or, sometimes, input.

An auditor or the legislature may consider that adherence to a particular process (compliance) is of greater value than the achievement of a specific result at a particular cost (outcome). Until recently, spending the allocated budget (input) and no more or less was considered inherently valuable. This kind of analysis complicates the process of value creation and of decision making beyond the classical model of the firm, which requires of the firm that it be profitable; that is that it meet its costs and generate a return to its owners that is commensurable with their investment. In reality, the interests of different stakeholders are neither equal nor equivalent.[13]

13 *Moore: 1994, 300-1.*

Table 3: Suggested performance indicators

	Traditional Financial Accounts			Extended Performance Accounts		
	Monetary	**Physical**	**Intangible**	**Structural**	**Relational**	**Human**
Tangible Resources	Cash Receivables Payables Securities	Property Plant Equipment Inventory	Intellectual Property Customer Lists Brands Contractual Agreements	Documented Operating Policies Documented Company Programmes (i.e. TQM, JIT, Six Sigma, SPC etc.)	Contractual Agreements with Alliance Partners and Joint Ventures	Employment Contracts Training Manuals In-house Learning and Development Programmes
Intangible, Knowledge Intensive Resources	Credit Rating Borrowing Capacity Strength of Balance Sheet	Plant Flexibility Tradability of Assets Quality of Inventory	Infrastructure Working Capital Management	New Product Development Management Processes and Programmes Information Systems and Processes Software Programs Organizational Structure and Culture Management Philosophy	Government Relations Community Relations Distribution and Supply Channels and Relations Customer Relations Financial Relations Industrial Relations Company Name and Brand	Employee Demographics Employee's Innovative Capacity Employee Diversity Learning and Development Abilities Educational and Work Related Qualifications Leadership and Top Mng Quality

It is accepted by economists that the firm operates under several constraints, related to resources (e.g. availability of essential inputs), output quantity or quality (e.g. delivery requirements or customer service standards or industry quality standards) or legal matters (e.g. environmental law, trade practices legislation). If the firm remains profitable within the existing constraints (and adapts as they change) it can be reasonably expected that it will meet the legitimate expectations of the shareholders (or owners). This is where the concept of economic profit can be introduced to reflect the balance between business profit and owner equity.[14] Profit maximization is not a universal goal; what a firm does is aimed at meeting a requirement for profitability in the end and the intent is generally to satisfice.

The constraints affecting the firm are similar to those affecting the department, which must also secure sufficient inputs, meet quantity and quality targets and expectations, and must stay within the law. It is now rare for departments to be exempted from legislation that binds the firm. In fact, there are tighter legal constraints upon the agency than operate upon the firm. The agency is also focused on meeting the legitimate expectations of its owners, which is generally achieved by satisficing. The concept of ownership is somewhat diluted and the concept of stakeholdership is perhaps more relevant, because of the particular accountabilities the agency has. Table 3 illustrates this.

14 Pappas and Hirschey: 1989, 9.

A similar web of accountabilities can be structured for the firm, as Table 4 shows. The differences are more of nomenclature, rather than of substance. The firm must achieve profitability before it can aim to satisfy other expectations; it is the sine qua non of survival. The equivalent obligation for the agency is to secure a budget that is sufficient to enable it to meet the expectations of stakeholders.

In each case, the concern is with inputs: to retain access to the capital it needs, the firm must generate income; the agency has the same task. Where they differ is in the means of achieving the goal and in the source of their income, using the word "income" in its broad sense. The firm sells goods and services, whereas the agency provides (for our purposes purchaser-provider arrangements can be included under this rubric) services (or, less often, goods), usually at no cost to the recipient.

The extent of income through user pays arrangements remains relatively small for most agencies. For large firms, that is not necessarily achieved entirely by selling products or services; in the 1980s, many companies used their corporate treasury to make money through investment. Some did well, many did not. The differences between the private and public sectors, essentially, are the absence of price signals for the agency and the absence or inadequate forms of contestability.

Questions to ask yourself to see if your value metrics are adequate include: are you getting timely, accurate information that enables you to gauge how well you are measuring up against both reality and perceptions? Are you bamboozled by overly complex measurement processes that hide from you what you need to see – until it is too late? Are your metrics a good vehicle to communicate your message to stakeholders, such as analysts or shareholders, for example? Are your metrics grounded in your understanding of risks and opportunities in the short, medium and long term or are you distracted by what I call the baubles, the bright shiny lights of the returns for the quarter?

How to lead stakeholders

You have mapped your stakeholders, you understand their needs, wants and expectations and you have developed appropriate metrics; what next? The strategy I propose requires that you achieve operational excellence, internal trust, external trust, with compliance integrated into all business processes – and that you make these the core of your value proposition. Then you need a plan to communicate the value proposition to relevant stakeholders, so that they do what you need them to do, because they want to. The approach I suggest relies on these elements:

1. Creating a value strategy for your business, with appropriate performance indicators.
2. Mapping and understanding groups of stakeholders that can affect the realisation of your value strategy.

3. Within these groups or from among those who have access to these groups, identify individuals who are influential – mavens, salesmen and connectors – who can help you to get your message to where it needs to be heard in a form that makes it likely that it will be understood.
4. Craft a message that is likely to convey to target stakeholder groups the essentials of your value strategy and why that strategy makes your business valuable to them. That message has to reflect an understanding of what the authorizing environment (see Figure 3) can live with and will accept.
5. Establish a coalition to promote that message and to influence decision-makers (see figures 4 and 5).

The last step is the most complex and difficult and I have developed an approach you may wish to adopt, which I have called a Coalition Building Model.

The Coalition Building Model

The literature suggests that successful cooperation requires partners to understand the environment in which the coalition or alliance will operate, what needs to be done, the process of collaboration, the partners' skills or flaws, and their intended and emerging goals. Also, three key processes are associated with success:

1. Senior management communicated and reiterated the learning intent.
2. Learning was disaggregated into a sequence of steps, arrayed in ... order of growing complexity.
3. The interface was designed with learning in mind.[15]

The Coalition Building Model (see figure 7) is intended to facilitate collaboration among interested parties who want to influence government policy, by proposing rules of engagement to which those parties can subscribe. It is relevant to this generic strategy and to the next. The tools to understand the environment, what needs to be done and the goals of stakeholders are provided elsewhere in this book. The Model is structured as a learning process.

The Coalition Building Model provides suggested rules of engagement that:

- require as a necessary and sufficient condition only that the parties share a common objective that can be stated succinctly and unambiguously;
- can work with a relatively low level of trust and mutual disclosure;
- allow for incremental agreement, building trust gradually;
- are principles based and not prescriptive;
- they allow for areas of divergence to be identified and dealt with later, if they are not on the critical path;

15 Doz and Hamel, Alliance Advantage: The Art of Creating Value through Partnering.

- are business-like and outcome focused, dealing with matters of detail only insofar as necessary to proceed to action; and
- create the potential for future collaboration on similar or unrelated issues.

The Model defines a process through which intending partners can move gradually from low risk, general principles, to explicit legal agreements, as collaboration progresses. The partners allow the agreed principles and statements of intent guide the process leading to agreement to detailed operational arrangements.

Figure 7: Coalition building model

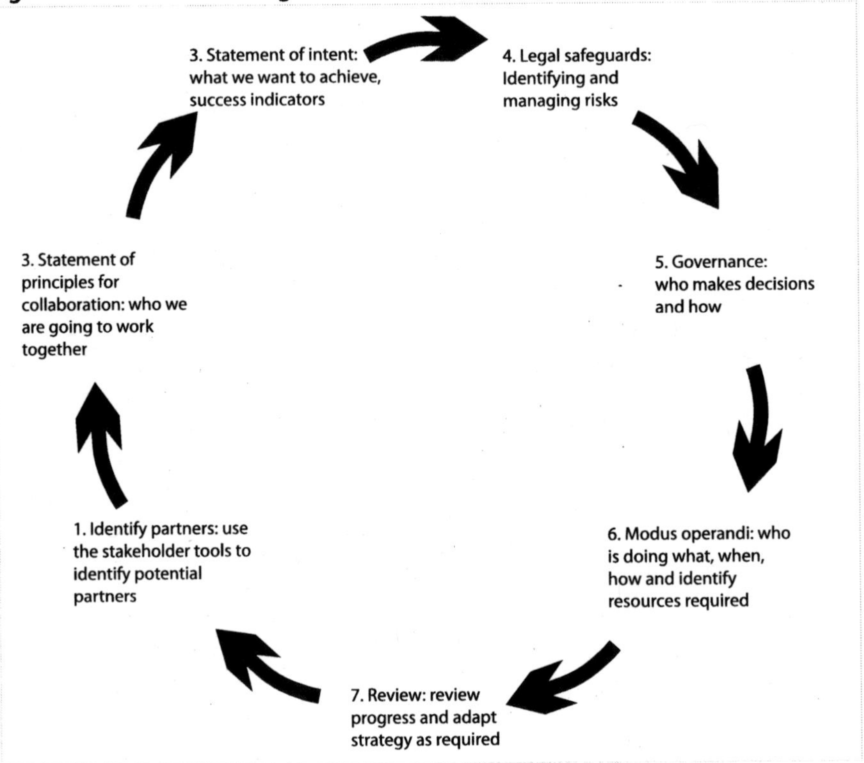

If you want to see something like this in action, you may want to visit www.nsif.gov.au, where a process similar to this one has been put to work to facilitate collaboration within the Australian federal government and across Australia's three levels of government, plus New Zealand. This type of process speeds up the process of building coalitions and enabling effective collaboration.

Such a process can be further enhanced by appropriate use of technology. For an example, I again refer you to Australia, specifically to www.govdex.gov.au. At that site you will see that GovDex was developed by the Australian Government to facilitate business process collaboration across agencies and jurisdictions. GovDex promotes effective and efficient information sharing, which is core to achieving collaboration. It provides governance, tools, methods and re-usable technical components that government agencies can use to assemble and deploy information services on their different technology platforms.

While GovDex enables a whole of government approach to IT service development and deployment, it is a platform that could be used to support any form of collaboration; in fact, it was originally developed for use in and by industry, but industry parties ignored its potential – the Australian Government did not. As at February 2008, GovDex has over two thousand years, in Australia and internationally. Developing this kind of capability within an industry or an industry sector could be a valuable step towards enabling safe and secure collaboration among competitors or among partners in a value chain.

Suggested reading

To make this work you will have to think like a civil servant – like someone who crafts, understands and works with policy. Let us start with the classic, Machiavelli's *The Prince*, always relevant and always useful as a guide to politics, at whatever level. Then, to get personal, you may want to read *Australia's Mandarins: the frank and the fearless*, by Patrick Weller. For a more philosophical perspective, try *Implementation* (third edition), edited by Jeffrey L. Pressman and Aaron Wildavsky, followed by The Private *Government of Public Money: Community and Policy Inside British Politics*, edited by Wildavsky and Hugh Heclo. I also suggest *The Politics of Regulation*, edited by Jacint Jordana and David Levi-Faur, and *Controlling Modern Government*, edited by Christopher Hood, Oliver James, B. Guy Peters and Colin Scott. If we want to cross the Atlantic, I suggest *The Federalists and the Origins of the U.S. Civil Service*, by Carl E. Prince, and *Federal Public Policy: Personal Accounts of Ten Senior Civil Service Executives*, by Theodore W. Taylor.

If all this civil service stuff gives you indigestion, read *Joining Forces*, by Mitchell Lee Marks and Phillip H. Mirvis. This is a book targeted at the private sector that discussed how to engineer, manage and benefit from mergers, acquisitions and alliances. It provides a logical, easy to follow step by step guide, starting with understanding what synergy is and why it is valuable, going on to the pre-combination phase, then to combination, post-combination and finally onto how to reap the rewards of "productive combination". In the endnotes to that book you will find many suggestions for further reading and pointers to useful resources.

Bibliography

I have tried to provide a comprehensive list of relevant reading on the topics covered in this book. To avoid duplication, where sufficient information to find a publication is provided in the text or in footnotes, I have generally not included that publication in the bibliography.

Adams, J. M. and Carfagna A. (2006). *Coming of age in a globalized world: the next generation*. Bloomfield (CT): Kumarian Press.

Argyris, C. (1977). "Double loop learning in organisations", *Harvard Business Review*, September/October, Vol. 55(5), 115 ff.

Argyris, C. and Schon, D.A. (1978). *Organisational learning: A theory of action perspective*. Reading (Mass.): Addison-Wesley.

Argyris, C. and Schon, D.A.(1985). *Strategy, change and defensive routines*. Marshfield (Mass.): Pitman.

Bandler, R. and Grindler, J. (1982). *Reframing*. Moab (Ut.): real People Press.

Boisot, M.H. (1998). *Knowledge assets: securing competitive advantage in the information economy*. Oxford: Oxford University Press.

Boyden, S. (1993). *Western civilization in biological perspective*. Oxford; Clarendon Press.

Callioni, P. (2003). "Creating value by managing knowledge", in *Australian studies in knowledge management*, Hasan, H. Handzic, M. (eds). Wollongong: Wollongong University Press.

Callioni, P. (2008). *Compliance and regulation in the international financial services industry*. Random Acres (UK): Global Professional Publishing.

Calvin, W.H. (1997). *How brains think*. London: Weidenfeld and Nicolson.

Cartwright, T.J. (1991). "Planning and chaos theory", *APA Journal*, Vol. 57, No.1, Winter 1991, 44-56.

Christensen, C.M. (1997). *The innovator's dilemma: when new technologies cause great firms to fail*. Boston (Mass): Harvard Business School Press.

Covey, S. (1999). *Principle centered leadership*. London: Simon and Schuster.

Davies, P. and Gribbin, J. (1992). The matter myth: dramatic discoveries that challenge our understanding of physical reality. New York: Simon & Schuster.

Dawkins, R. (1976). *The selfish gene*. Oxford: Oxford University Press.

Deacon, T. W. (1998). *The symbolic species*. New York: W.W. Norton.

de Geus, A. (1997). *The Living company: growth, learning and longevity in business*. Harvard (Mass.): Harvard Business School Press.

Drucker, P.F. (1992). *Managing the future*. London: ButterworthHeinemann.

Drucker, P.F. (1993). *Managing for results*. New York: Harper Collins.

Dyer, G. (2008). *Climate wars*. Melbourne: 2008.

Fairholm, G.W. (1994). *Leadership and the culture of trust*. Westport (CT): Greenwood Publishing Group.

Faris, S. (2009). *Forecast. The consequences of climate change from the Amazon to the Arctic*. Carlton North: Scribe Publications.

Ferguson, N. (2008). *The ascent of money*. New York: The Penguin Press.

Fernández-Armesto, F. (2002). *Civilizations*. New York: Touchstone.

Fernández-Armesto, F. (1998). *Truth: a history and guide for the perplexed*. London: Transworld Publishers Limited.

Friedman, T.L. (2008). *Hot, flat, and crowded*. New York: Farrar, Straus and Giroux.

Fukuyama, F. (1999). *The great disruption*. London: Profile books.

Galbraith, J.K. (1997).*The great crash 1929*. New York: Houghton Mifflin Company.

Gladwell, M. (2000). *The tipping point: how little things can make a big difference*. New York: Little, Brown.

Gladwell, M. (2008). *Outliers. The story of success*. New York: Little, Brown and Company.

Gleick, J. (1999). *Faster: The acceleration of just about everything*. New York: Pantheon.

Gould, S.J. (1996). *Dinosaur in a haystack*. London: Jonathan Cape.

Greenspan, A. (2007). *The age of turbulence: adventures in a new world*. New York: Penguin.

Gregersen, H. and Sailer, L. (1993). "Chaos theory and its implications for social research", *Human Relations*, Vol. 46, No. 7, 777-802.

Haeckel, S.H. (1999). *Adaptive enterprise: creating and leading sense-and-respond organizations*. Harvard: Harvard Business Press.

Hamel, G. and Prahalad, C.K. (1994). *Competing for the future: breakthrough strategies for seizing control of your industry and creating the markets of tomorrow*. Harvard (Mass): Harvard Business School Press.

Handy, C.B. (1995). *Beyond certainty : the changing worlds of organizations*. London: Hutchinson.

Harvey, J.B. (1974). "The Abilene paradox: the management of agreement", *Organizational Dynamics*, Vol. 3, 63-80.

Hopkins, A.G. (2002). *Globalization in world history*. London: Pimlico.

Huntington, S.P. (1997). *The clash of civilizations and the remaking of world order*. London: Touchstone.

Jackson, J.H. et al (1986). *Organization Theory: A Macro-perspective for Management*. Upper Saddle River (NJ): Prentice-Hall.

Janis, I.L. (1972). *Victims of groupthink*. Boston: Houghton Mifflin.

Kauffman, S.A. (1993). *The Origins of order: self-organization and selection in evolution*. New York: Oxford University Press.

Kauffman, S.A. (1996). *At home in the universe. The search for laws of self-organisation and complexity*. London: Penguin.

Koestler, A. (1989). *The sleepwalkers*. London: Arkana.

Krugman, P. (2009). *The return of depression economics and the crisis of 2008*. New York: W.W. Norton and Company.

Le Bon, G. (2002). *The crowd: a study of the popular mind*. Mineola, NY : Dover Publications.

Lovelock, J. (2007). *The revenge of Gaia*. London: Penguin Books.

Ormerod, P. (1997). *The death of economics*. New York: Wiley.

Ormerod, P. (2000). *Butterfly economics : a new general theory of social and economic behavior*. New York : Basic Books.

Ormerod, P. (2007). *Why most things fail: evolution, extinction and economics*. Hoboken (NJ): John Wiley.

Porter, M.E. (1980). *Competitive strategy*. New York: The Free Press.

Porter, M.E. (1985). *Competitive advantage*. New York: The Free Press.

Penrose, R. (1989). *The emperor's new mind*. London: Vintage.

Penrose, R. (1995). *Shadows of the mind*. London: Vintage.

Prigogine, I. (1980). *From being to becoming*. San Francisco: WH Freeman.

Prigogine, I. and Stengers, I. (1985). *Order out of chaos*. New York: Flamingo.

Putnam, R.D. (1993). *Making democracy work: civic traditions in modern Italy*. Princeton (NJ): Princeton University Press.

Putnam, R.D. (2000). *Bowling alone: the collapse and revival of American community*. New York: Simon & Schuster.

Ridley, M. (1996). *The origins of virtue*. London: Viking.

Said; E.W. (1994). *Orientalism*. New York: Vintage Books.

Salkowitz, R. (2008). *Generation blend*. Hoboken (NJ): 2008.

Sachs, J.D. (2008). *Common wealth*. New York: Penguin Books.

Salt, B. (2008). *Man drought and other social issues of the new century*. Prahran: Hardie Grant Books.

Schumpeter, J. (1975). *Capitalism, socialism, and democracy*. New York: Harper.

Simon, H.A. (1969). *The sciences of the artificial,* Second Edition. Cambridge (Mass): MIT Press.

Soros, G. (2008). *The credit crisis of 2008 and what it means*. New York: Public Affairs.

Stacey, R.D. (1993). *Strategic management and organisational dynamics*. London: Pitman.

Steele, E.J., Lindley, R.A. and Blanden, R.V. (1998). *Lamarck's signature*, by, Allen & Unwin: Sydney.

Tapscott , D. and Williams, A.D. (2006). *Wikinomics: how mass collaboration changes everything*. London: Penguin.

Tart, C. T. (1994). *Living the mindful life*. Boston (Mass): Shambala.

Tipler, F.J. (1995). *The physics of immortality*. London: Macmillan.

Tolle, E. (2005). *A new Earth*. Camberwell: Michael Joseph.

Tversky, A. (2004). *Preference, belief, and similarity: selected writings by Amos Tversky*; edited by Eldar Shafir. Cambridge (Mass.): MIT Press.

Weick, K.E. (1977). "Organization design: organizations as self-designing systems", *Organizational Dynamics*, Autumn 1977, pp. 31-46.

Weinberg, S. (1993). *The first three minutes*. London: Flamingo.

Wheatley, M.J. (1994). *Leadership and the new science*. San Francisco: Berrett-Koehler.

Wilson, E.O. (1999). *Consilience: the unity of knowledge*. New York, Random House 1999.

Wright, R. (2001). *Nonzero: the logic of human destiny*. New York: Vintage Books.

(2007) *How to use social media to engage employees: strategies to improve communication and collaboration*. Chicago: Melcrum Publishing.

Index

T